Thomas Boston

Human nature in its fourfold state of primitive integrity

All mankind in the future state. First American Edition

Thomas Boston

Human nature in its fourfold state of primitive integrity
All mankind in the future state. First American Edition

ISBN/EAN: 9783337102340

Printed in Europe, USA, Canada, Australia, Japan

Cover: Foto ©Lupo / pixelio.de

More available books at **www.hansebooks.com**

HUMAN NATURE

FOURFOLD STATE,

OF

Primitive Integrity, } Subsisting in { The Parents of Mankind in Paradise.
Entire Depravation, } { The Unregenerate.
Begun Recovery, and } { The Regenerate.
Consummate Happiness or Misery. } { All Mankind in the Future State.

IN SEVERAL

PRACTICAL DISCOURSES,

By the Eminently Pious and Learned
MR. THOMAS BOSTON,
Late Minister of the Gospel at *Etterick*.

First American Edition.

JOHN ii. 24, 25. *But Jesus did not commit himself unto them, because he knew all Men. And needed not that any should testify of Man: For he knew what was in Man.*
LUKE ix. 19. *Ye know not what manner of Spirit ye are of.*
PROVERBS xxvii. 19. *As, in Water, Face answereth to Face: So the Heart of Man to Man.*

Printed at Exeter,
By H. RANLET, FOR THOMAS AND ANDREWS,
Faust's Statue, No. 45, Newbury-Street, Boston.
1796.

RECOMMENDATIONS. iii

RECOMMENDATION by Mr. MICHAEL BOSTON, the Author's Grandson.

HUMAN NATURE in its FOURFOLD STATE, was the first Production of my venerable Ancestor, introduced to the Public. It made its first appearance in the year 1720. Since that period, it has undergone, at an average, one complete Edition every two years. Twenty thousand Copies of it have been exported to *America*, from one single City in *Scotland*, besides those that have been sent to the Continent from *England* and *Ireland*. The rapid sale of the Book upon its first publication, is a demonstrative proof of the esteem in which it was then held; and the uninterrupted demand for it still, shows that the Principles it inculcates, are yet held in repute. All that I need further to add, is, That this Edition is printed from that one Revised and Corrected by the Author himself, and may therefore be esteemed correct.

MICHAEL BOSTON.

Falkirk, Dec. 1784.

The Late Rev. Mr. JAMES HERVEY, in his *Dialogues*, Vol. I. *page* 343. gives the following

RECOMMENDATION of this Book.

'SEE this work of grace, and procedure of conversion, more copiously displayed, in a valuable little piece, intituled, *Human Nature in its Fourfold State*, by Mr. *Thomas Boston*; which, in my opinion, is one of our best books for common readers. The sentences are short, and the comparisons striking: The language is easy, and the doctrine evangelical: The method proper; the plan comprehensive; the manner searching, yet consolatory. Is another celebrated treatise is stiled, *The Whole Duty of Man*, I would call this, *The* WHOLE *of Man*; as it comprises, what he *was*, originally: what *he is*, by transgression: what he *should be*, through grace: and, then, what he *will be*, in glory.'

sons, is of as great use, in the conduct of human life, a[s] the knowledge of things; and it is most certain, that he wh[o] knows the various tempers, humours, and dispositions of me[n] who can find out their turn of thought, and penetrate into th[e] secret springs and principles of their actings, will not be at [a] loss to find out proper means for compassing his aims, will easil[y] preserve himself from snares, and either evite or overcome di[f]ficulties. But the knowledge of human nature, morally cons[i]dered, or, in other words, of the temper and disposition of th[e] soul in its moral powers, is of much greater value; as it is [of] use in the concerns of an unchangeable life and world; he wh[o] is possessed of so valuable a branch of knowledge, is thereb[y] capacitated to judge aright of himself, to understand tru[e] Christianity, and to conceive justly of perfect happiness, an[d] consummate misery.

The depravity of human nature is so plainly taught, yea in[culcated in sacred Scripture, and is so obvious to every thin[k]ing man's observation, who searches his own breast, and reflec[ts] duly on his temper and actings, that it is surprizingly strang[e] and wonderful, how it comes to pass, that this important trut[h] is so little understood, yea so much disbelieved, by men wh[o] bear the name of Gospel-Ministers. Are there not persons [to] be found in a neighbouring nation, in the character of preach[ers, appearing daily in pulpits, who are so unacquainted wit[h] their Bibles and themselves, that they ridicule the doctrine [of] original sin, as unintelligible jargon? If they are persons [of] a moral life and conversation, they seem to imagine, they ca[n]not become better than they are; if they are immoral, the[y] seem to indulge a conceit, that they can become virtuous, y[ea] religious, when they please. These are the men who talk [of] the dignity of human nature, of greatness of mind, noblene[ss] of soul, and generosity of spirit; as if they intended to persuad[e] themselves and others, that pride is a good principle, and [do] not know, that pride and selfishness are the bane of mankin[d,] productive of all the wickedness, and much of the misery [to] be found in this and in the other world; and is indeed tha[t] wherein the depravity of human nature properly consists.

Upright Adam's nature faintly adumbrated the divine, in a moderated self-esteem, an adequate self-love, and delightful reflection on his own borrowed excellency, regulated by a just esteem of, and supreme love to his adored Creator; whence a peaceful serenity of mind, a loving, compassionate, and benevolent disposition of soul, a depth of thought, and brightness of imagination, delightfully employed in the rapturous contemplation, of his beloved Maker's infinite perfections; thus bearing the divine image, and resembling God that made him. But he no sooner disobeyed the divine probatory command, than the scales were cast, his moderated self-esteem degenerated into pride, his adequate self-love shrunk into mere selfishness, and his delightful reflections on his own excellency, varied into the tickling pleasures of vanity and conceit; he lost view of the Author of his being, and thenceforth, instead of delighting in him, first dreaded and then despised him.

The modest, and therefore hitherto anonymous, author of the following discourses, Mr. THOMAS BOSTON, having handled this subject, in preaching to his own obscure parochial congregation of Etterick, in the sheriffdom of Selkirk, had a particular view to their benefit, in printing and publishing them; and therefore the stile and method is plain and simple, and the first edition printed on coarse paper; but the subject is so comprehensive and important, so well managed, and the book has been so well received, that it now appears in the world more embellished, as well as better corrected than formerly.

Let it suffice, to recommend it to those who have a right taste of genuine Christianity, that all the Author's notions flow so directly from the sacred fountain, that it is to be doubted, if he has had much recourse to any other helps, than his Bible and his GOD for assistance. Mean time, I am aware of an exception from these, who rank themselves among the polite part of mankind, as that there is the same harsh peculiarity of dialect in it, which is commonly to be found in books of practical divinity. But I beg leave to observe, That the dialect they except against, is borrowed from sacred scripture; and like as it has pleased GOD, by the foolishness of preaching to save them that believe; so also, to countenance what they are displeased with, by the operations of his Spirit, on the minds of true Christians, as their common experience witnesseth. However, I heartily wish, the exception were altogether removed, by some person's digesting into a methodical treatise, the views of human nature in its primitive perfection, in its depraved condition, and in its retrieved state, who is master of modern stile, and thoroughly understands the subjects discoursed in this book, that by becoming all things to all men, Some, viz. Of all ranks and kinds of men, may be gained

PREFACE.

I am not to declaim at large in favour of religion; this were to write a book by way of preface. Many able pens have been employed in recommending it to the world, by strong arguments drawn from its usefulness to society, its suitableness to the dignity of the rational nature, and the advantages arising to men from it, in this and the other world. But, after all, may not one be allowed to doubt, if religion be rightly understood by all its patrons? may not the beauties and excellencies of a precious gem be elegantly described by a naturalist or jeweller, who never saw the particular one he talked of, and knows little of its nature, less of the construction of its parts, and nothing of its proper use? Are there not men of bright parts, who reason finely in defence of religion, and yet are so much strangers to it, that they brand these who are so happy as to be possessed of it, with the hard name of Spiritualists, reckoning them a kind of Enthusiasts, unworthy of their regard? The truth is, Christianity is a mystery; mere reason does not comprehend it. There is a spiritual discerning, necessary to its being rightly understood; whence it comes to pass, that men of great learning and abilities, though they read the Scripture with attention, and comment learnedly upon them; yet do not, yea cannot, enter into the vein of thought peculiar to the inspired penman, because they share not of the same Spirit, wherefore it is, that the Apostle Paul asserts, the natural, that is, unregenerate man, not to know the things of GOD, neither indeed to be capable of knowing them, because they are spiritually discerned.

From what has been said, it is easy to conclude, That no pedantic apology on the part of the Author, for appearing in print, or fawning compliments to the courteous reader, on the part of the prefacer, are to be expected. The truth is, both the one and the other are rather little arts, vailing pedantry and conceit, than evidences of modesty and good sense. It is of more use to recommend the perusal of the book, to persons of all ranks and degrees, from a few suitable topics, than to shew wherein this Edition differs from the first.

That all mankind, however differenced by their rank and station in the world, have an equal concern in what is revealed concerning another and future world, will be readily owned; and it must be as readily granted, that however allowable it may be for men of learning and parts, to please themselves with fineness of language, justness of thought, and exact connection in writings upon other subjects; yet they ought not to indulge themselves in the same taste in discourses on divine things, lest they expose themselves to the just censure of acting with the same indiscretion, as a person in danger of famishing by hunger would be guilty of, if he perversly rejected plain wholesome food when offered to him, for no other reason than for want of palatable sauce, or order and splendor in serving it up.

The sacred book we call the Bible, has a peculiar sublimity in it, vailed with unusual dialect and seeming inconnection: but it is not therefore to be rejected by men who bear the name of Christians, as uncouth or unintelligible; true wisdom dictates quite another thing: it counsels us, by frequent reading, to acquaint ourselves well with it; become accustomed to its peculiar phrases, and search into its sublimities; upon this ground, that the matters contained in it, are of the utmost consequence to us, and when rightly understood, yield a refined delight, much superior to what is to be found in reading the best written books on the most entertaining subjects. What pleads for the parent, is a plea for the progeny; practical discourses upon divine subjects, are the genuine offspring of the sacred text, and ought therefore to be read carefully and with attention, by persons of all ranks and degrees, tho' they are indeed calculated for, and peculiarly adapted to such as move in low spheres of life.

Let it, however, be a prevailing argument with persons of all denominations, carefully to read books of practical divinity: That many of them are not written on the same motives and principles as other books are; the authors have often a peculiar divine call to publish them, and well-founded hope of their being useful to advance Christianity in the world. In consequence whereof it is that great numbers have reaped benefit by reading them, especially in childhood and youth; many have been converted by them; and it may be questioned, if ever there was a true Christian, since the Art of printing made these books common, who has not, in some stage of life, reaped considerable advantage from them. This book recommends itself in a particular manner, by its being a short substantial system of practical divinity, in so much, that it may with truth be asserted, that a person who is thoroughly acquainted with all that is here taught, may, without danger to his eternal interest, remain ignorant of other things, which pertain to the science called Divinity. It is therefore earnestly recommended to the serious and frequent perusal of all, but especially of such as are in that stage of life called youth, and are so stationed in the world, as not to be frequently opportuned to hear sermons, and read commentaries of the sacred text.

It is doubtless incumbent on masters of families to make some provision of spiritual as well as bodily food, for their children and servants; this is effectually done by putting practical books in their hands; and therefore this book is humbly and earnestly recommended as a family-book, which all the members of it are not only allowed, but desired to peruse.

PREFACE.

As to the difference betwixt this and the former edition, which gives it preference, it lies chiefly in the Author's not only having revised the ſtile, but the thought in many places; and corrected both, ſo as to ſet ſeveral important truths in a clearer light, and make the ſtile of the book now uniform, which formerly was not ſo, becauſe of the explications of peculiar words and phraſes in uſe amongſt practical divines, eſpecially of the church of Scotland, which were interſperſed throughout the former edition, and introduced by another hand, for the ſake of ſuch perſons as are not accuſtomed to them. It remains, that the prefacer not only ſubjoins his name, which was concealed in the firſt edition, as a teſtimony that he eſteems the Author, and values the book, but that he may thereby recommend it in a particular manner to the peruſal of perſons of his own acquaintance. If in his aſſiſting towards its being publiſhed, and in prefacing both editions, he has not run unſent, he has what will bear him up under all cenſures; the charitable will think no evil, and others will do as they pleaſe.

ROBERT WIGHTMAN, M. D. C. E.

Edinburgh, 18th March, 1799.

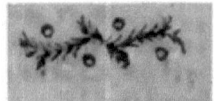

THE CONTENTS.

I. The state of INNOCENCE, or PRIMITIVE INTEGRITY, Discoursed from Ecc. vii. 29.

Of man's original righteousness,	Page 19
His understanding a lamp of light,	20
His will straight with the will of God,	ib.
His affections orderly and pure,	21
The qualities of this righteousness,	22
Of man's original happiness,	24
Man a glorious creature,	ib.
The favourite of heaven,	ib.
The covenant of works,	ib.
Lord of the world,	27
The forbidden tree, a stay to keep him from falling,	ib.
His perfect tranquility,	28
Life of pure delight,	ib.
Man immortal,	29
Instructions from this state,	30
Three sorts of persons reproved,	ib.
A lamentation over the ruins,	31

II. The State of NATURE, or state of ENTIRE DEPRAVATION.

HEAD I. The Sinfulness of Man's Natural State, discoursed from Gen. vi. 5.

That man's nature is corrupted, proven,	P. 37
From God's word,	ib.
From mens experience and observation,	40
Fallen Adam's image natural to men, in eleven particulars,	44
Of the corruption of the understanding,	49
Weakness with respect to spiritual things,	ib.
Three evidences of it,	50
Gross darkness in spiritual things,	ib.
Four evidences of it,	51
A bias in it to evil,	55
Six evidences of that bias,	ib.
Aversion to spiritual truths,	58
Three evidences thereof,	59
Proneness to lies and falsehood,	60
Man naturally high-minded,	62
Of the corruption of the will,	63
Utter inability for what is truly good,	ib.
Two evidences of it,	64

x   CONTENTS.

Averseness to good,	Page 65
Four evidences of it,	ib.
Proneness to evil,	68
Five evidences of it,	ib.
Enmity against God,	70
Against the being and nature of God,	71
Five queries, for conviction, on this head,	72
Against the Son of God,	73
In his prophetical office,	74
Two evidences of it,	ib.
In his priestly office,	76
Three evidences of it,	ib.
In his kingly office,	77
Three evidences of it,	ib.
A peculiar malignity against the priestly office, corrupt nature lying cross to the gospel-contrivance of salvation,	78
Four proofs of it,	79
Bent to the way of the law, as a covenant of works,	80
Four proofs of it,	81
Against the Spirit of God,	84
Against the law, as a rule of life,	85
Two evidences of it,	ib.
Contumacy against the Lord,	ib.
Perverseness in reference to the chief end,	86
Of the corruption of the affections,	87
Of the corruption of the conscience,	88
Of the corruption of the memory,	89
The body partaker of this corruption,	90
How man's nature was corrupted,	ib.
The doctrine of the corruption of nature, applied,	93
The natural man can do nothing but sin,	95
God takes special notice of the sin of our nature,	97
Evidences of men's overlooking the sin of their nature,	98
Wherein that sin is to be specially noticed,	100
Why it is to be specially noticed,	101
How to get a view of the corruption of nature,	103

HEAD II. The MISERY of Man's Natural State, Discoursed from Eph. ii. 3.   104

MAN's natural state, a state of wrath,	106
What this state of wrath is,	108
Wrath in the heart of God against the natural man,	ib.
Wrath in the word of God against him,	109
Wrath in the hand of God against him,	ib.
On his body and soul,	110
On his enjoyments,	111

He is under the power of Satan,	Page 111
Hath no security for a moment's safety,	112
Wrath against him at death, and at the general judgment,	ib.
The qualities of that wrath,	113
The doctrine of the state of wrath confirmed and vindicated,	115
Several instructions from it,	ib.
Alarm to the unregenerate,	122
They are under the covenant of works,	ib.
Their misery in that respect,	123
They are without God,	125
Their misery in that respect,	ib.
Instances of the wrath of God,	126
A view of the nature of God, whose wrath it is,	127
How to flee from wrath,	128
A few words to the saints, and a word to all,	129, 131

HEAD III. Man's Utter Inability to recover himself, Discoursed from Romans v. 6. John vi. 44. 132

ONLY two ways of man's recovering himself supposable, viz. the way of the law, and the way of the gospel,	133
Man unable to recover himself, in the way of the law,	ib.
He cannot keep the commands perfectly,	ib.
The perfection of law-obedience, fourfold,	134
He cannot satisfy the justice of God for his sin,	136
Object. God is merciful: we hope to be saved, if we do as well as we can, Answered,	137
Man unable to recover himself in the way of the gospel, to embrace and use the help offered for his recovery,	138
Proven by several arguments,	ib.
Object. (1.) If we be under an utter inability to do any good, how can God require us to do it? Answered,	140
Object. (2.) Why do you then call us to believe, repent, and use the means? Answered,	141
Object. (3.) The use of means needless, seeing we are utterly unable to help ourselves out of the state of sin and wrath: Answered,	142
Quest. Has God promised to convert and save them, who, in the use of means, do what they can, towards their own relief? Answered,	ib.
The conclusion of this head,	144

III. The State of GRACE, or begun Recovery.

HEAD I. Regeneration, Discoursed from 1 Pet. i. 23. Page 145

Of the nature of regeneration, 146
    Partial changes mistaken for this change, ib.
The change made in regeneration, what it is, 149
    In general and particular, ib. 151
The mind illuminated, and the will renewed, ib.
    Cured of its utter inability to good, 154
    Endued with a fixed aversion to evil, ib.
    Endued with a bent and propensity to good, 155
    Reconciled to the covenant of peace, 156
Disposed to receive Jesus Christ, ib.
The affections are changed, 157
The affections Rectified and **regulated** 157, 158
The conscience renewed, 159
The memory bettered by regenerating grace, 160
The body changed, in respect of use, 163
The whole conversation changed, ib.
The resemblance betwixt natural and spiritual generation, in nine particulars, 165
Trial of one's state, whether born again or not, 169
Some cases of doubting Christians resolved, 172
    Case (1.) The precise time and way of one's conversion not known, ib.
    Case (2.) Sin prevailing, 173
    Case (3.) Corruptions more violent than formerly, ib.
    Case (4.) Affections to the creature stronger than to the Creator----Glowing affections to God gone, 174
    Case (5.) Attainments of hypocrites and apostates, a terror, 176
    Case (6.) Falling short of the saints mentioned in Scripture, and of others, 177
    Case (7.) No child of God so tempted, ib.
    Case last. Strange and unusual affections, 179
The necessity of regeneration, ib.
    To qualify one to do good, 180
    To communion with God in duties, 182
    To make one meet for heaven, ib.
    To one's being admitted into heaven, 184
Advices to the unregenerate, 185

HEAD II. The Mystical Union between Christ and Believers, Discoursed from John xv. 5. Page 187

A General view of the Mistical Union, 188
The natural stock of all men, Adam, 191
   Originally a choice vine, 192
   Now a degenerate stock, ib.
Fruits growing on the branches of nature of the stock, 193
   A dead stock, 195
     The condition of the branches in that respect, ib.
   A killing stock, 196
     The condition of the branches in that respect, ib.
The supernatural stock, into which the branches are ingrafted, Jesus Christ, 198
The branches taken out of the natural stock, and grafted into the supernatural stock, the elect, 199
How cut off from the natural stock, in 12 particulars, 200
How ingrafted into Christ, 209
   Christ apprehends the sinner by his Spirit, 210
   The sinner apprehends Christ by faith, ib.
How one may know one's self to be apprehended of Christ, 212
The benefits flowing to believers from union with Christ, 214
   Justification, ib. Peace with God, and peace of conscience, 217. Adoption, 220. Sanctification, 221.
     Growth in Grace, 225
       Quest. If all true Christians be growing ones, what shall be said of these who, instead of growing, are going backward? Answered, ib.
       Qest. Do hypocrites grow at all? And if so, how shall we distinguish betwixt their growth, and the growth of the Christian? Answered, 226
     Fruitfulness, 227
     Acceptance of their fruits of holiness, 230
     Establishment, 232
     Support, 234
     The special care of the husbandman, 237
The duty of saints united to Christ, 239
A word to sinners, 242

IV. The Eternal State, or State of consummate Happiness or misery.

HEAD I. Death, discoursed from Job xxx. 23. 243
  THE certainty of death, 244
   Man's life vanity, 246
  A short-lived vanity, 247

A flying vanity, Page 248
The doctrine of death, a looking-glass, wherein to behold
the vanity of the world, 249
 A storehouse for contentment and patience, 250
 A bridle to curb lusts, conversant about the body, 252
 A spring of Christian resolution, 254
 A spur to incite to prepare for death, 255

Head II. The Difference betwixt the Righteous and the Wicked at death, Discoursed from Proverbs xiv. 32, 256

The wicked dying, are driven away, 257
 In what cases a wicked man may be willing to die, 259
  Whence they are driven, and whither, 260
  Driven away in their wickedness, 261
The hopelessness of their state at death, 262
 Their hopes of peace and pleasure in this life cut off, ib.
 They have no solid grounds to hope for eternal happiness, ib.
  Death roots up their delusive hopes of heaven, 263
 Makes their state absolutely and for ever hopeless, ib.
Caution against false Hopes: Characters of those Hopes, 264
 Exhortation to hasten out of a sinful state, 266
 To be concerned for the salvation of others, ib.
The state of the godly in death, a hopeful state, 267
 Christ, their best friend, is Lord of the other world, ib.
 They will have a safe passage to it, 268
  A joyful entrance into it, 270
Object. Many of the godly, when dying, full of fears, and have little hope? Answered, 271
  Death uncomfortable to them, in three cases, 273
Ten cases of saints anent death, Answered, 274
Considerations to bring saints in good terms with death, 277
Directions how to prepare for death, 278

Head III. The Resurrection, Discoursed from John v. 28, 29. 283

The possibility of the resurrection, ib.
 The certainty of the resurrection, 281
Who shall be raised, and, What shall be raised, 289
How the dead shall be raised, 290
 The difference betwixt the godly and the wicked, in their resurrection, 291
  The qualities of the raised bodies of the saints, 295
  The qualities of the raised bodies of the wicked, 297
Comfort to the people of God, 298
Terror to all natural men,

CONTENTS. xv

HEAD IV. The General Judgment, discoursed from Mat. xxv. 31, 32, 33, 34, 41. 46.   302

THAT there shall be a general judgment, proven,	303
Jesus Christ the Judge,	306
The coming of the Judge,	ib.
The summons given,	307
The Judge's sitting down on the tribunal,	ib.
The compearance of the parties,	309
The separation betwixt the righteous and the wicked,	310
The trial of the parties,	312
The books opened,	314
Sentence pronounced on the saints,	317
The saints judge the world,	319
Sentence of damnation on the ungodly,	ib.
The execution,	322
The general conflagration,	ib.
The place and time of the judgment, unknown,	324
Comfort to the saints,	ib.
Terror to unbelievers,	325
Exhortation to prepare for the judgment,	327

HEAD V. The Kingdom of Heaven, discoursed from Mat. xxv. 34.   328

THE nature of the kingdom of heaven,	330
The saints kingly power and authority,	ib.
Their ensigns of royalty,	331
White garments, on what occasion used: Much of heaven under them,	ib.
The country where this kingdom lies,	336
The royal city,	337
The royal palace,	ib.
The palace-garden	338
The royal treasures,	ib.
The temple in this kingdom,	339
The society there,	ib.
The society of the saints among themselves,	340
Society with the holy angels,	341
Glorious communion with God and Christ, the perfection of happiness,	342
The glorious presence of God and the Lamb,	ib.
The full enjoyment of GOD and the Lamb,	343
By sight,	344
They will see Christ, with their bodily eyes,	ib.
They will see God, with the eyes of the mind,	345
By experimental knowledge,	348

Fulness of joy unspeakable, 350
The eternal duration of this kingdom, 351
The saints admission to the kingdom, 352
　The quality in which they are introduced, 353
Trial of the claim to the kingdom of heaven, 354
Duty and comfort of the heirs of the kingdom, 356
Exhortation to these who have no right to it. 358

HEAD VI. Hell discoursed of, from Matth. xxv. 41.
THE curse under which the damned shall be shut up in hell, 361
　Their misery under that curse, 363
　　The punishment of loss, separation from God, ib.
　　The horror of separation from God, evinced by several considerations 365
　　The punishment of sense, departing into fire, 370
Hell-fire more vehement and terrible than any other, evinced by several considerations, ib.
Six properties of the fiery torments in hell, 372
　Three inferences from this doctrine, 375
Society with devils in this miserable state, 377
The eternity of the whole, 378
　What eternity is, ib.
　What is eternity in the state of the damned, 379
Reasonableness of the eternity of the punishment of the damned, 381
A measuring reed to measure our time, and endeavours for salvation by, 382
A balance to discover the lightness of what is falsely thought weighty, and the weight of what is falsly tho't light, 383
Exhortation to flee from the wrath to come, 384

STATE I.

NAMELY,

The State of Innocence or Primitive Integrity, in which Man was created.

Eccles. vii. 29.

Lo, this only have I found, That God hath made man upright: But they have sought out many inventions.

THERE are four things very necessary to be known by all that would see heaven. *First*, What man was in the state of innocence, as God made him. *Secondly*, What he is in the state of corrupt nature, as he hath unmade himself. *Thirdly*, What he must be in the state of grace, as created in Christ Jesus unto good works, if ever he be made a partaker of the inheritance of the saints in light. And, *Lastly*, What he shall be in his eternal state, as made by the Judge of all, either perfectly happy, or completely miserable, and that for ever. These are weighty points, that touch the vitals of practical godliness, from which most men, and even many professors, in these dregs of time, are quite estranged. I design therefore, under the divine conduct, to open up these things, and apply them.

I begin with the first of them, namely, The state of innocence: That, beholding man polished after the similitude of a palace, the ruins may the more affect us; we may the more prize that matchless Person, whom the Father has appointed the repairer of the breach; and that we may, with fixed resolves, betake ourselves to that way which leadeth to the city that hath unmoveable foundations.

In the text we have three things:

1. The state of innocence wherein man was created, *God hath made man upright*. By man here, we are to understand our first parents; the archetypal pair, the root of mankind, the compendized world, and the fountain from whence all generations have streamed, as may appear by comparing Gen. v. 1, 2. *In the day that God created man, in the likeness of God made he him, male and female created he them, and blessed them, as the root of mankind, and called their name Adam.* The original words are the same in our text, in this sense, man was made right, agreeable to the nature of God, whose work

B

is perfect, without any imperfection, corruption, or principle of corruption in his body or soul. He was made upright, that is, straight with the will and law of God, without any irregularity in his soul. By the set it got in its creation, it directly pointed towards God, as his chief end; which straight inclination was represented, as in an emblem, by the erect figure of his body, a figure that no other living creature partakes of. What David was in a gospel sense, that was he in a legal sense; one according to God's own heart, altogether righteous, pure and holy. GOD made him thus; he did not first make him, and then make him righteous; but in the very making of him, he made him righteous. Original righteousness was concreated with him: so that in the same moment he **was a man**, he was a righteous man, morally good; with the same breath that GOD breathed in him a living soul, he breathed in him a righteous soul.

2. Here is man's fallen state; *but they have sought out many inventions*. They fell off from their rest in GOD, and fell upon seeking inventions of their own, to mend their case; and they quite marred it. Their ruin was from their own proper motion; they would not abide as GOD had made them; but they sought out many inventions to deform and undo themselves.

3. Observe here the certainty and importance of those things; *Lo, this only have I found*, &c. Believe them, they are the result of a narrow search, and a serious inquiry performed by the wisest of men. In the two preceding verses, Solomon represents himself as in quest of goodness in the world: but the issue of it was, he could find no satisfying issue in his search after it; though it was not for want of pains; for he counted one by one to find out the account. *Behold this have I found*, saith the preacher, to wit, *that*, as the same word is read in our text, *yet my soul seeketh, but I find not*. He could make no satisfying discovery of it, which might stay his enquiry. He found good men very rare, one as it were among a thousand; good women more rare, not one good among his thousand wives and concubines, 2 Kings xi. 3. But could that satisfy the grand query, *Where shall wisdom be found?* No, it could not; and if the experience of others in this point run counter to Solomon's as it is no reflection on his discerning, it can as little decide the question; which will remain undetermined till the last day. But, amidst all this uncertainty, there is one point found out, and fixed: *This have I found*, Ye may depend upon it as most certain truth, and be fully satisfied in it: *Lo, this*; fix your eyes upon it, as a matter worthy of most deep and serious regard; to wit, that man's nature is now depraved, but that depravation was not from GOD, for he

made man upright; but for themselves, they have sought out many inventions.

DOCTRINE, *God made man altogether righteous.*

THIS is that state of innocence in which GOD set man down in the world. 'Tis described in the holy scriptures, with a running pen, in comparison of the following states; for it was of no continuance, but passed as a flying shadow, by man's abusing the freedom of his own will. I shall,

FIRST, Inquire into the righteousness of this state wherein man was created.

SECONDLY, Lay before you some of the happy concomitants, and consequences thereof.

LASTLY, Apply the whole.

Of Man's Original Righteousness.

FIRST, As to the righteousness of this state, consider, that as uncreated righteousness, the righteousness of GOD is the supreme rule; so all created righteousness, whether of men or angels, hath respect to a law as its rule, and is a conformity thereunto. A creature can no more be morally independent on GOD, in its actions and powers, than it can be naturally independent on him. A creature, as a creature, must acknowledge the Creator's will as its supreme law; for as it cannot be without him, so it must not be but for him, and according to his will: yet no law obliges, until it be revealed. And hence it follows, that there was a law which man, as a rational creature, was subjected to in his creation; and that this law was revealed to him. *God made man upright,* says the text. This presupposeth a law to which he was conformed in his creation; as when any thing is made regular, or according to rule, of necessity the rule itself is presupposed. Whence we may gather, that this law was no other than the eternal, indispensible law of righteousness, observed in all points by the second Adam: opposed by the carnal mind; some notions of which remain yet among the Pagans, who, *having not the law, are a law unto themselves,* Rom. ii. 15. In a word, this law is the very same which was afterwards summed up in the ten commandments, and promulgate on mount Sinai to the Israelites, called by us the moral law: and man's righteousness consisted in conformity to this law or rule. More particularly, there is a twofold conformity required of a man: a conformity of the powers of his soul to the law, which you may call habitual righteousness; and a conformity of all his actions to it, which is actual righteousness. Now, GOD made man habitually righteous; man was to make himself actually righteous: the former was the stock GOD put into his hand: the latter, the improvement he should have made of it. The sum of what I have said is, that the righteousness wherein man was created, was the conformity of all the faculties and powers of his soul to the moral law. This is what we call original righteousness, which man was originally endued with. We may take it up in these three things.

First, Man's understanding was a lamp of light. He had perfect knowledge of the law, and of his duty accordingly: he was made after GOD's image, and consequently could not want knowledge, which is a part thereof, Col. iii. 10. *The new man is renewed in knowledge, after the image of him that created him.* And indeed this was necessary to fit him for universal obedience; seeing no obedience can be according to the law, unless it proceed from a sense of the commandment of GOD requiring it. 'Tis true, Adam had not the law written upon tables of stone: but it was written upon his mind, the knowledge thereof being concreated with him. GOD impressed it upon his soul, and made him a law to himself, as the remains of it among the heathens do testify, Rom. ii. 14, 15. And seeing man was made to be the mouth of the creation, to glorify GOD in his works; we have ground to believe he had naturally an exquisite knowledge of the works of GOD. We have a proof of this in his giving names to the beasts of the field, and the fowls of the air, and these such as express their nature. *Whatsoever Adam called every living creature, that was the name thereof*, Gen. ii. 19. And the dominion which GOD gave him over the creatures, soberly to use and dispose of them according to his will, still in subordination to the will of GOD, seems to require no less than a knowledge of their natures. And besides all this, his perfect knowledge of the law, proves his knowledge in the management of civil affairs, which, in respect of the law of GOD, *a good man will guide with discretion*, Ps. cxii. 5.

Secondly, His will lay straight with the will of GOD, Eph. iv. 24. There was no corruption in his will, no bent nor inclination to evil; for that is sin properly and truly so called: hence the apostle says, Rom. vii. 7. *I had not known sin, but by the law, for I had not known lust, except the law had said, Thou shalt not covet.* An inclination to evil, is really a fountain of sin, and therefore inconsistent with that rectitude and uprightness which the text expressly says, he was endued with at his creation. The will of man then was directed, and naturally inclined to GOD and goodness, though mutably. It was disposed, by its original make, to follow the Creator's will, as the shadow does the body; and that was not left in an equal balance to good and evil: for at that rate he had not been upright, nor habitually conform to the law: which in no moment can allow the creature, not to be inclined towards God as his chief end, more than it can allow man to be a god himself. The law was impressed upon Adam's soul: now this according to the new covenant, by which the image of God is repaired, consists in two things: 1. Putting the law into the mind, denoting the knowledge of it: 2. Writing it in the heart, denoting inclinations in the will, answerable to the commands of the law, Heb. viii. 10. So that, as the will, when we consider it as renewed by grace, is by that grace natively inclined to the same holiness in all its parts which the law requires; so was the will of man, when we consider him as God made him at first, endued with natural inclinations to every thing commanded by the law. For if the regenerate are partakers of the divine nature, as undoubtedly they are; for so says the scripture, 2 Pet. i. 4. And if this divine nature can import no less than inclinations of the heart to holiness: then surely Adam's will could not want this inclination; for in him the image of God was perfect. It is true, 'tis said, Rom. ii. 14. 15. *That the Gentiles shew the work of the law written in their hearts:* but this denotes only their knowledge of that law, such as it is; but the apostle to the Hebrews, in the text cited, takes the word *heart*, in another sense, distinguishing it plainly from the mind. And it must be granted, that, when God promiseth in the new covenant, *To write his law in the hearts of his people*, it imports quite another thing than what Heathens have: for though they have notions of it in their minds, yet their hearts go another way; their will has got a set and a bias quite contrary to that law; and therefore, the expression suitable to the present purpose, must needs import, besides these notions of the mind, inclinations of the will going along therewith: which inclinations though mixed with corruption in the regenerate, were pure and unmixed in upright Adam. In a word, as Adam knew his master's pleasure in the matter of duty, so his will stood inclined to what he knew.

Thirdly, His affections were orderly, pure and holy; which is a necessary part of that uprightness wherein man was created. The apostle has a petition, 2 Thess. iii. 5. *The Lord direct your hearts unto the love of God;* that is, *The Lord straighten your hearts*, or make them lie straight to the love of God: and our text tells us, man was thus made straight, *The new man is created in righteousness and true holiness*, Eph. iv. 24. Now this holiness as it is distinguished from righteousness, may import the purity and orderliness of the affections. And thus the apostle, 1 Tim. ii. 8. will have men to pray, *lifting up holy hands, without wrath and doubting:* because, as troubled water is unfit to receive the image of the sun; so the heart, filled with impure and disorderly affections, is not fit for divine communications. Man's sensitive appetite was indeed naturally carried out towards objects grateful to the senses. For seeing man was made up of body and soul, and God made this man to glorify and enjoy him; and for this end to use his good creatures in subordination to himself: it is plain that man was naturally inclined both to spiritual and sensible good; yet to spiritual good, the chief good as his ultimate end. And therefore his sensitive motives and inclinations, were subordinate to his reason and will, which lay straight with the will of GOD, and were not, in the least, contrary to the same. Otherwise he should have been made up of contradictions; his soul being naturally inclined to GOD as the chief end, in the superior part thereof; and the same soul inclined to the creature as the chief end, in the inferior part thereof; as they call it: which is impossible; for man, at the same instant, cannot have two chief ends. Man's affections then in his primative state, were pure from all defilement, free from all disorder and distemper, because in all their motions they were duly subjected to his clear reason, and his holy will. He had also an executive power answerable to his will: a power to do the good which he knew should be done, and which he inclined to do even to fulfil the whole law of GOD. If it had not been so GOD would not have required of him perfect obedience; for to say, That the LORD gathereth where he hath not strawed, is but the blasphemy of a wicked heart, against a good and bountiful GOD, Mat. xxv. 24, 25.

From what has been said, it may be gathered, that the original righteousness explained was universal and natural: yet mutable.

First, It was universal; both with respect to the subject of it, the whole man and the object of it, the whole law. Universal I say, with respect to the subject of it; for this righteousness was diffused thro' the whole man; it was a blessed leaven that leavened the whole lump. There was not one wrong pin in the tabernacle of human nature, when GOD set it up, however shattered it is now. Man was then holy in soul, body and spirit: while the soul remained untainted, its lodging was kept pure and undefiled: the members of the body were consecrated vessels, and instruments of righteousness. A combat betwixt flesh and spirit, reason and appetite; nay the least inclination to sin, lust of the flesh in the inferior part of the soul, was utterly inconsistent with this uprightness, in which man was created: and has been invented to veil the corruption of man's nature, and to obscure the grace of God in JESUS CHRIST; it looks very like the language of fallen Adam, laying his own sin at his Maker's door, Gen iii. 12. *The woman whom thou gavest to be with me, she gave me of the tree, and I did eat.* But as this righteousness was universal in respect of the subject, because it spread through the whole man: so also it was universal, in respect of the object, the holy law. There was nothing in the law, but what was agreeable to his reason and will, as GOD made him: though sin hath now set him at odds with it: his soul was shapen out in length and breadth to the commandment, tho' exceeding broad: so that this original righteousness was not only perfect in parts, but in degrees.

Secondly, As it was universal, so it was natural to him, and not supernatural to him in that state. Not that it was essential to man as man: for then he could not have lost it, without the loss of his very being; but it was con-natural to him. He was created with it: and it was necessary to the perfection of man, as he came out of the hand of GOD; necessary to constitute him in a state of integrity. Yet,

Thirdly, It was mutable: it was a righteousness that might be lost, as is manifested by the doleful event. His will was not absolutely indifferent to good or evil; GOD set it towards good only: yet he did not so fix and confirm its inclinations, that it could not alter. No, it was moveable to evil: and that only by man himself, GOD having given him a sufficient power to stand in this integrity, if he had pleased. Let no man quarrel GOD's works in this: for if Adam had been unchangeably righteous, he behoved to have been so, either by nature or by free gift: by nature he could not be so, for that is proper to GOD, and incommunicable to any creature: if by free gift, then no wrong was done him, in with-holding of what he could not crave. Confirmation in a righteous state, is a reward of grace, given upon continuing righteous through the state of trial; and would have been given to Adam, if he had stood out the time appointed for probation by the Creator; and accordingly is given to the saints, upon the account of the merits of Christ, who was obedient even to the death. And herein believers have the advantage of Adam, that they can never totally nor finally fall away from grace.

Thus was man made originally righteous, being *created in God's own image*, Gen. i. 27. which consists in the positive qualities of *knowledge, righteousness and holiness*, Col. iii. 10. Eph. iv. 24. All that GOD made *was very good*, according to their several natures, Gen. i. 31. And so was man morally good, being made after the image of him who is, *good and upright*, Psalm xxv. 8. Without this, he could not have an-a sinner, which is absurd and horrible to imagine.

Of Man's Original Happiness.

SECONDLY, I shall lay before you some of those things, which did accompany or flow from the righteousness of man's primitive state. Happiness is the result of holiness; and as it was an holy, so it was an happy state.

First, Man was then a very glorious creature. We have reason to suppose, that as Moses' face shone when he came down from the mount; so man had a very lightsome and pleasant countenance, and beautiful body, while as yet there was no darkness of sin in him at all. But seeing GOD himself is glorious in his holiness, Exod. xv. 11. surely that spiritual comeliness, the LORD put upon man at his creation, made him a very glorious creature. O how did light shine in his holy conversation, to the glory of the Creator! while every action was but the darting forth of a ray and beam of that glorious, unmixed light, which GOD had set up in his soul; while that lamp of love, lighted from heaven, continued burning in his heart, as in the holy place; and the law of the LORD, put in his inward parts by the finger of GOD, was kept by him there, as in the most holy. There was no impurity to be seen without; no squint look in the eyes, after any unclean thing; the tongue spoke nothing but the language of heaven: and in a word, *the King's Son was all glorious within, and his cloathing of wrought gold.*

Secondly, he was the favourite of heaven. He shone brightly in the image of God, who cannot but love his own image, where-ever it appears. While he was alone in the world, he was not alone, for GOD was with him. His communion and fellowship was with his Creator, and that immediately: for as yet there was nothing to turn away the face of GOD from the work of his own hands; seeing sin had not as yet entered, which alone could make the breach.

By the favour of God, he was advanced to be confederate with heaven, in the first covenant, called, *The Covenant of Works*. God reduced the law, which he gave in his creation, into the form of a covenant, whereof perfect obedience was the condition: life was the thing promised, and death the penalty. As for the condition, one great branch of the natural law was, that men believe whatsoever God shall reveal, and do whatsoever he shall command: accordingly God making this covenant with man, extended his duty to the *not eating of* the tree of knowledge of good and evil; and the law thus extended, was the rule of man's covenant-obedience. How easy were these terms to him, who had the natural law written on his heart; and that inclining him to obey this positive law, revealed to him, it seems, by an audible voice, Gen. ii. 16. the matter whereof was so very easy? And indeed it was highly reasonable that the rule and matter of his covenant-obedience should be thus extended; that which was added, being a thing in itself indifferent, where his obedience was to turn upon the precise point of the will of God, the plainest evidence of true obedience, and it being in an external thing, wherein his obedience or disobedience would be most clear and conspicuous.

Now, upon this condition, God promised him life, the continuance of natural life, in the union of soul and body, and of spiritual life, in the favour of his Creator: He promised him also eternal life in heaven, to have been entered into, when he should have passed the time of his trial upon earth, and the Lord should see meet to transport him into the upper Paradise. This promise of life was included in the threatning of death, mentioned Gen. ii. 17. For while God says, *In the day thou eatest thereof thou shalt surely die;* it is in effect, *If thou do not eat of it, thou shalt surely live,* And this was sacramentally confirmed by another tree in the garden, called therefore, *The Tree of life;* which he was debarred from when he had sinned: Gen. iii. 22, 23. ——*Lest he put forth his hand, and take also of the tree of life, and eat, and live forever. Therefore the Lord God sent him forth from the garden of Eden.* Yet it is not to be thought, that man's life and death did hang only on this matter of the forbidden fruit, but on the whole law; for so says the apostle, Gal. iii. 10. *It is written, Cursed is every one that continueth not in all things, which are written in the book of the law to do them.* That of the forbidden fruit, was a revealed part of Adam's religion; and so behoved expresly to be laid before him: but as to the natural law, he naturally knew death to be the reward of disobedience; for the very Heathens were not ignorant of this, *knowing the judgment of God, that they which commit such things, are worthy of death,* Rom. i. 32. And moreover, the promise included in the threatnings, secured Adam's life according to the covenant, as long as he obeyed the natural law, with the addition of that positive command; so that he needed nothing to be expressed to him in the covenant, but what concerned the eating of the forbidden fruit, that eternal life in heaven was promised in this covenant, is plain from this, that the threatning was of eternal death in hell; to which when man had made himself liable, CHRIST was promised by his death to purchase eternal life; and CHRIST himself expounds the promise of the covenant of works of eternal life, while he promiseth the condition of that covenant, to a proud young man, who, though he had not Adam's stock, yet would needs enter into life in the way of working, as Adam was to have done under this covenant, Matth. xix. 17. *If thou wilt enter into life*, viz. eternal life, *by doing*, ver. 16. *keep the commandments.*

The penalty was death, Gen. ii. 17. *In the day that thou eatest thereof, thou shalt surely die.* The death threatned was such, as the life promised was; and that most justly, viz. *temporal, spiritual*, and *eternal death*. The event is a commentary on this: For that very day he did eat therof, he was a dead man in law; but the execution was stopped, because of his posterity then in his loins; and another covenant was prepared: However, that day his body got its death-wound, and became mortal. Death also seized his soul: He lost his original righteousness and the favour of GOD: witness the gripes and throws of conscience, which made him hide himself from GOD. And he became liable to eternal death, which would have actually followed of course, if a Mediator had not been provided, who found him bound with the cords of death, as a malefactor ready to be led to execution. Thus you have a short description of the covenant, into which the LORD bro't man, in the state of innocence.

And seemeth it a small thing unto you, that earth was thus confederate with heaven? This could have been done to none but him, whom the King of heaven delighted to honour. It was an act of grace worthy of the gracious God whose favourite he was; for there was grace and free favour in the first covenant, though *the exceeding riches of grace*, as the apostle calls it, Eph. ii. 7. was reserved for the second. It was certainly an act of grace, favour and admirable condescension in GOD, to enter into a covenant; and such a covenant with his own creature. Man was not at his own, but at GOD's disposal. Nor had he any thing to work with, but what he had received from GOD. There was no proportion betwixt the work and the promised reward. Before that covenant, man was bound to perfect obedience, in virtue of his natural dependence on GOD: & death was naturally the wages of sin; which the justice of GOD could and would have required, though there had never been any covenant betwixt GOD and man: But GOD was free; man could never have required eternal life as the reward of his work, if there had not been such a covenant. GOD was free to have disposed of his creature as he saw meet: and if he had stood in his integrity as long as the world should stand, and there had been no covenant promising eternal life to him upon his obedience; God might have withdrawn his supporting hand at last, and so made him creep back into the womb of nothing, whence almighty power had drawn him out. And what wrong could there have been in this, while God should have taken back what he freely gave? But now the covenant being made, God becomes debtor to his own faithfulness: If man will work, he may crave the reward on the ground of the covenant. Well might the angels then, upon his being raised to his dignity, have given him that salutation, *Hail thou that art highly favoured, the Lord is with thee.*

Thirdly, God made him *lord of the world,* prince of the inferior creatures, universal lord and emperor of the whole earth. His Creator gave him dominion over the fish of the sea, and over the fowls of the air, over all the earth, yea, and every living thing that liveth upon the earth: He *put all things under his feet,* Psal. viii. 6, 7, 8. He gave him a power soberly to use and dispose of the creatures, in the earth, sea, and air. Thus man was God's deputy-governor in the lower world; and this his dominion was an image of God's sovereignty. This was common to the man and the woman; but the man had one thing peculiar to him, viz. that he had dominion over the woman also, 1 Cor. xi. 7. Behold how the creatures came to him to own their subjection, and to do him homage as their lord; and quietly stood before him, till he put names on them as his own, Gen. ii. 19. Man's face struck an awe upon them; the stoutest creatures stood astonished, tamely and quietly adoring him as their lord and ruler. Thus was man *crowned with glory and honour,* Psal. viii. 5. The Lord dealt most liberally and bountifully with him, *put all things under his feet;* only be kept one thing, one tree in the garden, out of his hands, even the tree of knowledge of good and evil.

But, you may say, *And did he grudge him this?* I answer, Nay; but when he had made him thus holy and happy, he graciously gave him this restriction, which was in its own nature, a prop and stay to keep him from falling. And this I say, upon these three grounds: (1.) As it was most proper for the honour of God, who had made man lord of the lower world, to assert his sovereign dominion over all, by some particular visible sign; so it was most proper for man's safety. Man being set down in a beautiful Paradise, it was an act of infinite wisdom, and of grace too, to keep from him one single tree, as a visible testimony that he must hold all of his Creator, as his great Landlord; that so while he saw himself lord of the creatures, he might not forget that he was still God's subject. (2.) This was a memorial of his mutable state given in to him from heaven, to be laid up by him, for his great caution. For man was created with a free will to good which the *tree of life* was an evidence of: But his will was also free to evil, and the *forbidden tree* was to him a memorial thereof. It was in a manner, a continual watch-word to him against evil; a beacon set up before him, to bid him beware of dashing himself to pieces, on the rock of sin. (3.) GOD made man upright, directed towards GOD, as the chief end. He set him, like Moses on the top of the hill, holding up his hands to heaven; and as Aaron and Hur stayed up Moses' hand, Exod. xvii. 10, 11, 12. so GOD gave man an erect figure of body, and forbid him the eating of this tree, to keep him in that posture of uprightness wherein he was created. GOD made the beasts looking down towards the earth, to shew that their satisfaction might be brought from thence; and accordingly it does afford them what is commensurable to their appetite: But the erect figure of man's body, which looketh upward, shewed him, that his happiness lay above him, in GOD; and that he was to expect it from heaven, and not from earth. Now this fair tree, of which he was forbidden to eat, taught him the same lesson, that his happiness lay not in enjoyment of the creatures, for there was a want even in Paradise: So that the forbidden tree was, in effect, the hand of all the creatures, pointing man away from themselves to GOD for happiness. It was a sign of emptiness hung before the door of the creation, with that inscription, *This is not your rest.*

Fourthly, As he had a perfect tranquility within his own breast, so he had a perfect calm without. His heart had nothing to reproach him with; conscience then had nothing to do, but to direct, approve and feast him: And without, there was nothing to annoy him. The happy pair lived in perfect amity; and though their knowledge was vast, true and clear, they knew no shame. Though they were naked, there were no blushes in their faces; for sin, the seed of shame, was not yet sown, Gen. ii. 25. and their beautiful bodies were not capable of injuries from the air; so they had no need of clothes, which are originally the badges of our shame. They were liable to no diseases, nor pains: And though they were not to live idle, yet toil, weariness, and sweat of the brows, were not known in this state.

Fifthly, Man had a life of pure delight, and undreggy pleasure in this state. Rivers of pure pleasures run through it. The earth, with the product thereof, was now in its glory: nothing had yet come in, to mar the beauty of the creatures. God set him down, not in a common place of the earth, but in *Eden*; a place eminent for pleasantness, as the name of it imports: Nay, not only in *Eden*, but in the *garden of Eden*; the most pleasant spot of that pleasant place: a garden planted by GOD himself, to be the mansionhouse of this his favourite. As, when God made the other living creatures, he said, *Let the water bring forth the moving creature*, Gen. i. 20. And *Let the earth bring forth the living creature*, ver. 24. But, when man was to be made, he said, *Let us make man*, ver. 26. So, when the rest of the earth was to be furnished with herbs and trees, GOD said, *Let the earth bring forth grass, and the fruit-tree*, &c. Gen. i. 11. But of paradise it is said, *God planted it*, chap. ii. 8. which cannot but denote a singular excellency in that garden, beyond all other parts of the then beautiful earth. There he wanted neither for necessity nor delight: for there was *every tree that is pleasant to the sight, and good for food*, ver. 9. He knew not these delights which luxury has invented for the gratifying of lusts: but his delights were such as came out of the hand of GOD; without passing through sinful hands, which readily leave marks of impurity on what they touch. So his delights were pure, his pleasures refined. And yet may *I shew you a more excellent way, Wisdom had entered into his heart*: Surely then knowledge was pleasant unto his soul! What delight do some find in their discoveries of the works of nature, by the scraps of knowledge they have gathered! But how much more exquisite pleasure had Adam, while his piercing eyes read the book of GOD's works; which GOD laid before him, to the end he might glorify him in the same! And therefore he had surely fitted him for the work. But above all, his knowledge of GOD, and that as his GOD! And the communion he had with him, could not but afford him the most refined and exquisite pleasure in the innermost recesses of his heart. Great is that delight, which the saints find in these views of the glory of God, that their souls are sometimes let into, while they are compassed about with many infirmities! But much more may well be allowed to sinless Adam! No doubt he relished these pleasures at another rate.

Lastly, He was immortal. He would never have died, if he had not sinned; it was in case of sin that death was threatned, Gen. ii. 17. Which shews it to be the consequent of sin, and not of the sinless, human nature. The perfect constitution of his body, which came out of GOD's hand very good; and the righteousness and holiness of his soul, removed all inward causes of death: nothing being prepared for the grave's devouring mouth, but the vile body, Philip. iii. 21. And those who have sinned, Job xxiv. 19. And GOD's special care of his innocent creature, secured him against outward violence. The apostle's testimony is express, Rom. v. 12. *By one man sin entered into the world and death by sin*. Behold the door by which death came in! Satan wrought with his lies till he got it opened, and so death entered; and therefore is he said to have been *a murderer from the beginning*, John viii. 44.

Thus have I shown you the holiness and happiness of man in this state. If any say, What's all this to us, who never tasted of that holy and happy state? They must know it nearly concerns us, in so far as Adam was the root of all mankind, our common head and representative; who received from God our inheritance and stock to keep it for himself and his children, and convey it to them. The Lord put all mankind's stock, as it were in one ship; and, as we ourselves should have done, he made our common father the pilot. He put a blessing in the root, to have been, if rightly managed, diffused into all the branches. According to our text, making Adam upright, he made man upright; and all mankind had that uprightness in him; for, *if the root be holy, so are the branches*. But more of this afterwards. Had Adam stood, none would have quarrelled the representation.

Use I. For information. This shews us, (1.) That not God, but man himself was the cause of his ruin. God made him upright: his Creator set him up, but he threw himself down. Was the Lord's directing and inclining him to good, the reason of his woful choice? Or did heaven deal so sparingly with him, that his pressing wants sent him to hell to seek supply. Nay, man was, and is the cause of his own ruin. (2.) God may most justly require of men perfect obedience to his law, and condemn them for their not obeying it perfectly, though now they have no ability to keep it. In so doing, he gathers but where he has strawed. He gave man ability to keep the whole law; man has lost it by his own fault; but his sin could never take away that right which God hath to exact perfect obedience of his creature, and to punish in case of disobedience. (3.) Behold here the infinite obligation we lie under, to Jesus Christ the second Adam; who with his own precious blood has bought our escheat, and freely makes offer of it again to us, Hos. xiii. 9. and that with the advantage of everlasting security, that it can never be altogether lost any more, John x. 28, 29. Free grace will fix those, whom free-will shook down into a gulf of misery.

Use II. This reacheth a reproof to three sorts of persons. (1.) To these who hate religion in the power of it, wherever it appears; and can take pleasure in nothing, but in the world and their lusts. Surely those men are far from righteousness; they are haters of God, Rom. i. 30. for they are haters of his image. Upright Adam in Paradise, would have been a great eye-sore to all such persons as he was to the serpent, whose seed they prove themselves to be, by their malignity. (2.) It reproves those who put religion to shame, and those who are ashamed of religion, before a graceless world. There is a generation who make so bold with the God that made them, and can in a moment crush them, that they ridicule piety, and make a mock of seriousness. *Against whom do ye sport yourselves? Against whom make ye a wide mouth and draw out the tongue?* Isa. lvii. 4. It is not against God himself, whose image, in some measure repaired on some of his creatures, makes them fools in your eyes? But *be ye not mockers, lest your bonds be made strong,* Isa. xxviii. 22. Holiness was the glory God put on man, when he made him: but now sons of men turn that glory into shame, because they themselves glory in their shame. There are others that secretly approve of religion, and in religious company will profess it: who at other times, to be neighbour-like are ashamed to own it; so weak are they, that they are blown over with the wind of the wicked's mouth. A broad laughter, an impious jest, a silly gibe out of a profane mouth, is to many an unanswerable argument against religion and seriousness; for in the cause of religion, they are as silly doves without heart. O that such would consider that weighty word! Mark viii. 38. *Whosoever therefore shall be ashamed of me; and of my words, in this adulterous and sinful generation; of him also shall the son of man be ashamed, when he cometh in the glory of his Father with the holy angels.* (3.) It reproves the proud, self-conceited professor, who admires himself in a garment he hath patched together of rags. There are many, who, when once they have gathered some scraps of knowledge of religion, and have attained to some reformation of life, do swell big with conceit of themselves; a sad sign that the effects of the fall lie so heavy upon them, that they have not as yet come to themselves, Luke xv. 17. They have eyes behind, to see their attainments; but no eyes within, no eyes before, to see their wants, which would surely humble them; for true knowledge makes men to see, both what once they were, and what they are at present: and so is humbling, and will not suffer them to be content with any measure of grace attained; but puts them on to press forward, *forgetting the things that are behind,* Phil. iii. 13, 14. But those men are such a spectacle of commiseration, as one would be, that had set his palace on fire, and were glorying in a cottage he had built for himself out of the rubbish, tho' so very weak, that it could not stand against a storm.

Use. III. Of lamentation. Here was a stately building, man, carved like a fair palace, but now lying in ashes: let us stand and look on the ruins, and drop a tear. This is a lamentation, and shall be for a lamentation. Could we chuse but to weep, if we saw our country ruined, and turned by the enemy into a wilderness? If we saw our houses on fire, & our housholds perishing in the flames? But all this comes far short of the dismal sight, man fallen as a star from heaven. Ah! may not we now say, O that we were as in months past, when there were no stains in our nature, no clouds on our minds, no pollution in our hearts. Had we never been in better case, the matter had been less: but they that were brought up in scarlet, do now embrace dunghills. Where is our primative glory now! Once no darkness in the mind, no rebellion in the will, no disorder in the affections. But ah! *How is the faithful city become an harlot? Righteousness lodged in it; but now murderers. Our silver is become dross, our wine mixed with water.* That heart which was once the temple of God, is now turned into a den of thieves. Let our name be Ichabod, for the glory is departed. Happy wast thou, O man, who was like unto thee! No pain or sickness could affect thee, no death could approach thee, no sigh was heard from thee, till these bitter fruits were plucked off the forbidden tree. Heaven shone upon thee, and earth smiled; thou wast the companion of angels, and the envy of devils. But how low is he now laid, who was created for dominion, and made lord of the world! *The crown is fallen from our head: wo unto us that we have sinned.* The creatures that waited to do him service, are now since the fall, set in battle array against him; and the least of them having commission proves too hard for him. Waters overflow the old world; fire consumes Sodom: the stars in their courses fight against Sisera; frogs, flies, lice, &c. turn executioners to Pharoah and his Egyptians; worms eat up Herod: yea, man needs a league with the beasts, yea with the very *stones of the field*, Job v. 13. having reason to fear, that every one that findeth him will slay him. Alas! how are we fallen! How are we plunged into a gulf of misery! The sun has come down on us, death has come in at our windows; our enemies have put out our two eyes, and sport themselves with our miseries. Let us then lie down in our shame, and let our confusion cover us. Nevertheless there is hope in Israel concerning this thing. Come then, O sinner, look to Jesus Christ, the second Adam: quit the first Adam and his covenant: come over to the Mediator and Surety of the new and better covenant: and let our hearts say, *Be thou our ruler, and let this breach be under thy hand.* And let your eye trickle down, and cease not without any intermission, till the Lord look down and behold from heaven, Lam. iii. 49. 50.

The STATE of NATURE, or of ENTIRE DEPRAVATION.

HEAD I.

The SINFULNESS of Man's *Natural State*.

GENESIS vi. 5.

And God saw that the wickedness of Man was great in the earth, and that every imagination of the thoughts of his heart was only evil continually.

WE have seen what man was, as GOD made him, a lovely and happy creature: let us view him now as he hath unmade himself: and we shall see him a sinful and miserable creature. This is the sad state we were brought into by the fall: a state as black and doleful as the former was glorious: and this we commonly call, The state of nature, or man's natural state; according to that of the apostle, Eph. ii. 2. *& were by nature the children of wrath even as others.* And herein two things are to be considered; 1*st*, The sinfulness; 2*dly*, The misery of this state, in which all the unregenerate do live. I begin with the sinfulness of man's natural state, whereof the text gives us a full, though short account; *And God saw that the wickedness of man was great, &c.*

The scope and design of these words is, to clear GOD's justice, in bringing the flood on the old world. There are two particular causes of it taken notice of in the preceding verses. (1.) MIXT marriages, ver. 2. *The sons of God*, the posterity of Seth and Enos, professors of the true religion, married with the daughters of men, the profane, cursed race of Cain. They did not carry the matter before the Lord, that he might *chuse for them*, Psal. xlviii. 14. But without any respect to the will of GOD they chose; not according to the rules of their faith, but of their fancy; they saw that they were fair; and their marriage with them, occasioned their divorce from GOD. This was one of the causes of the deluge, which swept away the old world. Would to GOD all professors in our day, could plead not guilty; but tho' that sin brought on the del-

C

uge, yet the deluge hath not swept away that sin; which as of old, in our day, may justly be looked upon, as one of the causes of the decay of religion. It was an ordinary thing among the Pagans, to change their gods, as they changed their condition in a married lot; and many sad instances the Christian world affords of the same, as if people were of Pharaoh's opinion, That religion is only for those that have no other care upon their heads, Exod. v. 17. (2.) Great oppression, ver. 4. *There was giants in the earth in those days*, men of great stature, great strength and monstrous wickedness *filling the earth with violence*, ver. 11. But neither their strength nor treasures of wickedness, could profit them in the day of wrath. Yet the gain of oppression still carries many over the terror of this dreadful example. Thus much for the connexion, and what particular crimes that generation was guilty of. But every person that was swept away with the flood, could not be guilty of these things, and shall not the Judge of all the earth do right? Therefore in my text, there is a general indictment drawn up against them all, *The wickedness of man was great in the earth*, &c. And this is well instructed, for GOD saw it. Two things are laid to their charge here.

First, Corruption of life, wickedness, great wickedness. I understand this of the wickedness of their lives; for it is plainly distinguished from the wickedness of their hearts. The sins of their outward conversation, were great in the nature of them, and greatly aggravated by their attending circumstances: and this not only among those of the race of cursed Cain, but those of holy Seth; the wickedness of man was great. And then it is added, in the earth (1.) To vindicate GOD's severity, in that he not only cut off sinners, but defaced the beauty of the earth; and swept off the brute creatures from it by the deluge; that as men had set the marks of their impiety, GOD might set the marks of his indignation, on the earth. (2.) To shew the heinousness of their sin, in making the earth which GOD had so adorned for the use of man, a sink of sin, and a stage whereon to act their wickedness, in defiance of heaven. GOD saw this corruption of life: he not only knew it, and took notice of it, but he made them to know that he did take notice of it; and that he had not forsaken the earth, tho' they had forsaken heaven.

Secondly, Corruption of nature. *Every imagination of the thoughts of his heart was only evil continually*. All their wicked practices are here traced to the fountain-head; a corrupt heart was the source of all. The soul which was made upright in all its faculties, is now wholly disordered. The heart that was made according to GOD's own heart, is now the reverse of it, a forge of evil imaginations, a sink of inordinate affections, and a store-house of all impiety, Mark vii. 21, 22. Behold the heart of the natural man, as it is opened in our text. The mind is defiled; the thoughts of the heart are evil; the will and affections are defiled; the imagination of the thoughts of the heart *i. e.* whatsoever the heart frameth within itself by thinking, such as judgment, choice, purposes, devices, desires, every inward motion; or rather, the frame of thoughts of the heart, namely, the frame; make or mould of these, 1 Chron. xxix 18. is evil. Yea, and every imagination, every frame of his thoughts, is so. The heart is ever framing something; but never one right thing; the frame of thoughts, in the heart of man is exceeding various; yet are they never cast into a right frame; but is there not, at least, a mixture of good in them? No, they are only evil, there is nothing in them truly good and acceptable to GOD; nor can any thing be so that comes out of that forge; where not the Spirit of GOD, but *the prince of the power of the air worketh*, Eph. ii. 2. Whatever changes may be found in them, are only from evil to evil; for the imagination of the heart, or frame of thoughts in natural men, is evil continually, or every day; from the first day, to the last day in this state, they are in midnight darkness; there is not a glimmering of the light of holiness in them; not one holy thought can ever be produced by the unholy heart. O What a vile heart is this! O what a corrupt nature is this! the tree that always brings forth fruit, but never good fruit, whatever soil it be set in, whatever pains be taken on it, must naturally be an evil tree; and what can that heart be, whereof every imagination, every set of thoughts, is only evil, and that continually? Surely that corruption is ingrained in our hearts, interwoven with our very natures, has sunk into the marrow of our souls; and will never be cured, but by a miracle of grace. Now such is man's heart, such is his nature, till regenerating grace change it. GOD that searcheth the heart saw man's heart was so, he took special notice of it; and the faithful and true witness cannot mistake our case; though we are most apt to mistake ourselves in this point, and generally do overlook it.

Beware that there be not a thought in thy wicked heart, saying, what is that to us? Let that generation of whom the text speaks, see to that. For the Lord has left the case of that generation on record, to be a looking-glass to all after-generations; wherein they may see their own corruption of heart, and what their lives would be too, if he restrained them not; for *as in water face answereth to face so the heart of man to man*, Prov. xxvii. 19. Adam's fall has framed all men's hearts alike in this matter. Hence the apostle, Rom. iii. 10. proves the corruption of the natures, hearts, and lives of all men, from what the Psalmist says of the wicked in his day.

them that are under the law; that every mouth may be stopped, and all the world may become guilty before God. Had the history of the deluge been transmitted unto us, without the reason thereof in the text, we might thence have gathered the corruption and total depravation of man's nature; for what other quarrel could a holy and just GOD have with the Infants that were destroyed by the flood, seeing they had no actual sin? If we saw a wise man, who having made a curious piece of work, and heartily approved of it when he gave it out of his hand, as fit for the use it was designed for, rise up in wrath and break it all in pieces, when he looked on it afterwards; would we not thence conclude the frame of it had been quite marred since made, and that it does not serve for that use it was designed for? How much more, when we see the holy and wise GOD, destroying the work of his own hands, once solemnly pronounced by him very good, may we conclude that the original frame thereof is utterly marred, that it cannot be mended, but it must needs be new made, or lost altogether? Gen. vi. 6, 7. *And it repented the Lord that he had made man on the earth, and it grieved him at his heart; and the Lord said, I will destroy man* or blot him out; as a man doth a sentence out of a book, that cannot be corrected, by cutting off some letters, syllables, or words, and interlining others here and there; but must needs be wholly new framed. But did the deluge carry off this corruption of man's nature? Did it mend the matter? No, it did not. GOD in his holy providence, *That every mouth may be stopped and all the new world may become guilty before God,* as well as the old, permits that corruption of nature to break out in Noah, the father of the new world, after the deluge was over. Behold him as another Adam sinning in the fruit of a tree, Gen. ix. 20, 21. He *planted a vineyard and he drank of the wine, and was drunken, and he was uncovered within his tent.* More than that, GOD gives the same reason against a new deluge, which he gives in our text for bringing that on the world; *I will not,* saith he, *again curse the ground any more for man's sake, for the imagination of man's heart is evil from his youth,* Gen. viii. 21. Whereby it is intimated, that there is no mending the matter by this mean; and that if he would always take the same course with men that he had done, he would be always sending deluges on the earth, seeing the corruption of man's na-

That Man's Nature is corrupted.

ture remains still. But tho' the flood could not carry off the corruption of nature, yet it pointed at the way how it is to be done, viz. That men must be born of water and of the Spirit, raised from spiritual death in sin, by the grace of Jesus Christ, who came by water and blood; out of which a new world of saints arise in regeneration, even as the new world of sinners out of the waters, where they had long lain buried, as it were, in the ark. This we learn from 1 Pet. iii. 20, 21. where the apostle speaking of Noah's ark saith, *Wherein few, that is, eight souls, were saved by water. The like figure whereunto, even baptism doth also now save us.* Now the waters of the deluge being *a like figure to baptism*; it plainly follows, that they signified, as baptism doth, *the washing of regeneration, and renewing of the Holy Ghost.* To conclude then, these waters, tho' now dried up, may serve us for a looking-glass, in which to see the total corruption of our nature, and the necessity of regeneration. From the text thus explained, ariseth this weighty point of Doctrine, which he that runs may read in it, viz. *Man's nature is now wholly corrupted.* Now is there a sad alteration, a wonderful overturn, in the nature of man; where, at first, there was nothing evil; now there is nothing good. In prosecuting of this doctrine, I shall,

First, Confirm it.

Secondly, Represent this corruption of nature in its several parts.

Thirdly, Shew you how man's nature comes to be thus corrupted.

Lastly, Make application.

That Man's Nature is corrupted.

FIRST, I am to confirm the doctrine of the corruption of nature; to hold the glass to your eyes, wherein you may see your sinful nature? which, tho' GOD takes particular notice of it, many do quite overlook. And here we shall consult, 1. GOD's word. 2. Men's experience and observation.

I. For scripture proof, let us consider,

First, How the scripture takes particular notice of Adam's communicating his image to his posterity, Gen. v. 3. *Adam begat a son in his own likeness, after his image, and called his name Seth.* Compare with this ver. 1. of that chapter, *In the day that God created man, in the likeness of God made he him.* Behold here, how the image after which man was made, and the image after which he is begotten, are opposed. Man was made in the likeness of GOD; that is, a holy and righteous GOD made a holy & righteous creature; but fallen Adam begat a son not in the likeness of GOD, but in his own likeness;

that is, corrupt sinful Adam begat a corrupt sinful son. For as the image of GOD bore righteousness and immortality in it, as was cleared before, so this image of fallen Adam bore corruption and death in it, 1 Cor. xv. 49, 50. compare with ver. 28. Moses, in that fifth chapter of Genesis, being to give us the first bill of mortality, that ever was in the world, ushers it in with this, that dying Adam begat mortals. Having sinned, he became mortal, according to the threatening; and so he begat a son, in his own likeness, sinful, and therefore mortal; thus sin and death passed on all. Doubtless, he begat both Cain and Abel in his own likeness, as well as Seth. But it is not recorded of Abel; because he left no issue behind him, and his falling the first sacrifice to death in the world, was a sufficient document of it; nor of Cain, to whom it might have been thought peculiar, because of his monstrous wickedness; and besides all his posterity was drowned in the flood; but it is recorded of Seth, because he was the father of the holy seed; and from him all mankind since the flood has descended, and fallen Adam's own likeness with them.

Secondly, It appears from that scripture-text, Job xiv. 4. *Who can bring a clean thing out of an unclean? Not one.* Our first parents were unclean, how then can we be clean? How could our immediate parents be clean? Or, how shall our children be so? The uncleanness here aimed at, is a sinful uncleanness; for it is such as makes man's days full of trouble; and it is natural, being derived from unclean parents; *Man is born of a woman*, ver. 1. *And how can he be clean that is born of a woman?* Job. xxxv. 4. An omnipotent GOD, whose power is not here challenged, could bring a clean thing out of an unclean; and did so, in the case of the man Christ; but no other can. Every person that is born according to the course of nature, is born unclean. If the root be corrupt, so must the branches be. Neither is the matter mended, though the parents be sanctified ones; for they are but holy in part, and that by grace, not by nature; and they beget their children as men, not as holy men. Wherefore, as the circumcised parent begets an uncircumcised child, and after the purest grain is sown, we reap corn with the chaff; so the holiest parents beget unholy children, and cannot communicate their grace to them, as they do their nature; which many godly parents find true, in their sad experience.

Thirdly, Consider the confession of the Psalmist David, Psal. li. 6. *Behold I was shapen in iniquity, and in sin did my mother conceive me.* Here he ascends from his actual sin, to the fountain of it, namely, corrupt nature. He was a man according to GOD's own heart; but from the beginning it was not so with him. He was begotten in lawful marriage;

but when the lump was shapen in the womb, it was a sinful lump. Hence the corruption of nature is called the old man; being as old as ourselves, older than grace, even in those that are sanctified from the womb.

Fourthly, Hear our LORD's determination of the point, John iii. 5. *That which is born of the flesh, is flesh.* Behold the universal corruption of all mankind, all are flesh. Not that all are frail, though that is a sad truth too; yea, and our natural frailty is an evidence of our natural corruption; but that is not the sense of this text: but here is the meaning of it, all are corrupt and sinful, and that naturally; hence our LORD argues here, that because they are flesh, therefore they must be born again, or else they *cannot enter into the kingdom of God,* ver. 3. 5. And as the corruption of our nature evidenceth the absolute necessity of regeneration; so the absolute necessity of regeneration plainly proves the corruption of our nature; for why should a man need a second birth, if his nature were not quite marred in the first birth? Infants must be born again, for that is an except, John iii. 3. which admits of no exception. And therefore, they were circumcised under the old Testament; as having *the body of the sins of the flesh,* which is conveyed to them by natural generation, *to put off,* Col. ii. 11. And now by the appointment of Jesus Christ, they are to be baptised; which says they are unclean, and that there is no salvation for them, but by the *washing of regeneration, and renewing of the Holy Ghost,* Tit. iii. 5.

Fifthly, man certainly is sunk very low now, in comparison of what he once was, GOD made him but a *little lower than the angels;* but now we find him likened to the beasts that perish. He hearkened to a brute; and is now become like one of them. Like Nebuchadnezzar, his portion, in his natural state, is with the beasts, *minding only earthly things,* Phil. iii. 19. Nay brutes, in some sort, have the advantage of the natural man who is sunk a degree below them. He is more witless, in what concerns him most, than the stork, or the turtle, or the crane, or the swallow, in what is for their interest, Jer. viii. 7. He is more stupid than the ox or ass, Isa. i. 3. I find him sent to school, to learn of the ant or emmot, which having no guide or leader to go before her; no overseer or officer to compel or stir her up to work, no ruler, but may do as she lists, being under the dominion of none; yet *provideth her meet in the summer and harvest,* Prov. vi. 6, 7, 8. while the natural man has all these, and yet exposeth himself to eternal starving. Nay more than all this, the scripture holds out the natural man, not only as wanting the good qualities of those creatures; but as a compound of the evil qualities of the worst of the creatures, in which do concenter the fierceness of the lion, the craft of the fox, the unteachableness of the wild ass, the filthiness of the dog and swine, the poison of the asp, and such like. Truth itself calls them *serpents, a generation of vipers;* yea more, even *children of the devil,* Mat. xxi. 1.33. John viii. 44. Surely then, man's nature is miserably corrupted.

Lastly, *We are by nature children of wrath,* Eph. ii. 3. We are worthy of, as liable to the wrath of GOD; and this by nature; and therefore, doubtless, we are by nature sinful creatures. We are condemned before we have done good or evil; under the curse ere we know what it is. *But will a lion roar in the forest, while he hath no prey?* Amos iii. 4. that is, Will a holy and just GOD roar in his wrath against man, if he be not, by his sin, made a prey for wrath? No, he will not, he cannot. Let us conclude, then, that according to the word of God, man's nature is a corrupt nature.

II. If we consult experience, and observe the case of the world in these things that are obvious, to any person that will not shut his eyes against clear light; we will quickly perceive such fruits, as discover this root of bitterness: I shall propose a few things, that may serve to convince us in this point.

First, Who sees not a flood of miseries overflowing the world? And whether can a man go, where he shall not dip his foot, if he go not over head and ears in it? Every one at home and abroad, in city and country, in palaces and cottages, is groaning under some one thing or other, ungrateful to him. Some are oppressed with poverty, some chastned with sickness and pain, some are lamenting their losses: none wants a cross of one sort or another. No man's condition is so soft, but there is some thorn of uneasiness in it. And at length death, the wages of sin, comes after these its harbingers, and sweeps all away.

Now, what but sin has opened the sluice? There is not a complaint nor sigh heard in the world, nor a tear that falls from our eye, but it is an evidence that man is fallen as a star from heaven; for *God distributeth sorrow in his anger,* Job xxi. 17. This is a plain proof of the corruption of nature, forasmuch as those that have not yet actually sinned, have their share of these sorrows; yea, and draw their first breath in the world weeping, as if they knew this world, at first sight, to be a Bochim, the place of weepers. There are graves of the smallest, as well as of the largest size, in the church-yard; and there are never wanting some in the world, who' like Rachel, are weeping for their children, because they are not, Mat. ii. 18.

Secondly, Observe how early this corruption of nature begins to appear in young ones: Solomon observes, that even a *child is known by his doings,* Prov. xx. 11. It may soon be discerned, what way the bias of the heart lies: Do not the children of fallen Adam, before they can go alone, follow their father's footsteps? What a vast deal of little pride, ambition, curiosity, vanity, wilfulness, and averseness to good, appears in them! And when they creep out of infancy, there is a necessity of using the rod of correction, to drive away the foolishness that is bound up in their heart, Prov. xxii. 15. Which shews, that if grace prevail not, the child will be as Ishmael, *a wild ass-man,* as the word is, Gen. xvi. 13.

Thirdly, Take a view of the manifold gross outbreakings of sin in the world: *The wickedness of man is yet great in the earth.* Behold the bitter fruits of the corruption of our nature, Hos. iv. 2. *By swearing, and lying, and killing, and stealing, and committing adultery, they break out,* like the breaking forth of water, *and blood toucheth blood.* The world is filled with filthiness, and all manner of lewdness, wickedness and profanity. Whence is this deluge of sin on the earth, but from the breaking up of the fountains of *the great deep,* the heart of man; out of which proceed evil thoughts, adulteries, fornications, murders, thefts, covetousness, wickedness, &c. Mark vii. 21, 22. Ye will, it may be, thank GOD with a whole heart, that ye are not like these other men; and indeed ye have better reason for it, than I fear, ye are aware of; for *As in water, face answereth to face, so the heart of man to man,* Prov. xxvii. 19. As in looking into clear water, ye see your own face; so in looking into your own heart, ye may see other men's there; and looking into other men's, in them ye may see your own. So that the most vile and profane wretches that are in the world should serve you for a looking glass: in which you ought to discern the corruption of your own nature! and if you do so, ye would, with a heart truly touched, thank GOD, and not yourselves, indeed, that ye are not as other men, in your lives; seeing the corruption of nature is the same in you as in them.

Fourthly, Cast your eye upon these terrible convulsions the world is thrown into by the lust of men. Lions make not a prey of lions, nor wolves of wolves; but men are turned wolves to one another, biting and devouring one another. Upon how slight occasions will men sheath their swords in one another's bowels! The world is a wilderness, where the clearest fire men can carry about with them, will not fright away the wild beasts that inhabit it, and that because they are men, and not brutes, but one way or other they will be wounded. Since Cain shed the blood of Abel, the earth has been turned into a slaughter-house; and the chace has been continued since Nimrod began his hunting; on the earth, as in the sea, the greatest still devouring the lesser. When we see the world in such a ferment, every one stabbing another with words or swords, we may conclude there is an evil spirit among them. These violent heats among Adam's sons, speak the whole body to be distempered; the whole head to be sick, and the whole heart faint. They surely proceed from an inward cause, James vi. 1. *Lusts that war in our members.*

Fifthly, Consider the necessity of human laws, fenced with terrors and severities! to which we may apply what the apostle says, 1 Tim. i. 9. That *the law is not made for a righteous man, but for the lawless and disobedient, for the ungodly and for sinners,* &c. Man was made for society; and God himself said of the first man, when he had created him, that it was *not meet that he should be alone;* yet the case is such now, that, in society, he must be hedged in with thorns. And that from hence we may the better see the corruption of man's nature, consider, (1.) Every man naturally loves to be at full liberty himself; to have his own will for his law; and if he would follow his natural inclinations, would vote himself out of the reach of all laws, divine and human. And hence some, the power of whose hands has been answerable to their natural inclination, have indeed made themselves absolute, and above laws; agreeable to man's monstrous design at first, *to be as gods,* Gen. iii. 5. Yet, (2.) There is no man that would willingly adventure to live in a lawless society; and therefore, even pirates and robbers have laws among themselves, though the whole society cast off all respect to law and right. Thus men discover themselves to be conscious of the corruption of nature; not daring to trust one another, put upon security. (3.) How dangerous soever it is, to break through the hedge; yet the violence of lust makes many adventure daily to run the risk. They will not only sacrifice their credit and conscience, which last is highly esteemed in the world; but for the pleasure of a few moments, immediately succeeded with terror from within, they will lay themselves open to a violent death by the laws of the land wherein they live. (4.) The laws are often made to yield to mens lusts. Sometimes whole societies run into such extravagancies that, like a company of prisoners, they break off their fetters and put their guards to flight; and the voice of laws cannot be heard for the noise of arms. And seldom is there a time wherein there are not some persons so great and daring, that the laws dare not look their impetuous lusts in the face; which made David say, in the case of Joab, who had murdered Abner, *These men, the sons of Zeruiah, be too hard for me,* 2 Sam. iii. 39. Lusts sometimes grow too strong for laws, so that the law is slacked, as the pulse of a dying man, Hab. i. 3, 4 (5.) Consider what necessity often appears of amending old laws, and making new ones; which have their rise from new crimes that man's nature is very fruitful of. There would be no need of mending the hedge, if men were not like unruly beasts, still breaking it down. It is astonishing to see, what figure the Israelites, who were separated unto GOD, from among all the nations of the earth, do make in their history; what horrible confusions were among them, when there was no king in Israel, as you may see, Judges xviii. xix, xx. xxi. How hard it was to reform them, when they had the best of magistrates; and how quickly they turned aside again, when they got wicked rulers. I cannot but think, that one grand design of that sacred history, was to discover the corruption of man's nature, the absolute need of the Messiah, and his grace; and that we ought in the reading of it, to improve it to that end. How cutting is that word, the LORD has to Sam. concerning Saul, 1 Sam. ix. 17. *The same shall reign over*, or, as the word is, *shall restrain my people.* O the corruption of man's nature! the awe and dread of the GOD of heaven restrains them not; but they must have gods on the earth to do it, *to put them to shame*, Judges xviii. 7.

Sixthly, Consider the remains of that natural corruption in the saints. Though grace has entered, yet corruption is not quite expelled; though they have got the new creature, yet much of the old corrupt nature remains; and these struggle together within them, as the twins in Rebekah's womb, Gal. v. 17. They find it present with them at all times, and in all places even in the most retired corners. If a man have an ill neighbour, he may remove; if he have an ill servant, he may put him away at the term; if a bad yoke-fellow, he may sometimes leave the house, and be free of molestation that way. But should the saint go into a wilderness, or set up his tent in some remote rock in the sea, where never foot of man, beast, or fowl had touched, there will it be with him. Should he be, with Paul, caught up to the third heaven, it shall come back with him, 2 Cor. xii. 7. It follows him as the shadow doth the body; it makes a blot in the fairest line he can draw. It is like the fig tree in the wall, which, how nearly soever it was cut, yet still grew till the wall was thrown down; for the roots of it are fixed in the heart, while the saint is in the world, as with bands of iron and brass. It is especially active when he would do good, Rom. vii. 21. then the fowls come down upon the carcases. Hence, often, in holy duties, the spirit even of a saint, as it were, evaporates; and he is left, ere he is aware, like Michael, with an image in the bed, instead of an husband. I need not stand to prove the remains of the corruption of nature in the godly, to themselves, for they groan under it; and to prove it to them, were to hold out a candle to let men see the sun, and as for the wicked, they are ready to account mole-hills in the saint, as big as mountains; if not to reckon them all hypocrites. But consider these few things on this hand; (1.) If it be thus in the green tree, how must it be in the dry? The saints are not born saints, but made so by the power of regenerating grace. Have they got a new nature, and yet so much of the old remains with them? How great must that corruption be in others, where it is altogether unmixed with grace? (2.) The saints groan under the remains of it, as a heavy burden? Hear the apostle, Rom. vii. 24. *O wretched man that I am! Who shall deliver me from the body of this death?* What though the carnal man lives at ease and quiet, and the corruption of nature is not his burden; is he therefore free from it? No, no; only he is dead, and feels not the sinking weight. Many a groan is heard from a sick-bed, but never one from a grave. In the saint, as in the sick man, there is a mighty struggle; life and death striving for the mastery; but in the natural man, as in the dead corpse, there is no noise; because death bears full sway. (3.) The godly man resists the old corrupt nature; he strives to mortify it, yet it remains; he endeavours to starve it, and by that means to weaken it, yet it is active; how must it spread then, and strengthen itself in that soul, where it is not starved but fed? And this is the case of all unregenerate, who *make provision for the flesh, to fulfil the lusts thereof.* If the garden of the diligent afford him new work daily, in cutting off and rooting up, surely that of the sluggard must needs be all grown over with thorns.

Lastly, I shall add but one observe more, and that is, That in every man naturally the image of fallen Adam does appear. Some children, by their features and lineaments of their face, do as it were, father themselves; and thus we do resemble our first parents. Every one of us bear the image and impress of their fall upon him; and to evince the truth of this, I do appeal to the consciences of all in these following particulars.

1*st*. Is not a sinful curiosity natural to us? And is not this a print of Adam's image? Gen. iii. 6. Is not men naturally much more desirous to know new things, than to practice old known truths? How like to old Adam do we look in this, itching after novelties, and disrelishing old solid doctrines? We seek after knowledge rather than holiness; and study most to know these things, which are least edifying. Our wild and roving fancies need a bridle to curb them, while good solid affections must be quickened and spurred up.

iii. 2, 3, 6. I think this cannot be denied; for daily observation evinceth, that it is a natural principle, that stolen waters are sweet, and bread eaten in secret, is pleasant, Prov. ix. 17. The very heathens are convinced, that man was possessed with this spirit of contradiction, tho' they knew not the spring of it. How often do men give themselves the loose in these things, in which, if GOD had left them at liberty, they would have bound up themselves! but corrupt nature takes a pleasure in the very jumping over the hedge. And is it not a repeating of our father's folly, that men will rather climb for forbidden fruit, than gather what is shaken off the tree of good providence to them, when they have GOD's express allowance for it!

3*dly*, Which of all the children of Adam is not naturally disposed to hear the *instruction that causeth to err?* And was not this the rock our first parents split upon! Gen. iii. 4, 6. How apt is weak man, ever since that time, to parley with temptations! *God speaketh once, yea twice, yet man perceiveth it not,* Job xxxiii. 14. but readily doth he listen to Satan. Men might often come fair off if they would dismiss temptations with abhorrence, when first they appear: if they would nip them in the bud, they would soon die away; but alas! when we see the train laid for us, and the fire put to it, yet we stand till it run along, and we be blown up with its force.

4*thly,* Do not the eyes in our head often blind the eyes of the mind? And was not this the very case of our first parents? Gen. iii. 6. Man is never more blind than when he is looking on the objects that are most pleasant to the sense. Since the eyes of our first parents were opened to the forbidden fruit, mens eyes have been the gates of destruction to their souls; at which impure imaginations and sinful desires have entered the heart, to the wounding of the soul, wasting of the conscience, and bringing dismal effects sometimes on whole societies, as in Achan's case, Joshua vii. 21. Holy Job was aware of this danger: from these two little rowling bodies, which a very small splinter of wood will make useless; so as, with that King who durst not, with his ten thousand, meet him that came with twenty thousand against him, Luke xiv. 31, 32. He sendeth and desireth conditions of peace, Job xxxi. 1. *I have made a covenant with mine eyes,* &c.

5*thly,* Is it not natural for us, to care for the body even at the expence of the soul? This was one ingredient in the sin of our first parents, Gen. iii. 6. O how happy might we be, if we were but at half the pains about our souls, that we bestow upon our bodies! if that question, *What must I do to be saved?* Acts xvi. 30. did run but near as oft through our minds, as those other questions do, *What shall we eat; what shall we drink; wherewithal shall we be cloathed?* Mat. vi. 31. many a (now) hopeless case would turn very hopeful. But the truth is, most men live as if they were nothing but a lump of flesh; or as if their soul served for no other use, but like salt, to keep the body from corrupting: *They are flesh*, John iii. 6. *They mind the things of the flesh*, Rom. viii. 5. and *they live after the flesh*, ver. 13. If the consent of the flesh be got to an action, the consent of the conscience is rarely waited for; yea, the body is often served, when the conscience has entered a dissent.

6thly, Is not every one, by nature, discontent with his present lot in the world, or with some one thing or other in it? This also was Adam's case, Gen. iii. 5, 6. Some one thing is always missing; so that man is a creature given to changes. And if any doubt of this, let them look over all their enjoyments; and after a review of them, listen to their own hearts, and they will hear a secret murmuring for want of something; though perhaps, if they considered the matter aright, they would see that it is better for them to want, than to have that something. Since the hearts of our first parents flew out at their eyes, on the forbidden fruit, and a night of darkness was thereby brought on the world; their posterity have a natural disease, which Solomon calls, *The wandering of the desires*, or as the word is, *The walking of the soul*, Eccl. vi. 9. This is a sort of diabolical trance, wherein the soul traverseth the world; feeds itself with a thousand airy nothings; snatcheth at this and the other created excellency, in imagination and desire; goes here and there, and every where, except where it should go. And the soul is never cured of this disease, till overcoming grace bring it back, to take up its everlasting rest in God through Christ; but till this be, if man were set again in Paradise, the garden of the Lord; all the pleasures there would not keep him from looking, yea, and leaping over the hedge a second time.

7thly, Are we not far more easily impressed and influenced by evil counsels and examples, than by those that are good! You will see this was the ruin of Adam, Gen. iii. 6. Evil example, to this day, is one of Satan's master-devices to ruin men. And tho' we have by nature, more of the fox than of the lamb; yet that ill property some observe in this creature, viz. That if one lamb skip into a water, the rest that are near will suddenly follow, may be observed also in the dispotion of the children of men to whom it is very natural to embrace an evil way, because they see others upon it before them. Ill example has frequently the force of a violent stream, to carry us over plain duty; but especially, if the example be given by those we bear a great affection to; our affection, in that case, blinds our judgment; and what we would abhor in others, is complied with, to humor them. And nothing is more plain, than that generally men chuse rather to do what the most do, than what the best do.

8thly, Who of all Adam's sons need be taught the art of *sewing fig-leaves together*, to cover their nakedness? Gen. iii. 7. When we have ruined ourselves, and made ourselves naked, to our shame; we naturally seek to help ourselves by ourselves: and many poor gifts are fallen upon, as silly and insignificant as Adam's fig-leaves. What pains are men at, to cover their sin from their own consciences, and draw all the fair colours upon it that they can? And when once convictions are fastened upon them, so that they cannot but see themselves naked: it is as natural for them to attempt to spin a cover to it out of their own bowels, as for fishes to swim in the waters, or birds to fly in the air. Therefore the first question of the convinced is, *What shall we do?* Acts ii. 27. How shall we qualify ourselves? What shall we perform? Not minding that the new creature is GOD'S own workmanship, or deed, Eph. ii. 10. more than Adam thought of being clothed with skins of sacrifices, Gen. iii. 21.

9thly, Do not Adam's children naturally follow his footsteps, *in hiding themselves from the presence of the Lord*, Gen. iii. 8. We are every whit as blind in this matter as he was, who thought to hide himself from the presence of GOD among the shady trees of the garden. We are very apt to promise ourselves more security in a secret sin, than in one that is openly committed. *The eye of the adulterer waiting for the twilight, saying, No eye shall see me.* Job xxiv. 15. And men will freely do that in secret, which they would be ashamed to do in the presence of a child; as if darkness could hide from an all-seeing GOD. Are we not naturally careless of communion with GOD; ay, and averse to it? Never was there any communion betwixt GOD and Adam's children, where the LORD himself had not the first word. If he would let them alone, they would never inquire after him. Isaiah lvii. 18. *I hide me.*——Did he seek after a hiding GOD? Very far from it——He went on in the way of his heart.

10thly, How loth are men to confess sin, to take guilt and shame to themselves! And was it not thus in the case before us? Gen. iii. 10. Adam confesseth his nakedness, which he could not get denied; but not one word he says of his sins;

here was the reason of it, he would fain have hid it if he could. It is as natural for us to hide sin, as to commit it. Many sad instances thereof we have in this world; but a far clearer proof of it we shall get at the day of judgment, the day in which *God will judge the secrets of men*, Rom. ii. 16. Many a foul mouth will then be seen, which is now wiped, and saith, *I have done no wickedness*, Prov. xxx. 20.

Lastly, Is it not natural for us to extenuate our sin and transfer the guilt upon others? And when God examined our guilty first parents, did not Adam lay the blame on the serpent? Gen. iii. 12, 13. Now Adam's children need not be taught this hellish policy; before they can well speak, if they cannot get the fact denied, they will cunningly lisp out something to lessen their fault, and lay the blame upon another. Nay, so natural is this to men, that in the greatest of sins, they will lay the fault upon God himself; they will blaspheme his holy providence, under the mistaken name of misfortune, or ill luck; and thereby lay the blame of their sin at heaven's door. And was not this one of Adam's tricks after his fall? Gen. iii. 12. *And the man said, the woman whom thou gavest to be with me, she gave me of the tree, and I did eat*. Observe the order of the speech. He makes his apology in the first place; and then comes his confession; his apology is long; but his confession very short; it is all comprehended in a word, *And I did eat*. How pointed and distinct is his apology, as if he was afraid his meaning would have been mistaken? *The woman*, says he, or that woman, as if he would have pointed the judge to his own work, of which we read, Gen. ii. 22. There was but one woman then in the world; so that one would think he needed not be so nice and exact in pointing at her; yet she is as carefully marked out in his defence, as if there had been ten thousand. *The woman whom thou gavest me*; here he speaks as if he had been ruined with God's gifts. And to make the shift look the blacker, it is added to all this, *thou gavest to be with me*, a constant companion, to stand by me as a helper. This looks as if Adam would have fathered an ill design upon the Lord, in giving him this gift. And after all, there is a new demonstrative here, before the sentence is complete; he says not, *The woman gave me*, but *the woman, she gave me*; emphatically, as if he had said, She, even *She* gave me of the tree. This much for his apology. But his confession is quickly over, in one word, as he spoke it, *and I did eat*. And there is nothing here to point to himself, and as little to shew what he had eaten. How natural is this black art to Adam's posterity? He that runs may read it. So universally does Solomon's observe hold true, Prov. xvii. 3. *The foolishness of man perverteth his ways,* and his heart fretteth against the Lord. Let us then call fallen Adam, father; let us not deny the relation, seeing we bear his image.

And now to shut up this point, sufficiently confirmed by concurring evidence from the LORD's word, our own experience and observation; let us be perfuaded to believe the doctrine of the corruption of our nature; and to look to the second Adam, the blessed JESUS, for the application of his precious blood, to remove the guilt of this sin; and for the efficacy of his holy Spirit, to make us new creatures, knowing that *except we be born again, we cannot enter in to the kingdom of God.*

Of the Corruption of the Understanding:

SECONDLY, I proceed to inquire into the corruption of nature, in the several parts thereof. But who can comprehend it? Who can take the exact dimension of it, in its breadth, lenght, height, and depth? The heart is deceitful above all things, and desperately wicked; who can know it? Jer. xvii. 9. However, we may quickly perceive as much of it, as may be matter of deepest humiliation, and may discover to us the absolute necessity of regeneration. Man in his natural state is altogether corrupt. Both soul and body are polluted, as the apostle proves at large, Rom. iii. 10.----18. As for the soul, this natural corruption has spread itself thro' all the faculties thereof; and is to be found in the understanding, the will, the affections, the conscience, and the memory.

I. The understanding, that leading faculty is despoiled of its primitive glory, and covered over with confusion. We have fallen into the hands of our grand adversary, as Sampson into the hands of the Philistines, and are deprived of our two eyes. *There is none that understandeth*, Rom. iii. 11. *Mind and conscience are defiled*, Tit. i. 15. The natural man's apprehension of divine things is corrupt, Psal. l. 21. *Thou thoughtest that I was altogether such an one as thyself.* His judgment is corrupt, and cannot be otherwise, seeing his eye is evil; and therefore the scriptures, that shew that men did all wrong, say, *Every one did that which was right in his own eyes*, Judges xvii. 7. and xxi. 25. And his imaginations, or reasonings must be cast down, by the power of the word, being of a piece with his judgment, 2 Cor. x. 5. But, to point out this corruption of the mind or understanding more particularly, let these following things be considered.

First, There is a natural weakness in the minds of men, with respect to spiritual things. The apostle determines concerning every one that is not endued with the graces of the Spirit, *That he is blind, and cannot see afar off*, 2 Pet. i. 9.

D

Hence the Spirit of GOD, in the scripture, clothes, as it were, divine truths with earthly figures, even as parents teach their children, using similitudes, Hos. xi. 10. Which, though it doth not cure, yet doth evidence this natural weakness in the minds of men. But we want not plain proofs of it from experience. As, (1.) How hard a task is it to teach many people the common principles of our holy religion, and to make truths so plain as they may understand them? Here there must be *precept upon precept, precept upon precept; line upon line, line upon line*, Isa. xxviii. 9. Try the same persons in other things, they shall be found *wiser in their generation than the children of light*. They understand their work and business in the world as well as their neighbours, though they be very stupid and unteachable in the matters of GOD. Tell them how they may advance their worldly wealth, or how they may gratify their lusts, and they will quickly understand these things; tho' it is very hard to make them know how their souls may be saved; or how their hearts may find rest in JESUS CHRIST.——— (2.) Consider these who have many advantages, beyond the common gang of mankind; who have had the benefit of good education and instruction; yea, and are blest with the light of grace in that measure, wherein it is distributed to the saints on earth; yet how small a portion have they of the knowledge of divine things! What ignorance and confusion do still remain in their minds! How often are they mired, even in the matter of practical truths, and speak as a child in these things! it is a pitiful weakness, that we cannot perceive the things which GOD has revealed to us; and it must needs be a sinful weakness, since the law of GOD requires us to know and believe them. (3.) What dangerous mistakes are to be found amongst men, in their concerns of greatest weight! What woful delusions prevail over them! Do we not often see those, who otherwise are the wisest of men, the most notorious fools, with respect to their soul's interest, Matt. xi. 25. *Thou hast hid these things from the wise and prudent*. Many that are eagle-eyed, in the trifles of time, are like owls and bats in the light of life. Nay truly, the life of every natural man is but one continued dream and delusion; out of which he never awakes, till either by a new light darted from heaven into his soul, he come to himself, Luke xv. 17. or, *in hell he lift up his eyes*, chap. xvi. 24. 25. And therefore in scripture-account, be he never so wise, he is a fool and a simple one.

Secondly, Man's understanding is naturally overwhelmed with gross darkness in spiritual things. Man at the instigation of the devil, attempting to break out a new light in his mind; Gen. iii. 5. instead of that, broke up the door of the bottomless pit; so as by the smoke thereof, he was buried in darkness. When God at first had made man, his mind was a lamp of light: but now, when he comes to make him over again, in regeneration, he finds it darkness, Eph. v. 8. *Ye were sometimes darkness.* Sin has closed the windows of the soul; darkness is over all that region. It is the land of darkness, and shadow of death where the light is as darkness. The prince of darkness reigns there, and nothing but the works of darkness are framed there. We are born spiritually blind, and cannot be restored without a miracle of grace. This is thy case, whosoever thou art, if thou art not born again. And that you may be convinced in this matter take those following evidences of it.

Evidence 1. The darkness that was upon the face of the world before, and at the time when CHRIST came, arising as the Sun of righteousness upon the earth. When Adam, by his sin, had lost that primitive light wherewith he was endued in his creation, it pleased GOD to make a gracious revelation of his mind and will to him, touching the way of salvation, Gen. iii. 15. This was handed down by him and other godly fathers, before the flood: yet the natural darkness of the mind of man prevailed so far against that revelation, as to carry off all sense of true religion from the old world, except what remained in Noah's family, which was preserved in the ark. After the flood, as men multiplied on the earth, the natural darkness of mind prevails again, and the light decays till it died out among the generality of mankind, and is preserved only among the posterity of Shem. And even with them it was well near its setting, when GOD called Abraham from serving other gods, Josh. xxiv. 15. GOD gives Abraham a more clear and full revelation, and he communicates the same to his family, Gen. xvii. 19. Yet the natural darkness wears it out at length, save what of it was preserved among the posterity of Jacob. They being carried down into Egypt, that darkness prevailed so, as to leave them very little sense of true religion: and a new revelation behoved to be made them in the wilderness. And many a cloud of darkness got above that, now and then, during the time from Moses to CHRIST. When CHRIST came the world was divided into Jews and Gentiles. The Jews, and the true light with them, were within an inclosure, Psal. cxlvii. 19, 20. Betwixt them and the Gentile world, there was a partition-wall of GOD's making, namely the ceremonial law; and upon that there was reared up another of man's own making, namely, a rooted enmity betwixt the parties, Eph. ii. 14, 15. If we look abroad, without the inclosure: and except those proselytes of the Gentiles, who, by means of some rays of light breaking forth unto them from within the inclosure, having renounced idolatry, worshipped the true GOD, but did not conform to the Mosaical rites, we see nothing but dark places of the earth, full of the habitations of cruelty, Psal. lxxiv. 20. Gross darkness covered the face of the Gentile world; and the way of salvation was utterly unknown among them. They were drowned in superstition and idolatry; and had multiplied their idols to such a vast number, that above thirty thousand are reckoned to have been worshipped by those of Europe alone. Whatever wisdom was among their philosophers, the world by that wisdom knew not GOD, 1 Cor. i. 21. and all their researches in religion were but groping in the dark, Acts xvii. 27. If we look within the inclosure, and, except a few that were groaning and waiting for the Consolation of Israel, we will see a gross darkness on the face of that generation. Though to them were committed the oracles of GOD, yet they were most corrupt in their doctrine. Their traditions were multiplied, but the knowledge of these things wherein the life of religion lies, was lost: Masters of Israel knew not the nature and necessity of regeneration, John iii. 10. Their religion was to build on their birth privilege, as children of Abraham, Matth. iii. 9. to glory in their circumcision, and other external ordinances, Philip. iii. 2. 3. And to rest in the law, Rom. ii. 17. after they had, by their false glosses, cut it so short, as they might go well near to the fulfilling of it Matt. v.

Thus was darkness over the face of the world, when CHRIST, the true light, came into it; and so is darkness over every soul, till he, as the day-star, arise in the heart. The former is an evidence of the latter. What, but the natural darkness of mens minds, could still thus wear out the light of external revelation, in a matter upon which eternal happiness did depend? Men did not forget the way of preserving their lives, but how quickly did they lose the knowledge of the way of salvation of their souls, which are of infinite more weight and worth! When patriarchs and prophets teaching was ineffectual, men behoved to be taught of GOD himself, who alone can open the eyes of the understanding. But, that it might appear that the corruption of man's mind lay deeper than to be cured by mere external revelation, there were but very few converted by CHRIST's preaching, who spake as never man spake, John xii. 37. 38. The great cure on the generation remained to be performed, by the Spirit accompanying the preaching of the apostles; who, according to the promise, John xiv. 12. were to do great works. And if we look to the miracles wrought by our blessed LORD, we will find that, by applying the remedy to the soul, for the cure of bodily distempers, as in the case of a man sick of the palsy, Matth. ix.

2. be plainly discovered, that it was his main errand into the world, to cure the diseases of the soul. I find a miracle wrought upon one that was born blind, performed in such a way, as seems to have been designed to let the world see in it, as in a glass, their case and cure. John ix. 6. *He made clay, and anointed the eyes of the blind man with the clay.* What could more fitly represent the blindness of mens mind, than eyes closed up with earth? Isa. vi. 1. *Shut their eyes;* shut them up by *anointing* or *casting them with morter*, as the word would bear. And, chap. xliv. 18. *He hath shut their eyes:* the word properly signifies, *He hath plaistered their eyes;* as the house in which the leprosy had been, was to be plaistered, Lev. xiv. 42. Thus the LORD's word discovers the design of that strange work; and by it shews us, that the eyes of our understanding are naturally shut. Then the blind man must go and wash off this clay in the pool of Siloam; no other water will serve this purpose. If that pool had not represented him, whom the Father *sent* into the world, *to open the blind eyes,* Isa. xlii. 7. I think the evangelist had not given us the interpretation of the name, which, he says, signifies *sent*, John ix. 7. And so we may conclude, that the natural darkness of our minds is such, as there is no cure for, but from the blood and Spirit of JESUS CHRIST, whose eye-salve only can make us see, Rev. iii. 18.

Evid. 2. Every natural man's heart and life is a mass of darkness, disorder and confusion; how refined soever he appear in the sight of men. *For we ourselves also,* faith the apostle Paul, *were sometimes foolish, disobedient, deceived, serving divers lusts, and pleasures,* Tit. iii. 3. and yet at that time, which this text looks to, he was *blameless, touching the righteousness which is in the law,* Phil. iii. 6. This is a plain evidence that *the eye is evil, the whole body being full of darkness,* Mat. vi. 23. The unrenewed part of mankind, is rambling through the world, like so many blind men; who will neither take a guide, nor can guide themselves; and therefore are falling over this and the other precipiece, into destruction. Some are running after their covetousness, till they be pierced through with many sorrows; some sticking in the mire of sensuality; others dashing themselves on the rock of pride and self-conceit; every one stumbling on some one stone of stumbling or other: all of them are running themselves upon the sword-point of justice, while they eagerly follow, whither their unmortified passions and affections lead them; and while some are lying alone in the way, others are coming up, and falling headlong over them. And therefore, *Wo unto the (blind) world because of offences,* Matth. xviii. 7. Errors in judgment swarm in the world; because it is *night wherein all the beasts of the forest do creep forth.* All the unregenerate are utterly mistaken in the point of true happiness; for tho' Christianity hath fixed that matter in point of principle; yet nothing less than overcoming grace can fix it in the practical judgment. All men agree in the desire to be happy: but amongst unrenewed men, touching the way to happiness, there are almost as many opinions as there are men; they being *turned every one to his own way*, Isa. liii. 6. They are like the blind Sodomites about Lot's house, all were seeking to find the door, some grope one part of the wall for it, some another; but none of them could certainly say, he had found it; and so the natural man may stumble on any good but the chief good. Look into thine own unregenerate heart, and there thou wilt see all turned up-side down; heaven lying under, and earth atop; look into thy life: there thou mayest see, how thou art playing the madman, snatching at shadows, and neglecting the substance, eagerly flying after *that which is not*, and slighting that which is, and will be for ever.

Evid. 3. The natural man is always as a workman left without light; either trifling or doing mischief. Try to catch thy heart at any time thou wilt, and thou shalt find it either *weaving the spider's web, or hatching cockatrice-eggs*, Isa. lix. 5. roving through the world, or digging into the pit; filled with vanity, or else with vileness, busy doing nothing, or what is worse than nothing. A sad sign of a dark mind.

Evid. 4. The natural man is void of the saving knowledge of spiritual things. He knows not what a GOD he has to deal with; he is unacquainted with CHRIST; and knows not what sin is. The greatest graceless wits are blind as moles in these things. Ay, but some such can speak of them to good purpose; and so might these Israelites of the temptations, signs and miracles, their eyes had seen, Deut. xxix. 3. to whom nevertheless the LORD had not *given an heart to perceive, and eyes to see, and ears to hear, unto that day*, ver. 4. Many a man that bears the name of a Christian may make Pharaoh's confession of faith, Exod. v. 2. *I know not the Lord*, neither will they let go when he commands them to part with. GOD is with them as a prince in disguise among his subjects, who meets with no better treatment from them, than if they were his fellows, Psal. l. 21. Do they know CHRIST; or see his glory, and any beauty in him for which he is to be desired? if they did, they would not slight him as they do; a view of his glory would so darken all created excellency, that they would take him for, and instead of all, and gladly close with him, as he offereth himself in the gospel, John iv. 10. Psal. ix. 10. Matth. xiii. 44, 45, 50. Do they know what sin is, who hug the serpent in their bosom, hold fast deceit, refuse to let it go? I own indeed they may have a natural knowledge of those things as the unbelieving Jews had of CHRIST, whom they saw and conversed with: but there was spiritual glory in him, perceived by believers only, John i. 14. and in respect of that glory, the unbelieving world knew him not, ver. 10. But the spiritual knowledge of him they cannot have; it is above the reach of the carnal mind, 1 Cor. ii. 14. *The natural man receiveth not the things of the Spirit of God, for they are foolishness unto him; neither can he know them, for they are spiritually discerned.* He may indeed discourse of them; but no other way than one can talk of honey or vinegar, who never tasted the sweetness of the one, nor the sourness of the other. He has some notions of spiritual truths, but sees not the things themselves, that are wrapt up in the words of truth, 1 Tim. i. 7. *Understanding neither what they say, nor whereof they affirm.* In a word, natural men talk, like, confess they know not what. Thus may you see man's understanding naturally, is overwhelmed with gross darkness in spiritual things.

Thirdly, There is in the mind of a man a natural bias to evil, whereby it comes to pass, that what ever difficulties it finds, while occupied about things truly good, it acts with a great deal of ease in evil; as being in that case, in its own element, Jer. iv. 22. The carnal mind drives heavily in the thoughts of good; but furiously in the thoughts of evil. While holiness is before it, fetters are upon it; but when it has got over the hedge, it is as the bird got out of the cage, and becomes a free-thinker indeed. Let us reflect a little on the apprehension and imagination of the carnal mind; and we shall find incontestible evidence of this woful bias to evil.

Evidence, 1. As when a man, by a violent stroke on the head loseth his sight, there ariseth to him a kind of false light, whereby he perceiveth a thousand airy nothings, so man being struck blind to all that is truly good, and for his eternal interest, has a light of another sort brought into his mind; his eyes are opened, knowing evil, and so are the words of the tempter verified, Gen. iii. 5. The words of the Prophet are plain. *They are wise to do evil, but to do good they have no knowledge,* Jer. iv. 22. The mind of man has a natural dexterity to devise mischief; none are so simple as to want skill to contrive ways to gratify their lusts, and ruin their souls; though the power of every one's hand, cannot reach to put their devices in execution. None needs to be taught this black art; but as weeds grow up, of their own accord in the neglected ground, so doth this wisdom, which is *earthly, sensual, devilish,* James iii. 15. grow up in the minds of men, by virtue of the corruption of their nature. Why should we be surprised with the product of corrupt wits; their cunning devices to affront heaven, to oppose and run down truth and holiness, and to gratify their own and other mens lusts? They row with the stream, no wonder they make great progress; their stock is within them, and increaseth by using of it; and the works of darkness are contrived with the greater advantage, that the mind is wholly destitute of spiritual light, which, if it were in them, in any measure, would so far mar the work, 1 John iii. 9. *Whosoever is born of God doth not commit sin;* he does it not by art, for *his seed remaineth in him.* But on the other hand, *it is a sport for a fool to do mischief; but a man of understanding hath wisdom,* Prov. x. 23. To do wittily *wickedness nicely,* as the word imports is as a sport, or a play to a fool; it comes off with him easily; and why, but because he is a fool, and hath no wisdom; which would mar the contrivances of darkness? The more natural a thing is, it is done the more easily.

Evid. 2. Let the corrupt mind have but the advantage of one's being employed in, or present at some piece of service to God; that so the device, if not in itself sinful, yet may become sinful, by its unseasonableness; it shall quickly fall on some device or expedient, by its starting aside: which deliberation, in season, could not produce. Thus Saul, who wist not what to do, before the priest began to consult God, is quickly determined when once the priest's hand was in; his own heart then gave him an answer, and would not allow him to wait an answer from the Lord, 1 Sam. xiv. 18, 19. Such a devilish dexterity hath the carnal mind, in devising what may most effectually divert men from their duty to God.

Evid. 3. Doth not the carnal mind naturally strive to grasp spiritual things in imagination; as if the soul were quite immersed in flesh and blood, and would turn every thing into its own shape? Let men who are used to the forming of the most abstracted notion, look into their own souls, and they shall find this bias in their minds; whereof the idolatry, which did of old and still doth, so much prevail in the world, is an incontestable evidence. For it plainly discovers, that men naturally would have a visible deity, and see what they worship; and therefore they *changed the glory of the incorruptable God into an image,* &c. Rom. i. 23. The reformation of these nations, blessed be the Lord, for it, hath banished idolatry and images too out of our churches; but heart-reformation only can break down mental idolatry, and banish the more subtil and refined image-worship, and representation of the deity, of the minds of men. The world, in the time of its darkness, was never more prone to the former, than the unsanctified mind is to the latter. And hence are horrible, monstrous, and misshapen thoughts of GOD, CHRIST, the glory above, and all spiritual things.

Evid 4. What a difficult task is it to detain the carnal mind before the Lord! how averse is it to the entertaining of good thoughts, and dwelling in the meditation of spiritual things! if one be driven, at any time, to think of the great concerns of his soul, it is no harder work to hold in an unruly hungry beast, than to hedge in the carnal mind, that it get not away to the vanities of the world again. When GOD is speaking to men by his word, or they are speaking to him in prayer, doth not the mind often leave them before the LORD, like so many *idols that have eyes, but see not, and ears but hear not?* The carcase is laid down before GOD, but the world gets away the heart: though the eyes be closed, the man sees a thousand vanities; the mind, in the mean time, is like a bird got loose out of the cage, skipping from bush to bush; so that in effect, the man never comes to himself, till he be *gone from the presence of the Lord*. Say not, it is impossible to get the mind fixed. It is hard indeed, but not impossible. Grace from the LORD can do it, Psal. cviii. 1. Agreeable objections will do it. A pleasant speculation will arrest the minds of the inquisitive: the worldly man's mind is in little hazzard of wandering, when he is contriving of business, casting up his accounts, or telling his money: if he answer you not at first, he tells you, he did not hear you, he was busy; his mind was fixed. Were we admitted into the presence of a king to petition for our lives, we would be in no hazzard of gazing through the chamber of presence: But here lies the case, the carnal mind employed about any spiritual good, is out of its elements, and therefore cannot fix.

Evid. 5. But however hard it is to keep the mind on good thoughts, it sticks as glue to what is evil and corrupt like itself, 2 Pet. ii. 14. *Having eyes full of adultery and that cannot cease from sin.* Their eyes cannot cease from sin: so the words are constructed, that is, their hearts and minds venting by the eyes, what is within, are like a furious beast, which cannot be held in, when once it has got out its head. Let the corrupt imagination once be let loose on its proper object, it will be found hard work to call it back again, though both reason and will be for its retreat. For then it is in its own element; and to draw it off from its impurities, is as the drawing of a fish out of the water, or the renting of a limb from a man. It runs like fire set to a train of powder, that resteth not till it can get no further.

Evid. 6. Consider how the carnal imagination supplies the want of real objects to the corrupt heart; that it may make sinners happy, at least, in the imaginary enjoyment of their lusts. Thus the corrupt heart feeds itself with imagination-sins: the unclean person is filled with speculative impurities, having eyes full of adultery; the covetous man fills his heart with the world, though he cannot get his hands full of it; the malicious person, with delight, acts his revenge within his own breast; the envious man, within his own narrow soul, beholds, with satisfaction, his neighbour laid low enough; and every lust finds the corrupt imagination a friend to it in time of need. And this it doth, not only when people are awake, but sometimes even when they are asleep; whereby it comes to pass, that these sins are acted in dreams, which their hearts were carried out after, while they were awake. I know some do question the sinfulness of these things: But can it be thought they are consistent with that holy nature and frame of spirit, which was in innocent Adam, and in JESUS CHRIST, and should be in every man? It is the corruption of nature then, that makes filthy dreamers condemned, Jude 8. Solomon had experience of the exercise of grace in sleep: in a dream he prayed; in a dream he made the best choice: both were accepted of GOD, 1 Kings iii. 5,—15. And if a man may, in his sleep, do what is good and acceptable to GOD; why may he not also, when asleep, do that which is evil and displeasing to GOD? The same Solomon would have men aware of this; and prescribes the best remedy against it, namely, the law upon the heart Prov. vi. 20, 21. *When thou sleepest*: says he, ver. 22. *it shall keep thee*; to-wit, from the sinning in thy sleep: That is, from sinful dreams. For one's being kept from sin: not his being kept from affliction is the immediate proper effect of the law of GOD imprest upon the heart, Psal. cxix. 11. And thus the whole verse is to be understood, as appears from verse 23. *For the commandment is a lamp, and the law is light; and reproofs of instruction are the way of life*. Now, the law is a lamp of light, as it guides in the way of duty, and instructing reproofs from the law, are the way of life, as they keep from sin: neither do they guide into the way of peace, but as they lead into the way of duty; nor do they keep a man out of trouble, but as they keep him from sin. And remarkable is the particular, in which Solomon instanceth, namely, the sin of uncleanness; *To keep thee from the evil woman*, verse 24. Which is to be joined with verse 22. inclosing verse 23. in a parenthesis, as some versions have it. These things may suffice to convince us of the natural bias of the mind to evil.

Fourthly, There is in the carnal mind, an opposition to spiritual truths, and an aversion to the receiving of them. It is as little a friend to divine truths as it is to holiness. The truths of natural religion, which do, as it were, force their entry into the minds of natural men, they hold prisoners in unrighteousness, Rom. i. 18. And as for the truths of revealed religion there is *an evil heart of unbelief* in them, which opposeth their entry; and there is an armed force necessary to captivate the mind to the belief of them, 2 Cor. x. 4, 5. God has made a revelation of his mind and will to sinners, touching the way of salvation; he has given us the doctrine of his holy word: But do natural men believe it indeed? No, they do not; *For he that believeth not on the Son of God, believeth not God*; as is plain from 1 John v. 10. They believe not the promises of the word: they look on them, in effect, only as fair words; for these that receive them, are thereby made partakers of the divine nature, 2 Pet. i. 4. The promises are as silver cords, let down from heaven, to draw sinners unto God, and to waft them over into the promised land; but they cast them from them. They believe not the threatnings of the word. As men travelling in desarts, carry fire about with them, to fright away wild beasts; so God has made his law a fiery law: Deut. xxxiii. 2. hedging it about with threats of wrath: But men naturally are more brutish than beasts themselves; and will needs touch the fiery smoking mountain, though they should be thrust through with a dart. I doubt not but most, if not all of you, who are yet in the black state of nature, will here plead, Not guilty: But remember, the carnal Jews in Christ's time, were as confident as you are, that they believed Moses, John ix. 28, 29. — But he confutes their confidence, roundly telling them, John v. 46. *Had ye believed Moses, ye would have believed me.* Did ye believe the truths of God, ye durst not reject, as ye do him who is truth itself. The very difficulty you find in assenting to this truth, bewrays that unbelief I am charging you with. Has it not proceeded so far with some at this day, that it has steeled their foreheads with the impudence and impiety, openly to reject all revealed religion? Surely it is out of the abundance of the heart, their mouth speaketh. But though ye set not your mouths against the heavens, as they do, the same bitter root of unbelief is in all men by nature, and reigns in you, and will reign, till overcoming grace captivate your minds to the belief of the truth. To convince you in this point, consider these three things.

Evidence 1. How few are there who have been blest with an inward illumination, by the special operation of the Spirit of Christ, letting them into a view of divine truths, in their spiritual and heavenly lustre! How have you learned the truths of religion, which ye pretend to believe! Ye have them merely by the benefit of external revelation, and of your education; so that you are Christians, just because you were not born and bred in a Pagan, but in a Christian country. Ye are strangers to the inward work of the holy Spirit, bearing witness by and with the word in your hearts; and so you cannot have the assurance of faith, with respect to that outward divine revelation made in the word 1 Cor. ii. 10, 11, 12. And therefore ye are still unbelievers. *It is written in the prophets And they shall be all taught of God. Every man, therefore, that hath heard, and hath learned of the Father, cometh unto me,* says our LORD, John vi. 45. Now ye have not come to CHRIST, therefore ye have not been taught of GOD; ye have not been so taught, and therefore ye have not come; ye believe not. Behold the revelation from which the faith even of the fundamental principles in religion doth spring, Matth. xvi. 17, 18. *Thou art Christ the Son of the living God.—Blessed art thou, Simon Barjona; for flesh and blood hath not revealed it unto thee, but my Father which is in heaven.* If ever the Spirit of the LORD take a dealing with thee, to work in thee that faith, which is of the operation of GOD; it may be, as much time will be spent in razing the old foundation, as will make thee find a necessity of the working of his mighty power, & to enable thee to believe the very foundation-principles, which now thou thinkest thou makest no doubt of Eph. i. 19.

Evid. 2. How many professors have made shipwreck of their faith, such as it was, in time of temptation and trial! See how they fall, like stars from heaven, when Antichrist prevails, 2 Thes. ii. 11, 12. *God shall send them strong delusions, that they should believe a lie; that they all might be damned, who believed not the truth.* They fell into damning delusions, because they never really believed the truth, though they themselves, and others too, thought they did believe it. That house is built upon the sand, and that faith is but ill-founded, that cannot bear out, but is quite overthrown, when the storm comes.

Evid. 3. Consider the utter inconsistency of most men's lives, with the principles of religion which they profess; ye may as soon bring east and west together, as their practice. Men believe that fire will burn them and therefore they will not throw themselves into it: but the truth is, most men live as if they thought the gospel a mere fable; and the wrath of GOD revealed in his word against their unrighteousness and ungodliness, a mere scarecrow. If ye believe the doctrines of the word, how is it that ye are so unconcerned about the state of your souls before the LORD? Many live as they were born, and are like to die as they live, and yet live in peace. Do such believe the sinfulness and misery of a natural state? Do they believe they are *Children of wrath?*

Do they believe there is no salvation without regeneration? and no regeneration but what makes man a new creature! If you believe the promises of the word, why do you not embrace them, and labour to enter into the promised rest? What sluggard would not dig for a hid treasure, if he really believed he might so obtain it? Men will work and sweat for a maintenance; because they believe that by so doing they will get it: yet they will be at no tolerable pains for *the eternal weight of glory:* why, but because they do not believe the word of promise? Heb. iv. 1. 2. If you believe the threatenings, how is it that you live in your sins, live out of CHRIST and yet hope for mercy. Do such believe GOD to be the holy and just one, who will *by no means clear the guilty?* No, no, none believe, *none:* or next to none *believe what a just God the LORD is, and how severely he punisheth.*

Fifthly, There is in the mind of man a natural *proneness to lies and falshood,* which make for the safety of lusts. *They go astray as soon as they be born speaking lies,* Psal. lvii. 3. We have this with the rest of the corruption of our nature from our first parents. God revealed the truth to them but, through the solicitation of the tempter, they first doubted of it; they disbelieved it, and embraced a lie instead of it. And for an incontestible evidence hereof, we may see that first article of the devil's creed, *ye shall not surely die,* Gen. iii. 4. which was obtruded by him on our first parents, and by them received; naturally embraced by their posterity, and held fast, till a light from heaven oblige them to quit it. It spreads itself through the lives of natural men; who till their consciences be awakened, walk after their own lusts: still retaining the principle, *That they shall not surely die.* And this is often improved to that perfection, that the man can say, over the belly of the denounced curse, *I shall have peace tho' I walk in the imagination of mine heart, to add drunkenness to thirst,* Deut. xxix. 19. Whatever advantage the truths of GOD have over error by means of education, or otherwise; error has always with the natural man, this advantage against truth, namely, That there is something within him, which says, *O, that it were true;* so the mind lies fair for assenting to it. And here is the reason of it. The true doctrine is *the doctrine that is according to godliness,* 1 Tim. vi. 3. and *the truth which is after godliness,* Tit. i. 1. Error is the doctrine which is according to ungodliness; for there is never an error in the mind, nor an untruth vented in the world (in matters of religion) but what has an affinity with one corruption of the heart or other: according to that of the apostle, 2 Thess. ii. 21. *They believed not the truth, but had pleasure in unrighteousness.* So that truth and error being otherwise attended with equal advantages for their reception, error, by this means, has ready access to the minds of men in their natural state. Wherefore, it is nothing strange that men reject the simplicity of gospel-truths and institutions, and greedily embrace error and external pomp in religion; seeing they are so agreeable to the lusts of the heart, and the vanity of the mind of the natural man. And from hence also it is, that so many embrace atheistical principles; for none do it but in compliance with their irregular passions; none but these, whose advantage it would be, that there was no GOD.

Lastly, Man is naturally high-minded; for when the gospel comes in power to him, it is employed in *casting down imaginations, and every high thing that exalteth itself against the knowledge of God*, 2 Cor. x. 5. Lowliness of mind is not a flower that grows in the field of nature: but is planted by the finger of GOD in a renewed heart, and learned of the lowly JESUS. It is natural to man to think highly of himself, and what is his own; for the stroke he has got by his fall in Adam, has produced a false light, whereby mole-hills about him appear like mountains; and a thousand airy beauties present themselves to his deluded fancy. *Vain men would be wise*, so he accounts himself, and so he would be accounted of by others *though man be born like a wild ass's-colt*, Job. xi. 12. His way is right because it is his own: for *every way of a man is right in his own eyes*, Prov. xxi. 2. His state is good, because he knows no better: he is alive without the law, Rom. vii. 9. And therefore his hope is strong, and his confidence firm. It is another tower of Babel reared up against heaven; and shall not fall while the power of darkness can hold it up. The word batters it, yet it stands; one while breaches are made in it, but they are quickly repaired; at another time, it is all made to shake; but still it keeps up; till either GOD himself by his Spirit, raise an earthquake within the man, which tumbles it down; and leaves not one stone upon another, 2 Cor. x. 4, 5. or death batter it down and raze the foundations of it, Luke.xvi.23. And as the natural man thinks highly of himself, so he thinks meanly of GOD, whatever he pretends, Psalm l. 21. *Thou thoughtest that I was altogether such an one as thyself.* The doctrine of the gospel and the mystery of CHRIST are foolishness to him; and in his practice he treats them as such, 1 Corinth. i. 18. and ii. 14. He brings the word and the works of GOD in the government of the world, before the bar of his carnal reason, and there they are presumptuously censured and condemned, Hos. xiv. 9. Sometimes the ordinary restraint of providence is taken off, and Satan is permitted to stir up the carnal mind; and in that case it is like an ant's nest, uncovered and disturbed; doubts, denials, and hellish reasons crowd in it, and cannot be laid by all the arguments brought against them, till a power from on high captivate the mind, and still the mutiny of the corrupt principles.

Thus much of the corruption of the understanding: which although the half be not told, may discover to you the absolute necessity of regenerating grace. Call the understanding now Ichabod, for the glory is departed from it. Consider this, ye that are yet in the state of nature, and groan ye out your case before the LORD, that the Sun of righteousness may arise upon you, before you be shut up in everlasting darkness. What avails your worldly wisdom? What do your attainments in religion avail, while your understanding lies yet wrapt up in its natural darkness, and confusion, utterly void of the light of life? Whatever be the natural man's gifts or attainments, we must as in the case of the leper, Lev. xlii. 24. *pronounce him utterly unclean, his plague is in his head.* But that is not all; it is in his heart too, his will is corrupted, as I shall shew anon.

Of the Corruption of the Will.

II. The will, that commanding faculty, which sometimes was faithful and ruled with GOD, is now turned traitor, and rules with, and for the devil. God planted it in man wholly a right seed; but now it is *turned into the degenerate plant of a strange vine.* It was originally placed in a due subordination to the will of GOD as was shewn before, but now it is gone wholly aside. However some do magnify the power of free-will, a view of the spirituality of the law, to which acts of moral discipline do in no ways answer; and a deep insight into the corruption of nature, given by the inward operation of the Spirit, convincing of sin, righteousness and judgment, would make men find an absolute need of the power of free-grace, to remove the bands of wickedness from off the free-will. To open up this plague of the heart, I offer these following things to be considered.

First, There is, in the unrenewed will, an utter inability for what is truly good and acceptable in the sight of GOD. The natural man's will is in Satan's fetters; hemmed in within the circle of evil, and cannot move beyond it more than a dead man can raise himself out of his grave, Eph. ii. 1. We deny him not a power to chuse, pursue and act, what on the matter, is good; but though he can will what is good and right, he can will nothing aright and well. John. xv. 5. *Without me,* i. e. separate from me, as a branch from the stock, as both the word and context do carry it, ye can do nothing; to wit, nothing truly and spiritually good. His very choice and desire of spiritual things is carnal and selfish, John vi. 26. *Ye seek me because ye did eat of the loaves and were filled.* He not only comes not to Christ, but he cannot come, John vi. 44. And what can one do acceptable to GOD, who believeth not on him whom the Father hath sent? To evidence this inability for good in the unregenerate, consider these two things.

Evid. 1. How often does the light so shine before mens eyes; that they cannot but see the good they should chuse, and the evil they should refuse; and yet their hearts have no more power to comply with that light than if they were arrested by some invisible hand? They see what is right; yet they follow, and cannot but follow, what is wrong. Their conscience tells them the right way, and approves of it too; yet cannot their will be brought up to it: their corruption so chains them, that they cannot embrace it; so they sigh and go backward, over the belly of their light. And if it be not thus, how is it that the word, and way of holiness meets with such entertainment in the world? How is it that clear arguments and reason on the side of piety and a holy life, which bare in themselves even on the carnal mind, do not bring men over to that side? Although the being of a heaven and a hell, were but a *may-be*, it were sufficient to determine the will to the choice of holiness, were it capable to be determined thereto by mere reason; but men, knowing the judgment of GOD, that they which commit such things are worthy of death, not only do the same, but have pleasure in them that do them, Rom. i. 32. And how is it that these who magnify the power of free-will do not confirm their opinion before the world, by an ocular demonstration, in a practice as far above others in holiness, as the opinion of their natural abilities is above others? Or is it maintained only for the protection of lusts, which men may hold fast as long as they please; and when they have no more use for them, can throw them off in a moment, and leap out of Delilah's lap into Abraham's bosom? Whatever use some make of that principle, it does of itself and in its own nature, cast a broad shadow for a shelter to wickedness of heart and life. And it may be observed, that the generality of hearers of the gospel, of all denominations are plagued with it; for it is a root of bitterness, natural to all men; from whence do spring so much fearlessness about the soul's eternal state; so many delays and off-puts in that weighty matter, whereby much work is laid up for a death-bed by some; while others are ruined by a legal walk, and unacquaintedness with the life of faith, and the making use of CHRIST for sanctification; all flowing from the persuasion of sufficient natural abilities. So agreeable is it to corrupt nature.

Evid. 2. Let those, who, by the power of the spirit of bondage, having had the law laid out before them, in its spirituality, for their conviction, speak and tell, if they found themselves able to incline their hearts towards it, in that case: nay, if the more that light shone into their souls, they did not find their hearts more and more unable to comply with it. There are some, who have been brought unto the place of the breaking forth, who are yet in the devil's camp, that from their experience can tell, light let into the mind, cannot give life to the will, to enable it to comply therewith; and could give their testimony here, if they would. But take Paul's testimony concerning it, who, in his unconverted state was far from believing his utter inability for good; but learned it by experience, Rom. vii. 9, 10, 11, 13. I own, the natural man may have a kind of love to the law; but here lies the stress of the matter, he looks on the holy law in a carnal dress; and so, while he hugs a creature of his own fancy, he thinks he has the law, but in very deed he is without the law; for as yet he sees it not in its spirituality: if he did, he would find it the very reverse of his own nature, and what his will could not fall in with, till changed by the power of grace.

Secondly, There is in the unrenewed will an averseness to good. Sin is the natural man's element; he is loath to part with it, as the fishes are to come out of the water into dry land. He not only cannot come to CHRIST, but he will not come, John v. 40. He is polluted, and hates to be washen, Jer. xiii. 27. *Wilt thou not be made clean? When shall it once be?* He is sick, but utterly averse to the remedy; he loves his disease so, that he loaths the Physician. He is a captive, a prisoner, and a slave; but he loves his conqueror, his jailor and master; he is fond of his fetters, prison and drudgery; and has no liking to his liberty. For evidence of this averseness to good, in the will of man, I shall instance in some particulars.

Evid. 1. The untowardness of children. Do we not see them naturally, lovers of sinful liberty? How unwilling are they to be hedged in? How averse to restraint? The world can bear witness, that they are *as bullocks unaccustomed to the yoke*; and more, that it is far easier to bring young bullocks tamely to bear the yoke; than to bring young children under discipline, and make them tamely submit to the restraint of sinful liberty. Every body may see in this, as in a glass, that man is naturally wild and wilful, according to Zophar's observe, Job xi. 12. that *man is born like a wild ass's colt.* What can be said more? He is like a colt, the colt of an ass, the colt of a wild ass. Compare Jer. ii. 24. *A wild ass used to the wilderness, that snuffeth up the wind at her pleasure, in her occasion who can turn her away?*

Evid. 2. What pain and difficulty do men often find in bringing their hearts to religious duties? And what a task is it to the carnal heart to abide at them? It is a pain to it, to leave the world but a little, to converse with GOD. It is not easy to borrow time from the many things, to bestow it upon the one thing needful. Men often go to GOD in duties, with their faces toward the world; and when their bodies are on the mount of ordinances, their hearts will be found at the foot of the hill, *going after their covetousness,* Ezek. xxxiii. 31. They are soon wearied of well-doing; for holy duties are not agreeable to their corrupt nature. Take notice of them at their worldly business, set them down with their carnal company, or let them be sucking the breasts of a lust; time seems to them to fly, and drive furiously, so that it is gone ere they are aware. But how heavily does it drive, while a prayer, a sermon, or a sabbath lasts? The LORD's day is the longest day of all the week with many; and therefore they must sleep longer that morning, and go sooner to bed that night, than ordinarily they do; that the day may be made of a tolerable length; for their hearts say within them, *When will the sabbath be gone?* Amos viii. 5. The hours of worship are the longest hours of that day; hence when duty is over, they are like men eased of a burden; and when sermon is ended, many have neither the grace nor the good manners to stay 'till the blessing be pronounced, but like the beasts, their head is away as soon as one puts his hand to loose them; why, but because while they are at ordinances, they are, as Doeg, *detained before the Lord,* 1 Sam. xxii. 7.

Evid. 3. Consider how the will of the natural man doth *rebel against the light,* Job. xxiv. 13. Light sometimes entereth in, because he is not able to hold it out; but he loveth darkness rather than light. Sometimes by the force of truth, the outer door of understanding is broken up; but the inner door of the will remains fast bolted. Then lusts rise against light; corruption and conscience encounter, and fight as in the field of battle; till corruption getting the upper hand, conscience is forced to give back; convictions are murdered; and truth is made and held prisoner, so that it can create no more disturbance. While the word is preached or read, or the rod of GOD is upon the natural man, sometimes convictions are darted in on him, and his spirit is wounded, in greater or lesser measure; but these convictions not being able to make him fall, he runs away with the arrows sticking in his conscience; and at length, one way or other, gets them out, and licks himself whole again. Thus while the light shines, men, naturally averse to it, wilfully shut their eyes; till GOD is provoked to blind them judicially, and they become proof against the word and providences too: so they may go where they will, they can sit at ease; there is never a word from heaven to them, that goeth deeper than into their ears, Hos. iv. 17. *Ephraim is joined to his idols, let him alone.*

Evid. 4. Let us observe the resistance made by elect souls, when the Spirit of the LORD is at work, to bring them from the power of Satan unto GOD. Zion's King gets no subjects but by stroke of sword, in the day of his power, Psal. cx. 2, 3. None come to him, but such as are drawn by a divine hand, John vi. 44. When the LORD comes to the soul, he finds the strong man keeping the house, and a deep peace and security there, while the soul is fast asleep in the devil's arms. But the prey must be taken from the mighty, and the captive delivered. Therefore the LORD awakens the sinner, opens his eyes, and strikes him with terror, while the clouds are black above his head, and the sword of vengeance is held to his breast. Now he is at no small pains to put a fair face on a black heart, to shake off his fears, to make head against them, and to divert himself from thinking on the unpleasant and ungrateful subject of his soul's case. If he cannot so rid himself from them, carnal reason is called in to help, and urgeth that there is no ground for so great fear; all may be well enough yet; and if it be ill with him, it will be ill with many. When the sinner is beat from this, and sees no advantage of going to hell with company, he resolves to leave his sins, but cannot think of breaking off so soon; there is time enough, and he will do it afterwards. Conscience says, *To-day if ye will hear his voice, harden not your hearts;* but he cries, To-morrow, LORD, to-morrow, LORD; and, just now, LORD; till that now is never like to come. And thus, many times, he comes from his prayers and confessions, with nothing but a breast full of sharpest convictions; for the heart doth not always cast up the sweet morsel, as soon as confession is made with the mouth, Judges x. 10.——16. And when conscience obligeth them to part with some lusts, others are kept as right eyes and right hands; and there are rueful looks after those that are put away, as it was with the Israelites, who, with bitter hearts, did remember the fish they did eat in Egypt freely, Num. xi. 5. Nay, when he is so pressed, that he must needs say before the LORD, that he is content to part with all his idols; the heart will be giving the tongue the lie. In a word, the soul, in this case, will shift from one thing to another, like a fish with the hook in his jaws, till it can do no more,

Thirdly, There is in the will of man a natural proneness to evil, a woful bent toward sin. Men naturally are bent to backsliding from GOD, Hof. ii. 7. They hang as the word is towards backsliding; even as a hanging wall, whose breaking cometh suddenly at an instant. Set holiness and life upon the one side, sin and death upon the other; leave the unrenewed will to itself, it will chuse sin, and reject holiness. This is no more to be doubted, than that water, poured on the side of a hill, will run downward, but not upward, or that a flame will ascend and not descend.

Evidence 1. Is not the way of evil, the first way the children of men do go? Do not their inclinations plainly appear on the wrong side, while yet they have no cunning to hide them? In the first opening of our eyes in the world, we look a-squint hell-ward, not heaven-ward. As soon as it appears we are reasonable creatures, it appears we are sinful creatures, Psal. lviii. 3. *The wicked are estranged from the womb: they go astray as soon as they be born.* Prov. xxii. 15. *Foolishness is bound in the heart of a child: but the rod of correction shall drive it far from him.* Folly is bound in the heart, it is woven into our very nature. The knot will not loose, they must be broken asunder by strokes. Words will not do it, the rod must be taken to drive it away: and if it be not driven far away, the heart and it will meet and knit again. Not that the rod of itself will do this: the sad experience of many parents testifies the contrary; and Solomon himself tells you, Prov. xxvii. 22. *Though thou shouldst bray a fool in a mortar, among wheat, with a pestle, yet will not his foolishness depart from him:* It is so bound in his heart. But the rod is an ordinance of GOD, appointed for that end; which, like the word, is made effectual by the Spirit's accompanying his own ordinance. And this, by the way, shews that parents, in administring correction to their children, have need, first of all, to correct their own irregular passions; and look upon it as a matter of awful solemnity, setting about it with much dependance on the LORD, and following it with prayer for the blessing, if they would have it effectual.

Evid. 2. How easily are men led aside to sin? The children who are not persuaded to good, are otherwise simple ones; easily wrought upon: those whom the word cannot draw to holiness, are led by Satan at his pleasure. Profane Esau, that cunning man, Gen. xxv. 27. was as easily cheated of the blessing as if he had been a fool or an ideot. The more natural a thing is, it is the more easy: so CHRIST's yoke is easy to the saints, in so far as they are partakers of the divine nature: and sin is easy to the unrenewed man; but to learn to do good, is as difficult as for the Ethiopian to change his skin; because the will naturally hangs towards evil; but is averse to good. A child can cause a round thing to run, while he cannot move a square thing of the same weight; for the roundness makes it fit for motion, so that it goes with a touch. Even so, when men find the heart easily carried towards sin, while it is as a dead weight in the way of holiness; we must bring the reason of this from the natural set and disposition of the heart, whereby it is prone and bent to evil. Were man's will, naturally, but in an equal balance to good and evil, the one might be embraced with as little difficulty as the other; but experience testifies, it is not so. In the sacred history of the Israelites, especially in the book of Judges, how often do we find them forsaking JEHOVAH, the mighty GOD, and doting upon the idols of the nations about them? But did ever one of these nations grow fond of Israel's GOD, and forsake their own idols? No, no: though man is naturally given to changes, it is but from evil to evil, not from evil to good. Jer. ii. 10, 11. *Hath a nation changed their gods, which yet are no gods? But my people have changed their glory for that which doth not profit.* Surely the will of man stands not in equal balance, but has a cast to the wrong side.

Evid. 3. Consider how men go on still in the way of sin, till they meet with a stop, and that from another hand than their own; Isa. lvii. 17. *I hid me, and he went on frowardly in the way of his heart.* If GOD withdraw his restraining hand, and lay the reins on the sinner's neck, he is in no doubt what way to choose; for, observe it, the way of sin is the way of his heart; his heart naturally lies that way; it hath a natural propensity to sin. As long as GOD suffereth them, they walk in their own way, Acts xiv. 16. The natural man is so fixed in his woful choice, that there needs no more to shew he is off from GOD's way, but to tell he is upon his own.

Evid. 4. Whatever good impressions are made upon him, they do not last. Though his heart be firm as a stone, yea, harder than the nether mill-stone, in point of receiving of them; it is otherwise unstable as water, and cannot keep them. It works against the receiving of them; and, when they are made, it works them off, and returns to its natural bias; Hos. vi. 4. *Your goodness is as a morning cloud, and as the early dew, it goeth away.* The morning cloud promiseth a hearty shower, but, when the sun ariseth, it evanisheth: the sun beats upon the early dew, and it evaporates; so the husbandman's expectation is disappointed. Such is the goodness of the natural man. Some sharp affliction, or piercing conviction, obligeth him in some sort, to turn from his evil course: but his will not being renewed, religion is still against the grain with him, and therefore this goes off again, Psal. lxxviii. 34. 36. 37. Though a stone, thrown up into the air, may abide there a little while; yet its natural heaviness will bring it down to the earth again; and so do unrenewed men return to the wallowing in the mire; because although they were washed, yet their swinish nature was not changed. It is hard to cause wet wood take fire, hard to make it keep fire; but it is harder than either of these, to make the unrenewed will retain attained goodness; which is a plain evidence of the natural bent of the will to evil.

Evid. last. Do the saints serve the LORD now, as they were wont to serve sin in their unconverted state? Very far from it, Rom. vi. 20. *When ye were the servants of sin, ye were free from righteousness.* Sin got all, and admitted no partner; but now, when they are the servants of CHRIST, are they free from sin? Nay, there are still with them some deeds of the old man, shewing that he is but dying in them. And hence their hearts often misgive them, and slip aside unto evil, when they would do good, Rom. viii. 2. They need to watch, and keep their hearts with all diligence: and their sad experience teacheth them, that *He that trusteth in his own heart is a fool*, Prov. xxviii. 26. If it be thus in the green tree, how must it be in the dry?

Fourthly, There is a natural contrariety, direct opposition and enmity, in the will of man, to GOD himself, and his holy will, Rom. viii. 2. *The carnal mind is enmity against God; for it is not subject to the law of God, neither indeed can be.* The will was once GOD's deputy in the soul, set to command there for him, but now it is set up against him. If you would have the picture of it, in its natural state, the very reverse of the will of GOD represents it. If the fruit hanging before one's eyes, be but forbid, that is sufficient to draw the heart after it. Let me instance in the sin of profane swearing and cursing, to which some are so abandoned, that they take a pride in them; belching out horrid oaths and curses, as if hell opened with the opening of their mouths, or larding their speeches with minced oaths, as *faith, truth, faid ye, laid ye* and such like: and all this without any manner of provocation, though even that would not excuse them. Pray tell me, (1.) What profit is there here? A thief gets something in his hand for his pains; a drunkard gets a belly full; but what do ye get? Others serve the devil for pay; but ye are volunteers, that expect no reward, but your work itself, in affronting of heaven. And if you repent not, you will get your reward in full tale when you go to hell, your work will follow you. The drunkard shall not have a drop of water to cool his tongue there. Nor will the covetous man's wealth follow him into the other world; but ye shall drive on your old trade there. And an eternity shall be long enough to give you your heart's fill of it. (2.) What pleasure is there here but what flows from your trampling upon the holy law? Which of your senses doth swearing or cursing gratify? If it gratify your ears, it can only be by the noise it makes against the heavens. Though you had a mind to give up yourselves to all manner of profanity and sensuality, there is so little pleasure can be strained out of these, that we must needs conclude, your love to them, in this case, is a love to them, for themselves; a devilish unhired love, without any prospect of profit or pleasure from them otherwise. If any shall say, these are monsters of men, Be it so; yet alas! the world is fruitful of such monsters; they are to be found almost every-where. And allow me to say, They must be admitted as the mouth of the whole unregenerate world against heaven, Rom. iii. 14. *Whose mouth is full of cursing and bitterness.* Ver. 19. *Now we know, that what things-soever the law saith, it saith to them who are under the law, that every mouth may be stopped, and all the world may become guilty before* GOD.

I have a charge against every unregenerate man and woman, young or old, to be verified by the testimonies of the Scriptures of truth, and the testimony of their own conscience; namely, that whether they be professors or profane, whatever they be, seeing they are not born again, they are heart-enemies to GOD; to the Son of GOD, to the Spirit of GOD, and to the law of GOD. Hear this, ye careless souls, that live at ease in your natural state.

1st, Ye are enemies to GOD in your minds, Col. i. 21. Ye are not as yet reconciled to him, the natural enmity is not as yet slain, though perhaps it lies hid, and ye do not perceive it. (1.) Ye are enemies to the very being of GOD, Psal xiv. 1. *The fool hath said in his heart, There is no God,* The proud man would that none were above himself; the rebel, that there were no king; and the unrenewed man, who is a mass of pride and rebellion, that there were no GOD. He saith it in his heart, he wisheth it were so, though he be ashamed and afraid to speak it out. And that all natural men are such fools, appears from the Apostle's quoting a part of this Psalm, *that every mouth may be stopped,* Rom. iii. 10, 11, 12. 19. I own indeed, that while the natural man looks on GOD as the Creator and preserver of the world; because he loves his ownself, therefore his heart riseth not against the being of his benefactor: but this enmity will quickly appear, when he looks on GOD as the rector and judge of the world; binding him, under the pain of the curse, to exact holiness, and girding him with the cords of death, because of his sin. Listen in this case to the voice of the heart, and you will find it to be, *No God.* (2.) Ye are enemies to the nature of GOD, Job xxi. 14. *They say unto God, Depart from us; for we desire not the knowledge of thy ways.* Men set up to themselves an idol of their own fancy instead of GOD, and then fall down and worship it. They love him no other way, than Jacob loved Leah, while he took her for Rachel. Every natural man is an enemy to GOD, as he is revealed in his word. An infinitely holy, just, powerful and true Being, is not the GOD whom he loves, but the GOD whom he loaths. In effect men naturally are haters of GOD, Rom. i. 30. And if they could, they certainly would make him another than whatsoever is in GOD, is GOD; and therefore his attributes or perfections are not any thing really distinct from himself. If GOD's attributes be not himself, he is a compound being, and so not the first Being, which to say is blasphemous, for the parts compounding are before the compound itself; but he is *Alpha and Omega, the first and the last.*

Now upon this I would, for your conviction, propose to your consciences a few queries, (1.) How stand your hearts affected to the infinite purity and holiness of GOD? Conscience will give an answer to this, which the tongue will not speak out. If ye be not partakers of his holiness, ye cannot be reconciled to it. The Pagans finding they could not be like GOD in holiness, made their gods like themselves in filthiness; and thereby discovered what sort of a god the natural man would have. GOD is holy; can an unholy creature love his unspotted holiness? Nay, it is the righteous only that can *give thanks at the remembrance of his holiness.* Psal. lxxxvii. 12. God is light; can creatures of darkness rejoice therein? Nay, *every one that doth evil hateth the light,* John iii. 29. For, *What communion hath light with darkness?* 2 Cor. vi. 14. (2.) How stand your hearts affected to the justice of GOD? There is not a man, who is wedded to his lusts, as all the unregenerate are, but would be content with the blood of his body to blot that letter out of the name of GOD. Can the malefactor love his condemning judge? Or an unjustified sinner, a just GOD? No, he cannot, Luke vii. 47. *To whom little is forgiven, the same loveth little.* Hence seeing men cannot get the doctrine of his justice blotted out of the Bible, it is such an eye-sore to them, that they strive to blot it out of their minds. And they ruin themselves by presuming on his mercy, while they are not careful to get a righteousness, wherein they may stand before his justice; but *say in their heart, The Lord will not do good, neither will he do evil,* Zeph. i. 12. (3.) How stand ye affected to the omniscience and omnipresence of GOD? Men naturally would rather have a blind idol, than an all-seeing GOD; and therefore do what they can, as Adam did, to hide themselves from the presence of the LORD. They no more love an all-seeing, every-where-present GOD, than the thief loves to have the judge witness to his evil-deeds. If it could be carried by votes, GOD would be voted out of the world, and closed up in heaven: For the language of the carnal heart is, *The Lord seeth us not; the Lord hath forsaken the earth,* Ezek. vi. 12. (4.) How stand ye affected to the truth and veracity of GOD? There are but few in the world, that can heartily subscribe to that sentence of the Apostle, Rom. iii. 4. *Let God be true and every man a liar.* Nay truly, there are many, who in effect, do hope that GOD will not be true to his word. There are thousands who hear the gospel, that hope to be saved, and think all safe with them for eternity, who never had any experience of the new-birth, nor do at all concern themselves in that question, Whether they are born again, or not? A question that is like to wear out from among us at this day. Our LORD's words are plain and peremptory, *Except a man be born again, he cannot see the kingdom of God.* What are such hopes then, but real hopes that GOD, with profoundest reverence be it spoken, will recal his work, and that CHRIST will prove a false prophet? What else means the sinner, who, *when he heareth the words of the curse, blesseth himself in his heart, saying, I shall have peace, though I walk in the imagination of mine heart,* Deut. xxix 19. Lastly, How stand ye affected to the power of GOD? None but new creatures will love him for it, on a fair view thereof; though others may slavishly fear him, upon the account of it. There is not a natural man, but would contribute, to the utmost of his power, to the building of another tower of Babel, to hem it in. On these grounds, I declare every unrenewed man an enemy to GOD.

2dly, Ye are enemies to the SON of GOD. That enmity to CHRIST is in your hearts, which would have made you join the husbandmen, who killed the heir, and cast him out of the vineyard; if ye had been beset with their temptations, and no more restrained than they were. *Am I a dog,* you will say, to have treated my sweet Saviour? So said Hazael in another case: but when he had the temptation he was a dog to do it. Many call CHRIST their sweet Saviour, whose consciences can bear witness, they never sucked so much sweetness from him as from their sweet lusts, which are ten times sweeter to them than their Saviour. He is no other way sweet to them than as they abuse his death and sufferings for the peaceable enjoyment of their lusts; that they may live as they list in the world; and when they die, may be kept out of hell. Alas! it is but a mistaken CHRIST, this is sweet to you, whose souls loathe that CHRIST, who *is the brightness of the Father's glory, and the express image of his person.* It is with you as it was in the carnal Jews, who delighted in him while they mistook his errand into the world, fancying that he would be a temporal deliverer to them, Mal. iii. 1. But when he was come, and *set as a refiner and purifier of silver,* ver. 2. 3. and cast him as reprobate silver, who thought to have had no small honour in the kingdom of the Messiah! his doctrine galled their consciences, and they rested not till they imbrued their hands in his blood. To open your eyes in this point, which ye are so loth to believe, I will lay before you, the enmity of your hearts against CHRIST and all his offices.

1. Every unregenerate man is an enemy to CHRIST in his prophetical office. He is appointed of the Father, the great Prophet and Teacher; but not upon the world's call, who, in their natural state, would have unanimously voted against him: And therefore, when he came, he was condemned as a seducer and blasphemer. For evidence of this enmity, I will instance in two things.

Evid. 1. Consider the entertainment he meets with, when **he comes** to teach souls inwardly by his Spirit. Men do what they can to stop their ears, like the deaf adder, that they may not hear his voice. They always resist the Holy Ghost. They desire not the knowledge of his ways; and therefore bid him depart from them. The old calumny is often raised upon him on that occasion, John x. 20. *He is mad, why hear ye him?* Soul-exercise, raised by the spirit of bondage, is accounted by **many**, nothing else but distraction, and melancholy fits; men thus blaspheming the LORD's work, because they themselves are beside themselves, and cannot judge of these matters.

Evid. 2. Consider the entertainment he meets with, when he comes to teach men outwardly by his word.

(1.) His written word, the Bible, is slighted; CHRIST hath left it to us, as the book of our instructions, to show us what way we must steer our course, if we would come to Emmanuel's land. It is a lamp to light us through a dark world to eternal light. And he hath left us, to search it with that diligence, wherewith men dig into mines for silver and gold, John v. 39. But ah! how is this sacred treasure profaned by many! They ridicule the holy word, by which they must be judged at **the last day**; and will rather lose their souls than their jest, dressing up the conceit of their wanton wits in scripture-phrases; in which they act as mad a part, as one who would dig into a mine to procure metal to melt, and pour down in his own and his neighbor's throat. Many exhaust their spirits in reading romances, and their minds pursue them, as the flame doth the dry stubble; while they have no heart for, nor relish of the holy word, and therefore seldom take a Bible in their hands. What is agreeable to the vanity of their minds, is pleasant and taking: but what recommends holiness to their unholy hearts makes their spirits dull and flat. What pleasure will they find in reading of a profane ballad, or story book, to whom the Bible is tasteless, as the white of an egg? Many lay by their Bibles with their Sabbath-days clothes; and whatever use they have for their clothes, they have none for their Bibles, till the return of the Sabbath. Alas! the dust or finery about your Bibles is a witness now, and will, at the last day, be a witness of the enmity of your hearts against CHRIST as a prophet. Besides all this, among these who ordinarily read the scriptures, how few are there that read it as the word of the LORD to their souls, and keep communion with him in it. They do not make his statutes, their counsellors, nor doth their particular case send them to their Bibles. They are strangers to the solid comfort of the scriptures. And if at any time they be dejected, it is something else than the word that revives them; as Ahab was cured of his sullen fit, by the securing of Naboth's vineyard for him.

(2.) Christ's word preached is despised. The entertainment most of the world, to whom it has come, have always given it is that which is mentioned, Mat. xxii. 5. *They made light of it.* And for its sake they are despised whom he has employed to preach it; whatever other face men put upon their contempt of the ministry, John xv. 20. *The servant is not greater than his Lord: if they have persecuted me, they will also persecute you; if they have kept my sayings, they will keep yours also. But all these things will they do unto you for my name's sake.* That Levi was the son of the hated, seems not to have been without a mystery, which the world in all ages hath unriddled. But tho' the earthen vessel, wherein GOD has put the treasure, be turned, with many, into vessels wherein there is no pleasure, yet why is the treasure itself slighted? But slighted as it is, and that with a witness this day. LORD, who hath believed our report? To whom shall we speak? Men can without remorse, make to themselves silent Sabbaths, one after another. And alas! when they come to ordinances, for the most part, it is but to appear, as the word is, to be seen before the LORD, and to tread his courts, namely, as a company of beasts would do, if they were driven into them, Isa. i. 12. So little reverence and awe of GOD appears on their spirits. Many stand like brazen walls before the word, in whose corrupt conversation the preaching of the word makes no breach. Nay, not a few are growing worse and worse, under precept upon precept; and the result of all is, *They go and fall backward, and be broken, and snared, and taken,* Isa. xxviii. 13. What tears of blood are sufficient to lament that the gospel the grace of GOD is thus received in vain! We are but the voice of one crying; the speaker is in heaven and speaks to you from heaven by men: why do ye *refuse him that speaketh?* Heb. xii. 25. GOD has made our Master heir of all things, and we are sent to court a spouse for him. There is none so worthy as he; none more unworthy than they to whom this match is promised; but the Prince of darkness is preferred before the prince of peace. A dismal darkness overclouded the world by Adam's fall, more terrible than if the sun, moon and stars had been for ever wrapt up in blackness of darkness; and there we should have eternally lain, had not this grace of the gospel as a shining sun appeared to dispel it, Tit. ii. 11. But yet we fly like night-owls from it; and like the wild beasts, lay ourselves down in our dens; when the sun ariseth, we are struck blind with the light thereof; and, as creatures of darkness, love darkness rather than light. Such is the enmity of the hearts of men against Christ, in his prophetical office.

2. The natural man is an enemy to CHRIST in his priestly office. He is appointed of the Father *a Priest for ever*; that by his alone sacrifice and intercession, sinners may have peace with, and access to GOD; but CHRIST crucified is a stumbling-block, and foolishness to the unrenewed part of mankind, to whom he is preached, 1 Cor. i. 23. They are not for him, as the new and living way. Nor is he by the voice of the world, an High-Priest over the house of GOD. Corrupt nature goes quite another way to work.

Evidence 1. None of Adam's children naturally incline to receive the blessing in borrowed robes; but would always according to the spider's motto, owe all to themselves; and so climb up to heaven on a thread spun out of their own bowels. For they *desire to be under the law,* Gal. iv. 24. *And go about to establish their own righteousness,* Rom. x. 3. Man naturally looks on GOD as a great Master; and himself, as his servant, that must work and win heaven as his wages. Hence, when conscience is awakened, he thinks that, to the end he may be saved, he must answer the demands of the law; serve GOD as well as he can, and pray for mercy wherein he comes short. And thus many come to **duties, that** never come **out** of them to JESUS CHRIST.

Evid. 2. As men naturally think highly of their duties, that seem to them to be well done; so they look for acceptance with GOD according as their work is done, not according to the share they have in the blood of CHRIST. *Wherefore have we fasted, say they, and thou seest not?* They'll value themselves on their performances, and attainments; yea, their very opinions in religion, Phil. ii. 4. 5, 6, 7. taking to themselves, what they rob from CHRIST the great High-Priest.

Evid. 3. The natural man going to GOD in duties, will always be found, either to go without a Mediator, or with more than the only Mediator JESUS CHRIST. Nature is blind, and therefore venturous: it sets a man a-going immediately to GOD without CHRIST; to rush into his presence, and put their petitions in his hand, without being introduced by the secretary of heaven, or putting their requests into his hand. So fixed is this disposition in the unrenewed heart, that when many hearers of the gospel are conversed with upon the point of their hopes of salvation, the name of CHRIST will scarcely be heard from their mouths. Ask them how they think to obtain the pardon of sin? they will tell you, they beg and look for mercy, because GOD is a merciful GOD; and that is all they have to confide in. Others look for mercy for CHRIST's sake; but how do they know that CHRIST will take their plea in hand. Why, as the Papists have their mediators with the Mediator, so have they. They know he cannot but do it; for they pray, confess, mourn, and have great desires, and the like; and so have something of their own to commend them unto him: they were never made poor in spirit, and brought empty-handed to CHRIST, to lay the stress of all on his atoning blood.

3. The natural man is an enemy to CHRIST in his kingly office. The Father is appointed the Mediator King in Zion, Psal. ii. 6. And all to whom the gospel comes are commanded on their highest peril to kiss the Son, and submit themselves unto him, ver. 12. But the natural voice of mankind is, *Away with him,* as you may see, ver. 2, 3. *They will not have him to reign over them,* Luke xix. 14.

Evid. 1. The workings of corrupt nature to wrest the government out of his hands. No sooner was he born, but being born a King, Herod persecuted him, Matth. ii. And when he was crucified, they set up over his head his accusation written, *This is Jesus the King of the Jews,* Matth. xxvii. 37. Tho' his kingdom be a spiritual kingdom, and not of this world; yet they cannot allow him a kingdom within a kingdom which acknowledgeth no other head or supreme, but the royal Mediator. They make bold with his royal prerogatives, changing his laws, institutions and ordinances, modelling his worship according to the devices of their own hearts; introducing new offices and new officers into his kingdom, not to be found in the book of the manner of his kingdom; disposing of the external government thereof, as may best suit their carnal designs. Such is the enmity of the hearts of men against Zion's King.

Evid. 2. How unwilling are men, naturally, to submit unto and be hedged in by the laws and discipline of his kingdom! As a King, he is a law-giver, Isa. xxxiii. 22. and has appointed an external government, discipline and censors, to controul the unruly, and to keep his professed subjects in order, to be exercised by officers of his own appointment, Matth. xviii. 17, 18. 1 Cor. xii. 28. 1 Tim. v. 17. But these are the great eye-sores of the carnal world, who love sinful liberty, and therefore cry out, *Let us break their bands asunder, and cast away their cords from us,* Psal. ii. 3. Hence this work is found to be, in a special manner, a striving against the stream of corrupt nature, which, for the most part, puts such a face on the church, as if there were no King in Israel, every one doing that which is right in his own eyes.

Evid. 3. However natural men may be brought to feign submission to the King of saints, yet lusts always retain the throne and dominion in their hearts, and they are serving *divers lusts and pleasures,* Tit. iii. 3. None but these in whom CHRIST is formed, do really put the crown on his head, and receive the kingdom of CHRIST within them. His crown is *the crown wherewith his mother crowned him, in the day of his espousals.* Who are they whom the power of grace has not subdued, that will allow him to set up, and to put down, in their souls, as he will? Nay, as for others, any lord shall sooner get the rule over them, than the LORD of glory; they kindly entertain his enemies, and will never absolutely resign themselves to his government, till conquered in a day of power. Thus ye may see, that the natural man is an enemy to JESUS CHRIST in all his offices.

But O! how hard it is to convince men in this point! They are very loth to take with it. And in a special manner, the enmity of the heart against CHRIST in his priestly office, seems to be hid from the view of most of the hearers of the gospel. Yet there appears to be a peculiar malignity in corrupt nature against that office of his. It may be observed, that the Socinians, these enemies of our blessed LORD, allow him to be properly a Prophet and a King, but deny him to be properly a Priest. And this is agreeable enough to the corruption of our nature; for **under the** covenant of works, the LORD was known as a Prophet or Teacher, and also as a King or Ruler; but not at all as a Priest; so man knows nothing of the mystery of CHRIST, as the way to the Father, till it be revealed to him. And when it is revealed, the will riseth up against it; for corrupt nature lies cross the mystery of CHRIST, as the great contrivance of salvation, through a crucified Saviour, revealed in the gospel. For clearing of which weighty truths, let these four things be considered.

First, The soul's falling in with the grand device of salvation by JESUS CHRIST, and setting the matters of salvation on that footing before the LORD, is declared by the Scriptures of truth, to be an undoubted mark of a real saint, who is happy here, and shall be happy hereafter. Matth. xi. 6. "And blessed is he whosoever shall not be offended in me. 1 Cor. iii. 23. 24. But we preach CHRIST crucified, unto the Jews a stumbling block, and unto the Greeks foolishness; But unto them which are called, both Jews and Greeks, CHRIST, the power of GOD, and the wisdom of GOD. Philip. iii. 3. For we are the circumcision, which worship GOD in the Spirit, and rejoice in CHRIST JESUS, and have no confidence in the flesh." Now, how could this be, if nature could comply with that grand device.

Secondly, Corrupt nature is the very reverse of the gospel-contrivance. In the gospel, GOD promiseth JESUS CHRIST, as the great means of reuniting man to himself; he has named him as the Mediator, one in whom he is well pleased; and will have none but him, Matth. xvii. 5. But nature will have none of him, Psal. lxxxi. 11. GOD appointed the place of meeting for their reconciliation, namely, the flesh of CHRIST; accordingly, GOD was in CHRIST, 2 Cor. v. 29. as the tabernacle of meeting, to make up the peace with sinners; but natural men, though they should die for ever, will not come thither, John v. 40. *And ye will not come unto me, that ye might have life.* In the way of the gospel, the sinner must stand before the LORD in an imputed righteousness; but corrupt nature is for an inherent righteousness; and therefore, so far as natural men follow after righteousness, they follow after the law of righteousness, Rom. ix. 31, 32. and not after the LORD our righteousness. Nature is always for building up itself, and to have some grounds for boasting; but the great design of the gospel, is to exalt grace, to depress nature, and exclude boasting, Rom. iii. 27. The sum of our natural religion is, to do good from and for ourselves, John v. 44. The sum of the gospel religion, is to deny ourselves, and to do good from and for CHRIST, Philip. i. 21.

Thirdly, Every thing in nature, is against believing in Jesus Christ. What beauty can the blind man discern in a crucified Saviour, for which he is to be desired? How can the will, naturally impotent, yea, and averse to good, make choice of him? Well may the soul then say to him in the day of the spiritual siege, as the Jebusites said to David in another case, *Except thou take away the blind and the lame, thou shalt not come in hither,* 2 Sam. v. 6. The way of nature is to go into one's self for all; according to the fundamental maxim of unsanctified morality, That a man should trust in himself; Which, according to the doctrine of faith, is mere foolishness. For so it is determinded, Prov. xviii. 26. *he that trusteth in his own heart, is a fool.* Now faith is the soul's going out of itself for all; and this nature, on the other hand determines to be foolishness, 1 Cor. i. 18. 23. Wherefore there is need of the working of mighty power, to cause sinners to believe, Eph. i. 19. Isa. liii. 1. We see promises of welcome to sinners, in the gospel covenant, are ample, large and free, clogged with no conditions, Isa. lv. 1. Rev. xxii. 17. If they cannot believe his bare word, he has given them his oath upon it, Ezek. xxxiii. 11. And for their greater assurance, he has appended seals to his sworn covenant, namely, the holy sacraments. So that no more could be demanded of the most faithless person in the world, to make us believe him, than the Lord hath condescended to give us, to make us believe himself. This plainly speaks nature to be against believing, and these who flee to Christ for refuge, to have need of strong consolation, Heb. vi. 18. to blame their strong doubts, and propensity to unbelief. Farther, also it may be observed, how, in the word sent to a secure, graceless generation, their objections are answered aforehand: and words of grace are heaped one upon another, as ye may read, Isa. lv. 7, 8. 9. Joel ii. 13. Why? Because the Lord knows, that when these secure sinners are throughly wakened, doubts, fears, and carnal reasonings against believing, will be within their breasts, as thick as dust in a house, raised by sweeping a dry floor.

Lastly, Corrupt nature is bent towards the way of the law, or covenant of works: and every natural man, so far as he sets himself to seek after salvation, is engaged in that way; and will not quit it, till beat from it by divine power. Now the way of salvation by works, and that of free grace in Jesus Christ, are inconsistent, Rom. xi. 6. *And if by grace, then it is no more of works; otherwise grace is no more grace. But if it be of works then it is no more grace; otherwise work is no more work,* Gal. iii. 13. *And the law is not of FAITH; but the man that DOTH them, shall live in them.* Wherefore, if the will of man naturally incline to the way of salvation by the law; it lies cross to the gospel contrivance. And that such is the natural bent of our hearts will appear, if these following things be considered.

1. The law was Adam's covenant, and he knew no other, as he was the head and representative of all mankind, that were brought into it with him, and left under it by him, tho' without strength to perform the condition thereof. Hence, this covenant is ingrained in our nature: and tho' we have lost our father's strength, yet we still incline to the way he was set upon, as our head and representative in that covenant; that is, by doing to live. This is our natural religion, and the principle which men naturally take for granted, Matth. xix. 11. *What good thing shall I DO, that I may have eternal life?*

2. Consider the opposition that has always been made in the world against the doctrine of free-grace in JESUS CHRIST, by men setting up for the way of works; thereby discovering the natural tendency of the heart. It is manifest, that the great design of the gospel-contrivance, is to exalt the free grace of GOD in JESUS CHRIST, Rom. iv. 16. *Therefore it is of faith, that it might be by grace.* See Eph. i. 6. and chap. ii. 7, 9. All gospel-truths center in CHRIST; so that to learn the truth is, to learn CHRIST, Eph. iv. 20. And to be truly taught is, to be taught as the truth is in JESUS, ver. 21. All dispensations of grace and favour from heaven, whether to nations or particular persons, have still had something about them, proclaiming a freedom of grace; as in the very first separation made by the divine favour, Cain, the elder brother, is rejected; and Abel, the younger, accepted. This shines through the whole history of the Bible; but as true as it is, this has been the point principally opposed by corrupt nature. One may well say, that of all errors in religion, since CHRIST, the Seed of the woman, was preached, this of works, in opposition to free-grace in him, was the first that lived; and it is likely to be the last that dies. There have been vast numbers of errors, which sprung up, one after another, whereof at length, the world became ashamed and weary; so that they died out. But this has continued from Cain, the first author of this heresy, unto this day; and never wanted some that clave to it, even in the times of greatest light. I do not without ground, call Cain the author of it; For when Abel brought the sacrifice of atonement, a bloody offering of the firstlings of his flock, like the Publican, *smiting on his breast* and saying, *God be merciful to me a sinner,* Cain advanced with his thank offering of the first-fruit of the ground, Gen. iv. 3, 4. like the proud

F

Pharisee, with his *God I thank thee*. For what was the cause of Cain's wrath, and of his murdering of Abel? Was it not that he was accepted of GOD, for his work? Gen. iv. 4, 5. *And wherefore slew he him? Because his own works were evil, and his brother's righteous*, 1 John iii. 22. That is done in faith, and accepted; when his were done without faith, and therefore rejected, as the Apostle teacheth, Heb. xi. 4. And so he wrote his indignation against justification and acceptance with GOD, through faith, in opposition to works, in the blood of his brother, to convey it down to posterity. And since that time, the unbloody sacrifice has often swimmed in the blood of those that rejected it. The promise made to Abraham, of the *seed* in which all nations should be blessed, was so overclouded among his posterity in Egypt, that the generality of them saw no need of that way of obtaining the blessing till GOD himself confuted their error, by a fiery law from mount Sinai, *which was added because of transgressions, till the Seed should come*, Gal. iii. 19. I need not insist to tell you, how Moses and the Prophets had still much ado, to lead the people off the conceit of their own righteousness; Deut. xi. is entirely spent on that purpose. They were very gross in that point, in our Saviour's time. In the time of the Apostles, when the doctrine of free grace was most clearly preached, that error lifted up its head, in face of clearest light; witness the Epistle to the Romans and Galatians; And, since that time, it has not been wanted; Popery being the common sink of former heresies, and this the heart and life of that delusion. And, finally, it may be observed, that always as the church declined from her purity otherwise, the doctrine of free grace was obscured proportionably.

3. Such is the natural propensity of man's heart, to the way of the law, in opposition to CHRIST; that, as the tainted vessel turns the taste of the purest liquor put into it, so the natural man turns the very gospel into law; and transforms the covenant of grace into a covenant of works. The ceremonial law was to the Jews a real gospel; which held blood, death, and translation of guilt before their eyes continually, as the only way of salvation: yet their very table *i. e.* their altar, with the several ordinances pertaining thereto, Mal. i. 12. was *a snare unto them*, Rom. ii. 9. While they use it to make up the defects in their obedience to the moral law, and cleave to it so, as to reject Him, whom the altar and sacrifices pointed them to as the substance of all: even as Hagar, whose it was only to serve, was by their father brought into her mistress's bed; not without a mystery in the purpose of GOD, *for these are the two covenants*, Gal. iv. 24. Thus is the doctrine of the gospel corrupted by Papists, and

other enemies to the doctrine of free grace. And indeed, however natural mens heads may be set right in this point, as surely as they are out of CHRIST, their faith, repentance and obedience, such as they are, are placed by them in the room of CHRIST and his righteousness, and so trusted to, as if by these they fulfilled a new law.

4. Great is the difficulty in Adam's sons their parting with the law, as a covenant of works. None part with it in that respect, but these whom the power of the Spirit of grace separates from it. The law is our first husband, and gets every one's virgin love. When CHRIST comes to the soul, he finds it married to the law; so as it neither can, nor will be married to another, till it be obliged to part with the first husband as the apostle teacheth. Rom. vii. 1, 2, 3, 4. Now that ye may see what sort of a parting this is, consider,

(1.) It is a death, Rom. vii. 4. Gal. iii. 19. Intreaties will not prevail with the soul here; it saith to the first husband, as Ruth to Naomi, *The Lord do so to me, and more also, if ought but death part thee and me.* And here sinners are true to their word; they die to the law, ere they be married to CHRIST. Death is hard to every body: but what difficulty do ye imagine must a loving wife, on her death-bed, find in parting with her husband, the husband of her youth, and with the dear children she has brought forth to him: the law is that husband; all the duties performed by the natural men, are these children. What a struggle as for life, will be in the heart ere they be got parted? I may have occasion to touch upon this afterwards. In the mean time, take the Apostle's short, but pithy description of it, Rom. x. 3. *For they being ignorant of God's righteousness, and going about to establish their own righteousness, have not submitted themselves to the righteousness of God.* They go about to establish their own righteousness, like an eager disputant in schools, seeking to establish the point in question: or like a tormentor, extorting a confession from one upon the rack. They go about to establish it to make it stand; their righteousness is like a house built upon the sand; it cannot stand, but they will have it to stand: it falls, they set it up again, but still it tumbles down on them; yet they cease not to go about to make it stand. But wherefore all this pains about a tottering righteousness? Because, such as it is, it is their own. What ails them at CHRIST's righteousness? Why, that would make them free grace's debtors for all; and that is what the proud heart by no means can submit to. Here lies the stress of the matter, Psal. x. 4. *The wicked through the pride of his countenance will not seek,* to read it without the supplement, that is, in other terms, *he cannot dig, and to beg he is ashamed*. Such is the struggle ere the soul die to the law. But what speaks yet more of this woful disposition of the heart, nature oft-times gets the mastery of the disease; ; insomuch that the soul, which was like to have died to the law, while convictions were sharp and piercing, fatally recovers of the happy and promising sickness; and, what is very natural cleaves more closely than ever to the law, even as a wife brought back from the gates of death would cleave to her husband. This is the issue of the exercise of many about their soul's case: they are indeed brought to follow duties more closely; but they are as far from CHRIST as ever, if not farther.

(2.) It is a violent death, Rom. vii. 4. *Ye are become dead to the law*, being killed, slain, or put to death, as the word bears. The law itself has a great hand in this; the husband gives the wound, Gal. ii. 19. *I through the law am dead to the law*. The soul that dies this death, is like a loving wife matched with a rigorous husband: she does what she can to please him, yet he is never pleased; but tosseth, harrasseth, and beats her till she brake her heart, and death sets her free; as will afterwards more fully appear. Thus it is made evident, that mens hearts are naturally bent to the way of the law, and lie cross to the gospel-contrivance; and the second article of the charge, against you that are unregenerate, is verified, namely, that ye are enemies to the Son of GOD.

3*dly*, Ye are enemies to the Spirit of GOD. He is the Spirit of holiness; the natural man is unholy, and loves to be so, and therfore *resists the Holy Ghost*, Acts vii. 51. The work of the Spirit is to convince the world of *sin, righteousness, and judgment*, John xvi. 8. But O how do men strive to ward off these convictions, as ever they would ward off a blow, threatning their loss of a right-eye, or a right-hand! If the Spirit of the LORD dart them in, so as they cannot evite them: the heart says, in effect, as Ahab to Elijah, whom he both hated and feared, *Hast thou found me, O mine enemy?* And indeed they treat him as an enemy, doing their utmost to stifle convictions, and to murder these harbingers, that come to prepare the LORD's way into the soul. Some fill their hands with business, to put their convictions out of their heads, as Cain, who fell a building of a city: some put them off with delays and fair promises, as Felix did: some will sport them away in company, and some sleep them away. The holy Spirit is the Spirit of sanctification: whose work is to subdue lusts, and burn up corruption: how then can the natural man whose lusts are to him as his limbs, yea, as his life, fail of being an enemy to him?

Lastly, Ye are enemies to the law of GOD. Tho' the natural man desires to be under the law, as a covenant of works, chusing that way of salvation in opposition to the mystery of CHRIST; yet as it is a rule of life, requiring universal holiness, and discharging all manner of impurity, he is an enemy to it: *Is not subject to the law of God, neither indeed can be*, Rom. viii. 7. For, (1.) There is no unrenewed man, who is not wedded to some one lust or other, which his heart can by no means part with. Now, that he cannot bring up his inclinations to the holy law, he would feign have the law brought down to his inclinations: a plain evidence of the enmity of the heart against it. And therefore, *to delight in the law of God, after the inward man*, is proposed in the word as a mark of a gracious soul, Rom. vii. 22. Psal. i. 2. It is from this natural enmity of the heart against the law, that all the Pharisaical gloss upon it have arisen: whereby the commandment, which is in itself exceeding broad, has been made narrow to the intent it might be the more agreeable to the natural disposition of the heart. (2.) The law laid home to the natural conscience, in its spirituality, irritates corruption. The nearer it comes, nature riseth the more against it. In that case, it is as oil to the fire, which instead of quenching it, makes it flame the more: *When the commandment came, sin revived*, says the Apostle, Rom. vii. 9. What reason can be assigned for this, but the natural enmity of the heart against the holy law? Unmortified corruption, the more it is opposed, the more it rageth. Let us conclude then, that the unregenerate are heart-enemies to GOD, his Son, his Spirit, and his law; that there is a natural contrariety, opposition and enmity in the will of man, to GOD himself, and his holy will.

Fifthly, There is, in the will of man, contumacy against the LORD. Man's will is naturally wilful in an evil course. He will have his will, though it should ruin him; it is with him, as with the leviathan, Job xli. 29. *Darts are counted as stubble; he laugheth at the shaking of a spear*. The LORD calls to him by his word, says to him, as Paul to the jaylor, when he was about to kill himself, *Do thyself no harm*. Sinners, *Why will ye die?* Ezek. xviii. 31. But they will not hearken, *Every one turneth to his course, as the horse rusheth into the battle*, Jer. viii. 6. We have a promise of life in form of a command, Prov. iv. 4: *Keep my commandments and live*: it speaks impenitent sinners to be self-destroyers, wilful self-murderers. They transgress the command of living; as if one's servant should wilfully starve himself to death, greedily drink up a cup of poison, which his master commands him to forbear: even so do they: they will not live, they will die. Proverbs viii. 36. *All they that hate me love death*. O what a heart is this! It is a stony heart, Ezek. xxxvi. 26. hard and inflexible, as a stone: mercies melt it not, judgments break it not; yet it will break ere it bow. It is an insensible heart; tho' there be upon the sinner a weight of sin, which makes the earth to stagger; although there is a weight of wrath on him, which makes the devil to tremble: yet he goes lightly under the burden; he feels not the weight more than a stone: till the spirit of the LORD quicken him, so far as to feel it.

Lastly, The unrenewed will is wholly perverse in reference to man's chief and highest end. The natural man's chief end is not his GOD, but himself. Man is a mere relative, dependent, borrowed being: he has no being nor goodness originally from himself; but all he hath is from GOD, as the first cause and spring of all perfection, natural or moral: dependence is woven into his very nature; so that if GOD should totally withdraw from him, he would dwindle into a mere nothing. Seeing then whatever man is, he is of him; surely in whatever he is, he should be to him; as the waters which come from the sea, do of course return thither again. And thus man was created, directly looking to GOD, as his chief end: but falling into sin, he fell off from GOD, and turned into himself; and like a traitor usurping the throne, he gathers in the rents of the crown to himself: Now, this infers a total apostasy, and universal corruption in the man; for where the chief and last end is changed, there can be no goodness there. This is the case of all men in their natural state. Psal. xiv. 2, 3. *The Lord looked down,---to see if there were any that did--- seek God. They are all gone aside*, viz. from GOD; they seek not GOD, but themselves. And though many fair shrewds of morality, are to be found amongst them, yet *there is none that doeth good, no not one*; for though some of them run well, they are still off the way; they never aim at the right mark. They are lovers *of their ownselves*, 2 Tim. iii. 2. *more than God*, verse 4. Wherefore JESUS CHRIST, having come into the world, to bring men back to GOD again, came to bring them out of themselves, in the first place, Matth. xvi. 25. The godly groan under the remains of this woful disposition of the heart; they acknowledge it, and set themselves against it, in its subtile and dangerous insinuations. The unregenerate, though most insensible of it, are under the power thereof; and whithersoever they turn themselves, they cannot move, without the circle of self; they seek themselves, they act for themselves; their natural civil and religious actions from whatever spring they come, do all run into, and meet in the dead sea of self.

Most men are so far from making GOD their chief end, in their natural and civil actions; that in these matters, GOD is not in all their thoughts. Their eating and drinking, and such like natural actions, are for themselves; their own pleasure or necessity, without any higher end, Zech. vii. 6. *Did ye not eat for yourselves?* They have no eye to the glory of GOD in these things, as they ought to have, 1 Cor. x. 31. They do not eat and drink, to keep up their bodies for the LORD's service; they do them not, because GOD has said, *Thou shalt not kill:* neither do these drops of sweetness GOD has put into the creature, raise up their souls towards that ocean of delight that is in the Creator, tho' they are indeed a sign hung out at heaven's door, to tell men of the fulness of goodness that's in GOD himself, Acts xiv. 16. But it is self, and not GOD, that is sought in them by natural men. And what are the unrenewed man's civil actions, such as buying, selling, working, &c. but fruit to himself? Hos. x. 1. so marrying and giving in marriage, are reckoned amongst the sins of the old world, Mat. xxiv. 38. for they had no eye to GOD therein, to please him; but all they had in view, was to please themselves, Gen. vi. 3. Finally, Self is natural men's highest end, in their religious actions. They perform duties for a name, Matth. vi. 1, 2. or some other *worldly interest*, John vi. 26. Or if they be more refined; it is their peace, and at most their salvation from hell and wrath, or their own eternal happiness, that is their chief and highest end, Mat. xix. 16 --22. Their eyes are held, that they see not the glory of GOD. They seek GOD indeed, but not for himself, but for themselves. They seek him not at all, but for their own welfare: so their whole life is woven into one web of practical blasphemy; making GOD the means, and self their end, yea, their chief end.

And thus have I given you some rude draughts of man's will, in his natural state, drawn by Scripture and men's own experience. Call it no more Naomi, but Marah: for bitter it is, and a root of bitterness. Call it no more free-will, but slavish lust: free to evil, but free from good, till regenerating grace loose the bands of wickedness. Now, since all must be wrong, and nothing can be right, where the understanding and will are so corrupt; I shall briefly dispatch what remains as follow of course, on the corruption of those prime faculties of the soul.

The Corruption of the Affections, the Conscience and the Memory. The body partaker of this Corruption.

III. The affections are corrupted. The unrenewed man's affections are wholly disordered and distempered, they are as the unruly horse, that either will not receive, or violently runs away with the rider. So man's heart naturally is a mother of abominations, Mark vii. 21, 22, *For from within, out of the heart of men, proceed evil thoughts, adulteries, fornications, murders, thefts, covetousness*, &c. The natural man's affections are wretchedly misplaced; he is a spiritual monster. His heart is there, where his feet should be, fixed on the earth; his heels are lifted up against heaven, which his heart should be set on, Acts ix. 5. His face is towards hell, his back towards heaven; and therefore GOD calls him to turn. He loves what he should hate, and hates what he should love: joys in what he ought to mourn for, and mourns for what he should rejoice in: glorieth in his shame, and is ashamed of his glory; abhors what he should desire, and desires what he should abhor, Prov. ii. 13, 14, 15. They hit the point indeed, as Caiaphas did, in another case who cried out on the Apostles as men that *turned the world upside-down*, Acts xvii. 6. For that is the work the gospel has to do in the world, where sin has put all things so out of order, that heaven lies under, and earth a-top. If the unrenewed man's affections be set on lawful objects, then they are either excessive, or defective. Lawful enjoyments of the world have sometimes too little, but mostly too much of them: either they get not their due; or, if they do, it is measure *pressed down, and running over*. Spiritual things have always too little of them. In a word, they are always in or over; never right, only evil.

Now here is a three-fold cord against heaven and holiness, not easily broken; a blind mind, a perverse will, and disorderly, distempered affections. The mind swelled with self conceit, says the man should not stoop; the will, opposite to the will of GOD, says he will not; and the corrupt affections, rising against the LORD, in a defence of the corrupt will, say, he shall not. Thus the poor creature stands out against GOD and goodness, till a day of power come, in which he is made a new creature.

IV. The conscience is corrupt and defiled, Tit. i. 15. It is an evil eye, that fills one's conversation with much darkness and confusion; being naturally unable to do its office; till the LORD, by letting in a new light to the soul awaken the conscience; it remains sleepy and unactive. Conscience can never do its work, but according to the light it hath to work by. Wherefore seeing the natural man cannot spiritually discern spiritual things, 1 Cor. ii. 14. the conscience naturally is quite useless in that point; being cast into such a deep sleep, that nothing but a saving illumination from the LORD can set it on work in that matter. The light of the natural conscience in good and evil, sin, and duty, is very defective therefore tho' it may check for grosser sins; yet as to the more subtil workings of sin, it cannot check for them, because it discerns them not. Thus conscience will fly in the face of many, if at any time they be drunk, swear, neglect prayer, or be guilty of any gross sin; who otherwise have a profound peace; tho' they live in the sin of unbelief, are strangers to spiritual worship, and the life of faith. And natural light being but faint and languishing in many things which it doth reach, conscience in that case shoots like a stitch in one's side, which quickly goes off; its incitements to duty, and checks for and struggles against sin, are very remiss, which the natural man easily gets over. But because there is a false light in the dark mind, the natural conscience following the same, will call *evil good, and good evil.* Isa. v. 20. And so it is often found like a blind and furious horse, which doth violently run down himself, his rider, and all that doth come in his way, John xvi. 2. *Whosoever killeth you, will think that he doth God service.* When the natural conscience is awakened by the Spirit of conviction, it will indeed rage and rore, and put the whole man in a dreadful consternation, awfully summon all the powers of the soul to help in a strait; make the stiff heart to tremble, and the knees to bow; set the eyes a-weeping, the tongue a-confessing; and oblige the man to cast out the **goods** into the sea, which it apprehends are like to sink the ship of the soul, tho' the heart still goes after them. But yet it is an evil conscience, which natively leads to despair, and will do it effectually, as in Judas's case; unless either lusts prevail over it, to lull it asleep, as in the case of Felix, Acts xxiv. 25. or the blood of CHRIST prevail over it, sprinkling and purging it from dead works, as is the case of all true converts, Heb. ix. 14. and x. 23.

Lastly, Even the memory bears evident marks of this corruption. What is good and worthy to be minded, as it makes but slender impression, so that impression easily wears off; the memory, as a leaking vessel, lets it slip, Heb. ii. 1. As a sieve that is full, when in the water, lets all go when it is taken out; so is the memory, with respect to spiritual things. But how does it retain what ought to be forgotten? Naughty things so bear in themselves upon it, that though men would fain have them out of mind, yet they stick there like glue. However forgetful men be in other things, it is hard to forget an injury. So the memory often furnishes new fuel to old lusts; makes men in old age to re-act the sins of their youth, while it presents them again to the mind with delight, which thereupon licks up the former vomit. And thus it is like the riddle, that lets through the pure grain, and keeps the refuse. Thus far of the corruption of the soul.

The body itself also is partaker of this corruption and defilement, so far as it is capable thereof. Wherefore the Scripture calls it sinful flesh, Rom. viii. 3. We may take this up in two things. (1.) The natural temper; or rather distemper on the bodies of Adam's children, as it is an affect of original sin; so it hath a native tendancy to sin, leads the soul into snares, yea, is itself a snare to the soul. The body is a furious beast, of such metal, that if it be not beat down, kept under, and brought into subjection, it will cast the soul into much sin and misery, 1 Cor. ix. 27. There's vileness in the body, Phil. iii. 21. which as to the saints, will never be removed, until it be melted down in a grave, and cast into a new mould, at the resurrection to come forth a spiritual body: and will never be carried off from the bodies of those who are not partakers of the resurrection to life. (2.) It serves the soul in many sins. Its members are instruments of weapons of unrighteousness, whereby men fight against GOD, Rom. vi. 13. The eyes and ears are open doors, by which impure motions and sinful desires enter the soul: *The tongue is a world of iniquity: An unruly evil, full of deadly poison,* James iii. 6. 8. By it the impure heart vents a great deal of its filthiness. *The throat is an open sepulchre,* Rom. iii. 13. The feet runs the devil's errands, ver. 15. The belly is made a god, Philip. iii. 19. not only by drunkards and riotous livers, but by every natural man, Zech. vii 6. So the body naturally is an agent for the devil; and a magazine of armour against the LORD.

To conclude, man by nature is wholly corrupted: From the sole of the foot even unto the head, there is no soundness in him. And as in a dunghill, every part contributes to the corruption of the whole; so the natural man, while in that state, grows still worse and worse. The soul is made worse by the body, and the body by the soul: and every faculty of the soul serves to corrupt another more and **more.** Thus much for the second general head.

How Man's Nature was corrupted.

Thirdly, I shall shew how man's nature comes to be **thus** corrupted. The heathens perceived that man's nature was corrupted; but how sin had entered, they could not tell. But the Scripture is very plain in that point, Rom. v. 12. 19. *By one man sin entered into the world. By one man's disobedience, many were made sinners.* Adam's sin corrupted man's nature and leavened the whole lump of mankind. We putrified in Adam, as our root was poisoned, and so the branches were envenomed; the vine turned the vine of Sodom, and so the grapes became grapes of gall. Adam, by his sin, became

his disobedience, **were made** sinners, as Levi, in the loins of Abraham paid tithes, Heb. vii. 9. His first sin is imputed to us; therefore justly are we left under the want of his original righteousness, which, being given to him as a common person, he cast off, by his sin; and this is necessarily followed in him and us, by the corruption of the whole nature; righteousness and corruption being two contraries, one of which must needs always be in man as a subject capable thereof. And Adam, our common father, being corrupt, we are so too; for, *Who can bring a clean thing out of an unclean?*

Although it is sufficient to evince the righteousness of this dispensation, that it was from the LORD, who doth all things well; yet to silence the murmurings of proud nature, let these few things further be considered. (1.) In the covenant wherein Adam represented us, eternal happiness was promised to him and his posterity, upon condition of this, that is, Adam's perfect obedience, as the representative for all mankind; whereas, if there had been no covenant, they could not have pleaded eternal life, upon their most perfect obedience, but might have been, after all, reduced to nothing, notwithstanding, by the natural justice, they would have been liable to GOD's eternal wrath, in case of sin. Who in that case would not have consented to that representation? (2.) Adam had a power to stand given him, being made upright. He was as capable to stand for himself, and all his posterity, as any after him could be for themselves. This trial of mankind, in their head, would soon have been over, and the crown won to them all, had he stood; whereas, had his posterity been independent on him, and every one left to act for himself, the trial would have been continually a-carrying on as men came into the world. (3.) He had natural affections the strongest to engage him, being our common father. (4.) His one stock was in the ship, his all lay at stake as well as ours. He had no seperate interest from ours; for if he forgot ours, he behoved to have forgot his own. (5.) If he had stood, we should have had the light of his mind, the righteousness of his will, and holiness of his affections, with entire purity transmitted unto us; we could not have fallen; the crown of glory, by his obedience, would have been for ever secured to him and his. This is evident from the nature of a federal representation; and no reason can be given why, seeing we are lost by Adam's sin, we should not have been saved by his obedience. On the other hand, it is reasonable that, he falling, we should with him bear the loss. *Lastly*, Such as quarrel this dispensation, must renounce their part in CHRIST; for we are no otherwise made sinners by Adam, than we are made righteous by CHRIST; from whom we have both imputed and inherent righteousness. We no more made choice of the second Adam, for our head and representative, in the second covenant than we did of the first Adam in the first covenant.

Let none wonder that such an horrible change would be brought on by one sin of our first parents, for thereby they turned away from GOD, as their chief end; which necessarily infers an universal depravation. Their sin was a complication of evils, a total apostacy from GOD, a violation of the whole law. By it they broke all the ten commands at once. (1.) They chose new gods. They made their belly their god, by their sensuality; self their god by their ambition; yea, and the devil their GOD, believing him, and disbelieving their Maker. (2.) Though they received, yet they observed not that ordinance of GOD, about the forbidden fruit. They contemned that ordinance so plainly enjoined them, and would needs carve out to themselves, how to serve the LORD. (3.) They took the name of the LORD their GOD in vain; despising his attributes, his justice, truth, power, &c. They grosly profaned that sacramental tree; abused his word, by not giving credit to it; abused that creature of his, which they should not have touched, and violently misconstrued his providence; as if GOD, by forbidding them that tree, had been standing in the way of their happiness; and therefore he suffered them not to escape his righteous judgment. (4.) They remembered not the Sabbath, to keep it holy; but put themselves out of a condition to serve GOD aright on his own day. Neither kept they that state of holy rest, wherein GOD had put them. (5.) They cast off their relative duties; Eve forgets herself, and acts without advice of her husband, to the ruin of both; Adam instead of admonishing her to repent, yields to the temptation, & confirms her in her wickedness. They forgot all duty to their posterity. They honoured not their Father in heaven; and therefore their days were not long in the land which the LORD their GOD gave them. (6.) They ruined themselves, and all their posterity. (7.) Gave up themselves to luxury and sensuality. (8.) Took away what was not their own, against the express will of the great owner. (9.) They bore false witness, and lied against the LORD, before angels, devils, and one another; in effect giving out that they were hardly dealt by, and that heaven grudged their happiness. (10) They were discontent with their lot, and coveted an evil covetousness to their house; which ruined both them and theirs. Thus was the image of GOD on man defaced all at once.

The Doctrine of the Corruption of Nature applied.

USE I. For information. Is man's nature wholly corrupted? Then,

1. No wonder the grave open its devouring mouth for us, as soon as the womb hath cast us forth; and that the cradle be turned into a coffin, to recieve the corrupt lump: for we are all, in a spiritual sense, dead-born; yea, and filthy, Psal. xiv. 3. noisome, rank, and stinking as a corrupt thing, as the word imports. Let us not complain of the miseries we are exposed to at our entrance, nor of the continuance of them, while we are in the world. Here is the venom that has poisoned all the springs of earthly enjoyments we have to drink of. It is the corruption of man's nature, that brings forth all the miseries of human life in churches, states, families; in mens souls and bodies.

2. Behold here, as in a glass, the spring of all the wickedness, profanity, and formality in the world; the source of all the disorders in thy own heart and life. Every thing acts like itself, agreeable to its own nature; and so corrupt man acts corruptly. You need not wonder at the sinfulness of your own heart and life, nor at the sinfulness and perverseness of others; if a man be crooked, he cannot but halt; and if the clock be set wrong, **how** can it point the hour right.

3. See here, why sin is so pleasant, and religion such a burden to carnal spirits: sin is natural, holiness not so. Oxen cannot feed in the sea, nor fishes in the fruitful fields. A swine brought into a palace, would get away again, to wallow in the mire. A corrupt nature tends even to impurity.

4. Learn from this the nature and necessity of regeneration. *First*, This discovers the nature of regeneration in these two things, (1.) It is not a partial but a total change, tho' imperfect in this life. Thy whole nature is corrupted, and therefore the cure must go thro' every part. Regeneration makes not only a new head for knowledge, but a new heart, and new affections for holiness. *All things become new*, 2 Cor. v. 17. If one having received many wounds; should be cured of them all, save one only, he might bleed to death by that one as well as a thousand. So if the change go not through the

whole man it is naught. (2.) It is not a change made by human industry, but by the mighty power of the Spirit of GOD. A man must be *born of the Spirit*, John iii. 5. Accidental diseases may be cured by men, but these which are natural, not without a miracle, John ix. 39. The change brought upon men by good education, or forced upon them by a natural conscience, tho' it may pass among men for a saving change, it is not so; for our nature is corrupt, and none but the GOD of nature can change it. Tho' a gardiner in grafting a pear-branch into an apple-tree, may make the apple-tree bear pears, yet the art of man cannot change the nature of the apple-tree; so one may pin a new life to his old heart, but he can never change the heart. *Secondly*, This also shews the necessity of regeneration. It is absolutely necessary in order to salvation, John iii. 3. *Except a man be born again, he cannot see the kingdom of God.* No unclean thing can enter the new Jerusalem; but thou art wholly unclean, while in thy natural state. If every member of thy body were disjointed, each joint behoved to be loosed, ere the members could be set right again. This is the case of thy soul, as thou hast heard; and therefore thou must be born again; else thou shalt never see heaven, unless it be far off, as the rich man in hell did. Decieve not thyself: no mercy of GOD, no blood of CHRIST will bring thee to heaven, in thy unregenerate state: for GOD will never open a fountain of mercy, to wash away his own holiness and truth: nor did CHRIST shed his precious blood, to blot out the truths of GOD, or to overturn GOD's measures about the salvation of sinners. Heaven! What would ye do there, that are not born again? Ye that are no ways fitting for CHRIST the head. That would be a strange sight, a holy head and members wholly corrupt! a head full of treasures of grace, members wherein are nothing but treasures of wickedness! a head obedient to death, and heels kicking against heaven! Ye are no ways adapted to the society above, more than beasts for converse with men. Thou art a hater of true holiness: and at the first sight of a saint there, would cry out, *Hast thou found me, O mine enemy?* Nay, the unrenewed man, if it were possible he could go to heaven in that state, he would no otherwise go to it, than now he comes to the duties of holiness, that is, leaving his heart behind him.

USE II. For lamentation. Well may we lament thy case, O natural man, for it is the saddest case one can be in, out of hell. It is time to lament for thee; for thou art dead already, dead while thou livest: thou carriest about with thee a dead soul in a living body; and because thou art dead, thou canst not lament thy own case. Thou art loathsome in the sight of GOD; for thou art altogether corrupt. Thou hast no good in thee; thy soul is a mass of darkness, rebellion, and vileness before the LORD. Thou thinkest, perhaps, that thou hast a good heart to GOD, good inclination, and good desires; but GOD knows there is nothing good in thee, but every imagination of thine heart is only evil. Thou canst do no good, thou canst do nothing but sin. For,

First, Thou art *the servant of sin,* Rom. vi. 17. and therefore *free from righteousness,* ver. 20. Whatever righteousness be, poor souls, thou art free of it; thou dost not, thou canst not meddle with it. Thou art under the dominion of sin, a dominion where righteousness can have no place. Thou art a child and servant of the devil, tho' thou be neither wizzard nor witch: seeing thou art yet in the state of nature. John viii. 44. *Ye are of your father the devil.* And to prevent any mistake, consider, that sin and satan have two sorts of servants, (1.) There are some employed, as it were, in coarser work: those bear the devil's mark in their fore-heads, having no form of godliness; but are profane, grossly ignorant, mere moralists, not so much as performing the external duties of religion, but living to the view of the world; as sons of earth, only *minding earthly things,* Phil. iii. 19. (2.) There are some employed in a more refined sort of service to sin, who carry the devil's mark in their right hand; which they can, and do hide from the view of the world. These are close hypocrites, who sacrifice as much to the corrupt mind, as the other to the flesh, Eph. ii. 3. These are ruined by a more undiscernable trade of sin; pride, unbelief, self-seeking, and the like swarm in, and prey upon their corrupted, wholly corrupted souls. Both are servants of the same house; the latter as far as the former from righteousness.

Secondly, How is it possible thou shouldst be able to do any good, thou whose nature is wholly corrupt? Can fruit grow where there is no root? Or can there be an effect without a cause? *Can the fig-tree bear olive berries? either a vine figs.* If thy nature be wholly corrupt, as indeed it is, all thou dost is certainly so too; for no effect can exceed the virtue of its cause. *Can a corrupt tree bring forth good fruit?* Matth. vii. 18.

Ah! what a miserable spectacle is he that can do nothing but sin? Thou art the man, whosoever thou art, that art yet in thy natural state. Hear, O sinner, what is thy cause.

First, Innumerable sins compass thee about. Mountains of guilt are lying upon thee. Floods of impurities overwhelm thee. Living lusts of all sorts roll up and down in the dead sea of thy soul; where no good can breathe, because of the corruption there. Thy lips are unclean; the opening of thy mouth is as the opening of an unripe grave, full of stench and rottenness, Rom. iii. 13. *Their throat is an open sepulchre.* Thy natural actions are sin, for *when ye did eat, and when ye did drink, did not ye eat for yourselves, and drink for yourselves?* Zech. vii. 6. Thy civil actions are sin, Prov. xxi. 4. *The plowing of the wicked is sin.* Thy religious actions are sin, Prov. xv. 8. *The sacrifice of the wicked is an abomination to the Lord.* The thoughts and imaginations of thy heart, are only evil. A deed may be soon done, a word soon spoken, a thought swiftly passeth thro' the heart; but each is an Item in thy accounts. O sad reckoning! as many thoughts, words, actions; as many sins. The longer thou livest, thy accounts swell the more. Should a tear be dropt for every sin, thine head behoved to be waters, and thine eyes a fountain of tears; for nothing but sin comes from thee. Thy heart frames nothing but evil imaginations; there is nothing in thy life, but what is framed by thine heart; and therefore there is nothing in thy heart or life but evil.

Secondly, All thy religion, if thou hast any, is lost labour; as to acceptance with GOD, or any saving effect to thyself. Art thou yet in thy natural state? Truly then thy duties are sins, as was just now hinted. Would not the best wine be lothsome in a vessel wherein there is no pleasure? So is the religion of an unregenerate man. Under the law, the garment which the flesh of the sacrifice was carried in, though it touched other things, did not make them holy; but he that was unclean touching any thing, whether common or sacred, made it unclean. Even so thy duties cannot make thy corrupt soul holy, tho' they in themselves be good; but thy corrupt heart defiles them and makes them unclean. Haggai ii. 12, 13, 14. Thou wast wont to divide thy works into two sorts; some good, some evil; but thou must count again and put them all under one head; for GOD writes on them all, *only evil.* This is lamentable: It will be no wonder to see those beg in harvest, who fold their hands to sleep in seed-time; but to be labouring with others in the spring, and yet have nothing to reap when the harvest comes, is a very sad case; and will be the case of all professors living and dying in their natural state.

Lastly. Thou canst not help thyself. What canst thou do to take away thy sin, who art wholly corrupt? Nothing truly but sin. If a natural man begin to relent, drop a tear for his sin, and reform, presently the corrupt heart apprehends at least, a merit of congruity; he has done much himself, he thinks, and GOD cannot but do more for him on that account. In the mean time he does nothing but sin; so that the congruous merit is the leper that must be put out of the ramp: the dead soul buried out of sight; and the corrupt lump cast into the pit. How canst thou think to recover thyself by any thing thou canst do? Will mud and filth wash out filthiness? and wilt thou purge out sin by sinning? Job took a potsherd to scrape himself, because his hands were as full of boils as his body. This is the case of thy corrupt soul; not to be recovered but by JESUS CHRIST, whose strength was dried up like a potsherd, Psal. xxii. 15. Thou art poor indeed, extremely miserable and poor, Rev. iii. 17. Thou hast no shelter but a refuge of lies; no garment for thy soul, but filthy rags; nothing to nourish it but husks that cannot satisfy. More than that, thou hast got such a bruise in the loins of Adam, which is not yet cured, that thou art without strength, Rom. v. 6. unable to do or work for thyself; nay, more than all this, thou canst not so much as seek aright, *but liest helpless, as an infant exposed in the open field!* Ezek. xvi. 5.

USE III. I exhort you to believe this sad truth. Alas, it is evident, it is very little believed in the world. Few are concerned to get their corrupt conversation changed; but fewer, by far, to get their nature changed. Most men know not what they are, nor what spirits they are of; they are as the eye, which seeing many things, never sees itself. But until ye know, every one the plague of his own heart, there is no hope of your recovery. Why will ye not believe it? Ye have plain scripture-testimony for it; but you are loth to entertain such an ill opinion of yourselves. Alas! that is the nature of your disease, Rev. iii. 17. *Thou knowest not that thou art wretched, and miserable, and poor, and blind, and naked.* LORD open their eyes to see it, before they die of it, and in hell lift up their eyes, and see what they will not see now.

I shall shut up this weighty point of the corruption of man's nature, with a few words to another doctrine from the text.

DOCT. *God takes special notice of our natural corruption, or the sin of our nature.* This he testifies two ways, 1. By his word, as in the text, *God saw that every imagination of the thoughts of man's heart, was only evil continually,* see Psal. xiv. 2, 3. 2. By his works GOD writes his particular notice of it, and displeasure with it, as in many of his works, so especially in these two:

(1.) In the death of the infant children of men. Many miseries they have been exposed to; they were drowned in the deluge, consumed in Sodom by fire and brimstone; they have been slain with the sword, dashed against the stones, and are still dying ordinary deaths. What is the true cause of this? On what ground doth a holy GOD thus pursue them? Is it the sin of their parents? That may be the occasion of the LORD's raising the process against them; but it must be their own sin, that is the ground of the sentence passing on them; for, *the soul that sinneth, it shall die*, saith GOD, Ezek. xviii. 4. Is it their own actual sin? They have none. But as men do with toads and serpents, which they kill at first sight, before they have done any hurt, because of their venomous nature; so is it in this case.

(2.) In the birth of the elect children of GOD. When the LORD is about to change their nature, he makes the sin of their nature lie heavy on their spirits. When he minds to let out the corruption, the lance gets full depth in their souls, reaching to the root of sin, Rom. vii. 7, 8, 9. The flesh, or corruption of nature is pierced, being crucified, as well as the affections and lusts, Gal. v. 24.

USE. Let us then have a special eye upon the corruption and sin of our nature. GOD sees it; O that we saw it too, and *that* sin were ever before us! What avails it to notice other sins, while this mother-sin is not noticed? Turn your eyes inward to the sin of your nature. It is to be feared, many have this work to begin yet; that they have shut the door, while the grand thief is yet in the house undiscovered. This is a weighty point; and in the handling of it,

I. I shall, for conviction, point at some evidence of mens overlooking the sin of their nature, which yet the LORD takes particular notice of. (1.) Mens looking on themselves with such confidence, as if they were in no hazard of gross sins. Many would take it very heinously, to get such a caution, as CHRIST gave his Apostles, Luke xxi. 34. *Take heed of surfeiting and drunkeness.* If any should suppose them to break out in gross abominations they would be ready to say, *Am I a dog?* It would raise the pride of their hearts, but not their fear and trembling; because they know not the corruption of their nature. (2.) Untenderness towards those that fall. Many in that case cast off all bowels of Christian compassion; for they do not consider themselves, lest they also be tempted, Gal. vi. 1. Mens passions are often highest against the faults of others, when sin sleeps soundly in their own breasts. Even good David, when he was at his worst, was most violent against the faults of others. While his conscience was asleep under his guilt, in the matter of Uriah; the Spirit of the LORD takes notice, that his *anger was greatly kindled against the man,* in the parable, 2 Sam. xii. 5. And on good grounds it is thought, it was at the same time that he treated the Ammonites so cruelly, as is related, ver. 31. *Putting them under* saws of iron, and under harrows of iron, and under axes of iron and making them pass through the brick kiln. Grace makes men zealous against sin in others, as well as in themselves: but eyes turned inward to the corruption of nature, clothe them with pity and compassion; and fill them with thankfulness to the LORD, that they themselves were not the persons left to be such spectacles of human frailty. (3.) There are not a few, who, if they be kept from affliction in worldly things, and from gross out-breakings in their conversation, know not what it is to have a sad heart. If they meet with a cross, which their proud hearts cannot stoop to bear, they will be ready to say, O to be gone; but the corruption of their nature never makes them long for heaven. Lusts scandalously breaking out at a time, will mar their peace; but the sin of their nature never makes them a heavy heart. (4.) Delaying of repentance, in hopes to set about it afterwards. Many have their own appointed time for repentance and reformation, as if they were such complete masters over their lusts that they can allow them to gather more strength, & yet overcome them. They take up resolutions to amend without an eye to JESUS CHRIST, union with him, & strength from him; a plain evidence they are strangers to themselves: and so they are left to themselves, and their flourishing resolutions wither; for as they see not the necessity, so they get not the benefit of dew from heaven to water them. (5.) Mens venturing frankly on temptations, and promising liberally on their own heads. They cast themselves fearlessly into temptation, in confidence of coming off fairly: but were they sensible of the corruption of their nature, they would beware of entering on the devil's ground: as one girt about with bags of gunpowder, would be loth to walk where sparks of fire are flying, lest he should be blown up. Self-jealousing well becomes Christians: *Lord, is it I?* They that know the deceit of their bow, will not be very confident that they shall hit the mark. (6.) Unacquaintedness with heart plagues. The knowledge of the plagues of the heart, is a rare qualification. There are indeed some of them written in such great characters, that he who runs may read them; but there are others more subtile, which few do discern. How few are there, to whom the bias of the heart to unbelief is a burden? Nay, they perceive it not. Many have had sharp convictions of other sins, that were never to this day convinced of their unbelief; tho' that is the sin specially aimed at in a thorough conviction, John xi. 8, 9. *He will reprove the world of sin, — because they believe not on me.* A disposition to establish our own righteousness is a weed that naturally grows in every man's heart; but few sweat at the plucking of it **up**: it lurks undiscovered. The bias of the heart to the way of the covenant of works, is a hidden plague of the heart to many. All the difficulty they find is, in getting up their heart to duties: they find no difficulty in getting their hearts off them, and over them to JESUS CHRIST. How hard is it to slave men off from their own righteousness? Yet it is very hard to convince them of their leaning to it at all. *Lastly*, Pride and self-conceit. A view of the corruption of nature would be very humbling; and oblige him that has it, to reckon himself the chief of sinners. Under greatest attainments and enlargements, it would be ballast to his heart, and hide pride from his eyes. The want of thorough humiliation, piercing to the sin of one's nature is the ruin of many professors; for digging deep makes great difference betwixt wise and foolish builders, Luke vi. 48, 49.

II. I will lay before you a few things, in which ye should have a special eye to the sin of your nature. (1.) Have a special eye to it in your application to JESUS CHRIST. Do you find any need of CHRIST, which sends you to him as the Physician of souls? O forget not your disease when you are with the Physician. They never yet knew well their errand to CHRIST, that went not to him for the sin of their nature: for his blood to take away the guilt of it, and his Spirit to break the power of it. Tho' in the bitterness of your souls, you should lay before him a catalogue of your sins of omission and commission, which might reach from earth to heaven; yet if the sin of your nature were wanting in it, assure yourselves, you have forgot the best part of the errand a poor sinner has to the Physician of souls. What would it have availed the people of Jericho, to have set before Elisha all the vessels in their city full of the water that was naught, if they had not led him forth to the spring, to cast in the salt there? 2 Kings ii. 19, 20, 21. The application is easy. (2.) Have a special eye towards it in your repentance whether initial or progressive, in your first repentance, and in the renewing of your repentance afterwards. Tho' a man be sick, there is no fear of death, if the sickness strike not his heart: and there is as little fear of the death of sin, as long as the sin of our nature is not touched. But if ye would repent indeed, let the streams lead you up to the fountain; and mourn over your corrupt nature, as the cause of all sin, in heart, lip, and life, Psalm li. 4, 5. *Against thee, thee only have I sinned, and done this evil in thy sight.* —— *Behold, I was shapen in iniquity, and in sin did my mother conceive me.* (4.) Have a special eye upon it in your mortification, Gal. v. 24. *And they that are Christ's have crucified the flesh.* It is the root of bitterness that must be struck at, which the ax of mortification must be laid to; else we labour in vain. In vain do men go about to purge the streams, while they are at no pains about the muddy fountain; It is vain religion to attempt to make the life truly good, while the corruption of nature retains its ancient vigour, and the power of it is not broken. *Lastly*, Ye are to eye it in your daily walk. He that would walk aright, must have one eye upward to JESUS CHRIST; and another inward to the corruption of his own nature. It is not enough that we look about us, we must also look within us. There the wall is weakest; there our greatest enemy lies; and there are grounds for daily watching and mourning.

III. I shall offer some reasons, why we should especially notice the sin of our nature.

1. Because of all sins it is the most extensive and diffusive. It goes through the whole man, and spoils all. Other sins mar particular parts of the image of GOD; but this doth at once deface the whole. A disease affecting any particular member of the body is ill; but that which affects the whole is worse. The corruption of nature is the poison of the old serpent, cast into the fountain of action, and so infects every action, every breathing of the soul.

2. It is the cause of all particular lusts, and actual sins in our hearts and lives. It is the spawn which the great Leviathan has left in the souls of men; from whence comes all the fry of actual sins and abominations. Mark vii. 21. *Out of the heart of men proceed evil thoughts, adulteries,* &c. It is the bitter fountain: particular lusts are but running rivulets from it, which bring forth into the life, a part only, and not the whole of what is within. Now the fountain is still above the streams: so where the water is good, it is best in the fountain; where it is ill, it is worst there. The corruption of nature being that which defiles all, itself must needs be the abominable thing.

3. It is virtually all sin: for it is the seed of all sins, which want but the occasion to set up their heads: being in the corruption of nature, as the effect in the virtue of its cause. Hence it is called *a body of death,* Rom. vii. 24. as consisting of the several members, belonging to such *a body of sins,* Col. ii. 11. whose life lies in spiritual death. It is the cursed ground, fit to bring forth all manner of noxious weeds. As the whole nest of venomous creatures must needs be more dreadful, than any few of them that come creeping forth; so the sin of thy nature, that mother of abominations, must be worse than any particular lusts, that appear stirring in thy heart and life. Never did every sin appear in the conversation of the vilest

wretch that ever lived, but look thou into thy corrupt nature, and there thou mayest see all and every sin in the seed and root thereof. There is a fulness of all unrighteousness there, Rom. i. 29. There is atheism, idolatry, blasphemy, murder, adultery, and whatsoever is vile. Possibly none of these appear to thee in thy heart: but there is more in that unfathomable depth of wickedness, than thou knowest. Thy corrupt heart is like an ant's nest, on which, while the stone lieth, none of them appear: but take off the stone, stir them up, but with the point of a straw, you will see what a swarm is there, and how lively they be. Just such a sight would thy heart afford thee, did the LORD but withdraw the restraint upon it, and suffer Satan to stir it up by temptation.

4. The sin of our nature is, of all sins, the most fixed and abiding. Sinful actions, tho' the guilt and stain of them may remain, yet in themselves they are passing. The drunkard is not always at his cup, nor the unclean person always acting lewdness. But the corruption of nature is an abiding sin: it remains with men in its full power by night and by day, at all times, fixed as with bands of iron and brass: till their nature be changed by converting grace, and the remains of it continue with the godly, until the death of the body. Pride, envy, covetousness, and the like are not always stirring in thee. But the proud, envious, carnal nature is still with thee even as the clock that is wrong is not always striking wrong; but the wrong set continues with it, without great intermission.

5. It is the great reigning sin, Rom. vi. 12. *Let not sin therefore reign in your mortal body, that you should obey it in the lust thereof.* There are three things you may observe in the corrupt heart. (1.) There is the corrupt nature; the corrupt set of the heart whereby men are unapt for all good, and fitted for all evil. This the apostle here calls, sin which reigns. (2.) There are particular lusts, or dispositions of that corrupt nature which the apostle calls the lusts thereof; such as pride, covetousness, &c. (3.) There is one among these, which is, like Saul amongst the people higher by far than the rest, namely is *sin which doth so easily beset us*, Heb. xii. 1. This we usually call the predominant sin, because it doth, as it were, reign over other particular lusts; so that other lusts must yield to it. These three are like a river which divides itself into many streams, whereof one is greater than the rest. The corruption of nature is the river-head, which has many particular lusts, in which it runs: but it mainly disburdens itself into what is commonly called one's predominant sin. Now all of these being fed by the sin of our nature; it is evident that sin is the

great reigning sin which never loseth its superiority over particular lusts, that live and die with it, and by it. But as in some rivers, the main stream runs not always in one and the same channel: so particular predominants may be changed, as lust in youth may be succeeded by covetousness in old age. Now, what doth it avail to reform in other sins, while the great reigning sin remains in its full power? What tho' some particular lust be broken? If that sin, the sin of our nature keep the throne it will set up another in its stead: as when a water-course is stopt in one place, while the fountain is not damned up, it will stream forth another way. And thus some cast off their prodigality, but covetousness comes up in its stead: some cast away their profanity, and the corruption of nature sends not its main stream that way as before; but it runs in another channel, namely in that of a legal disposition, self-righteousness, or the like, so that the people are ruined by their not eying the sin of their nature.

Lastly, It is an hereditary evil, Psal. li. 5. *In sin did my mother conceive me.* Particular lusts are not so, but in the virtue of their cause. A prodigal father may have a frugal son: but this disease is necessarily propagated in nature, and therefore hardest to cure. Surely then the word should be given out against this sin, as against the King of Israel, 1 Kings. xxii. 31. Fight neither with small nor great, save only with this; for this sin being broke, all other sins are broken with it; and while it stands entire, there is no victory.

IV. That ye may get a view of the corruption of your nature, I would recommend to you three things. (1) Study to know the spirituality and extent of the law of GOD, for that is the glass wherein you may see yourselves. (2.) Observe your hearts all times, but especially under temptation. Temptation is a fire that brings up the scum of the vile heart; do ye carefully mark the first risings of corruption. *Lastly,* Go to GOD thro' JESUS CHRIST, for illumination by his Spirit. Lay out your soul before the LORD, as willing to know the vileness of your nature; say unto him, *That which I know not, teach thou me,* and be willing to take in light from the word. Believe, and you shall see. It is by the word the Spirit teacheth, but without the Spirit's teaching, all other teaching will be to little purpose. Tho' the gospel should shine about you like the sun at noon-day; and this great truth be never so plainly preached; you will never see yourselves aright, until the Spirit of the LORD light his candle within your breast: the fulness and glory of CHRIST, the corruption and vileness of our nature, are never rightly learned, but where the Spirit of CHRIST is the teacher.

And now to shut up this weighty point, let the consideration of what is said, commend CHRIST to you all. Ye that are brought out of your natural state of corruption unto CHRIST, be humble; still coming to CHRIST, and improving your union with him, to the further weakening of the remains of this natural corruption. Is your nature changed? It is but in part so. The day was ye could not stir: now ye are cured; but remember the cure is not perfected, ye still go halting. And tho' it were better with you than it is, the remembrance of what you were by nature should keep you low. Ye that are yet in your natural state, take with it: believe the corruption of your nature; and let CHRIST and his grace be precious in your eyes. O that ye would at length be serious about the state of your souls! What mind ye to do? Ye must die; ye must appear before the judgment-seat of GOD. Will ye lie down, and sleep another night at ease, in this case? Do it not; for before another day you may be sisted before GOD's dreadful tribunal, in the grave cloaths of your corrupt state; and your vile souls cast into the pit of destruction, as a corrupt lump, to be for ever buried out of GOD's sight. For I testify unto you all, there is no peace with GOD, no pardon, no heaven for you, in this state: there is but a step betwixt you and eternal destruction from the presence of the LORD: if the brittle thread of your life, which may be broke with a touch, ere you are aware, be indeed broken while you are in this state; you are ruined for ever, and without remedy. But come speedily to JESUS CHRIST; he has cleansed as vile souls as yours; and he will yet *cleanse the blood that he hath not yet cleansed*, Joel iii. 21. Thus far the sinfulness of man's natural state.

HEAD II.

The Misery of Man's Natural State.

EPHESIANS ii. 3.

———— were by nature the children of wrath, even as others.

HAVING shewed you the sinfulness of man's natural state, I come now to lay before you the misery of it. A sinful state cannot but be a miserable state. If sin go before, wrath follows of course. Corruption and destruction are so knit together, that the Holy Ghost calls destruction, even eternal destruction, corruption, Gal. vi. 8. *He that soweth to his flesh, shall of the flesh reap corruption,* that is everlasting destruction; as is clear from its being opposed to life everlasting, in the following clause. And so the Apostle having shown the Ephesians their real state by nature, viz. that they were dead in sins and trespasses, altogether corrupt; he tells them in the words of the text, their relative state, namely, that the pit was digged for them, while in that state of corruption: being dead in sins, they were by nature children of wrath, even as others.

In the words **we have four things,**

1. The misery of a natural state; it is a state of wrath, as well as a state of sin. We were, says the Apostle, children of wrath, bound over, and liable to the wrath of GOD; under **wrath in** some measure; and in wrath, bound over to more, even the full measure of it in hell, where the floods of it go over the prisoners for ever. Thus Saul, in his wrath, adjudging David to die, 1 Sam. xx. 31. and David in his wrath passing sentence of death against the man in the parable, 2 Sam. xii. 5. say each of them, of his supposed criminal, *He shall surely die:* or, as the words in the first language are, *he is a son of death.* So the natural man is a child of wrath, a son of death. He is a malefactor dead in law, lying in chains of guilt: a criminal held fast in his fetters, till the day of execution: which will not fail, unless a pardon be obtained from his God, who is his judge and party too. By that means, indeed, children of wrath may become children of the kingdom. The phrase in the text, however common it is in holy language, is very significant. And as it is evident, that the Apostle calling natural men, the children of disobedience, ver. 2. means more than that they were disobedient **children;** for such may the LORD's own children be: so to be children of wrath is more than simply to be liable to, or under wrath. JESUS CHRIST was liable to, and under wrath; but I doubt we have any warrant to say, he was a child of wrath. The phrase seems to intimate, that men are, whatsoever they are in their natural state, under the wrath of GOD; that they **are wholly under wrath: wrath is,** as it **were** woven into their very nature, and mixeth itself with the whole of the man; who is, if I may so speak, a very lump of wrath, a child of hell, **as the iron** in the fire is all fire. For men naturally are children of wrath, come forth, so to speak, out of the womb of wrath; Jonah's gourd was the son of a night, which we render came up in a night, Jonah iv. 10. as if it had come out of the womb of the night, as we read of the womb of the morning, Psal. cx. 3. and so the birth following the belly whence it came, was soon gone. The sparks of fire are called sons of the burning coal, Job v. 7. marg. Isa.

xxi. 10. *O my threshing, and the corn, or son of my floor, threshen in the floor of wrath, and, as it were, brought forth by it.* Thus the natural man is a child of wrath: *it comes into his bowels like water, and like oil into his bones,* Psal. cix. 18. For though Judas was the only son of perdition amongst the Apostles; yet all men, by nature, are of the same family.

2. There is the rise of this misery; men have it by nature. They owe it to their nature, not to their substance or essence; for that neither is nor was sin, and therefore cannot make them children of wrath, tho' for sin it may be under wrath; not to their nature as qualified, at man's creation, by his Maker, but to their nature, as vitiated and corrupted by the fall. To the vicious quality, or corruption of their nature, whereof before which is their principle of action, and ceasing from action, the only principle is an unregenerate state. Now by this nature, men are children of wrath; as in time of pestilential infection, one draws in death together with the disease then raging. Wherefore seeing from our first being as children of Adam, we be corrupt children, shapen in iniquity, conceived in sin; we are also, from that moment, children of wrath.

3. The universality of this misery. All are by nature children of wrath; *We,* saith the Apostle, *even as others;* Jews as well as Gentiles. Those that are now by grace, the children of God, were by nature, in no better case, than those that are still in their natural state.

Lastly, There is a glorious and happy change intimated here; we were children of wrath but are not so now; grace has brought us out of that fearful state. This the apostle says of himself and other believers. And thus, it well becomes the people of God to be often standing on the shore, looking back to the red sea of the state of wrath, they were sometimes weltering in, even as others.

DOCTRINE, *The state of nature is a state of wrath.* Every one in a natural unregenerate state, is in a state of wrath. We are born children of wrath; and continue so, until we be born again. Nay, as soon as we were children of Abraham we were children of wrath.

I shall usher in what I am to say on this point, with a few observes touching the universality of this state of wrath; which may serve to prepare the way of the word into your consciences.

Wrath has gone as wide as ever sin went. When angels sinned, the wrath of God brake in upon them as a flood; *God spared not the angels which sinned, but cast them down to hell*, 2 Pet. ii. 4. And thereby it was demonstrated, that no natural excellency in the creature will shield it from the wrath of GOD; if once it becomes a sinful creature. The finest and the nicest piece of the workmanship of heaven, if once the Creator's image upon it be defaced by sin, GOD can and will dash it to pieces, in his wrath; unless satisfaction be made to justice, and that image be repaired; neither of which the sinner himself can do. Adam sinned; and the whole lump of mankind was leavened, and bound over to the fiery oven of GOD's wrath. And from the text ye may learn, (1.) That ignorance of that state cannot free men from it; the Gentiles that knew not GOD, *were by nature children of wrath, even as others*. A man's house may be on fire, his wife and children perishing in the flames; while he knows nothing of it, and therefore is not concerned about it. Such is your case, O ye that are ignorant of these things! **wrath** is silently sinking into your souls, while you are blessing yourselves, saying, *Ye shall have peace*. Ye need not a more certain token, that ye are *children of wrath*, than that ye never yet saw yourselves such. Ye cannot be the children of GOD, that never yet saw yourselves children of the devil. Ye cannot be in the way to heaven, that never saw yourselves by nature in the road to hell. Ye are grosly ignorant of your state by nature; and so ignorant of GOD, and of CHRIST, and your need of him; and tho' ye look on your ignorance as a covert from wrath; yet take it out of the mouth of GOD himself, that it will ruin you if it be not removed, Isa. xxvii. 11. *It is a people of no understanding; therefore he that made them, will not have mercy on them*. See 2 Thess. i. 8. Hos. iv. 6. (2.) No outward privileges can exempt men from this state of wrath; for the Jews, **the** children of the kingdom, GOD's peculiar people, were children of wrath even as others. Tho' ye be church-members, partakers of all church-privileges; tho' ye be descended of godly parents, of great and honourable families; be what ye will ye are by nature heirs of hell, children **of** wrath. (3.) No profession, nor attainments in a profession of religion, do or can exempt a **man** from this state of wrath. Paul was one of the strictest sect of the Jewish religion, Acts xxvi. 5. yet a child of wrath, even as others, till he was converted. The close hypocrite, and the profane, are alike as to their state; however different their conversations be; and they will be alike in their fatal end, Psal. cxxv. 5. *As for such as turn aside unto their crooked ways, the Lord shall lead them forth with the workers of iniquity*. (4.) Young ones that are yet but setting out in the world, have not that to do, to make themselves children of wrath, by following the graceless **mul-**

titude. They are children of wrath by nature; so it is done already; they were born heirs of hell; they will indeed make themselves more so, if they do not, while they are young, flee from that wrath they were born to, by fleeing to JESUS CHRIST. *Lastly*, Whatever men are now by grace, they were even as others, by nature. And this may be a sad meditation to them, that have been at ease from their youth, and have had no changes.

Now these things being premised, I shall, in the first place, shew what this state of wrath is; next confirm the doctrine; and then apply it.

I. I am to shew what this state of wrath is. But who can fully describe the wrath of an angry GOD? None can do it. Yet so much of it must be discovered, as may serve to convince men of the absolute necessity of fleeing to JESUS CHRIST, out of that state of wrath. Anger in men is a passion, and commotion of the spirit for an injury received, with a desire to resent the same. When it comes to a height, and is fixed in one's spirit, it is called wrath. Now there are no passions in GOD, properly speaking; they are inconsistent with his absolute unchangeableness, and independency; and therefore Paul and Barnabas, to remove the mistake of the Lycaonians, who thought they were gods, tell them, they were men of like passions with themselves, Acts xiv. 15. Wrath then is attributed to GOD, not in respect of the affection of wrath, but the effects thereof. Wrath is a fire in the bowels of a man, tormenting the man himself; but there is no perturbation in GOD. His wrath does not in the least mar that infinite repose and happiness, which he hath in himself. It is a most pure undisturbed act of his will, producing dreadful effects against the sinner. It is little we know of an **infinite** GOD; but condescending to our weakness, he is pleased to speak of himself to us after the manner of men. Let us therefore notice man's wrath, but remove every thing in our consideration of the wrath of GOD, that argues imperfection; and so we may attain to some view of it, however scanty. By this means we are led to take up the **wrath** of GOD against the natural man, in these three.

First, There is wrath in the heart of GOD against him. The LORD approves him not, but is displeased with him. Every natural man lies under the displeasure of GOD; and that is heavier than mountains of brass. Although he be pleased with himself, and others be pleased with him too; yet GOD looks down on him, as displeased. *First*, His person is under GOD's displeasure; *Thou hatest all workers of iniquity*, Psal. v. 5. A godly man's sin is displeasing to GOD, yet his person is still *accepted in the beloved.* Eph. i. 6. But *God is angry with the wicked every day*, Pf. vii. 11. A fire of wrath burns continually against him, in the heart of GOD. They are as dogs and swine, most abominable creatures in the sight of GOD. Tho' their natural state be gilded over with a shining profession, yet they are abhorred of GOD; they are to him as *smoke in his nose.* Isa. lxv. 5. and lukewarm water, to be *spewed out of his mouth*, Rev. iii. 16. *whited sepulchres,* Mat. xxiii. 27. *a generation of vipers,* Matth. 12. 34. and a *people of his wrath,* Isa. x. 6. *Secondly,* He is displeased with all they do; It is impossible for them to please him, being unbelievers, Heb. xi. 6. He hates their persons; and so hath no pleasure in, but is displeased with their best works, Isa. lvi. 3. *He that sacrificeth a lamb as if he cut off a dog's neck,* &c. Their duty, as done by them, is *an abomination to the Lord*, Prov. xv. 8. And as men turn their back upon them whom they are angry with; so the LORD's refusing communion with the natural man in his duties, is a plain indication of this wrath.

Secondly, There is wrath in the word of GOD against him: When wrath is in the heart, it seeks a vent by the lips, so GOD fights against the natural man with *the sword of his mouth,* Rev. ii. 16. The LORD's word never speaks good of him, but always curseth or condemneth him. Hence it is, that when he is awakened, the word read or preached often increaseth his horror. *First,* It condemns all his actions, together with his corrupt nature. There is nothing he does but the law declares it to be sin. It is a rule of perfect obedience from which he always in all things, declines; and so it rejects every thing he doth as sin. *Secondly,* It pronounceth his doom, and denounceth GOD's curse against him, Gal. iii. 10 *For as many as are of the works of the law are under the curse; for it is written, Cursed is every one that continueth not in all things, which are written in the book of the law to do them.* Be he never so well in the world, it pronounceth a woe from heaven against him, Isa. iii. 11. The Bible is a quiver filled with arrows of wrath against him, ready to be poured in on his soul. GOD's threatnings in his word, hang over his head as a black cloud, ready to shower down on him every moment. The word is indeed the saint's security against wrath, but it binds the natural man's sin and wrath together, as a certain pledge of his ruin, if he continue in that state. So the conscience being awakened, and perceiving this tie made by the law, the man is filled with terrors in his soul.

Thirdly, There is wrath in the hand of GOD against the

natural man. He is under heavy strokes of wrath already, and is liable to more.

1*st*, There is wrath on his body. It is a piece of cursed clay, which wrath is sinking into by virtue of the threatning of the first covenant, Gen. ii. 17. *In the day that thou eatest thereof, thou shalt surely die.* There is never a disease, gripe nor stitch, that effects him, but it comes on him with the sting of GOD's indignation in it. They are all cords of death, sent before to bind the prisoner.

2*dly*, There is wrath upon his soul. (1.) He can have no communion with GOD; he is *foolish, and shall not stand in God's sight*, Psal. v. 5. When Adam sinned, GOD turned him out of paradise; and natural men are, as Adam left them, banished from the gracious presence of the LORD: and can have no access to him in that state. There is war betwixt heaven and them; and so all commerce is cut off, *They are without God in the world*, Eph. ii. 12. The sun is gone down on them, and there is not the least glimpse of favour towards them from heaven. (2.) Hence the soul is left to pine away in its iniquity. The natural darkness of their minds, the averseness to good in their wills, the disorder of their affections, and distemper of their consciences, and all their natural plagues, are left upon them in a penal way; and being so left, increase daily. GOD casts a portion of worldly goods to them, more or less; as a bone is thrown to a dog; but, alas! his wrath against them appears, in that they get no grace. The Physician of souls comes by them, and goes by them, and cures others beside them; while they are consuming away in their iniquity, and ripening daily for utter destruction. (3.) They lie open to fearful additional plagues on their souls, even in this life. *First*, Sometimes they meet with deadning strokes; silent blows from the hand of an angry GOD: arrows of wrath that enter into their souls without noise; Isa. vi. 10. *Make the heart of this people fat, and make their ears heavy, and shut their eyes lest they see with their eyes,* &c. GOD strives with them for a while, and convictions enter their consciences; but they rebel against the light; and by a secret judgment, they are knocked on the head; so that, from that time, they do, as it were, live and rot above ground. Their hearts are deadned; their affections withered; their consciences stupified; and their whole souls blasted; *cast forth as a branch and withered*, John xv. 16. They are plagued with judicial blindness. They shut their eyes against the light, and they are given over to the devil, the god of this world to be blinded more, 2 Cor. iv. 4. Yea, *God sends them strong delusion, that they should believe a lie,*

2 Thess. ii. 11. even conscience, like a false light on the shore leads them upon rocks; by which they are broken in pieces. They harden themselves against God; and he gives up with them, and leaves them to Satan and their own hearts, whereby they are hardned more and more. They are often given up unto vile affections, Rom. i. 26. The reins are laid on their necks; and they are left to run into all access, as their furious lusts draw them. Secondly, Sometimes they meet with quicking strokes, whereby their souls become like mount Sinai; where nothing is seen, but fire and smoak; nothing heard, but the thunder of God's wrath, and the voice of the trumpet of a broken law, waxing louder and louder: which makes them like Pashur, Jer. xx. 4. *A terror to themselves.* God takes the filthy garments of their sins, which they were wont to sleep in securely; overlays them with brimstone, and sets them on fire about their ears; so they have a hell within them.

3dly, There is wrath on the natural man's enjoyments. Whatever be wanting in his house, there is one thing that is never wanting there, Prov. iii. 33. *The curse of the Lord is in the house of the wicked.* Wrath is on all that he has; on the bread that he eats, the liquor he drinks, and clothes which he wears, *His basket and store are cursed,* Deut. xxviii. 17. Some things fall wrong with him; and that comes to pass by virtue of his wrath; other things go according to his wish, and there is wrath in that too; for it is a snare to his soul, Prov. i 32. *The prosperity of fools shall destroy them.* This wrath turns his blessings into curses, Mal. ii. 2. *I will curse your blessings; yea, I have cursed them already.* The holy law is a killing letter to him, 2 Cor. iii. 6. The ministry of the gospel, *a savour of death unto death,* chap. ii 15. In the sacrament of the Lord's supper, *He eateth and drinketh damnation to himself,* 1 Cor. xi. 29. Nay, more than all that, Christ himself is to him, *a stone of stumbling and a rock of offence,* 1 Pet. ii. 8. Thus wrath follows the natural man, as his shadow doth his body.

4thly, He is under the power of Satan, Acts xxvi. 18. The devil has overcome him, so he is his by conquest; his lawful captive, Isa. xlix. 24. The natural man is condemned already, John iii. 18. and therefore under the heavy hand of him that hath the power of death, that is the devil. And he keeps his prisoner, in the prison of a natural state, bound hand and foot, Isa. lxi. 1. laden with divers lusts, as chains wherewith he holds him fast. Thou needest not, as many do, call on the devil to take thee; for he has a fast hold of thee already as a child of wrath.

Lastly, The natural man has no security for a moment's safety from the wrath of GOD, its coming on him to the uttermost. The curse of the law denounced against him, has already tied him to the stake: so that the arrows of justice may pierce his soul; and in him may meet all the miseries and plagues that flow from the avenging wrath of GOD. See how he is set as a mark to the arrows of wrath, Psalm vii. 11, 12, 13. *God is angry with the wicked every day. If he turn not, he will whet his sword: he hath bent his bow and made it ready; he hath also prepared for him the instruments of death.* Doth he lie down to sleep? There is not a promise, he knows of, or can know, to secure him that he shall not be in hell ere he awake. Justice is pursuing, and cries for vengeance on the sinner; the law casts the fire-balls of its curses, continually upon him: wasted and long-tired patience is that which keeps in his life: he walks amidst enemies armed against him: his name may be *Magor Missabib, i. e. teror round about*, Jer. xx. 3. Angels, devils, men, beasts, stones, heaven, and earth, are in readiness, on a word of command from the LORD, to ruin him.

Thus the natural man lives, but he must die too; and death is a dreadful messenger to him. It comes upon him armed with wrath, and puts three sad charges in his hand. (1.) Death chargeth him to bid an eternal farewell to all things in this world; to leave it, and make way to another world. Ah! what a dreadful charge must this be to a child of wrath! He can have no comfort from heaven for GOD is his enemy; and as for the things of the world, and the enjoyment of his lusts, which were the only springs of his comfort; these are in a moment dried up to him for ever. He is not ready for another world; he was not thinking of removing so soon; or if he was, yet he has no portion secured to him in another world, but that which he was born to, and was increasing all his days, namely, a treasure of wrath. But go he must; his clay-god, the world, must be parted with, and what has he more? There was never a glimmering of light, or favour from heaven, to his soul: and now the wrath that did hang in the threatning as a cloud like a man's hand, is darkning the face of the whole heaven above him; and if he *look unto the earth, from whence all his light was wont to come, behold trouble and darkness, dimness of anguish; and he shall be driven to darkness,* Isa. viii. 22. (2.) Death chargeth soul and body to part till the great day. His soul is required of him, Luke xii. 20. O what a miserable parting must this be to a child of wrath! care was indeed taken to provide for the body, things necessary for this life: but alas! there is nothing laid up for another life to it; nothing to be a seed of glorious resurrection; as it lived, so it must die, and rise again sinful flesh; fuel for the fire of GOD's wrath. As for the soul, he was never solicitous to provide for it. It lay in the body, dead to GOD, and all things truly good; and so must be carried out into the pit, in the grave-clothes of its natural state: for now that death comes, the companions in sin must part. (3.) Death chargeth the soul to compear before the tribunal of GOD, while the body lies to be carried to the grave, Eccles. xii. 7. *The spirit shall return unto God who gave it.* Heb. ix. 27. *It is appointed unto all men once to die, but after this the judgment.* Well were it for the sinful soul, if it might be buried together with the body. But that cannot be: it must go and receive its sentence; and shall be shut up in the prison of hell, while the cursed body lies imprisoned in the grave till the day of the general judgment.

When the end of the world, appointed of GOD is come; the trumpet shall sound, and the dead arise. Then shall the weary earth, at the command of the Judge, cast forth the bodies; the cursed bodies of these that lived and died in their natural state; *The sea, death, and hell, shall deliver up their dead*, Rev. xx. 13. Their miserable bodies & souls shall be re-united, and they sisted before the tribunal of CHRIST. Then shall they receive that fearful sentence, *Depart from me, ye cursed, into everlasting fire prepared for the devil and his angels*, Matth. xx. 41. Whereupon *they shall go away into everlasting punishment*, ver. 49. They shall be eternally shut up in hell, never to get the least drop of comfort, nor the least ease of their torment. There they will be punished with the punishment of loss; being excommunicated for ever from the presence of GOD, his angels and saints. All means of grace, all hopes of a delivery, shall be for ever cut off from their eyes. They shall not have *a drop of water to cool their tongues*, Luke xvi. 24, 35. They shall be punished with the punishment of sense. They must not only depart from GOD, but depart into fire, into everlasting fire. There the worm, that shall gnaw them, shall never die; the fire that shall scorch them, shall never be quenched. GOD shall, thro' all eternity, hold them up with the one hand, and pour the full vials of wrath into them with the other.

This is that state of wrath natural men live in; being under much of the wrath of GOD, and liable to more. But for a further view of it, let us consider the qualities of that wrath (1.) it is irresistable, there is no standing before it, *Who may stand in thy sight, when once thou art angry?* Psal. lxxxvi. 7. Can the worm, or the moth, defend itself against him that designs to crush it? As little can worm man stand before an angry GOD. Foolish man indeed practically bids a defiance

H

to heaven: but the LORD often, even in this world, opens such sluices of wrath on them, as all their might cannot stop; they are carried away thereby, as with a flood. How much more will it be so in hell? (2.) It is unsupportable. What one cannot resist, he will see himself to bear: but, *Who shall dwell with devouring fire? Who shall dwell with everlasting burning?* GOD's wrath is a weight that will sink men into the lowest hell. It is a burden no man is able to stand under. *A wounded spirit who can bear it?* Prov. xviii. 14. (3.) It is unavoidable to such as go on impenitently in their sinful course. *He that being often reproved, hardeneth his neck, shall suddenly be destroyed, and that without remedy,* Prov. xxix. 1. We may now fly from it indeed, by flying to JESUS CHRIST: but such as fly from CHRIST, shall never be able to avoid it. Whither can men fly from an avenging GOD? Where will they find a shelter? The hills will not bear them; the mountains will be deaf to their loudest cries; when they cry to them, to hide them from the wrath of the Lamb. (4.) It is powerful and fierce wrath, Psalm xc. 11. *Who knoweth the power of thine anger? Even according to thy fear, so is thy wrath.* We are apt to fear the wrath of man more than we ought; but no man can apprehend the wrath of GOD to be more dreadful than it really is: the power of it can never be known to the utmost: seeing it is infinite, and properly speaking has no utmost: how fierce soever it be, either on earth, or in hell, GOD can still carry it further. Every thing in GOD is most perfect in its kind; and therefore no wrath is so fierce as his. O sinner, how wilt thou be able to endure that wrath which will tear thee in pieces, Psal. l. 22. and grind thee to powder, Luke xx. 18. The history of the two she-bears, that tare the children of Bethel, is an awful one, 2 Kings ii. 23, 24. But the united force of the rage of lions, leopards, and she-bears bereaved of their whelps, is not sufficient to give us even a scanty view of the power of the wrath of GOD, Hos. xiii. 7, 8. *Therefore I will be unto them as a lion; as a leopard by the way will I observe them. I will meet them as a bear that is bereaved of her whelps, and will rent the caul of their heart,* &c. (5.) It is penetrating and piercing wrath. It is burning wrath, and fiery indignation. There is no pain more exquisite, than that which is caused by fire; and no fire so piercing as the fire of GOD's indignation, that burns into the lowest hell, Deut. xxxii. 22. The arrows of men's wrath can pierce flesh, blood and bones, but cannot reach the soul; but the wrath of GOD will sink into the soul, and so pierce a man in the most tender part. Like as when a person is thunder-struck, oft-times there is not a wound to be seen in the skin; yet life is gone and the bones are, as it were, melts-ed; so GOD's wrath can penetrate into, and melt one's soul within him, when his earthly comforts stand about him entire and untouched as in Belshazzar's case, Dan. v. 6. (6.) It is *constant* wrath, running parallel with the man's continuance in an unregenerate state; constantly attending him, from the womb to the grave. There are few so dark days, but the sun sometimes looketh out from under the clouds: but the wrath of GOD is an abiding cloud on the subjects of it, John iii. 36. *The wrath of GOD abideth on him that believeth not.* (7.) It is *eternal*. O miserable soul! If thou fly not from this wrath unto JESUS CHRIST, thy misery had a beginning, but it shall never have an end. Should devouring death wholly swallow thee up, and for ever hold thee fast in a grave, it would be kind; but thou must live again, and never die; that thou mayest be ever dying, in the hands of the living GOD. Cold death will quench the flame of man's wrath against us, if nothing else do it; but GOD's wrath, when it has come on the sinner, millions of ages will still be the wrath to come, Mat. iii. 7. 1 Thess. i. 10. As the water of a river is still coming, how much soever of it has passed. While GOD is, he will pursue the quarrel. *Lastly*, Howsoever dreadful it is, and tho' it be eternal, yet it is most just wrath; it is a clear fire, without the least smoke of injustice. The sea of wrath raging with greatest fury against the sinner is clear as chrystal. The Judge of all the earth can do no wrong. He knows no transports of passion, for they are inconsistent with the perfection of his nature. *Is God unrighteous, who taketh vengeance? I speak as a man, God forbid; for then, how shall God judge the world?* Rom. iii. 5, 6.

The Doctrine of the State of Wrath, confirmed and vindicated.

II. I shall confirm the doctrine. Consider (1.) How peremptory the threatning of the first covenant is; *In the day thou eatest thereof, thou shalt surely die*, Gen. ii. 17. Hereby sin and punishment being connected, the veracity of GOD ascertains the execution of the threatning: Now all men being by nature under this covenant, the breach of it lays them under the curse. (2.) The justice of GOD requires that a child of sin be a child of wrath; that the law being broken, the sanction thereof should take place. GOD, as man's Ruler and Judge, cannot but do right, Gen. xviii. 25. 'Now it is a righteous thing with GOD to recompence sin with wrath', 2 Thess. i. 6. *He is of purer eyes, than to behold evil*, Hab. i. 13. And *he hates all the workers of iniquity*, Psal. v. 6. (3.) The horrors of a natural conscience prove this. There is a conscience in the breasts of men, which tell them they are sinners, and therefore liable to the wrath of GOD. Let men, at any time soberly commune with themselves, and they will find they have the witness in themselves, *knowing the judgment of God that they which commit such things are worthy of death*, Rom. i. 32. (4.) The pangs of the new birth, the work of the spirit of bondage on elect souls in order to their conversion, demonstrate this. Hereby their natural sinfulness and misery, as liable to the wrath of GOD, are plainly taught them; filling their hearts with fear of that wrath. Now that this spirit of bondage is no other than the Spirit of GOD, whose work is to convince of sin, righteousness and judgment, John xvi. 8. this testimony must needs be true; for the Spirit of truth cannot witness an untruth. Meanwhile, true believers being freed from the state of wrath, *receive not the spirit of bondage again to fear, but receive the Spirit of adoption*, Rom. iii. 15. And therefore if fears of that nature do arise, after the soul's union with CHRIST, they came from the saint's own spirit, or from a worse. *Lastly*, The sufferings of CHRIST plainly prove this doctrine. Wherefore was the Son of GOD, a Son under wrath, but because the children of men were children of wrath? He suffered the wrath of GOD, not for himself, but for those that were liable to it in their own persons. Nay, this not only speaks us to have been liable to wrath, but also that wrath must have a vent in the punishing of sin. If this was done in the green tree, what will become of the dry? What a miserable case must a sinner be in, that is out of CHRIST, that is not vitally united to CHRIST, and partakes not of his Spirit? GOD who spared not his own Son, surely will not spare such an one.

But the unregenerate man, who has no great value for the honour of GOD, will be apt to rise up against his Judge, and in his own heart condemn his procedure. Nevertheless the Judge being infinitely just, the sentence must be righteous. And therefore, to stop thy mouth, O proud sinner, and to still thy clamour against the righteous Judge; consider, *First*, Thou art a sinner by nature, and it is highly reasonable that guilt and wrath be as old as sin. Why should not GOD begin to vindicate his honour, as soon as vile worms begin to impair it? Why should not a serpent bite the thief, as soon as he leaps over the hedge? Why should not the threatening take hold of the sinner, as soon as he casts away the command? The poisonous nature of the serpent affords men sufficient ground to kill it, as soon as ever he can reach it; and, by this time thou mayest be convinced, that thy nature is a very compound of enmity against GOD. *Secondly*, Thou hast not only an enmity against God, in thy nature; but hast discovered it, by actual sins, which are in his eye acts of hostility. Thou hast brought forth thy lust into the field of battle against thy Sovereign Lord. And now, that thou art such a criminal, thy condemnation is just: for, besides the sin of thy nature, thou hast done that against heaven, which if thou hadst done against men, thy life behoved to have gone for it: and shall not wrath from heaven overtake thee? (1.) Thou art guilty of high treason, and rebellion against the king of heaven. The thought and wish of thy heart, which he knows as well as the language of thy mouth, has been, *no God*, Psal. xiv. 1. Thou hast rejected his government, blown the trumpet, and set up the standard of rebellion against him; being one of these that say, *We will not have this man to reign over us*, Luke xix. 14. Thou hast striven against, and quenched his Spirit; practically disowned his laws proclaimed by his messengers; stopped thine ears at their voice, and sent them away mourning for thy pride. Thou hast conspired with his grand enemy the devil. Altho' thou art a sworn servant of the King of glory, daily receiving of his favours, and living on his bounty; thou art holding a correspondence, and hast contracted a friendship with his greatest enemy, and art acting for him against thy Lord; for, *The lusts of the devil ye will do*, John viii. 44. (2.) Thou art a murderer before the Lord. Thou hast laid the stumbling-block of thine iniquity before the blind world; and hast ruined the souls of others by thy sinful course. And tho' thou dost not see now: the time may come, when thou shalt see the blood of thy relations, neighbours, acquaintances and others upon thy head, Matth. xviii. 2. *Wo unto the world because of offences.—Wo to that man by whom offence cometh.* Yea, thou art a *self-murderer* before God. Prov. viii. 36. *He that sinneth against me wrongeth his own soul: all they that hate me, love death*, Ezek. xviii. 31. *Why will ye die?* The laws of men go as far as they can against the self-murderer, denying his body a burial-place amongst others, and confiscating his goods: what wonder is it the law of God is so severe against soul-murderers? Is it strange, that they who will needs depart from God now, cost what it will, be forced to depart from him at last, into everlasting fire? But what is yet more criminal, thou art guilty of the murder of the Son of God, for the Lord will reckon thee amongst those that pierced him, Rev. i. 7. Thou hast rejected him as well as the Jews did; and by thy rejecting him, thou hast justified their deed. They indeed did not acknowledge him to be the Son of God, but thou dost. What they did against him, was in a state of humiliation; but thou hast acted against him, in his state of exaltation. These things will aggravate thy condemnation. What wonder then, if the voice of the **Lamb change** to the roaring of the lion against the traitor and **murderer**.

Object. But some will say, is there not a vast disproportion betwixt our sin and that wrath you talk of? I answer, No; GOD punishes no more than the sinner deserves. To rectify your mistake, in this matter, consider (1.) The vast rewards GOD has annexed to obedience. His word is no more full of fiery wrath against sin, than it is of gracious rewards to the obedience it requires. If heaven be in the promises, it is altogether equal that hell be in the threatnings. If death were set in the balance with life, eternal misery with eternal happiness, where were the proportion? Moreover sin deserves the misery, but our best works do not deserve the happiness; yet both are set before us; sin and misery, holiness and happiness. What reason is there then to complain? (2.) How severe soever the threatnings be, yet all has enough ado to reach the end of the law. *Fear him,* says our LORD, *which after he hath killed, hath power to cast into hell; yea, I say unto you, fear him,* Luke xii. 5 This bespeaks our dread of divine power and majesty; but how few fear him indeed! The LORD knows the sinners hearts to be exceedingly intent upon fulfilling their lusts; they cleave so fondly to those fulsome breasts, that a small force does not suffice to draw them from them. They that travel through deserts, where they are in hazard from wild beasts, have need to carry fire along with them; and they have need of a hard wedge that have knotty timber to cleave; so a holy law must be fenced with a dreadful wrath, in a world lying in wickedness. But who are they that complain of that wrath as too great, but those to whom it is too little to draw them off from their sinful courses? It was the man who pretended to fear his lord, because he was an austere man, that kept his pound laid up in a napkin; and so he was condemned out of his own mouth, Luke, xix. 20, 21, 22. Thou art that man, even thou whose objection I am answering. How can the wrath thou art under, and liable to, be too great, while yet it is not sufficient to awaken thee to fly from it? Is it time to relax the penalties of the law, when men are trampling the commands of it under foot? (3.) Consider how GOD dealt with his own Son, whom he spared not, Rom. viii. 32. The wrath of GOD seized on his soul and body both, and brought him into the dust of death. That his sufferings were not eternal, flowed from the quality of the sufferer, who was infinite; and therefore able to bear at once, the whole load of wrath; and upon that account, his sufferings were infinite in value. But in value, they must be protracted to an eternity. And confidence can a rebel-subject have to quarrel, for his part, a punishment executed on the King's Son? (4.) The sinner doth against GOD what he can. *Behold thou hast done evil things as thou couldst,* Jer. iii. 5. That thou hast not done more and worse, thanks to him who restrained thee; to the chain which the wolf was kept in by, not to thyself. No wonder GOD shew his power on the sinner, who puts forth his power against GOD, as far as it will reach. The unregenerate man puts no period to his sinful course; and would put no bounds to it neither, if he were not restrained by divine power for wise ends; and therefore it is just he be for ever under wrath. (5.) It is infinite majesty sin strikes against: and so it is, in some sort, an infinite evil. Sin riseth in its demerit, according to the quality of the party offended. If a man wound his neighbour, his goods must go for it; but if he wound his prince, his life must go to make amends for that. The infinity of GOD makes infinite wrath the just demerit of sin. GOD is infinitely displeased with sin; and when he acts, he must act like himself, and shew his displeasure by proportionable means. *Lastly,* Those that shall lie for ever under his wrath, will be eternally sinning; and therefore must eternally suffer; not only in respect of divine judicial procedure; but because sin is its own punishment, in the same manner that holy obedience is its own reward.

The Doctrine of the Misery of Man's Natural State applied.

Use (1.) Of Information. Is our state by nature a state of wrath? Then,

1. Surely we are not born innocent. These chains of wrath, which by nature are upon us, speak us to be born criminals. The swaddling bands wherewith infants are bound hand and foot as soon as they are born, may put us in mind of the cords of wrath, with which they are held prisoners, as **children of wrath.**

2. What desperate madness is it for sinners to go on in their sinful course: what is it but to heap coals of fire on thine own head, and lay more and more fuel to the fire of wrath, to treasure up unto thyself wrath against the day of wrath, Rom. ii. 5. Thou mayest perish, when his wrath is kindled but a little, Psalm ii. 12. Why wilt thou increase it yet more? Thou art already bound with such cords of death, as will not easily be loosed: what need is there of more? Stand, careless sinner, and consider this.

3. Thou hast no reason to complain, as long as thou art out of hell, *Wherefore doth a living man complain?* I am,

ii. 39. If one who has forfeited his life, be banished his native country, and exposed to many hardships; he may well bear all patiently, seeing his life is spared. Do ye murmur, for that ye are under pain or sickness? Nay, bless God ye are not there, where the worm never dieth. Dost thou grudge that thou art not in so good a condition in the world, as some of thy neighbours are? Be thankful rather, that ye are not in the case of the damned. Is thy substance gone from thee? Wonder that the fire of God's wrath hath not consumed thyself. Kiss the rod, O sinner, and acknowledge mercy; for God punisheth us less than our iniquities deserve. Ezra. ix. 13.

4. Here is a memorandum, both for poor and rich (1.) The poorest that go from door to door, and hath not one penny left them by their parents, were born to an inheritance. Their first father Adam left them children of wrath; and continuing in their natural state they cannot miss of it; *For this is the portion of a wicked man from God, and the heritage appointed to him by God*, Job. xx. 29. An heritage, that will furnish them, with an habitation, who have not where to lay their heads; they shall be cast into utter darkness, Mat. xxv. 30. for to them is reserved the blackness of darkness for ever, Jude 13. where their bed shall be sorrow: *They shall lie down in sorrow*, Isa. l. 11. their food shall be judgment, for God will feed them with judgment. Ezek. xxxiv. 16. and their drink shall be the red wine of God's wrath, the dregs whereof all the wicked of the earth shall wring out, and drink them, Psal. lxxv. 8. I know, that these who are destitute of worldly goods, and withal void of the knowledge and grace of God, who therefore may be called the devil's poor, will be apt to say here, We hope God will make us suffer all our misery in this world, and we shall be happy in the next; as if their miserable outward condition in time, would secure their happiness in eternity. A gross and fatal mistake! And this is another inheritance they have, viz. *lies, vanity, and things wherein there is no profit*, Jer. xvi. 19. But. *the hail shall sweep away the refuge of lies*, Isa. xxviii. 17. Dost thou think, O sinner, that God who commands judges on earth, not to respect the person of the poor in judgment, Lev. xix 15. will pervert judgment for thee? Nay, know for certain, however miserable thou art here, thou shalt be eternally miserable hereafter, if thou livest and diest in thy natural state. (2.) Many that have enough in the world, have far more than they know of. Thou hadst, it may be, O unregenerate man, an estate, a good portion, or large stock left thee by thy father; thou hast improven it, and the sun of prosperity shines upon thee; so that thou canst say with E-

sau, Gen. xxxiii. 9. *I have enough.* But know, thou hast more than all that, an inheritance thou dost not consider of; thou art a child of wrath, an heir of hell. That is an heritage which will abide with thee, amidst all the changes in the world; as long as thou continuest in an unregenerate state. When thou shalt leave thy substance to others, this shall go along with thyself, into another world. It is no wonder a slaughter-ox be fed to the full, and is not toiled as others are, Job xxi. 30. *The wicked is reserved to the day of destruction; they shall be brought forth to the day of wrath.* Well then, Rejoice, let thine heart chear thee, walk in the ways of thine heart, and in the sight of thine eyes; live above reproofs and warnings from the work of GOD; shew thyself a man of a fine spirit, by casting off all fear of GOD; mock at seriousness; live like thyself, a child of wrath, an heir of hell: *But know thou, that for all these thing God will bring thee into judgment.* Eccles. xi. 9. Assure thyself, thy breaking shall come suddenly, at an instant, Isa xxx. 13. *For as the crackling of thorns under a pot, so is the laughter of a fool,* Eccles. vii. 6. The fair blaze, and great noise they make, is quickly gone; so shall thy mirth be. And then that wrath that is now silently sinking into thy soul, shall make a fearful hissing.

5. Wo to him, that, like Moab, hath been at ease from his youth, Jer. xlviii. 11. and never saw the black cloud of wrath hanging over his head. There are many who have no changes, therefore they fear not GOD, Psal. lv. 19. They have lived in a good belief, as they call it, all their days; that is, they never had power to believe an ill report of their souls state. Many have come by their religion too easily; and as it came lightly to them, so it will go from them, when their trial comes. Do ye think men flee from wrath, in a morning-dream? Or will they flee from the wrath, they never saw pursuing them.

6. Think it not strange if ye see one in great distress about his soul's condition, who was wont to be as jovial, and as little concerned about salvation, as any of his neighbours. Can one get a right view of himself, as in a state of wrath, and not be pierced with sorrows, terrors, anxiety? When a weight, quite above one's strength, lies upon him, and he is alone, he can neither stir hand nor foot; but when one comes to lift it off him, he'll struggle to get from under it. Thunder-claps of wrath from the word of GOD conveyed to the soul by the Spirit of the LORD, will surely keep a man awake.

Lastly, It is no wonder wrath come upon churches and nations, and upon us in this land, and that infants and children yet unborn smart under it. Most of the society are yet children of wrath; few are fleein from it, or taking the way to prevent it; but people of all ranks are helping it on. The Jews rejected CHRIST; and their children have been smarting under wrath these sixteen hundred years. GOD grant, that the bad entertainment given to CHRIST and his gospel, by this generation, be not pursued with wrath on the succeeding one.

USE (2.) Of exhortation. And here, 1. I shall drop a word to these who are yet in an unregenerate state. 2. To those that are brought out of it. 3. To all indifferently.

I. To you that are yet in an unregenerate state, I would sound the alarm, and warn you to see to yourselves, while yet there is hope. O ye children of wrath, take no rest in this dismal state; but flee to JESUS CHRIST the only refuge. Haste and make your escape thither. The state of wrath is too hot a climate for you to live in, Micah ii. 10. *Arise ye and depart, for this is not your rest.* O sinner knowest thou where thou art? Dost thou not see thy danger? The curse has entered into thy soul; wrath is thy covering; the heavens are growing blacker and blacker above thy head; the earth is weary of thee; the pit is opening her mouth for thee; and should the thread of thy life be cut this moment, thou art henceforth past all hopes for ever. Sirs, if we saw you putting a cup of poison to your mouth, we would fly to you and snatch it out of your hands; If we saw the house on fire about you, while ye were fast asleep in it, we would run to you, and drag you out of it. But alas! ye are in ten thousand times greater hazard; yet we can do no more but tell you your danger; invite, exhort, beseech, and obtest you, to look to yourselves; and lament your stupidity and obstinacy, when we cannot prevail with you to take warning. If there were no hope of your recovery, we should be silent, and would not torment you before the time; but tho' ye be lost and undone, there is hope in Israel concerning this thing. Wherefore, I cry unto you in the name of the LORD, and in the words of the prophet, Zech. ix. 12. *Turn ye to the strong-hold, ye prisoners of hope.* Flee to JESUS CHRIST out of this your natural state.

Motive 1. While ye are in this state, ye must stand or fall according to the law or covenant of works. If ye understood this aright, it would strike through your hearts, as a thousand darts. One had better be a slave to the Turks, condemned to the galleys, or under Egyptian bondage, than be under the covenant of works now. All mankind were brought under it in Adam, as we heard before! and thou in thy unregenerate state art still where Adam left thee. It is true, there is another covenant brought in; but what is that to thee, who art not brought into it? Thou must need be under one of the two covenants; either under the law, or under grace. That thou art not under grace, the dominion of sin over thee, manifestly evinceth; therefore thou art under the law, Rom. vi. 14. Do not think GOD has laid aside the first covenant, Matth. v. 17. 18. Gal. iii. 10. No, he will magnify the law, and make it honourable. It is broken indeed on thy part; but it is absurd to think, that therefore your obligation is dissolved. Nay, thou must stand and fall by it, till thou canst produce thy discharge from GOD himself, who is thy party in that covenant; and this thou canst not pretend to, seeing thou art not in CHRIST.

Now, to give you a view of your misery, in this respect, consider these following things, (1.) Hereby ye are bound over to death, in virtue of the threatening of death in that covenant, Gen. ii. 17. The condition being broken, ye fall under the penalty: So it concludes you under wrath. (2.) There is no salvation for you under this covenant, but on a condition impossible to be performed by you. The justice of GOD must be satisfied for the wrong you have done already. GOD hath written this truth in characters of the blood of his Son. Yea, and you must perfectly obey the law for the time to come. So faith the law, Gal. iii. 12. *The man that doth them, shall live in them.* Come then, O sinner, see if thou canst make a ladder, whereby thou mayst reach the throne of GOD; stretch forth thine arms, and try, if thou canst fly on the wings of the wind, catch hold of the clouds and pierce thro' the visible heavens; and then either climb over, or break thro' the jasper walls of the city above. These things shalt thou do, as soon as thou shalt reach heaven in thy natural state, or under this covenant. (3.) There is no pardon under this covenant. Pardon is the benefit of another covenant, with which thou hast nothing to do, Acts xiii. *And by him all that believe are justified from all things from which ye could not be justified by the law of Moses.* As for thee, thou art in the hand of a merciless creditor, which will take thee by the throat, saying, *Pay what thou owest*; and cast thee into prison, there to remain, till thou hast paid the utmost farthing; unless thou beest so wise as to get a cautioner in time, who is able to answer for all thy debt, and get up thy discharge; this JESUS CHRIST alone can do. Thou abidest under this covenant, and pleadest mercy; but what is thy plea founded on? There is not one promise of mercy or pardon in that covenant. Dost thou plead mercy, for mercy sake? Justice will step in betwixt it and thee; and plead GOD's covenant-threatning, which he cannot deny. (4.) There's no place for repentance in this covenant, so as the sinner can be helped by it. For as soon as thou sinnest, the law lays its curse on thee, which is a dead weight thou canst by no means turow off; no, not tho' thine head were waters, and thine eyes a fountain of tears, to weep day and night for thy sin. That is what the law cannot do, in that it is weak through the flesh, Rom. viii. 3. Now thou art another profane Esau, that hath sold the blessing; and there is no place for repentance, though thou seekest it carefully with tears while under that covenant. (5.) There is no accepting of the will for the deed under this covenant, which was not made for good will, but good works. The mistake in this point ruins many. They are not in CHRIST, but stand under the first covenant; & yet they will plead this privilege. This is just as if one having made a feast for those of his own family, when they sit down at table, another man's servant that has run away from his master, should presumptuously come forward and sit down among them; would not the master of the feast give such a stranger that check, *Friend how camest thou in thither?* And since he is none of his family, command him to be gone quickly. Though a master accept the good will of his own child for the deed, can a hired servant expect that privilege? (6.) Ye have nothing to do with CHRIST, while under this covenant. By the law of GOD, a woman cannot be married to two husbands at once; either at death or divorce must dissolve the first marriage, ere we can be married to CHRIST, Rom. vii. 4. The law is the first husband; JESUS CHRIST, who raiseth the dead, marries the widow, that was heart broken, and slain by the first husband. But while the soul is in the house with the first husband, it cannot plead a marriage-relation to CHRIST; nor the benefits of a marriage-covenant, which is not yet entered into: Gal. v. 4. *Christ is become of no effect to you, whosoever of you are justified by the law ye are fallen from grace.* Peace, pardon, and such like benefits are all benefits of the covenant of grace. And ye must not think to stand off from CHRIST, and the marriage-covenant with him, and yet plead these benefits: more than one man's wife can plead the benefit of a contract of marriage past betwixt another man and his own wife. *Lastly,* See the bill of exclusion, past in the court of heaven, against all under the covenant of works, Gal. iv. 30. *The son of the bond-woman shall not be heir.* Compare ver. 24. Heirs of wrath must not be heirs of glory. Whom the first covenant hath power to exclude out of heaven, the second covenant cannot bring into it.

Objection. Then it is impossible for us to be saved. *Answer,* It is so, while you are in that state. But if you would be out of that dreadful condition, hasten out of that state. If a murderer be under sentence of death, so long as he lives within the kingdom, the laws will reach his life; but if he can make his escape, and get over the sea, into the dominions of another prince; our laws cannot reach him there. This is what we would have you to do, flee out of the kingdom of darkness, into the kingdom of GOD's dear Son; out of the dominion of the law, into the dominion of grace; then all the curses of the law, or covenant of works, shall never be able to reach you.

Motive 2. O ye children of wrath, your state is wretched, for ye have lost GOD; and that is an unspeakable loss. Ye are without GOD in the world, Eph. ii 12. Whatever you may call yours, you cannot call GOD yours. If ye look to the earth, perhaps you can tell us, that land, that house, or that herd of cattle, is yours. But let us look upward to heaven, is that GOD, that grace, that glory ours? Truly, you have neither part nor lot in that matter. When Nebuchadnezzar talks of cites and kingdoms, O how big does he speak! *Great Babylon that I have built----my power----my majesty*! but he tells a poor tale when he comes to speak of GOD, saying, *Your God*, Dan. ii. 47. and iv. 30. Alas! sinner, whatever thou hast, GOD is gone from thee. O the misery of a godless soul! Hast thou lost GOD? Then, (1.) The sap and substance of all that thou hast in the world, is gone. The godless man, have what he will, is one that hath not, Mat. xxv. 29. I defy the unregenerate man to attain to soul-satisfaction, whatever he possesseth, since GOD is not his GOD. All his days he eateth in darkness; in every condition, there is a secret dissatisfaction haunts his heart like a ghost; the soul wants something, tho' perhaps it knoweth not what it is; and so it will be always, till the soul return to GOD, the fountain of satisfaction. (2.) Thou canst do nothing to the purpose for thyself, for GOD is gone; his soul is departed from thee, Jer. vi. 8. like a leg out of joint, hanging by, whereof a man hath no use, as the word there used doth bear. Losing GOD, thou hast lost the fountain of good; and so all grace, all goodness all the saving influences of his Spirit. What canst thou do then? What fruit canst thou bring forth, more than a branch cut off from the stock? John xv. 5. Thou art become unprofitable, Rom. iii. 12. as a filthy rotten thing, fit only for the dunghill. (3.) **Death** has come up into thy windows, yea, and has settled on thy face; for GOD, in whose favour is life, Psal. xxx. 5. is gone from thee, and so the soul of thy soul is departed. What a lothsome lump is the body, when the soul is gone? Far more lothsome is thy soul in this case. Thou art dead while thou livest. Do not deny it, seeing thy speech is laid, thine eyes closed, and all spiritual motion in thee ceaseth. Thy true friends, who see thy case, do lament, because thou art gone into the land of silence. (4.) Thou hast not a steady friend among all the creatures of God; for now that thou hast lost the Master's favour, all the family is set against thee. Conscience is thine enemy; the word never speaks good of thee: God's people loathe thee, so far as they see what thou art, Psal. xv. 22. The beasts and stones of the field are banded together against thee, Job v. 23. Hos. ii. 18. Thy meat, drink, clothes, grudge to be serviceable to the wretch that has lost God, and abuseth them to his dishonour. The earth groaneth under thee; yea the whole creation groaneth and travaileth in pain together, because of thee, and such as thou art, Rom. viii. 22. Heaven will have nothing to do with thee; *For there shall in no wise enter into it any thing that defileth*, Rev. xxi. 24. Only hell from beneath is moved for thee, to meet thee at thy coming, Isa. xiv. 9. *Lastly*, Thy hell is begun already. What makes hell, but exclusion from the presence of God? *Depart from me ye cursed*. Now ye are gone from God already, with the curse upon you. That shall be your punishment at length, if ye return not, which is now your choice. As a gracious state is a state of glory in the bud; so a graceless state is hell in the bud; which if it continue, will come to perfection at length.

Motive 3. Consider the dreadful instances of the wrath of God; and let them serve to awaken thee to flee out of this state. Consider (1.) How it has fallen on men. Even in this world, many have been set up as monuments of divine vengeance; that others might fear. Wrath has swept away multitudes, who have fallen together by the hand of an angry God. Consider how the Lord spared not the old world, bringing in the flood upon the world of the ungodly: and turning the cities of Sodom and Gomorrah into ashes, condemned them with an overthrow, making them an example unto those that after should live ungodly, 2 Pet. ii. 5. 6. But it is yet more dreadful to think of that weeping, wailing, and gnashing of teeth, amongst those, who in hell lift up their eyes, but cannot get a drop of water to cool their tongues. Believe these things and be warned by them; lest destruction come upon thee, for a warning to others. (2.) Consider how wrath fell upon the fallen angels, whose case is absolutely hopeless. They were the first that ventured to break the hedge of the divine law; and God set them up for monuments of his wrath against sin. They once left their own habitation, and were never allowed to look in again at the hole of the door; but they are reserved in everlasting chains, under darkness unto the judgment of the great day, Jude 6. *Lastly*, Behold how an angry God dealt with his own Son, standing in the room of elect sinners, Rom. viii. 32. *God spared not his own Son.* Sparing-mercy might have been expected, if any at all. If any person could have obtained it, surely his own Son would have got it; but he spared him not. The Father's delight is made a man of sorrows: he who is the wisdom of GOD becomes sore amazed, ready to faint away with a fit of horror. The weight of this wrath makes him sweat great drops of blood. By the fierceness of this fire, his heart was like wax melted in the midst of his bowels. Behold here how severe GOD is against sin; the sun was struck blind with this terrible sight; rocks were rent, graves opened; death, as it were, in the excess of astonishment, letting its prisoners slip away. What is a deluge, a shower of fire and brimstone on Sodomites, the terrible noise of a dissolving world, the whole fabric of heaven and earth falling down at once, angels cast down from heaven into the bottomless pit? What are all these, I say, in comparison with this? GOD suffering! groaning, dying upon a cross! infinite holiness did it, to make sin look like itself, viz. infinitely odious. And will men live at ease, while exposed to this wrath.

Lastly, Consider what a GOD he is with whom thou hast to do, whose wrath thou art liable unto: He is a GOD of infinite knowledge and wisdom; so that none of thy sins, however secret, can be hid from him. He infallibly finds out all means whereby wrath may be executed, toward the satisfying of justice. He is of infinite power, and so can do what he will against the sinner. How heavy must the strokes of wrath be, which are laid on by an omnipotent hand! infinite power can make the sinner prisoner, even when he is in his greatest rage against heaven. It can bring again the several parcels of dust, out of the grave; put them together again, reunite the soul and the body, sist them before the tribunal, hurry them away to the pit, and hold them up with the one hand, thro' eternity, while they are lashed with the other. He is infinitely just, and therefore must punish: it were acting contrary to his nature to suffer the sinner to escape wrath. Hence the executing of this wrath is pleasing to him; for tho' the LORD hath no delight in the death of the sinner as it is the destruction of his own creature; yet he delights in it, as it is the execution of justice. *Upon the wicked he shall rain snares, fire and brimstone, and an horrible tempest.* Mark the reason, *For the righteous Lord loveth righteousness.* Psal. xi. 6, 7. *I will cause my fury to rest upon them, and I will be comforted,* Ezek. v. 13. *I also will laugh at your calamity,* Prov. i. 26. *Finally,* He lives for ever, to pursue the quarrel. Let us therefore conclude, *It is a fearful thing to fall into the hands of the living God!*

Be awakened then, O young sinner; be awakened. O old sinner, who art yet in the state thou wast born in. Your security is none of God's allowance; it is the sleep of death; Rise out of it ere the pit close its mouth on you. It is true, you may put on a breastplate of iron; make your bow brass, and your heart as an adamant; who can help it? But God will break that brazen bow, and make that adamantine heart, at last, to fly into a thousand pieces. Ye may, if ye will labour to put these things out of your heads, that ye may yet sleep in a sound skin, tho' in a state of wrath. Ye may run away with the arrows sticking in your consciences to your work to work them away; or to your beds, to sleep them out; or to company, to sport and laugh them away; but convictions so stifled, will have a fearful resurrection: and the day is coming, when the arrows of wrath shall so stick in thy soul, as thou shalt never be able to pluck them out thro' the ages of eternity, unless thou take warning in time.

But if any desire to flee from the wrath to come; and for that end, to know what course to take; I offer them these few advices, and obtest and beseech them as they love their own souls, to fall in with them. (1.) Retire yourselves into some secret place, and there meditate on this your misery. Believe it, and fix your thoughts on it. Let each put the question to himself, How can I live in this state? How can I die in it? How will I rise again, and stand before the tribunal of God in it? (2.) Consider seriously the sin of your nature, heart and life. A kindly sight of wrath flows from a deep sense of sin. They who see themselves exceeding sinful, will find no great difficulty to perceive themselves to be heirs of wrath. (3.) Labour to justify God in this matter. To quarrel with God about it, and to rage like a wild bull in a net, will but fix you the more in it. Humiliation of soul, before the Lord, is necessary for an escape. God will not sell deliverance, but freely gives it to those, who see themselves altogether unworthy of his favour. *Lastly*, Turn your eyes, O prisoners of hope, towards the Lord Jesus Christ; and embrace him as he offereth himself in the gospel. *There is no salvation in any other*, Acts iv. 12. God is a consuming fire; ye are children of wrath: if the Mediator interpose not betwixt him and you, ye are undone for ever. If ye would be safe, come under his shadow: one drop of that wrath cannot fall there, for he delivereth us from the wrath to come, 1 Thes. i. 10. Accept of him in his covenant, wherein he offereth himself to thee: and so thou shalt, as the captive woman, redeem thy life by marrying the Conqueror. His blood will quench that fire of wrath, which burns against thee: in the white raiment of his righteousness thou shalt be safe; for no storm of wrath can pierce it.

II. I shall drop a few words to the saints.

First, Remember, that at that time, namely, when ye were in your natural state, ye were without CHRIST, having no hope, and without GOD in the world. Call to mind that state ye were in formerly, and review the misery of it. There are five memorials, I may thence give into the whole assembly of the saints, who are no more children of wrath; but heirs of GOD, and joint heirs with CHRIST, tho' as yet in their minority. (1.) Remember, that in the day our LORD took you by the hand, ye were in no better condition than others. O what moved him to take you, when he past by your neighbours! he found you children of wrath, even as others; but he did not leave you so. He came into the common prison, where you lay in your fetters, even as others; and from amongst the multitude of condemned malefactors, he picked out you, commanded your fetters to be taken off, put a pardon in your hand, and brought you into the glorious liberty of the children of GOD, while he left others in the devil's fetters. (2.) Remember there was nothing in you to engage him to love you, in the day he first appeared for your deliverance. Ye were children of wrath, even as others, fit for hell, and altogether unfit for heaven; yet the King brought you into the palace; the King's Son made love to you a condemned criminal, and espoused you to himself, on the day in which ye might have been led forth to execution. *Even so, Father, for so it seemeth good in thy sight,* Matth. ix. 26. (3.) Remember, ye were fitter to be loathed than loved in that day. Wonder, that when he saw you in your blood, he looked not at you with abhorrence, and passed by you. Wonder that ever such a time could be a time of love, Ezek. xvi. 8. (4.) Remember, ye are decked with borrowed feathers. It is his comliness which is upon you, ver. 14. It was he that took off your prison-garments, and clothed you with robes of righteousness, garments of salvation; garments wherewith ye are arrayed as the lilies, which toil not neither do they spin. He took the chains from off your arms, the rope from about your neck; put you in such a dress as ye may be fit for the court of heaven, even to eat at the King's table. (5.) Remember your faults this day, as Pharaoh's butler, who had forgotten Joseph. Mind how you have forgotten, and how unkindly you have treated him, who remembered you in your low estate. *Is this your kindness to your friend?* In the day of your deliverance, did ye think, ye could have thus requited him, your LORD?

I

Secondly, Pity the children of wrath, the world that lies in wickedness. Can ye be unconcerned for them, ye who were once in the same condition? Ye have got ashore indeed, but your fellows are yet in hazard of perishing; and will not ye make them all possible help for their deliverance? What they are, ye sometimes were. This may draw pity from you, and engage you to use all means for their recovery. See Tit. iii. 1, 2, 3.

Thirdly, Admire that matchless love, which brought you out of the state of wrath. CHRIST's love was active love, he loved thy soul from the pit of corruption. It was no easy work to purchase the life of the condemned sinner; but he gave his life for thy life. He gave his precious blood to quench that flame of wrath, which otherwise would have burnt thee up. Men get the best view of the stars, from the bottom of a deep pit; from this pit of misery into which thou wast cast by the first Adam, thou mayst get the best view of the Sun of righteousness, in all his dimensions. He is the second Adam, who took thee out of the horrible pit, and out of the miry clay. How broad were the skirts of that love, which covered such a multitude of sins! behold the length of it, reaching from everlasting to everlasting, Psal. cii. 17. The depth of it, going so low as to deliver thee from the lowest hell, Psal. lxxxi. 13. The height of it, in raising thee up to sit in heavenly places, Eph. ii. 6.

Fourthly, Be humble, carry low sails, walk softly all your years. Be not proud of your gifts, graces, privileges or attainments; but remember ye were children of wrath, even as others. The peacock walks slowly, hangs down his starry feathers, while he looks to his black feet. Look ye to the hole of the pit, whence ye are digged, walk humbly as it becomes free grace's debtors.

Lastly, Be wholly for your LORD. Every wife is obliged to be dutiful to her husband; but double ties lie upon her who was taken from a prison or a dunghill. If your LORD has delivered you from wrath, ye ought, upon that very account, to be wholly his: to act for him, to suffer for him, and to do whatever he calls you to. The saints have no reason to complain of their lot in the world, whatever it be. Well may they bear the cross for him, by whom the curse was taken away from them. Well may they bear the wrath of men in his cause, who has freed them from the wrath of GOD; and chearfully go to a fire for him, by whom hell-fire is quenched to them. Soul and body, and all thou hadst in the world, were sometimes under wrath; he has removed that wrath: shall not all these be at his service? That thy soul is not overwhelmed with the wrath of GOD, is owing purely to

JESUS CHRIST; and shall it not then be a tempel for his Spirit? That thy heart is not filled with horror and despair, is owing to him only; to whom then should it be devoted but to him alone? That thine eyes are not blinded with the smoak of the pit, thy hands are not fettered with chains of darkness, thy tongue is not broiling in the fire of hell, and thy feet are not standing in that lake which burns with fire and brimstone, is owing purely to JESUS CHRIST; and shall not these eyes be employed for him, these hands act for him, that tongue speak for him, and these feet speedily run his errands? To him who believes that he was a child of wrath even as others, but is now delivered by the blessed JESUS; nothing will appear too much, to do or suffer for his deliverer, when he has a fair call to it.

III. To conclude with a word to all; let no man think lightly of sin, which lays the sinner open to the wrath of GOD. Let not the sin of our nature, which wreaths the yoke of GOD's wrath, so early about our necks, seem a small thing in our eyes. Fear the LORD, because of his dreadful wrath. Tremble at the thought of sin, against which GOD has such fiery indignation. Look on his wrath, and stand in awe, and sin not. Do you think this is to press you to slavish fear? If it were so, one had better be a slave to GOD with a trembling heart; than a free man to the devil, with a seared conscience and a heart of adamant. But it is not so, you may love him, and thus fear him too; yea, ye ought to do it though ye were saints of the first magnitude. See Psal. cxix. 10. Matth. x. 28. Luke xii. 5. Heb. xii. 28, 29. Altho' ye have past the gulf of wrath, being in JESUS CHRIST; yet it is but reasonable your hearts shiver, when ye look back to it. Your sin still deservs wrath even as the sins of others; and it would be terrible to be in a fiery furnace; altho' by a miracle, we were so fenced against it, as that it could not harm us.

HEAD III.

Man's utter Inability to recover himself.

ROMANS v. 6.

For when we were yet without strength, in due time Christ died for the ungodly.

JOHN vi. 44.

No man can come to me, except the Father which hath sent me, draw him.

WE have now had a view of the total corruption of man's nature, and that load of wrath which lies on him, that gulph of misery he is plunged into, in his natural state. But there is one part of his misery that deserves particular consideration; namely, his utter inability to recover himself, the knowledge of which is necessary for the due humiliation of a sinner. What I design here is, only to propose a few things, whereby to convince the unregenerate man of this his inability; that he may see an absolute need of CHRIST, and of the power of his grace.

As a man that is fallen into a pit, cannot be supposed to help himself out of it, but by one of two ways; either by doing all himself alone, or taking hold of, and improving the help offered him by others; so an unconverted man cannot be supposed to help himself out of that state, but either in the way of the law, or covenant of works, by doing all himself without CHRIST; or else in the way of the gospel, or covenant of grace, by exerting his own strength to lay hold upon, and to make use of the help offered him by a Saviour. But alas! the unconverted man is dead in the pit, and cannot help himself, either of these ways. Not the first way; for the first text tells us, that when our LORD came to help us, we were without strength, unable to recover ourselves. We were ungodly; therefore under a burden of guilt and wrath; yet without strength, unable to stand under it; and unable to throw it off, or get from under it; so that all mankind had undoubtedly perished, had not CHRIST died for the ungodly, and brought help to them who could never have recovered themselves. —But when CHRIST comes and offereth help to sinners, cannot they take it? Cannot they improve help when it comes to their hands? No, the second text tells us, they cannot; *No man can come unto me* (i. e.) believe in me, John vi. 35. *except the Father draw him.* This is a drawing which enables them to come, who till then could not come; and therefore could not help themselves, by improving the help offered. It is a drawing, which is always effectual; for it can be no less than hearing and learning of the Father, which whoso partakes of, cometh to CHRIST, ver. 25. Therefore, it is not drawing in the way of mere moral suasion, which may be, yea, and always is, ineffectual: but it is drawing by mighty power, Eph. i. 9. absolutely necessary for them that have no power in themselves, to come and take hold of the offered help.

Hearken then, O unregenerate man, and be convinced, that as thou art in a most miserable state by nature; so thou art utterly unable to recover thyself, any manner of way. Thou art ruined; and what way wilt thou go to work, to recover thyself? Which of these two ways wilt thou chuse; Wilt thou try it alone? Or wilt thou make use of help? Wilt thou fall on the way of works, or on the way of the gospel? I know very well, thou wilt not so much as try the way of the gospel, till once thou hast found the recovery impracticable, in the way of the law. Therefore we shall begin, where corrupt nature teaches men to begin, viz. at the way of the law of works.

I. Sinner, I would have thee believe that thy working will never effect it. Work and do thy best, thou shalt never be able to work thyself out of this state of corruption and wrath. Thou must have CHRIST, else thou shalt perish eternally. It is only CHRIST in you, can be the hope of glory. But if thou wilt needs try it, then I must lay before thee, from the unalterable word of the living GOD, two things which thou must do for thyself. And if thou canst do them, it must be yielded, that thou art able to recover thyself; but if not, then thou canst do nothing this way, for thy recovery.

FIRST, *If thou wilt enter into life, keep the commandments,* Mat. xix. 17. That is, if thou wilt, by doing enter into life, then perfectly keep the ten commands. For the scope of these words is, to beat down the pride of man's heart; and to let him see the absolute need of a Saviour, from the impossibility of keeping the law. The answer is given, suitable to the address. Our LORD checks him for his compliment, *Good master,* ver. 16. telling him, *There is none good but one, that is God,* ver. 17. As if he had said, You think yourself a good man, and me another? but where goodness is spoken of, men and angels may veil their faces before the good GOD. And as to his question, wherein he discovereth his legal disposition, Christ does not answer him, saying, *Believe and thou shalt be saved*; that would not have been so seasonable, in the case of one who thought he could do well enough for himself, if he but knew what good things he should do; but, suitable to the humour the man was in, he bid him *keep the commandments*; keep them nicely and accurately, as those that watch malefactors in prison, lest any of them escape, and their life go for theirs. See then, O unregenerate man, what canst thou do in this matter; for, if thou wilt recover thyself in this way, thou must perfectly keep the commandments of God.

And (1) Thy obedience must be perfect, in respect of the principal of it; that is, thy soul, the principle of action, must be perfectly pure, and altogether without sin. For the law requires all moral perfection; not only actual, but habitual, and so condemns original sin; impurity of nature, as well as of actions. Now if thou canst bring this to pass, **thou shalt be** able to answer that question of Solomon's so as never one of Adam's posterity could yet answer it, Prov. 22. 9. *Who can say, I have made my heart clean?* But if thou canst not, the very want of this perfection is a sin; and so lays thee open to the curse, and cuts thee off from life. Yea, it makes all thine actions, even thy best actions sinful; *For who can bring a clean thing out of an unclean?* Job xiv. 4. And dost thou think, by sin to help thyself out of sin and misery? (2.) Thy obedience must also be perfect in parts. It must be as broad as the whole law of God; if thou lackest one thing, thou art undone; for the law denounceth the curse on him that continueth not in every thing written therein, Gal. iii. 10. Thou must give internal and external obedience to the whole law; keep all the commands, in heart and life. If thou breakest any one of them, that will insure thy ruin. A vain thought or idle word, will still shut thee up under the curse. (3.) It must be perfect in respect of degrees, as was the obedience of Adam, while he stood in his innocence. This the law requires, and will accept of no less, Mat. xxii. 37. *Thou shalt love the Lord thy God, with all thy heart, and with all thy soul, and with all thy mind.* If one degree of that love required by the law, be wanting; if each part of thy obedience be not screwed up to the greatest height commanded; that want is a breach of the law, and so leaves thee still under the curse. One may bring as many buckets of water to a house that is on fire, as he is able to carry; and yet it may be consumed; and will be so, if he bring not as many as will quench the fire. Even so, although thou shouldst do what thou art able, in keeping the commands; if thou fail in the least degree of obedience which the law enjoins, thou art certainly ruined for ever; unless thou take hold of CHRIST, renouncing all thy righteousness as filthy rags. See Rom. x. 5. Gal. iii. 10. *Lastly*, It must be perpetual, as the man CHRIST's obedience was, who always did the things that pleased the Father; for the tenor of the law is, *Cursed is he that continueth not in all things written in the law, to do them.* Hence tho' Adam's obedience was for a while absolutely perfect; yet because at length he tripped in one point, *viz.* in eating the forbidden fruit, he fell under the curse of the law. If one should live a dutiful subject to his prince, till the close of his days, and then conspire against him; he must die for his treason. Even so, tho' thou shouldst, all the time of thy life live in perfect obedience to the law of GOD; and only at the hour of death entertain a vain thought, or pronounce an idle word; that idle word or vain thought, would blot out all thy former righteousness, and ruin thee: namely, in this way, in which thou art seeking to recover thyself.

Now such is the obedience those must perform, if thou wouldst recover thyself in the way of the law. But tho' thou shouldst thus obey, the law takes thee down in the state of wrath, till another demand of it be satisfied, *viz.*

SECONDLY, Thou must pay what thou owest. It is undeniable thou art a sinner; and whatever thou mayest be in time to come, justice must be satisfied for thy sin already committed. The honour of the law must be maintained, by thy suffering the denounced wrath. It may be thou hast changed thy course of life, or art now resolved to do it, and set about the keeping of the commands of GOD: but what hast thou done, or what wilt thou do, with the old debt? Your obedience to GOD, tho' it were perfect, is a debt due to him, for the time wherein it is performed; and can no more satisfy for former sins, than a tenant's paying the current year's rent, can satisfy the master for all bygones. Can the paying of new debts acquit a man from old accounts? Nay, deceive not yourselves, you will find these laid up in store with GOD, and sealed up amongst his treasures, Deut. xxxii. 34. It remains then that either thou must bear that wrath, to which, for thy sin, thou art liable, according to the law: or else, thou must acknowledge thou canst not bear it, and thereupon have recourse to the surety the LORD JESUS CHRIST. Let me now ask thee, Art thou able to satisfy the justice of GOD? Canst thou pay thy own debt? Surely not: for, seeing he is an infinite GOD, whom thou hast offended; the punishment, being suited to the quality of the offence, must be infinite. But so it is, thy punishment or sufferings for sin cannot be infinite in value, seeing thou art a finite creature: therefore they must be infinite in duration or continuance; that is, reco-

must be eternal. And so all thy sufferings in this world, are but an earnest of what thou must suffer in the world to come.

Now sinner if thou canst answer these demands, thou mayest recover thyself in the way of the law. But art thou not conscious of thy inability to do any of these things, much more to do them all? Yet if thou do not all, thou dost nothing. Turn then to what course of life thou wilt, thou art still in a state of wrath. Screw up thy obedience to the greatest height thou canst; suffer what GOD lays upon thee, yea add, if thou wilt to the burden, and walk under all, without the least impatience; yet all this will not satisfy the demands of the law; and therefore thou art still a ruined creature. Alas! sinner, what art thou doing, while thou strivest to help thyself; but dost not receive and unite with JESUS CHRIST? Thou art labouring in the fire, wearying thyself for very vanity; labouring to enter into heaven by the door, which Adam's sin so bolted, as neither he, nor any of his lost posterity can ever enter by it. Dost thou not see the flaming sword of justice keeping thee off from the tree of life? Dost thou not hear the law denouncing a curse on thee for all thou art doing; even for thy obedience, thy prayers, thy tears, thy reformation of life, &c. because, being under the law's dominion, thy best works are not so good, as it requires them to be under the pain of the curse? Believe it, sirs, if you live and die out of CHRIST, without being actually united to him as the second Adam, a life-giving Spirit, and without coming under the covert of his atoning blood; though ye should do the utmost that any man on earth can do, in keeping the commands of GOD, ye shall never see the face of GOD in peace. If you should from this moment, bid an eternal farewell to this world's joy, and all the affairs thereof; and henceforth busy yourselves with nothing, but the salvation of your souls: If you should go into some wilderness, live upon the grass of the field, and be companions to dragons and owls: If you should retire to some dark cavern of the earth, and weep there for your sins, until you have wept yourselves blind; yea, wept out all the moisture of your body; if ye should confess with your tongue, until it cleave to the roof of your mouth; pray, till your knees grow hard as horns: fast, till your body become like a skeleton; and after all this give it to be burnt, the word is gone out of the LORD's mouth in righteousness, and cannot return; you should perish for ever, notwithstanding of all this, as not being in CHRIST, John xiv. 6. *No man cometh unto the Father but by me.* Acts iv. 19. *Neither is there salvation in any other.* Mark xvi. 16. *He that believeth not shall be damned.*

Object. But GOD is a merciful GOD, and he knows we are not able to answer his demands; we hope therefore to be saved, if we do as well as we can, and keep the commands as well as we are able. *Ans.* (1.) Though thou art able to do many things, thou art not able to do one thing aright; thou canst do nothing acceptable to GOD, being out of CHRIST, John xv. 5. *Without me ye can do nothing.* An unrenewed man, as thou art, can do nothing but sin; as we have already evinced. Thy best actions are sin, and so they increase thy debt to justice; how then can it be expected they should lessen it? (2.) If GOD should offer to save men upon condition that they did all they could do, in obedience to his commands, we have ground to think, that these who would betake themselves to that way, should never be saved. For where is the man, that does as well as he can? Who sees not many false steps he has made, which he might have evited; There are so many things to be done, so many temptations to carry us out of the road of duty, and our nature is so very apt to be set on fire of hell, that we would surely fail, even in some point, that is within the compass of our natural abilities. But (3.) Though thou shouldst do all thou art able to do, in vain dost thou hope to be saved in that way. What word of GOD is this hope of thine founded on? It is neither founded on law nor gospel, and therefore it is but a delusion. It is not founded on the gospel; for the gospel leads the soul out of itself, to JESUS CHRIST for all; and it establisheth the law, Rom. iii. 31. whereas this hope of yours cannot be established, but on the ruin of the law, which GOD will magnify and make honourable. and hence it appears, that it is not founded on the law neither. When GOD set Adam a working for happiness to himself and his posterity, perfect obedience was the condition required of him; and a curse was denounced in case of disobedience. The law being broken by him, he and his posterity were subjected to the penalty, for sin commited; and withal still bound to perfect obedience; for it is absurd to think that man's sinning and suffering for his sin, should free him from his duty of obedience to his Creator. When CHRIST came in the room of the elect, to purchase their salvation, the same were the terms. Justice had the elect under arrest; if he minds to deliver them the terms are known. He must satisfy for their sin, by suffering the punishment due to it; he must do what they cannot do, viz. obey the law perfectly, and so fulfil all righteousness. Accordingly, all this he did, and so became the end of the law for righteousness to every one that believeth, Rom. x. 4. And now dost thou think, GOD will abate of these terms to thee, when his own Son got no abatement of them? Expect it not, though thou shouldst beg it with tears of blood: for if they prevailed, they behoved to prevail against the truth, justice and honour of GOD, Gal. iii. 10. 22. *Cursed is every one that continueth not in all things, which are written in the book of the law, to do them.—And the law is not of faith, but the man that doth them, shall live in them.* It is true, that GOD is merciful; he cannot but be merciful, unless he save you in a way that is neither consistent with his law nor gospel? Hath not his goodness and mercy sufficiently appeared, in sending the Son of his love, to do what the law could not do, in that it was weak through the flesh? He has provided help for them that cannot help themselves: but thou, insensible of thine own weakness, wilt needs think to recover thyself by thine own works; while thou art no more able to do it, than to remove mountains of brass out of their place.

Wherefore I conclude thou art utterly unable to recover thyself, by the way of works, or of the law. O that thou wouldst conclude the same concerning thyself!

II. Let us try next, what the sinner can do to recover himself, in the way of the gospel; It is likely, thou thinkest, that howbeit thou canst not do all, by thyself alone; yet JESUS CHRIST offering thee help, thou canst of thyself embrace it, and use it to thy recovery. But, O sinner, be convinced of thine absolute need of the grace of CHRIST, for truly there is help offered, but thou canst not accept of it; there is a rope cast out to hale ship-wrecked sinners to land; but alas! they have no hands to catch hold of it. They are like infants exposed in the open field that must starve, though their food be lying by them, unless one put it into their mouths. To convince natural men of this, let it be considered,

First, That although CHRIST is offered in the gospel, yet they cannot believe in him. Saving faith is the faith of GOD's elect; the special gift of GOD to them, wrought in them by his spirit. Salvation is offered to them that will believe in CHRIST; but how can ye believe? John v. 44. It is offered to these that will come to CHRIST; but no man can come unto him, except the Father draw him. It is offered to them that will look to him as lifted up on the pole of the gospel, Isa. xlv. 22. But the natural man is spiritually blind, Rev. iii. 17. and as to the things of the Spirit of GOD, he cannot know them, for they are spiritually discerned, 1 Cor. ii. 14. Nay, whosoever will he is welcome; let him come, Rev. xxii. 17. But there must be a day of power on the sinner, before the will be willing, Psalm cx. 3.

Secondly, Man naturally has nothing, wherewithal to improve, to his recovery, the help brought in by the gospel.

He is cast away in a state of wrath; but is bound hand and foot, so that he cannot lay hold of the cords of love, thrown out to him in the gospel. The most skilful artificer cannot work without instruments, nor can the most cunning musician play well on an instrument that is out of tune. How can one believe, how can he repent, whose understanding is darkness, Eph. v. 8. whose heart is a stony heart, inflexible, insensible, Ezek. xxxvi. 26. whose affections are wholly disordered and distempered; who is averse to good, and bent to evil? The arms of natural abilities are too short to reach supernatural help; hence those who most excel in them, are oft-times most estranged from spiritual things, Matt. xi. 25. *Thou hast hid these things from the wise and prudent.*

Thirdly, Man cannot work a saving change on himself; but so changed he must be, else he can neither believe nor repent, nor ever see heaven. No action can be without a suitable principle. Believing, repenting, and the like, are the product of the new nature; and can never be produced by the old corrupt nature. Now, what can the natural man do in this matter? He must be unregenerate, begotten again into a lively hope; but as the child cannot be active in his own generation, so a man cannot be active, but passive only in his own regeneration. The heart is shut against CHRIST; man cannot open it; only GOD can do it by his grace, Acts xvi. 14. He is dead in sin; he must be quickened, raised out of his grave; who can do this but GOD himself? Eph. ii. 1, 5. Nay, he must be created in CHRIST JESUS unto good works, Eph. ii. 10. These are works of omnipotency, and can be done by no less power.

Fourthly, Man, in his depraved state, is under an utter inability to do any thing truly good, as was cleared before at large; how then can he obey the gospel? His nature is the very reverse of the gospel; how can he, of himself, fall in with that device of salvation, and accept the offered remedy? The corruption of man's nature infallibly concludes his utter inability, to recover himself any manner of way; and whoso is convinced of the one, must needs admit the other; for they stand and fall together. Were all the purchase of CHRIST offered to the unregenerate man, for one good thought; he cannot command it, 2 Cor. iii. 5. *Not that we are sufficient of ourselves, to think any thing as of ourselves.* Were it offered on condition of a good word, yet how can ye, being evil, *speak good things?* Mat. xii. 35. Nay, were it left to yourselves, to chuse what is easiest; Christ himself tells you, John xv. 5. *Without me, ye can do nothing.*

Lastly, The natural man cannot but resist the LORD, offering to help him; howbeit that resistance is infallibly overcome in the elect, by converting grace. Can the stony heart chuse but to resist the stroke? There is not only an inability, but an enmity and obstinacy in man's will by nature. God knows, natural man, whether thou knowest it or not, that thou art obstinate, and thy neck is an iron sinew, and thy brow brass, Isa. xlviii. 4. and cannot be overcome, but by him, who hath broken the gates of brass, and cut the bars of iron in sunder. Hence is there such hard work in converting a sinner. Sometimes he seems to be caught in the net of the gospel; yet quickly he slips away again. The hook catcheth hold of him; but he struggles, till getting free of it, he makes away with a bleeding wound. When good hopes are conceived of him, by these that travail in birth, for the forming of CHRIST in him; there is oft-times nothing brought forth but wind. The deceitful heart makes many a shift to avoid a Saviour, and to cheat the man of his eternal happiness. Thus the natural man lies sunk in a state of sin and wrath, utterly unable to recover himself.

Object. (1.) If we be under an utter inability to do any good, how can GOD require us to do it? *Ans.* GOD making man upright, Eccles. vii. 29. gave him a power to do every thing he should require of him; this power man lost by his own fault. We were bound to serve GOD, and do whatsoever he commanded us, as being his creatures; and also, ye were under the superadded tye of a covenant, for that effect. Now, we having, by our own fault, disabled ourselves; shall GOD lose his right of requiring our task because we have thrown away the strength he gave us, wherewithal to perform it?—— Has the creditor no right to require payment of his money, because the debtor has squandered it away, and is not able to pay him? Truly, if GOD can require no more of us than we are able to do; we need no more to save us from wrath, but to make ourselves unable for every duty, and to incapacitate ourselves for serving of GOD any manner of way, as profane men frequently do; and so the deeper one is immersed in sin, he will be the more secure from wrath; for where GOD can require no duty of us, we do not sin in omitting it; and where there is no sin, there can be no wrath. (As to what may be urged by the unhumbled soul, against the putting of our stock in Adam's hand, the righteousness of that dispensation was cleared before.) But, moreover, the unrenewed man is daily throwing away the very remains of natural abilities; that light and strength which are to be found amongst the ruins of mankind. Nay, farther, he will not believe his own utter inability to help himself; so that out of his own mouth he will be condemned. Even those who make their natural impotency to good, a cover for their sloth, do, with others, delay the

Objections answered. 141

to GOD from time to time; under convinc-
promises of reformation, which afterwards
; and delay their repentance to a death-bed,
help themselves in a moment; which speaks
m a due sense of their natural inability, what-

can require of men the duty they are not a-
n in justice punish them for their not doing
g of their inability. If he have power to ex-
edience, he has also power to cast the insol-
prison, for his not paying it. Further, tho'
have no gracious abilities, yet they want
es, which nevertheless they will not improve.
things they can do, which they do not, they
; and therefore their damnation will be just.
bility to good is voluntary; they will not
r, John v. 40. They will not repent, they
viii. 51. So they will be justly condemned,
not turn to GOD, nor come to CHRIST,
ains better than their liberty, and darkness
John iii. 19.
hy do you then preach CHRIST to us;
e to him, to believe, repent, and use
ation? *Ans.* Because it is your duty so
our duty to accept of CHRIST as he is
spel; to repent of your sins, and to be holy
conversation. These things are commanded
d his command, not your ability, is the mea-
. Moreover, these calls and exhortations,
it GOD is pleased to make use of, for con-
and working grace in their hearts; to them,
aring, Rom. x. 17. while they are unable to
as the rest of mankind are. Upon very good
at the command of GOD, who raiseth the
graves and cry in his name, *Awake thou that
from the dead, and Christ shall give thee light,*
d seeing the elect are not to be known and
n others before conversion, as the sun shines
's face, and the rain falls on the rocks as well
plains; so we preach CHRIST to all, and
it a venture, which GOD himself directs as
Moreover, these calls and exhortations are not
, even to those that are not converted by
ersons may be convinced, though they be
lthough they be not sanctified by these means,
restrained by them, from running into that
ness which otherwise they would arrive at,

The means of grace serve, as it were to embalm many dead souls which were never quickened by them, though they do not restore them to life; yet they keep them from smelling so rank as otherwise they would do. *Finally*, Though ye cannot recover yourselves; nor take hold of the saving help offered to you in the gospel; yet even by the power of nature, ye may use the outward and ordinary means, whereby CHRIST communicates the benefits of redemption to ruined sinners, who are utterly unable to recover themselves out of the state of sin and wrath. Ye may, and can, if ye please, do many things, that would set you in a fair way for help from the LORD JESUS CHRIST. Ye may go so far on, as to be not far from the kingdom of GOD, as the discreet scribe had done, Mark xii. 34. though, it would seem, he was destitute of supernatural abilities. Though, ye cannot cure yourselves, yet ye may come to the pool, where many such diseased persons as ye are, have been cured; ye have none to put you into it, yet ye may lie at the side of it; and who knows but the LORD may return, and leave a blessing behind him, as in the case of the impotent man, recorded, John v. 5, 6, 7, 8. I hope Satan does not chain you to your houses, nor stake you down in your fields on the LORD's day; but ye are are at liberty, and can wait at the posts of wisdom's door if ye will. And when ye come thither, he doth not beat drums at your ears, that ye cannot hear what is said; there is no force upon you, obliging you to apply all you hear to others; ye may apply to yourselves what belongs to your state and condition; and when you go home, you are not fettered in your houses, where perhaps no religious discourse is to be heard; but ye may retire to some separate place, where ye can meditate, and pose your conscience with pertinent questions upon what ye have heard. Ye are not possessed with a dumb devil, that ye cannot get your mouths opened in prayer to GOD. Ye are not so driven out of your beds to your worldly business, and from your worldly business to your beds again; but ye might, if ye would, bestow some prayers to GOD upon the case of your perishing souls. Ye may examine yourselves, as to the state of your souls, in a solemn manner, as in the presence of GOD; ye may discern that ye have no grace, and that ye are lost and undone without it; and may cry unto GOD for it. These things are within the compass of natural abilities, and may be practised where there is no grace. It must aggravate your guilt, that you will not be at so much pains about the state and case of your precious souls. And if ye do not what you can do, ye will be condemned not only for your want of grace, but for your despising of it.

Object. (3.) But all this is needless, seeing we are utterly unable to keep ourselves out of the state of sin and wrath. *Ans.* Give no place to that delusion, which puts asunder what GOD hath joined, namely, the use of means, and a sense of our own impotency. If ever the Spirit of GOD graciously influence your souls, ye will become thoroughly sensible of your absolute inability, and yet enter upon a vigorous use of means. Ye will do for yourselves, as if ye were to do all; and yet overlook all ye do, as if ye had done nothing. Will ye do nothing for yourselves, because ye cannot do all? **Lay** down no such impious conclusion against your own souls. **Do** what you can, and it may be, while ye are doing what ye can for yourselves, GOD will do for you what ye cannot. *Understandest thou what thou readest?* said Philip to the Eunuch: *How can I,* said he, *except some man should guide me,* Acts viii. 30, 31. He could not understand the scripture he read; yet he could read it; he did what he could, he read; and while he was reading, GOD sent him an interpreter. The Israelites were in a great strait at the red sea; and how could they help themselves, when upon the one hand were mountains, and on the other, the enemies garrison; when Pharaoh and his host were behind them, and the red sea before them? What could they do? *Speak unto the children of Israel,* saith the LORD to Moses, *that they go forward,* Exod. xiv. 15. For what end should they go forward? Can they make a passage to themselves through the sea? No; but let them go forward saith the LORD; though they cannot turn sea to dry land, yet they can go forward to the shore; and so they did; and when they did what thy **could,** GOD **did for them** what they could not do.

Quest. Has GOD promised to convert and save **them who** in the use of means, do what they can towards their own relief? *Ans.* We may not speak wickedly for GOD; natural men being strangers to the covenants of promise, Eph. ii. 12. have no such promise made **to them**: Nevertheless, they **do** not act rationally, unless they **exert** the powers they have, and do what they can. For, (1.) **It is** possible this course may succeed with them. If ye do what ye can, it may be GOD will do for you what you cannot do for yourselves. This is sufficient to determine a man, in a matter of the utmost importance, such as this is, Acts viii. 22. *Pray God, if perhaps the thoughts of thy heart may be forgiven thee.* Joel ii. 14. *Who knoweth if he will return?* If success may be, the trial should be. If, in a wreck at sea, all the sailors and passengers had betaken themselves each to a broken board for safety, and one of them should see all the rest perish, notwithstanding of their utmost endeavours to save themselves, yet the very possibility of escaping by that means, would determine that one still to do his best with his board. Why then do ye not reason with yourselves as the four lepers did, who sat at the gates of Samaria, 2 Kings vii. 3, 4. Why do ye not say, If we sit still, not doing what we can, we die; let us put it to a trial, if we be saved, we shall live; if not, we shall but die. (2.) It is probable this course may succeed. God is good and merciful; he loves to surprise men with his grace, and is often found of them that sought him not, Isa. lxv. 1. If ye do thus, ye are so far in the road of your duty; and ye are using the means which the Lord is wont to bless, for men's spiritual recovery; ye lay yourselves in the way of the great Physician, and so it is probable ye may be healed. Lydia went, with others, to the place where prayer was wont to be made; and the Lord opened her heart, Acts xvi. 13, 14. Ye plow and sow, though nobody can tell you for certain, that ye will get so much as your seed again; ye use means for the recovery of your health, though ye are not sure they will succeed. In these cases, probability determines you; and why not in this also? Importunity, we see, does very much with men; therefore pray, meditate, desire help of God; be much at the throne of grace, supplicating for grace, and do not faint. Though God regard not you, who, in your present state, are but one mass of sin; universally depraved, and vitiated in all the powers of your soul: yet he may regard his own ordinance. Though he regards not your prayers, your meditations, &c. yet he may regard prayer, meditation, and the like means of his own appointment, and so bless them to you. Wherefore, if ye will not do what ye can; ye are not only dead, but you declare yourselves unworthy of eternal life.

To conclude, let the saints admire the freedom and power of grace, which came to them in their helpless condition, made their chains fall off, the iron gate to open to them, raised the fallen creatures, and brought them out of the state of sin and wrath, wherein they would have lain and perished, had they not been mercifully visited. Let the natural man be sensible of his utter inability to recover himself. Know thou art without strength; and canst not come to Christ, till thou be drawn. Thou art lost, and canst not help thyself. This may shake the foundation of thy hopes, who never sawest thy absolute need of Christ and his grace; but thinkest to shift for thyself, by thy civility, morality, drowsy wishes and duties; and by a faith and repentance, which have sprung up out of thy natural powers, without the power and efficacy of the grace of Christ. O be convinced of thy absolute need of Christ, and his overcoming grace; believe thy utter inability to recover thyself; and so thou mayst be humbled, shaken out of thy self-confidence, and lie down in dust and ashes, groaning out thy miserable case before the LORD. A kindly sense of thy natural impotency, the impotency of depraved human nature, would be a step towards a delivery.—— Thus far of man's natural state, the state of entire depravation.

STATE III.

NAMELY,

The State of Grace; or Begun Recovery.

HEAD I.

REGENERATION.

1 PET. i. 23.

Being born again, not of corruptible Seed, but of incorruptible, by the Word of God, which liveth and abideth for ever.

WE proceed now to the state of grace, the state of begun recovery of human nature, into which, all that shall partake of eternal happiness, are translated, sooner or later, while in this world. It is the result of a gracious change, made upon those who shall inherit eternal life; which change may be taken up in these two, (1.) In opposition to their natural real state, the state of corruption, there is a change made upon them in regeneration, whereby their nature is changed. (2.) In opposition to their natural relative state, the state of wrath, there is a change made upon them, in their union with the LORD JESUS CHRIST; by which they are set beyond the reach of condemnation. These therefore, namely, regeneration, and union with CHRIST, I design to handle, as the great and comprehensive changes on a sinner, constituting him in the state of grace.

The first of these we have in the text, together with the outward and ordinary means, by which it is brought about. The apostle here, to excite the saints to the study of holiness, and particularly of brotherly love, puts them in mind of their spiritual original. He tells them they were born again; and that of one incorruptible seed, the word of GOD. This speaks them to be brethren, partakers of the same new nature; which is the root from which holiness, and particularly brotherly love, doth spring. We are once both sinners; we must be born again, that we may be saints. The simple word signifies to be begotten; and so it may be read, Mat. xi. 11. *to be conceived*, Mat. i. 20. and *to be born*, Matth. ii. 1. Accordingly the compound word used in the text, may be taken in its full latitude, the last notion presupposing the two former, and so regeneration is a supernatural real change on the whole man, fitly compared to natural or corporal generation, as will afterwards appear. The ordinary means of regeneration, called the seed, whereof the new creature is formed, is not corruptible seed. Of such, indeed, our bodies are generated; but the spiritual seed, of which the new creature is generated, is incorruptible; namely, *the word of God, which liveth and abideth for ever.* The sound of the word of GOD passeth even as other sounds do; but the word lasteth, liveth and abideth, in respect of its everlasting effects, on all upon whom it operates. This word, which by the gospel is preached unto you, ver. 25. impregnated by the Spirit of GOD, is the means of regeneration; and by it are dead sinners raised to life.

DOCTRINE, *All men in the state of grace are born again.* All gracious persons, namely, such as are in a state of favour with GOD, and endued with gracious qualities and dispositions, are regenerate persons. In discoursing this subject, I shall shew what regeneration is; Next, Why is it so called, and then apply the doctrine.

Of the Nature of Regeneration.

I. For the better understanding of the nature of regeneration, take this along with you in the first place, That as there are false conceptions in nature, so there are also in grace; and by these, many are deluded, mistaking some partial changes made upon them, for this great and thorough change. To remove such mistakes, let these few things be considered, (1.) Many call the church their mother, whom GOD will not own to be his children, Cant. i. 6. *My mother's children* (i.e. false brethren) *were angry with me.* All that are baptized are not born again. Simeon was baptized, yet still in the gall of bitterness, and in the bond of iniquity, Acts viii. 13. 23. Where Christianity is the religion of the country, many will be called by the name of CHRIST, who have no more of him but the name; and no wonder, seeing the devil had his goats among CHRIST's sheep, in these places, where but few professed the Christian religion, 1 John ii. 19. *They went out from us, but they were not of us.* (2.) Good education is not regeneration. Education may chain up men's lusts, but cannot change their hearts. A wolf is still a ravenous beast, though it be in chains. Joash was very devout during the life of his good tutor Jehoiada; but afterwards he quickly shewed what spirit he was of, by his sudden apostacy, 2 Chron. xxiv. 2. 17, 18. Good example is of mighty influence to change the outward man; but that change often goes off, when one changes his company; of which the world affords many sad instances. (2.) A turning from open profanity, to civility and sobriety, falls short of this saving change. Some are, for a while, very loose, especially in their younger years; but at length they reform, and leave their profane courses. Here is a change, yet but such an one, as may be found in men, utterly void of the grace of GOD, and whose righteousness is so far from exceeding, that it doth not come up to the righteousness of the Scribes & Pharisees. (4.) One may engage in all the outward duties of religion and yet not be born again. Tho' lead be cast into various shapes, is remains still but a base metal. Men may escape the pollutions of the world, and yet be but dogs and swine, 2 Pet. ii. 20. 22. All the external acts of religion are within the compass of natural abilities. Yea, hypocrites may have the counterfeit of all the graces of the Spirit; for we read of true holiness, Eph. iv. 23. and faith unfeigned, 1 Tim. i. 5 which shews us, that there is a counterfeit holiness, and a feigned faith; (5.) Men may advance to a great deal of strictness in their own way of religion; and yet be strangers to the new birth, Acts xxvi. 5. *After the most strictest sect of our religion, I lived a Pharisee.* Nature has its own unsanctified strictness in religion. The Pharisees had so much of it, that they looked on CHRIST, as little better than a mere libertine. A man whose conscience hath been awakened, and who lives under the felt influence of the covenant of works, what will he not do, that is within the compass of natural abilities? It was a truth, tho' it came out of a hellish mouth, that *skin for skin, all that a man hath, will he give for his life,* Job ii. 4. (6.) One may have sharp soul-exercises and pangs, and yet die in the birth. Many have been in pain, that have but, as it were, brought forth wind. There may be sore pangs and throws of conscience, which turn to nothing at last. Pharaoh and Simon Magus had such convictions, as made them desire the prayers of others for them. Judas repented himself; and under terrors of conscience, gave back his ill-gotten pieces of silver. All is not gold that glisters. Trees may blossom fairly in the spring, on which no fruit is to be found in the harvest; and some have sharp soul-exercises, which are nothing but fore-tastes of hell.

The new birth, however in appearance hopefully begun, may be marred two ways. *First*, Some like Zarah, Gen. xxxviii. 28, 29. are brought to the birth, but go back again. They have sharp convictions for a while; but these go off, and they turn as careless about their salvation, as profane as ever: and usually worse than ever, their last state is worse than their first, Mat. xii. 45. They get awakening grace, but not converting grace; and that goes off by degrees, as the light of the declining day, till it issue in midnight darkness. *Secondly*, Some, like Ishmael, come forth too soon; they are born before the time of the promise, Gen. xvi. 1, 2. compare Gal. iv. 22. and downward. They take up with a mere law-work, and stay not till the time of the promise of the gospel. They snatch at consolation, not waiting till it be given them; and foolishly draw their comfort from the law that wounded them. They apply the healing plaister to themselves, before their wound be sufficiently searched. The law, that rigorous husband, severely beats them and throws in curses and vengeance upon their souls; then they fall a re-forming, praying, mourning, promising and vowing, till this ghost be laid; which done they fall asleep again in the arms of the law; but they are never shaken out of themselves and their own righteousness, nor brought forward to JESUS CHRIST. *Lastly*, There may be a wonderful moving of the affections, in souls that are not at all touched with regenerating grace. Where there is no grace, there may notwithstanding be a flood of tears, as in Esau, who found no place of repentance, though he sought it carefully with tears, Heb. xii. 17. There may be great flashes of joy; as in the hearers of the word represented in the parable by the stony ground, who anon with joy receive it, Matth. xiii. 20. There may be also great desire after good things, and great delight in them too; as in these hypocrites described, Isa. lviii. 2. *Yet they seek me daily, and delight to know my ways.—They take delight in approaching unto God.* See how high they may sometimes stand, who yet fall away, Heb. vi. 4, 5, 6. They may be enlightened, taste of the heavenly gift, be partakers of the holy Ghost, taste the good word of GOD, and the powers of the world to come. Common operations of the divine Spirit, like a land-flood, make a strange turning of things upside down. And when they are over, all runs again in the ordinary channel. All these things may be, where the sanctifying Spirit of CHRIST is never rests upon the soul, but the stony heart still remains; and in that case, these affections cannot but wither, because they have no root.

But regeneration is a real thorough change, whereby the man is made a new creature, 2 Cor. v. 17. The LORD GOD makes the creature a new creature, as the goldsmith melts down the vessel of dishonour, and makes it a vessel of honour. Man is, in respect of his natural state, altogether disjointed by the fall; every faculty of the soul is, as it were, dislocated: in regeneration the LORD looseth every joint, and sets it right again. Now this change made in regeneration is,

1. A change of qualities or dispositions: it is not a change of the substance, but of the qualities of the soul. Vicious qualities are removed, and the contrary dispositions are brought in their room. *The old man is put off*, Eph. iv. 22. *the new man put on*. ver. 24. Man lost none of the rational faculties of his soul by sin; he had an understanding still, but it was darkened; he had still a will, but it was contrary to the will of GOD. So in regeneration there is not a new substance created, but new qualities are infused; light instead of darkness, righteousness instead of unrighteousness.

2. It is a supernatural change; he that **is born again, is born of the Spirit**, John iii. 5. Great changes may be made by the power of nature, especially when assisted by external revelation. And nature may be so elevated by the common influences of the Spirit, that one may thereby be turned into another **man**, as Saul **was**, 1 Sam. x. 6. who yet never becomes a new **man**. But in regeneration nature itself is changed, and we become partakers of the divine nature; and this must needs be a supernatural change. How can we that are dead in trespasses and sins, renew ourselves, more than a dead man can raise himself out of his grave? Who but the sanctifying Spirit of CHRIST, can form CHRIST in a soul, changing it into the same image? Who, but the Spirit of sanctification can give the new heart? Well may we say, when we see a man thus changed, *This is the finger of God.*

3. It is a change into the likeness **of** GOD, 2 Cor. iii. 18. *We---beholding as in a glass the glory of the Lord, are changed into the same image.* Every thing that generates, generates its like; **the child bears** the image of the parent; and they that are **born of** GOD, **bear** GOD's image. Man aspiring to be as GOD, made himself like the devil. In his natural state he resembles the devil, as a child doth the father, John viii. 44. *Ye are of your father the devil.* But when this happy change comes, the image of Satan is defaced, and the image of GOD restored. CHRIST himself who is the brightness of his Father's glory, is the pattern after which the new creature is made, Rom. viii. 29. *For whom he did foreknow, he also did predestinate to be conformed to the image of his Son,*

Hence he is said to be conformed in the regenerate, Gal. iv. 19.

4. It is an universal change; all things become new, 2 Cor. vi. 17. It is a blest leaven, that leavens the whole lump, the whole spirit, and soul and body. Original sin infects the whole man; and regenerating grace, which is the salve, goes as far as the sore. This fruit of the Spirit is in all goodness; goodness of the mind, goodness of the will, goodness of the affections, goodness of the whole man. One gets not only a new head to know religion, or a new tongue to talk of it; but a new heart to love and embrace it, in the whole of his conversation. When the LORD opens the sluice of grace on the soul's new birth-day, the waters run through the whole man, to purify and make him fruitful. In these natural changes spoken of before, they are, as it were, pieces of new cloth put into an old garment; a new life sewed to an old heart; but the gracious change is a thorough change, a change both of heart and life.

5. Yet it is but an imperfect change. Though every part of the man is renewed, there is no part of him perfectly renewed. As an infant has all the parts of a man, but none of them are come to their perfect growth; so regeneration brings a perfection of parts, to be brought forward in the gradual advances of sanctification, 1 Pet. ii. 2. *As new-born babes, desire the sincere milk of the word, that ye may grow thereby.* Although in regeneration there is a heavenly light let into the mind, yet there is still some darkness there; though the will is renewed, it is not perfectly renewed, there is still some of the old inclination to sin remaining; and thus it will be, till that which is in part be done away, and the light of glory come. Adam was created at his full stature, but they that are born must have their time to grow up; so they that are born again, do come forth into the new world of grace but imperfectly holy: though Adam being created upright was at the same time perfectly righteous, without the least mixture of sinful imperfection.

Lastly, Nevertheless it is a lasting change, which never goes off. The seed is incorruptible, saith the text; and so is the creature that is formed of it. The life given in regeneration, whatever decays it may fall under, can never be utterly lost; His seed remaineth in him, who is born of GOD, 1 John iii. 9. Though the branches should be cut down, the root shall abide in the earth: and being watered with the dew of heaven, shall sprout again; for, *The root of the righteous shall not be moved,* Prov. xii. 3. But to come to particulars,

First, In regeneration the mind is favingly enlightened: There is a new light let into the understanding, so that they who were sometimes darkness, *are now light in the* LORD, Eph. v. 8. The beams of the light of life, make their way into the dark dungeon of the heart; then night is over, and the morning-light is come, which will shine more and more unto the perfect day. Now the man is illuminated.

1. In the knowledge of GOD. He has far other thoughts of GOD, than ever he had before, Hof. ii. 20. *I will even betrothe thee unto me in faithfulness, and thou shalt know the Lord.* The Spirit of the LORD brings him back to that question, What is GOD? And catechiseth him anew upon that grand point, so as he is made to say, *I have heard of thee by the hearing of the ear; but now mine eye seeth thee,* Job xlii. 5. The spotless purity of GOD, his exact justice, his all-sufficiency, and other glorious perfections revealed in his word, are, by this new light, discovered to the soul, with a plainness and certainty that doth as far exceed the knowledge it had of these things before, as occular demonstration exceeds common fame; For now he sees what he only heard of before.

2. He is enlightened in the knowledge of sin. He hath other thoughts of it, than he was wont to have. Formerly his sight could not pierce through the cover Satan laid over it; but now the Spirit of GOD strips it before him, wipes off the paint and fairding: and he sees it in its native colours, as the worst of evils; *exceeding sinful,* Rom. vii. 12. O what deformed monsters do formerly beloved lusts appear! Were they right eyes, he would pluck them out; were they right hands, he would consent to their cutting off. He sees how offensive sin is to GOD, how destructive it is to the soul; and calls himself fool, for fighting so long against the LORD, and harbouring that destroyer as a bosom-friend.

3. He is instructed in the knowledge of himself. Regenerating grace causeth the prodigal to come to himself, Luke xv. 17. and makes men full of eyes within, knowing every one the plague of his own heart. The mind being savingly enlightened, the man sees how desperately corrupt his nature is; what enmity against GOD and his holy law has long lodged there; so that his soul lothes itself. No open sepulchre, no puddle, so vile and loathsome in his eyes as himself, Ezek. xxxvi. 31. *Then shall ye remember your own evil ways, and your doings that were not good, and shall lothe yourselves in your own sight.* He is no worse than he was before; but the sun is shining: and so these pollutions are seen, which he could not discern, when there was no dawning in him; as the word is, Isa. viii. 20. while as yet the day of grace was not broken with him.

4. He is enlightened in the knowledge of **Jesus Christ**, 1 Cor. i. 23, 24. *But we preach Christ crucified,* **unto the Jews** *a stumbling block, and unto the Greeks foolishness; but unto them that are called, both Jews and Greeks, Christ, the power of God, and the wisdom of God.* The truth is, unregenerate men, though capable of discoursing of Christ, have not, properly speaking, the knowledge of him, but only an opinion, a good opinion of him; as one has of many controverted points of doctrine, wherein he is far from certainty. As when ye meet with a stranger upon the road, he behaving himself discreetly, we conceive a good opinion of him; and therefore willingly converse with him; but yet ye will not commit your money to him; because, though you have a good opinion of the man, he is a stranger to you, ye do not know him. So many they think well of Christ, but they will never commit themselves to him; seeing they know him not. But saving illumination carries the soul beyond opinion, to the certain knowledge of Christ and his excellency, 1 Thes. i. 5. *For our gospel came not unto you in word only, but also in power, and in the Holy Ghost, and in much assurance.* The light of grace thus discovers the suitableness of the mystery of Christ, to the divine perfections, and to the sinner's case. Hence the regenerate admire the glorious plan of salvation through Christ crucified, lay their whole weight upon it, and heartily acquiesce therein; for whatever he be to others, he is to them *Christ the power of God, and the wisdom of God.* But unrenewed men, not seeing this, are offended in him; they will not venture their souls in that bottom, but betake themselves to the broken boards of their own righteousness. The same light convincingly discovers a superlative worth, a transcendent glory and excellency in Christ; which darken all created excellencies, as the rising sun makes the stars to hide their heads; and so it engages the merchantman to sell all that he hath, to buy the one pearl of great price, Matth. xiii. 45, 46. makes the soul well **content to** take Christ for all, and instead of all. Even as an **unskil**ful merchant, to whom one offereth a pearl of great price, for all his petty wares, dares not venture on the bargain; for though he thinks, that one pearl may be more worth than all he has, yet he is not sure of it; but when a jeweller comes to him, and assures him that it is worth double all his wares; he then greedily embraceth the bargain, and chearfully parts with all that he has, for that pearl. *Finally,* This illumination in the knowledge of Christ, convincingly discovereth to man a fulness in him, sufficient for the supply of all his wants; enough to satisfy the boundless desires of an immortal soul. They are persuaded such fulness is in him, and that it

order to be communicated; they depend upon it, as a certain truth; and therefore their souls take up their eternal rest in him.

5. The man is instructed in the knowledge of the vanity of the world, Psal. cxix. 96. *I have seen an end of all perfection.* Regenerating grace elevates the soul, sets it, as it were, amongst the stars, from whence this earth cannot but appear a little, yea a very little thing! even as heaven appeared before, while the soul was immersed in the earth. Grace brings a man into a new world; while this world is reputed but a stage of vanity, an howling wilderness, a valley of tears. GOD hath hung the sign of vanity at the door of all created enjoyments; yet how do men throng into the house, calling and looking for somewhat that is satisfying; even after it has been a thousand times told them, there is no such thing in it, it is not to be got there: Isa. lvi. 10. *Thou art wearied in the greatness of thy ways; yet saidst thou not, There is no hope.* Why are men so foolish? The truth of the matter lies here, they do not see by the light of grace, they do not spiritually discern that sign of vanity. They have often indeed made a rational discovery of it; but can that truly wean the heart from the world? Nay, no more than painted fire can burn off the prisoner's bands. But the light of grace is the light of life, powerful and efficacious.

Lastly, To sum up all in one word, in regeneration the mind is enlightened in the knowledge of spiritual things, 1 John ii. 20. *Ye have an unction from the holy One,* that is, from JESUS CHRIST, Rev. iii. 18. It is an allusion to the sanctuary, whence the holy oil was brought to anoint the priests, *and ye knew all things,* viz. necessary to salvation. Tho' men be not book-learned, if they be born again, they are Spirit-learned; for all such are taught of GOD, John vi. 45. The Spirit of regeneration teacheth them what they knew not before; and what they did know, as by the ear only, he teacheth them over again, as by the eye. The light of grace is an overcoming light, determining men to assent to divine truths on the mere testimony of GOD. It is no easy thing for the mind of man, to acquiesce in divine revelation. Many pretend great respect to the scriptures; whom nevertheless, the clear scripture-testimony will not divorce from their preconceived opinions. But this illumination will make mens minds run, as captives, after CHRIST's chariot-wheels; which for their part, shall be allowed to drive over, and cast down their own imaginations, and every high thing that exalteth itself against the knowledge of GOD, 2 Cor. x. 5. It will make them receive the kingdom of GOD as a little child, Mark x. 15. who thinks he has sufficient ground to believe any thing, if his father do but say it is so.

Secondly, The will is renewed. The LORD takes away the stony heart, and gives a heart of flesh, Ezek. xxxvi. 26. And so, of stones raiseth up children to Abraham. Regenerating grace is powerful and efficacious, and gives the will a new set. It does not indeed force it; but sweetly, yet powerfully draws it, so that his people are willing in the day of his power, Psal. cx. 3. There is heavenly oratory in the Mediator's lips, to persuade sinners, Psal. xlv. 2. *Grace is poured into thy lips.* There are cords of a man, and bands of love, in his hands, to draw them after him, Hos. xi. 4. Love makes a net for elect souls, which will infallibly catch them, and hale them to land. The cords of CHRIST's love are strong cords: and they need to be so; for every sinner is heavier than a mountain of brass; and Satan, together with the heart itself, draw the contrary way. But love is strong as death; and the LORD's love to the soul he died for, is strongest love; which acts so powerfully, that it must come off victorious.

1. The will is cured of its utter inability to will what is good. While the opening of the prison to them that are bound, is proclaimed in the gospel, the Spirit of GOD comes to the prison-door, opens it, goes to the prisoner, and by the power of his grace makes his chains fall off; breaks the bond of iniquity, wherewith he was held in sin, so as he could neither will nor do, any thing truly good; brings him forth into a large place, *Working in him both to will and to do, of his good pleasure*, Phil. ii. 13. Then it is that the soul, that was fixed to the earth, can move heavenward; the withered hand is restored, and can be stretched out.

2. There is wrought in the will a fixed aversion to evil. In regeneration, a man gets a new spirit put within him, Ezek. xxxvi. 26. and that spirit lusteth against the flesh, Gal. v. 17. The sweet morsel of sin, so greedily swallowed down, he now lothes, and would fain be rid of it; even as willingly as one that had drunk a cup of poison, would throw it up again. When the spring is stopt, the mud lies in the well unmoved; but when once the spring is cleared, the waters springing up, will work the mud away by degrees. Even so, while a man continues in an unregenerate state, sin lies at ease in the heart; but as soon as the LORD strikes the rocky heart, with the rod of his strength in the day of conversion, grace is in him a well of water springing up into everlasting life, John iv. working away natural corruption, and gradually purifying the heart, Acts xv. 9. The renewed will riseth up against sin, strikes at the root thereof, and the branches too. Lusts are

now grevious, and the soul endeavours to starve them; the corrupt nature is the source of all evil, and therefore the soul will be often laying it before the great Physician. O what sorrow, shame and self-lothing fill the heart, in the day that grace makes its triumphant entrance into it? For now the mad-man is come to himself, and the remembrance of his follies cannot but cut him to the heart.

Lastly, The will is endued with an inclination, bent, and propensity to good. In its depraved state, it lay quite another way, being prone and bent to evil only: but now, by a pull of the omnipotent, all-conquering arm, it is drawn from evil to good, and gets another set. And as the former set was natural; so this is natural too, in respect of the new nature given in regeneration, which has its own holy lustings as well as the corrupt old nature hath its sinful lustings, Gal. v. 17. The will, as renewed, inclines and points towards GOD and godliness. When GOD made man, his will, in respect of its intention, was directed towards GOD, as his chief end; in respect of its choice, it pointed towards that which GOD willed. When man unmade himself, his will was framed into the very reverse hereof: he made himself his chief end, and his own will his law. But when man is new made, in regeneration, grace rectifies this disorder in some measure, tho' not perfectly indeed; because we are but renewed in part, while in this world. It brings back the sinner, out of himself, to GOD as his chief end, truly, though not perfectly, Psalm lxxiii. 25. *Whom have I in heaven but thee? and there is none upon earth, that I desire besides thee.* Phil. i. 21. *For me to live is Christ.* It makes him to deny himself, and whatever way he turns, to point habitually towards GOD, who is the center of the gracious soul, its home, its dwelling-place in all generations, Psal. xc. 1. By regenerating grace, the will is framed into conformity to the will of GOD. It is conformed to his preceptive will, being endued with holy inclinations; agreeable to every one of his commands. The whole law is impressed on the gracious soul; every part of it is written over on the renewed heart. And although remaining corruption makes such blots in the writing, that oft-times the man himself cannot read it; yet he that wrote it, can read it at all times; it is never quite blotted out, nor can be. What he has written, it shall stand; *For this is the covenant,—I will put my laws into their mind, and write them in their hearts,* Heb. viii. 10. And it is a covenant of fault, a perpetual covenant. It is also conformed to his providential will; so that the man will no more be master of his own process, nor carve out his lot for himself. He learns to say from his heart, *The will of the Lord be done,* he shall chuse our *inheritance for us*, Psalm xlvii. 4. Thus the will is disposed to fall in with those things, which, in its depraved state, it could never be reconciled to.

Particularly. (1.) The LORD is reconciled to the covenant of peace. The LORD GOD promiseth a covenant of peace to sinners; a covenant which he himself hath framed, and registrated in the Bible; but they are not pleased with it; nay an unrenewed heart cannot be pleased with it. Were it put into their hands, to frame it according to their mind, they would blot many things out of it, which GOD has put in; and put in many things GOD has kept out. But the renewed heart is entirely satisfied with the covenant, 2 Sam. xxiii. 5. *He hath made with me an everlasting covenant, ordered in all things and sure: this is all my salvation, and all my desire.* Though the covenant could not be brought down to their depraved will, their will is, by grace, brought up to the covenant; they are well pleased with it; there is nothing in it they would have out, nor is any thing left out of it, which they would have in. (2.) The will is disposed to receive CHRIST JESUS the LORD. The soul is content to submit to him. Regenerating grace undermines, and brings down the towering imaginations of the heart, raised up against its rightful LORD; it breaks the iron sinew, which kept the sinner from bowing to him, and disposed him to be no more stiff-necked but to yield to himself. He is willing to take on the yoke of CHRIST'S commands, to take up the cross and to follow him. He is content to take CHRIST on any terms, Ps. cx. 3. *Thy people shall be willing in the day of thy power.*

Now, the mind being savingly enlightened and the will renewed, the sinner is thereby determined and enabled to answer the gospel-call. So the main work in regeneration is done, the fort of the heart is taken; there is room made for the LORD JESUS CHRIST, in the innermost parts of the soul; the outer-door of the will being now opened to him, as well as the inner-door of the understanding. In one word, CHRIST is passively received into the heart; he is come into the soul by his quickening spirit, whereby spiritual life is given to the man, who in himself was dead to sin. And his first vital act we may conceive to be an active receiving of JESUS CHRIST, discerned in his glorious excellencies; that is, a believing on him, a closing with him, as discerned, offered, and exhibited in the word of his grace, the glorious gospel; the immediate effect of which is union with him, John i. 12, 13. *To as many as received him, to them gave he power, or privilege, to become the sons of God, even to them that believe on his Name, which were born not of blood, nor of the will of the flesh, nor of the will of man, but of* GOD. Eph iii. 17. *That Christ*

drawn, runs; and being effectually called, comes.

Thirdly, In regeneration, there is a happy **change** made on the affections; they are both rectified and regulated.

1. This change rectifies the affections, placing them on suitable objects, 2 Thess. iii. 5. *The Lord direct your **hearts** into the love of God.* The regenerate men's desires are rectified; they are set on GOD himself, and the things above. He who before cried with the word, *Who will shew us any good?* he changes his note, and says, *Lord lift up the light of thy countenance upon us,* Psal. iv. 6. Sometimes he saw no beauty in CHRIST, for which he was to be desired; but now he is all desires, he is altogether lovely. Cant. v. 16. The main stream of his desires is turned to run towards GOD; for there is the one thing he desireth, Psalm xxvii. 4. He desires to be holy, as well as to be happy; and rather to be gracious than great. His hopes which before were low, and staked down to things on earth, are now raised, and set on the glory which is to be revealed. He entertains the hope of eternal life, founded on the word of promise, Tit. i. 2. Which hope he has, as an anchor of the soul, fixing the heart under trials, Heb. vi. 18. And it puts him upon purifying himself, even as GOD is pure, John iii. 3. For he is begotten again into a lively hope, 1 Pet. i. 3. His love is raised and set on GOD himself, Psal. xxviii. 1. on his holy law, Psal. cxix. 97. Though it strike against his most beloved lust, he says, *The law is holy, and the commandment holy, and just, and good,* Rom. vii. 12. He loves the ordinances of GOD, Psal. lxxxiv. 1. *How amiable are tabernacles, O Lord of hosts?* Being passed from death unto life, he loves the brethren, 1 John iii. 14. the people of GOD, as they are called, 1 Pet. i. 10. He loves GOD for himself, and what is GOD's for his sake. Yea, as being a child of GOD, he loves his own enemies. His heavenly Father is compassionate and benevolent; he maketh the sun to rise on the evil and the good, and sendeth rain on the just, and on the unjust; and therefore he is in the like manner disposed, Mat. v. 44, 45. His hatred is turned against sin in himself and others, Psal. ci. 3. *I hate the work of them that turn aside, it shall not cleave to me.* He groans under the remains of it, and longs for deliverance, Rom. vii. 24. *O wretched man that I am! Who shall deliver me from the body of this death?* His joys and delights are in GOD the LORD, in the light of his countenance, in his law, and in his people;

because they are like him. **Sin** is what he chiefly fears; it is a fountain of sorrow to him **now**, though formerly a spring of pleasure.

9. It regulates the affections placed on suitable objects. Our affections when placed on the creature, are naturally exorbitant: when we joy in it, we are apt to over-joy; and when we sorrow, we are ready to sorrow over-much: but grace bridles these affections, clips their wings, and keeps them within bounds, that they overflow not at all their banks. It makes a man hate his father and mother, and wife and children, yea, and his own life also, comparatively; that is, to love them less than he loves GOD, Luke xiv. 26. It also sanctifies lawful affections; bringing them forth from right principles to right ends. There may be unholy desires after CHRIST and his grace; as when men desire CHRIST, not from any love to him, but merely out of love to themselves. Give us of your oil, said the foolish virgins, for our lamps are gone out, Mat. xxv. 8. There may be an unsanctified sorrow for sin, as when one sorroweth for it, not because it is displeasing to GOD, but only because the wrath annexed to it, as did Pharaoh, Judas, and others. So a man may love his father and mother, from mere natural principles, without any respect to the command of GOD binding him thereto. But grace sanctifies the affections in such cases, making them to run in a new channel of love to GOD, respect to his commands, and regard to his glory. Again, grace screws up the affections, where they are too low. It gives the chief seat in them to GOD; & pulls down all other rivals, whether persons or things, making them lie at his feet, Psal. lxxiii. 25. *Whom have I in heaven but thee? and there is none upon earth, that I desire besides thee.* He is loved for himself; and other persons or things, for his sake. What is lovely in them, to the renewed heart, is some ray of the divine goodness appearing in them; for unto gracious souls they shine only by borrowed light. This accounts for the saints loving all men, and yet hating those that hate GOD, and contemning the wicked as vile persons. They hate and contemn them for their wickedness; there is nothing of GOD in that, and therefore nothing lovely nor honourable in it; but they love them for their commendable qualities, or perfections, whether natural or moral; because, in whomsoever these are, they are from GOD, and can be traced to him as their fountain. Finally, regenerating grace sets the affections so firmly on GOD; that the man is disposed, at GOD's command, to quit his hold of every thing else, in order to keep his hold of CHRIST; to hate father and mother, in comparison with CHRIST, Luke xiv. 26. It makes even lawful enjoyments, like Joseph's

mantle, to hang loose about a man; that he may quit them when he is in hazard to be ensnared by holding them.

If the stream of our affections was never thus turned, we are doubtless going down the stream into the pit. If the lust of the eye, the lust of the flesh, and the pride of life, have the throne in our hearts, which should be possessed by the Father, Son, and Holy ghost; if we never had so much love to GOD, as to ourselves; if sin has been somewhat bitter to us, but never so bitter as suffering, never so bitter as the pain of being weaned from it; truly we are strangers to this saving change. For grace turns the affections up-side down, whenever it comes into the heart.

Fourthly, The conscience is renewed. Now, that a new light is set up in the soul in regeneration; conscience is enlightened, instructed, and informed. That candle of the LORD, Prov. xx. 27. is now snuffed and brightened; so as it shines, and sends forth its light into the most retired corners of the heart; discovering sins which the soul was not aware of before; and, in a special manner, discovering the corruption or depravity of nature, that seed and spawn whence all actual sins proceed. This produces the new complaint, Rom. vii. 24. *O wretched man that I am! who shall deliver me from the body of this death?* That conscience which lay sleeping in the man's bosom before, is now awakened, and makes its voice to be heard through the whole soul: and therefore there is no more rest for him in the sluggard's bed; he must get up and be doing, arise, haste and escape for his life. It powerfully incites to obedience, even in the most spiritual acts, which lay not within the view of the natural conscience; and powerfully restrains from sin, even from these sins which do not lie open to the observation of the world. It urgeth the sovereign authority of GOD, to which the heart is now reconciled, and which it willingly acknowledges: and so it engageth the man to his duty, whatever be the hazard from the world; for it fills the heart so with the fear of GOD, that the force of the fear of man is broken. This hath engaged many to put their life in their hand, and follow the cause of religion they once contemned, and resolutely walk in the path they formerly abhorred, Gal. i. 23. *He which persecuted us in times past, now preacheth the faith which once he destroyed.* Guilt now makes the conscience to smart. It hath bitter remorse for sins past, which fills the soul with anxiety, sorrow and self-lothing. And every new reflection on these sins, is apt to affect, and make its wounds bleed afresh with regret. It is made tender, in point of sin and duty, for the time to come; being once burnt, it dreads the fire, and fears to break the hedge, where it was formerly bit by the serpent.

Finally, The renewed conscience drives the sinner to JESUS CHRIST, as the only physician that can draw out the sting of guilt; and whose blood alone can purge the conscience from dead works, Heb. ix. 14. refusing all ease offered to it from any other hand. And this is an evidence, that the conscience is not only fired, as it may be in an unregenerate state; but oiled also with regenerating grace.

Fifthly, As the memory wanted not its share of depravity, it is also bettered by regenerating grace. The memory is weakened with respect to those things that are not worth their room therein; and men are taught to forget injuries, and drop their resentments, Matth. v. 44, 45. *Do good to them that hate you, and pray for them which despitefully use you.—That ye may be, i. e.* appear to be *the children of your Father which is in heaven*. It is strengthened for spiritual things. We have Solomon's receipt for an ill memory, Prov. iii. 1 *My son*, saith he *forget not my law*. But how shall it be kept in mind? *Let thine heart keep my commandments*. Grace makes a heart-memory, even where there is no good head memory, Psal. cxix. 11. *Thy word have I hid in mine heart*. The heart truly touched with the powerful sweetness of truth, will help the memory to retain what is so relished. Did divine truths make deeper impressions on our hearts, they would thereby impress themselves with more force on our memories, Psal. cxix. 93. *I will never forget thy precepts, for with them thou hast quickned me*. Grace sanctifies the memory. Many have large, but unsanctified memories, which serve only to gather knowledge, whereby to aggravate their condemnation; but a renewed memory serves to remember his commandments to do them, Psal. ciii. 18. It is a sacred store-house, from whence a Christian is furnished in his way to Zion; for faith and hope are often supplied out of it, in a dark hour. It is the store-house of former experiences; and these are the believer's way-marks, by noticing of which he comes to know where he is, even in a dark time, Psal. xlii. 6. *O my God, my soul is cast down within me; therefore will I remember thee from the land of Jordan*, &c. It also helps the soul to godly sorrow and self-loathing, presenting old guilt anew before the conscience; and making it bleed afresh, tho' the sin be already pardoned, Psal. xxv. 7. *Remember not the sins of my youth*. And where unpardoned guilt is lying on the sleeping conscience, it is often employed to bring in a word, which in a moment sets the whole soul afire: as when Peter remembered the words of JESUS, he went out and wept bitterly, Mat. xxvi. 75. The word of GOD laid up in a sanctified memory, enables a man to resist temptations, puts the sword in his hand his spiritual enemies, and is a light to direct his steps in the way of religion and righteousness.

Sixthly, There is a change made on the body, and the members thereof, in respect of their use; they are consecrated to the LORD. Even the body is for the LORD, 1 Cor. vi. 13. It is the temple of the holy Ghost, ver. 19. The members thereof, that were formerly instruments of unrighteousness unto sin, become instruments of righteousness unto GOD, Rom. vi. 13. *Servants to righteousness unto holiness,* ver. 19. the eye that conveyed sinful imaginations into the heart, is under a covenant, Job xxxi. to do so no more; but to serve the soul in viewing the works, and reading the word of GOD. The ear that had often been death's porter, to let in sin, is turned to be the gate of life, by which the word of life enters the soul. The tongue that set on fire the whole course of nature, is restored to the office it was designed for by the Creator; namely, to be an instrument of glorifying him, and setting forth his praise. In a word, the whole man is for GOD, in soul and body, which by this blessed change are made his.

Lastly, This gracious change shines forth in the conversation. Even the outward man is renewed. A new heart makes newness of life. When the King's daughter is all glorious within, her cloathing is of wrought gold, Psal. xlv. 13. The single eye makes the whole body full of light, Matth. vi. 22. This change will appear in every part of one's conversation, particularly in these following things.

1. In the change of his company. Tho' sometimes he despised the company of the saints, now they are the excellent, in whom is all his delight, Psal. xvi. 3. *I am a companion of all that fear thee,* saith the royal Psalmist, Psal. cxix. 63. A renewed man joins himself with the saints; for he and they are like-minded, in that which is their main work and business: they have all one new nature; they are travelling to Immanuel's land, and converse together in the language of Canaan. In vain do men pretend to religion, while ungodly company is their choice; for, *A companion of fools shall be destroyed,* Prov. xiii. 20. Religion will make a man shy of throwing himself into an ungodly family, or any unnecessary familiarity with wicked men; as one that is clean, will beware of going into an infected house.

wealth, and family. It is a just exception made against the religion of many, namely, that they are bad relatives, they are ill husbands, wives, masters, servants, &c. How will we prove ourselves to be new creatures, if we be still just such as we were before, in our several relations, 2 Cor. v. 17. *Therefore if any man be in Christ, he is a new creature: old things are passed away; behold all things are become new.* Real godliness will gain a testimony to a man, from the consciences of his nearest relations, tho' they know more of his sinful infirmities, than others do, as we see in that case, 2 Kings iv. 1. *Thy servant, my husband, is dead: and thou knowest that thy servant did fear the Lord.*

3. In the way of his following his wordly business, there is a great change. It appears to be no more his all, as sometimes it was. Tho' saints apply themselves to wordly business, as well as others; yet their hearts are not swallowed up in it. It is evident they are carrying on a trade with heaven, as well as a trade with earth, Philip. iii. 20. *For our conversation is in heaven.* And they go about their employment in the world as a duty laid upon them by the LORD of all; doing their lawful business, as the will of GOD, Eph. vi. 7. Working, because he has said *Thou shalt not steal.*

4. They have a special concern for the advancement of the kingdom of CHRIST in the world: they espouse the interests of religion, and prefer Jerusalem above their chief joy, Psal. cxxxvii. 6. How privately soever they live, grace makes them a public spirit, which will concern itself in the ark and work of GOD; in the gospel of GOD; and in the people of GOD; even those of them whom they never saw in the face. As children of GOD, they naturally care for these things. They have a new and unwonted concern for the spiritual good of others. And no sooner do they taste of the power of grace themselves, but they are inclined to set up to be agents for CHRIST and holiness in this world; as appears in the case of the woman of Samaria, who when CHRIST had manifested himself to her, went her way into the city, and saith unto the men, *Come see a man which told me all things that ever I did: Is not this the Christ?* John iv. 28, 29. They have seen and felt the evil of sin, and therefore pity the world lying in wickedness. They would fain pluck the brands out of the fire, remembering that they themselves were plucked out of it. They will labour to commend religion to others, both by word and example; and rather deny themselves their liberty in things indifferent, than by the uncharitable use of it, destroy others, 1 Cor. viii. 13. *Therefore if meat make my brother to offend, I will*

forth while the world standeth, lest I make my brother to offend.

5. In their use of lawful comforts, there is a great change. They rest not in them, as their end; but use them, as means to help them in their way. They draw their satisfaction from the higher springs, even while the lower springs are running. Thus Hannah having obtained a son, rejoiced not so much in the gift as in the giver, 1 Sam. ii. 1. *And Hannah prayed, and said, My heart rejoiceth in the Lord.* Yea, when the comforts of life are gone, they can subsist without them, & rejoice in the LORD altho' the fig-tree do not blossom, Hab. iii. 17, 18. Grace teacheth to use the conveniences of a present life passingly; and to shew a holy moderation in all things. The heart, which formerly immersed itself in these things without fear, is now shy of being over-much pleased with them; and being apprehensive of danger, uses them warily; as the dogs of Egypt run while they lap their water out of the river Nile, for fear of the crocodiles that are in it.

Lastly, This change shines forth in the man's performance of religious duties. He who lived in the neglect of them, will do so no more, if once the grace of GOD enter into his heart. If a man be new-born, he will desire the sincere milk of the word, 1 Pet. ii. 2. Whenever the prayerless person gets the Spirit of grace, he will be in him a Spirit of supplication, Zech. xii. 10. It is as natural for one that is born again to fall a-praying, as for the new born babe to fall a-crying, Acts ix. 11. *Behold, he prayeth.* His heart will be a temple for GOD, and his house a church. His devotion, which before was superficial and formal, is now spiritual and lively; forasmuch as heart and tongue are touched with a live-coal from heaven; and he rests not in the mere performing of duties, as careful only to get his task done: but in every duty seeking communion with GOD in CHRIST, justly considering them as means appointed of GOD for that end, and reckoning himself disappointed if he miss of it. Thus far of the **nature of** regeneration.

The Resemblance betwixt natural and spiritual Generation.

II. I come to shew why this change is called regeneration, a being born again. It is so called, because of the resemblance betwixt natural and spiritual generation, which lies in the following particulars.

First, Natural generation **is a** mysterious thing; and so is spiritual generation, John iii. 8. *The wind bloweth where it* *listeth, and thou hearest the sound thereof, but canst not tell whence it cometh, and whither it goeth; so is every one that is born of the Spirit.* The work of the spirit is felt, but his way of working is a mystery we cannot comprehend. A new light is let into the mind, and the will is renewed; but how that light is conveyed thither, how the will is fettered with cords of love, and how the rebel is made a willing captive, we can no more tell, than we can tell, how the bones do grow in the womb of her that is with child, Eccl. xi 5. As a man hears the sound of the wind, and finds it stirring, but knows not where it begins, & where it ends; so is every one that is born of the Spirit; he finds the change that is made upon him, but how it is produced he knoweth not. One thing he may know that whereas he was blind, **now** he seeth; but the seed of grace doth spring and grow **up,** he knoweth **not** how, Mark iv. 26, 27.

Secondly, In both, **the** creature **comes** to a being, it had not before. The child is not, till he be generate; and a man has no gracious being, no being in grace, till he be regenerate. Regeneration is not so much the curing of a sick man, **as** the quickning of a dead man, Eph. ii. 1. 5. Man in his depraved state, is a mere non-entity in **grace**; and is brought into a new being, by the power of him, **who** calleth things that be **not**, as though they were; being **created** in JESUS CHRIST unto good **works,** Eph. ii. 10. Therefore our LORD JESUS, to give ground of hope to the Laodiceans, in their wretched and miserable state, proposeth himself as the beginning of the creation of GOD, Rev. iii. 14. Namely, the active beginning of it; for all things were made by him at first, John i. 3. From whence they might gather, that seeing he made them when they were nothing, he could make them over again, when they were worse than nothing; the same hand that made them his creatures, could make them new creatures.

Thirdly, As the child is merely passive in generation, so is the child of GOD in regeneration. The one contributes nothing to its own generation; neither does the other contribute any thing, by way of efficiency, to its regeneration: for tho' a man may lay himself down at the pool yet he hath no hand in moving of the water, no efficacy in performing of the cure. One is born the child of a king, another the child of a beggar: the child has no hand at all in this difference. GOD leaves some in their depraved state; others he brings into a state of grace or regeneracy. If thou be thus honoured, no thanks to thee; for who maketh thee to differ from another? 1 Cor. iv. 7.

Fourthly, There is a wonderful contexture of parts in both births. Admirable is the structure of man's body, in which there is such a variety of organ's; nothing wanting, nothing superfluous. The psalmist considering his own body, looks on it as a piece of marvelous work; *I am fearfully and wonderfully made*, saith he, *and curiously wrought in the lower parts of the earth*, Psal. cxxxix. 14, 15. That is, in the womb, where I know not how the bones do grow, more than I know what is a-doing in the lower parts of the earth. In natural generation, we are curiously wrought, as a piece of needle-work, as the word imports: even so it is in regeneration, Psal. xlv. 14. *she shall be brought unto the King, in raiment of nee-dee-work*, raiment curiously wrought. It is the same word in both texts. And what that raiment is, the Apostle tells us, Eph. iv. 24. It is the new man, which after GOD, is created in righteousness and true holiness. This is the raiment, he saith in the same place, we must put on: not excluding the imputed righteousness of CHRIST. Both are curiously wrought, as master-pieces of the manifold wisdom of GOD. O the wonderful contexture of graces in the new creature! O glorious creature, new made after the image of GOD! It is grace for grace in CHRIST, which makes up the new man, John i. 16. Even as in bodily generation, the child has member for member in the parent; has every member the parent has, in a certain proportion.

Fifthly, All this in both cases hath its rise from that which is in itself very small and inconsiderable. O the power of GOD, in making such a creature of the corruptible seed! and much more in bringing forth the new creature from so small beginnings: it is as the little cloud like a man's hand which spread till heaven was black with clouds and wind, and there was a great rain, 1 Kings xiii. 44, 45. A man gets a word at a sermon, which hundreds desire him hear, and let slip; but it remains with him, works in him, and never leaves him, till the little word be turned upside-down by it; that is, till he become a new man. It is like the vapour that got up into Ahasuerus' head, and cut off sleep from his eyes, Esther vi. 1. which proved a spring of such motions, as never ceased, until Mordica, in royal pomp, was brought on horseback thro' the street, proud Haman trudging at his foot; the same Haman afterwards hanged, Mordica advanced, and the church delivered from Haman's hellish plot. The grain of mustard-seed becometh a tree, Mat. xiii. 21, 22. GOD loves to bring great things out of small beginnings.

Sixthly, Natural generation is carried on by degrees. Job x. 10. *Hast thou not poured me out as milk, and cruddled me like cheese?* So is regeneration. It is with the soul ordinarily, in regeneration, as with the blind man cured by our LORD, who first saw men as trees walking, afterwards saw every man clearly, Mat. viii. 23, 24, 25. It is true, regeneration being, strictly speaking, a passing from death to life, the soul is quickened in a moment; like as, when the embryo is brought to perfection in the womb, the soul is infused into the lifeless lump. Nevertheless, we may imagine somewhat like conception in spiritual generation, whereby the soul is prepared for quickning; and the new creature is capable of growth, 1 Pet. ii. 2. And of life more abundantly, John x. 10.

Seventhly, In both there are new relations. The regenerate may call GOD, Father; for they are his children, John i. 12, 13. begotten of him, 1 Pet. i. 3. The bride, the Lamb's wife, that is the church, is their mother, Gal. iv. 27. They are related, as brethren, as sisters, to angels and glorified saints, the family of heaven. They are of the heavenly flock; and the meanest of them, the base things of the world, 1 Cor. i. 28. the kinless things, as the word imports, who cannot boast of the blood that runs in their veins, are yet by their new birth, near of kin with the excellent in the earth.

Eighthly, There is a likeness betwixt the parent and the child. Every thing that generates, generates its like; and the regenerate are partakers of the divine nature, 2 Pet. i. 4. the moral perfections of the divine nature, are in measure and degree communicated to the renewed soul, and thus the divine image is retrieved; so that, as the child resembles the father, the new creature resembles GOD himself, being holy as he is holy.

Lastly, As there is no birth without pain, both to the mother and to the child; so there is great pain in bringing forth the new creature. The children have more or less of these birth-pains, whereby they are pricked in their heart, Acts ii. 37. The soul has sore pains when under conviction and humiliation: *A wounded spirit who can bear?* The mother is pained, Zion travails, Isa. lxvi. 8. she sighs, groans, crieth and hath hard labour, in her ministers and members, to bring forth children to her LORD, Gal. iv. 19. *My little children, of whom I travail in birth again, until Christ be formed in you.* And never was a mother more feelingly touched with joy, than a man-child was born into the world, than she is upon the new birth of her children. But what is more remarkable than all this, we read not only of our LORD JESUS CHRIST's travail or toil of soul, Isa. liii. 11. but what lies more directly to our purpose of his pains, or pangs, as of one travailing in child-birth; so the word used, Acts ii. 24.

properly signifies. Well may he call the new creature, as Rachel called her dear-bought son Benoni, *i. e.* The son of my sorrow; and as she called another, Naphtali, *i. e.* my wrestling; for the pangs of that travail put him to strong crying and tears, Heb. v. 7. yea, in an agony and bloody sweat, Luke xxii. 44. And, in the end, he died of these pangs; they became to him the pains of death, Acts ii. 24.

The doctrine of Regeneration applied.

Use I. By what is said, you may try whether you are in the state of grace or not. If ye be brought out of the state of wrath or ruin, into the state of grace or salvation; ye are new creatures, ye are born again. But ye will say, How shall we know whether we be born again or not?

Ans. Did you ask me, if the sun were risen, and how you should know, whether it were risen or not? I would bid you look up to the heavens, and see it with your eyes. And would you know if the light be risen in your heart? Look in, and see. Grace is light, and discovers itself: Look into thy mind, see if it has been illuminated in the knowledge of GOD. Hast thou been inwardly taught what GOD is? Were thine eyes ever turned inward to see thyself; the sinfulness of thy depraved state; the corruption of thy nature; the sins of thy heart and life? Wast thou ever let into a view of the exceeding sinfulness of sin? Have thine eyes seen King JESUS in his beauty; the manifold wisdom of GOD in him, his transcendent excellency, and absolute fulness and sufficiency, with the vanity and emptiness of all things else? Next, What change is there on thy will? Are the fetters taken off, wherewith it was sometimes bound up from moving heavenwards? And has thy will got a new set? Dost thou find an aversion to sin, and a proneness to good wrought in thy heart? Is thy soul turned towards GOD, as thy chief end? Is thy will new moulded into some measure of conformity to the preceptive and providential will of GOD? Art thou heartily reconciled to the covenant of peace, and fixedly disposed to the receiving of CHRIST, as he is offered in the gospel? And as to a change on your affections, are they rectified & placed on right objects? Are your desires going on after GOD? Are they to his name and remembrance of him? Isa. xxvi. 8. Are your hopes in him? Is your love set upon him, and your hatred set against sin? Does your offending a good GOD, affect your heart with sorrow, and do you fear sin more than suffering? Are your affections regulated? Are they, with respect to created comforts brought down as being too high; and with respect to GOD in CHRIST, screwed up, as being too low? Has he the chief seat in your heart? And are all your lawful worldly comforts, and enjoyments laid at his feet? Has thy conscience been enlightened and awakened, refusing all ease, but from the application of the blood of a Redeemer? Is thy memory sanctified, thy body consecrated to the service of GOD? And art thou now walking in newness of life? Thus ye may discover, whether ye are born again or not.

But, for your further help in this matter, I will discourse a little of another sign of regeneration, namely, The love of the brethren; an evidence whereby the weakest and most timorous saints have often had comfort, when they could have little or no consolation from other marks proposed to them. This the Apostle lays down, 1 John iii. 14. *We know* **that we** *have passed from death unto life, because we love the brethren.* It is not to be thought, that the Apostle by the brethren in this place, means brethren by a common relation to the first Adam, but to the second Adam, CHRIST JESUS; because, however true it is, that universal benevolence, a good-will to the whole race of mankind, takes place in the renewed soul, as being a lively lineament of the divine image; yet the whole context speaks of those that are the sons of GOD, ver. 1, 2. children of GOD, ver. 10. born of GOD, ve. 9. distinguishing betwixt the children of GOD, and the children of the devil, ver. 10. betwixt these that are of the devil, ver. 8. 12. and these that are of GOD, ver. 10. And the text itself comes in as a reason why we should not marvel that the world hates the brethren, the children of GOD, ver. 13. How can we marvel at it, seeing the love of the brethren is an evidence of one's having passed from death to life? And therefore it were absurd to look for that love amongst the men of the world, who are dead in trespasses and sins. They cannot love the brethren; no marvel then that they hate them. Wherefore it is plain, that by brethren here, are meant brethren by regeneration.

Now, in order to set this mark of regeneration in a true light, consider these three things: (1.) This love to the brethren, is a love to them as such. Then do we love them in the sense of the text, when the grace or image of GOD in them, is the chief motive of our love to them. When we love the godly for their godliness, the saints for their sanctity or holiness; then we love GOD in them, & so may conclude, we are born of GOD: for, *Every one that loveth him that begat, loveth him also that is begotten of him,* 1 John v. 1. Hypocrites may love saints, on account of a civil relation to them; because of their obliging conversation; for their being of the same opinion with themselves in religious matters; and on many other such like accounts, whereby wicked men may be induced to love the godly. But happy they, who can love them for naked grace in them; for their heaven-born temper and disposition; who can pick this pearl out of a dung-hill of infirmities in and about them; lay hold on it, and love them for it. (2.) It is a love that will be given to all, in whom the grace of GOD appears. They that love one saint, because he is a saint, will have love to all the saints, Eph. i. 15. They will love all who, to their discerning, bear the image of GOD. They that cannot love a gracious person in rags, but confine their love to those of them who wear gay cloathing, have not this love to the brethren in them. Those who can confine their love to a party, to whom GOD has not confined his grace, are souls too narrow to be put among the children. In what points soever men differ from us, in their judgment or way, yet if they appear to agree with us, in love to GOD, and our SAVIOUR JESUS CHRIST, and in bearing his image; we will love them as brethren, if we ourselves be of the heavenly family. And (3.) If this love be in us, the more grace any person appears to be possessed of, he will be the more beloved by us. The more vehemently the holy fire of grace doth flame in any, the hearts of true Christians will be the more warmed in love to them. It is not with the saints as with many other men, who make themselves the standard for others; and love them so far as they think they are like themselves. But, if they seem to out-shine, and darken them, their love is turned to hatred and envy; and they endeavour to detract from the due praise of their exemplary piety; because nothing relisheth with them in the practice of religion, that goes beyond their own measure. What of the life and power of religion appears in others, serves only to raise the serpentine grudge in their Pharisaical hearts.— But, as for them that are born again, their love and affection to the brethren, bears proportion to the degrees of the divine image they discern in them.

Now, if ye would improve these things to the knowledge of your state, I would advise you, (1.) To set apart some time, when ye are at home, for a review of your case, and try your state, by what has been said. Many have comfort and clearness as to their state, at a sermon, who in a little time lose it again; because, while they hear the word preached, they make application of it; but do not consider of these things more deliberately and leisurely, when alone. The action is too sudden and short, to give lasting comfort. And it is often so indeliberate, that it has bad consequences.— Therefore, set about this work at home, after earnest and serious prayer to GOD, for his help in it. Complain not of your want of time, while the night follows the busy day; or of place, while the fields and out-houses are to be got. (2.) Renew your repentance before the LORD. Guilt lying on the conscience, unrepented of, may darken all your evidences and marks of grace. It provokes the Spirit of grace to depart; and when he goes, our light ceases. It is not fit time for a saint to read his evidences, when the candle is blown out by some conscience-wounding guilt.

Lastly, Exert the powers of the new nature; let the graces of the divine Spirit in you, discover themselves by action. If ye would know whether there is a sacred fire in your breast, or not, ye must blow the coal; for although it be, and be a live-coal, yet if it be under the ashes, it will give you no light. Settle in your hearts a firm purpose, through the grace that is in CHRIST JESUS, to comply with every known duty, and watch against every known sin; having a readiness of mind to be instructed in what ye know not. If gracious souls would thus manage their inquiries into their state, it is likely they would have a comfortable issue. And if others would take such a solemn review, and make trial of their state impartially, fitting themselves before the tribunal of their own consciences, they might have a timely discovery of their own naughtiness. But the neglect of self-examination leaves most men under sad delusions, as to their state; and deprives many saints of the comfortable sight of the grace of GOD in them.

But that I may afford some further help to true Christians, in their inquiries into their state, I shall propose and briefly answer some cases or doubts, which may possibly hinder some persons from the comfortable view of their happy state. The children's bread must not be with-held, tho' while it is reached to them, the dogs should snatch at it.

Case 1. I doubt if I be regenerate, because I know not the precise time of my conversion; nor can I trace the particular steps, in the way in which it was brought to pass. *Ans.* Though it is very desirable, to be able to give an account of the beginning, and the gradual advances of the LORD's work upon our souls, as some saints can distinctly do; however, the manner of the Spirit's working is still a mystery; yet this is not necessary to evidence the truth of grace. Happy he that can say, in this case, as the blind man in the gospel, *One thing I know, that whereas I was blind, now I see.* Like as when we see flames, we know there is fire, though we know not how or when it began; so the truth of grace in us may be discerned, though we know not how, or when, it was wrought into our hearts. If thou canst perceive the happy change, which is wrought on thy soul; if thou findest thy mind is enlightened, duly inclined to comply with the will of GOD in all things, especially to fall in with the divine plan of salvation through a crucified Redeemer; in vain dost thou trouble thyself, and refuse comfort, because thou knowest not, how and what way it was brought about.

Case 2. If I were a new creature, sin could not prevail against me as it doth. *Ans.* Though we must not lay pillows, for hypocrites to rest their heads upon, who indulge themselves in their sins, and make the doctrine of GOD's grace subservient to their lusts, lying down contentedly in the bond of iniquity, like men that are fond of golden chains; yet it must be owned, the just man falleth seven times a-day, and iniquity may prevail against the children of GOD. But, if thou art groaning under the weight of the body of death, the corruption of thy nature; loathing thyself for the sins of thy heart and life; striving to mortify thy lusts; fleeing daily to the blood of CHRIST for pardon; and looking to his Spirit for sanctification; though thou mayst be obliged to say with the Psalmist, *Iniquities prevail against me:* Yet thou mayst add with him, *As for our transgressions thou shalt purge them away,* Pf. lxv. 3. The new creature doth not yet possess the house alone; it dwells beside an ill neighbour; namely, remaining corruption, the relicts of depraved nature. These struggle together for the mastery: *The flesh lusteth against the Spirit, and the Spirit against the flesh,* Gal. v. 1. And sometimes corruption prevails, bringing the child of GOD into captivity to the law of sin, Rom. vii. 23. Let not therefore the prevailing of corruption, make thee in this case conclude, thou art none of GOD's children; but let it humble thee to be the more watchful, and to thirst the more intensely after JESUS CHRIST, his blood and Spirit; and that very disposition will evidence a principle of grace in thee, which seeks the destruction of sin, that prevails so often against thee.

Case 3. I find the motions of sin in my heart, more violent, since the LORD began his work in my soul, than they were before that time. Can this consist with a change of my nature? *Ans.* Dreadful is the case of many, who, after GOD has had a remarkable dealing with their souls, tending to their reformation, have thrown off all bonds, and have become grosly and openly immoral and profane; as if the devil had returned into their hearts, with seven spirits worse than himself.— All I shall say to such persons is, that their state is exceeding dangerous; they are in danger of sinning against the Holy Ghost. Therefore let them repent, before it be too late.— But if it be not thus with you; though corruption is stirring itself more violently than formerly, as if all the forces of hell were raised, to hold fast, or give back a fugitive; I say, these stirrings may consist with a change of your nature. When the restraint of grace is newly laid upon corruption, it is no wonder if this last acts more vigorously than before, warring against the law of the mind, Rom. vii. 23. The motions of sin may really be most violent, when a new principle is bro't in to cast it out. And, as the sun, sending its beams through the window, discovers the motes in the house, and their motions, which were not seen before; so the light of grace may discover the rising and actings of corruption, in another manner than ever the man saw them before; though they really do not rise nor act more vigorously. Sin is not quite dead in the regenerate soul, it is but dying; and, dying a lingering death, being crucified, no wonder there be great fightings, when it is sick at the heart, and death is at the door. Besides, temptations may be more in number, and stronger, while Satan is striving to bring you back who are escaped, than while he endeavored only to retain you: *After ye were illuminated, ye endured a great fight of afflictions*, says the Apostle to the Hebrews, chap. x. 32. But cast not away your confidence. Remember his grace is sufficient for you; and the GOD of peace will bruise Satan under your feet shortly. Pharaoh and his Egyptians never made such a formidable appearance against the Israelites, as at the Red-sea, after they were brought out of Egypt; but then were the pursuers nearest to a total overthrow, Exod. xiv. Let not this case therefore make you raze your foundations, but be ye emptied of yourselves, and strong in the LORD, and in the power of his might; and ye shall come off victorious.

Case 4 But when I compare my love to GOD, with my love to some created enjoyments, I find the pulse of my affections, beat stronger to the creature than the Creator. How then can I call him father? Nay, alas! these turnings of heart within me, and glowings of affection to him, I sometimes had, are gone; so that I fear, all the love I ever had to the LORD, has been but a fit and flash of affection, such as hypocrites often have. *Ans.* It cannot be denied, that the predominant love of the world, is a certain mark of an unregenerate state, 1 John ii. 15. *If a man love the world, the love of the Father is not in him.* Nevertheless, these are not always the strongest affections, which are most violent. A man's affection may be more moved on some occasions by an object that is little regarded, than by another, that is exceedingly beloved; even as a little brook sometimes makes a greater noise than a great river. The strength of our affections is to be measured by the firmness and fixedness of the root; not by the violence of their actings. Suppose a person meeting with a friend who has been long abroad, finds his affection more vehemently acting towards his friend on that occasion, than towards his own wife and children; will he therefore say, that he loves his friend more than them? Surely no. Even so, although the Christian may find himself more moved in his love to the creature, than in his love to GOD, yet he is not therefore to be said to love the creature more than GOD; seeing love to GOD is always more firmly rooted in a gracious heart, than love to any created enjoyment whatsoever; as appears when competition arises in such a manner, that the one or the other is to be forgone. Would you then know your case? Retire into your own hearts, and there lay the two in the balance, and try which of them weighs down the other. Ask thyself, as in the sight of GOD, whether thou wouldst part with CHRIST for the creature, or part with the creature for CHRIST, if thou wert left to thy choice in the matter? If you find your heart disposed to part with what is dearest to you in the world for CHRIST, at his call, you have no reason to conclude, you love the creature more than GOD; but on the contrary, that you love GOD more than the creature; albeit you do not feel such violent motions in the love of GOD, as in the love of some created thing, Matth. x. 37. *He that loveth father or mother more than me, is not worthy of me.* Luke xiv. 26. *If any man come to me, and hate not his father and mother,—he cannot be my disciple.* From which texts compared, we may infer, that he who hates, *i. e.* is ready to part with father and mother for CHRIST, is, in our LORD's account, one that loves them less than him; and not one who loves father and mother more than him. Moreover ye are to consider, there is a twofold love to CHRIST. (1.) There is a sensible love to him, which is felt as a dart in the heart; and makes a holy love-sickness in the soul, arising either from want of enjoyment, as in the case of the spouse, Cant. v 8. *I charge you, O daughters of Jerusalem, if ye find my beloved, that ye tell him, that I am sick of love:* or else from the fulness of it, as in that case, Cant. ii. 5. *Stay me with flagons, comfort me with apples; for I am sick of love.* These glowings of affections, are usually wrought in young converts, who are ordinarily made to sing in the days of their youth, Hos. ii. 14. While the fire-edge is on the young convert, he looks on others reputed to be godly, and not finding them in such a temper and disposition as himself, he is ready to censure them; and think there is far less religion in the world, than indeed there is. But when his own cup comes to settle below the brim, and he finds that in himself, which made him question the state of others, he is more humbled, and feels more and more the necessity of daily recourse to the blood of CHRIST for pardon, and to the Spirit of CHRIST for sanctification; and thus grows downwards, in humiliation, self-loathing, and self-denial. (2.) There is a rational love to CHRIST, which, without these sensible emotions felt in the former case, evidences itself by a dutiful regard to the divine authority and command. When one bears such a love to CHRIST, though the vehement stirrings of affection be wanting, yet he is truly tender of offending a gracious GOD; endeavours to walk before him unto all pleasing; and grieved at the heart, for what is displeasing unto him, 1 John v. 3. *For this is the love of God, that we keep his commandments.* Now, although that sensible love doth not always continue with you, ye have no reason to account in a hypocritical fit, while the rational love remains with you, more than a faithful and loving wife needs question her love to her husband, when her fondness is abated.

Case 5. The attainments of hypocrites and apostates are a terror to me; and come like a shaking storm on me, when I am about to conclude from the marks of grace which I seem to find in myself, that I am in the state of grace. *Ans.* These things should indeed stir us up to a most serious and impartial examination of ourselves: but ought not to keep us in a continued suspense as to our state. Sirs, ye see the out-side of hypocrites, their duties, their gifts, their tears, &c. but ye see not their in-side: ye do not discern their hearts, the bias of their spirits. Upon what ye see of them, ye found a judgment of charity, as to their state: and ye do well to judge charitably in such a case, because ye cannot know the secret springs of their actings: But ye are speaking, and ought to have a judgment of certainty, as to your own state; and therefore are to look in to that part of religion, which none in the world but yourselves can discern in you; and which ye can as little see in others. An hypocrite's religion may appear far greater than that of a sincere soul; but that which makes the greatest figure in the eyes of men, is often least worth before GOD. I would rather utter one of those groans the Apostle speaks of, Rom. viii. 26. Than shed Esau's tears, have Balaam's prophetic spirit, or the joy of the stony ground hearers. The fire that shall try every man's work will try, not of what bulk it is, but of what sort it is Cor. iii. 13. Now, ye may know what bulk of religion another has; & what tho' it be more bulky than your own? GOD doth not regard that; Why then do you make such a matter of it? It is impossible for you, without divine revelation, certainly to know of what sort another man's religion is; but ye may certainly know what sort your own is of, without extraordinary revelation; otherwise the Apostle would not exhort the saints to give diligence to make their calling and election sure, 2 Pet. i. 10. Therefore the attainments of hypocrites and apostates, should not disturb you in your sense enquiry into your own state. But I'll tell you two things, wherein the meanest saints go beyond the most refined hypocrites. (1.) In denying themselves, renouncing all confidence in themselves, and their own works, acquiescing in, being well-pleased with, and venturing their souls upon God's plan of salvation thro' Jesus Christ, Mat. v. 3. *Blessed are the poor in spirit, for theirs is the kingdom of heaven.* And chap. ix. 6. *Blessed is he whosoever shall not be offended in me.* Phil. iii. 3. *We are the circumcision which worship God in the spirit, and rejoice in Christ Jesus, and have no confidence in the flesh.* (2.) In a real hatred of sin; being willing to part with every lust, without exception, and comply with every duty the Lord makes, or shall make known to them, Psal. cxix. 6. *Then shall I not be ashamed, when I have respect unto all thy commandments.* Try yourselves by these.

Case 6. I see myself fall so far short of the saints mentioned in the scriptures, and of several excellent persons of my own acquaintance; that, when I look on them, I hardly look on myself as one of the same family with them. *Ans.* It is indeed matter of humiliation, that we get not forward to that measure of grace and holiness, which we see is attainable in this life. This should make us more vigorously press towards the mark; but surely it is from the devil, that weak Christians make a rack for themselves of the attainments of the strong. And to yield to this temptation, is as unreasonable, as for a child to dispute away his relation to his father, because he is not of the same stature with his elder brethren. There are saints of several sizes in Christ's family; some fathers, some young men, and some little children, 1 John ii. 13, 14.

Case 7. I never read in the word of God, nor did I ever know of a child of God so tempted, and so left of God as I am and therefore no saint's case being like mine, I cannot but conclude I am none of their number. *Ans.* This objection arises to some, from their unacquaintedness with the scriptures and with experienced Christians. It is profitable in this case, to impart the matter to some experienced Christian friend; or to some godly minister. This has been a blessed mean of peace to some persons; while their case, which appeared to be singular, has been evinced to have been the case of other saints. The scriptures give instances of very horrid temptations, wherewith the saints have been assaulted. Job was tempted to blaspheme; this was the great thing the devil aimed at in the case of that saint, Job i. 11. *He will curse thee to thy face.* Chap. ii. 9. *Curse God and die.* Asaph was tempted to think it was in vain to be religious, which was in effect to throw off all religion, Psal. lxxiii. 13. *Verily I have cleans-*

ed my heart in vain. Yea, CHRIST himself was tempted to cast himself down from a pinnacle of the temple, and to worship the devil, Mat. iv. 6, 9. And many of the children of GOD have not only been attacked with, but have actually yielded to very gross temptations for a time. Peter denied CHRIST, and cursed and swore that he knew him not, Mark xiv. 7. Paul, when a persecutor, compelled even the saints to blaspheme, Acts xxvi. 10, 11. Many of the saints can, from their sad experience, bear witness to very gross temptations, which have astonished their spirits, made their very flesh to tremble, and sickened their bodies. Satan's fiery darts make terrible work, and will cost pains to quench them, by a vigorous managing of the shield of faith, Eph. vi. 16. Sometimes, he makes such desperate attacks, that never was one more put to it, in running to and fro without intermission, to quench the fire-balls incessantly thrown into his house, by an enemy designing to burn the house about him; than the poor tempted saint is, to repel satanical injections. But these injections, these horrid temptations, though they are a dreadful affliction, they are not the sins of the tempted unless they make them theirs by consenting to them. They will be charged upon the tempter alone, if they be not consented to; and will no more be laid to the charge of the tempted party, than a bastard's being laid down at the chaste man's door, will fix guilt upon him.

But, suppose neither minister nor private Christian, to whom you go, can tell you of any who has been in your case, yet you ought not thence to infer, that your case certainly is singular, far less to give over hopes; for it is not to be thought, that every godly minister, or private christian, has had the experience of all the cases a child of GOD may be in. And we need not doubt, but some have had distresses known only to GOD, and their own consciences; and so, to others these distresses are as if they had never been. Yea, and tho' the scriptures do contain suitable directions for every case a child of GOD can be in; and these illustrated with a sufficient number of examples; yet it is not to be imagined, there are in the scriptures, perfect instances of every particular case incident to the saints. Therefore, howbeit you cannot find an instance of your case in the scriptures; yet bring your case to it, and you shall find suitable remedies prescribed there for it. And study rather to make use of CHRIST for your case, who has salve for all sores; than to know if ever any was in your case. Though one should shew you an instance of your case, in an undoubted saint; yet none could promise it would certainly give you ease: for a scrupulous conscience would readily find out some difference. And if nothing but a perfect conformity of another's case to yours, will satisfy, it will be hard, if not impossible to satisfy you. For it is with peoples cases, as with their natural faces; tho' the faces of all men are of one make, and some are so very like others, that at first view we are ready to take them for the same; yet if you view them more accurately, you will see something in every face, distinguishing it from all others, though possibly you cannot tell what it is: Wherefore I conclude, that if you can find in yourselves the marks of regeneration, proposed to you from the word; you ought to conclude, you are in the state of grace, though your case were singular, which is indeed unlikely.

Case last, The afflictions I meet with are strange and unusual. I doubt if ever a child of GOD, was trysted with such dispensations of providence as I am. *Ans.* Much of what was said on the preceeding case, may be helpful in this. Holy Job was assaulted with this temptation, Job v. 1. *To which of the saints wilt thou turn?* But he rejected it, and held fast his integrity. The Apostle supposeth Christians may be tempted to think strange concerning the fiery trial, 1 Pet. iv. 12. But they have need of larger experience than Solomon's who will venture to say, *See! this is new*, Eccl. i. 10. And what though, in respect of the outward dispensations of providence, it happen to you according to the work of the wicked? You may be just notwithstanding, according to Solomon's observe, Eccles. viii. 14. Sometimes we travel in ways, where we cannot perceive the prints of the foot of man or beast; yet we cannot from thence conclude, that there was never any there before us; so albeit thou canst not perceive the footsteps of the flock in the way of thine affliction, thou must not therefore conclude, thou art the first that ever travelled that road. But what if it were so, that thou wert indeed the first? Some saint or other behoved to be the first, in drinking of each bitter cup the rest have drunk of. What warrant have you or I, to limit the holy One of Israel to a trodden path, in his dispensations towards us? *Thy way is in the sea, and thy path in the great waters; and thy footsteps are not known*, Psal. lxxvii. 19. If the LORD should carry you to heaven, by some retired road, and let you in at a back-door, so to speak; you would have no ground to complain. Learn to allow sovereignty a latitude; be at your duty; and let no afflictions cast a vail over any evidences you otherwise have for your being in the state of grace; for, *No man knoweth either their love or hatred, by all that is before them*, Eccl. ix 1.

Use II. Ye that are strangers to this new birth, be convinced of the absolute necessity of it. Are all in the state of grace born again? Then ye have neither part nor lot in it, who are not born again. I must tell you in the words of our LORD and Saviour, and O that he would speak them to your hearts, Ye must be born again, John iii. 7. And for your conviction, consider these few things.

First, Regeneration is absolutely necessary to qualify you to do any thing really good and acceptable to GOD. While you are not born again, your best works are but glistering sins; for though the matter of them is good, they are quite marred in the making. Consider, (1.) That without regeneration there is no faith; and, *Without faith, it is impossible to please God*, Heb. xi. 6. Faith is a vital act of the new-born soul. The Evangelist, shewing the different entertainment our LORD JESUS had from different persons, some receiving him, some rejecting him, points at regenerating grace, as the true rise of that difference, without which never one would have received him. He tells us that as many as received him, were these which were born of GOD, John i. 11, 12, 13. Unregenerate men may presume, but true faith they cannot have. Faith is a flower that grows not in the field of nature. As the tree cannot grow without a root, neither can a man believe, without the new nature, whereof the principle of believing is a part. (2) Without regeneration, a man's works are dead works. As is the principle, so must the effects be: if the lungs be rotten, the breath will be unsavoury; and he who, at best, is dead in sin, his works, at best, will be but dead works. *Unto them that are defiled and unbelieving, is nothing pure----being abominable and disobedient; and unto every good work, reprobate*, Tit. i. 15, 16. Could we say of a man, that he is more blameless in his life, than any other in the world; that he macerates his body with fasting; and has made his knees as horns with continual praying; but he is not born again: that exception would mar all. As if one should say, There is a well proportioned body, but the soul is gone; it is but a dead lump. This is a melting consideration. Thou dost many things materially good, but GOD saith, All these things avail not, as long as I see the old nature reigning in the man, Gal. vi. 15. *For, in Jesus Christ, neither circumcision availeth any thing, nor uncircumcision, but a* **new** *creature*.

If thou art not born again, (1.) All thy reformation is naught in the sight of GOD. Thou hast shut the door, but the thief is still in the house. It may be thou art not what once thou wast, yet thou art not what thou must be, if ever thou seest heaven; for, *Except a man be born again, he cannot see the kingdom of God*, John iii. 3. (2.) Thy prayers are an abomination to the LORD, Prov. xv. 8. It may be, others admire thy seriousness; thou criest as for thy life: but GOD accounts of the opening of thy mouth, as one would account of the opening of a grave full of rottenness, Rom. iii. 13. *Their throat is an open sepulchre.* Others are affected with thy prayers, which seem to them as if they would rend the heavens; but God accounts them as the howling of a dog: *They have not cried unto me with their heart, when they howled upon their beds,* Hos. vii. 14. Others take thee for a wrestler and prevailer with God; but he can take no delight in thee nor thy prayers neither, Isa. lxvi. 3. *He that killeth an ox, as if he slew a man: he that sacrificeth a lamb, as if he cut off a dog's neck;—he that burneth incense, as if he blessed an idol.* Why that? Because thou art yet in the gall of bitterness and bond of iniquity. (3.) All thou hast done for God, and his cause in the world, though it may be followed with temporal rewards, yet is lost as to divine acceptance. This is clear from the case of Jehu, who was indeed rewarded with a kingdom, for his executing due vengeance upon the house of Ahab, as being a work good for the matter of it, because it was commanded of God, as you may see, 2 Kings x. 13. Yet he was punished for it, in his posterity, because he did it not in a right manner, Hos. i. 4. *I will avenge the blood of Jezreel upon the house of Jehu.* God looks mainly to the heart; and if so, truly albeit thy outward appearance be fairer than that of many others, yet the hidden man of thy heart is loathsome; thou lookest well before men, but art thou, as Moses was, *fair to God,* as the margin hath it, Acts vii. 20. O what a difference is there betwixt the characters of Asa and Amaziah: *The high places were not removed: nevertheless, Asa his heart was perfect with the Lord all his days.* 1 Kings xv. 14. *Amaziah did that which was right in the sight of the Lord, but not with a perfect heart,* 2 Chron. xxv. 2. It may be, thou art zealous against sin in others, and dost admonish them to their duty, and reprove them for their sin; and they hate thee, because thou dost thy duty: But I must tell thee, God **hates thee too,** because thou dost it not in a right manner; and that thou canst never do, whilst thou art not born again. *Lastly,* All thy struggles against sin, in thine own heart and life, are naught. The proud pharisee afflicted his body with fasting, and God struck his soul, in the meantime, with a sentence of condemnation, Luke xviii. Balaam struggled with his covetous temper to that degree, that though he loved the wages of unrighteousness, yet he would not win them by cursing Israel; but he died the death of the wicked, Numb. xxxi. 8. All thou dost, while in an unregenerate state, is for thyself; and therefore it will fair with thee, as with a subject who, having reduced the rebels, put the crown on his own head; and therefore looseth all his good service, and his head too.

Object. If it be thus with us, then we need never perform any religious duty at all. *Ans.* The conclusion is not just. No inability of thine can loose thee from the duty God's law lays on thee: and there is less evil in thy doing thy duty, than there is in the omitting of it. But there is a mids betwixt omitting of duty, & the doing of it as thou dost it. A man ordereth masons to build a house, if they quite neglect the work, that will not be accepted; if they fall on and build upon the old rotten foundation, neither will that please, but they must raze the old foundation, and build on firm ground: Go thou and do likewise. In the meantime, it is not in vain for thee, even for thee, to seek the LORD; for tho' he regards thee not, yet he may have respect to his own ordinance, and do thee good thereby, as was said before.

Secondly, Without regeneration there is no communion with GOD. There is a society on earth, whose fellowship is with the Father and with the Son JESUS CHRIST, 1 John i. 5. But out of that society all the unregenerate are excluded; for they are all enemies to GOD, as ye heard before at large. Now, *Can two walk together, except they be agreed?* Amos iii. 3. They are all unholy; and, *What communion hath light with darkness—Christ with Belial?* 2 Cor. vi. 14, 15. They may have a shew and semblance of holiness, but they are strangers to true holiness, and therefore without GOD in the world. How sad is this case, to be employed in religious duties, but to have no fellowship with GOD in them! Ye would not be content with your meat, unless it fed you; nor with your clothes unless they kept you warm: And how can you satisfy yourselves with your duties, while they are not effectual to your communion with GOD?

Thirdly, Regeneration is absolutely necessary to qualify you for heaven. None go to heaven but they that are made meet for it, Col. i. 12. As it was with Solomon's temple, 1 Kings vi. 7. so it is with the temple above. It is built of stone, made ready before it is brought thither; namely of lively stones, 1 Pet. ii. 5. wrought for the same thing. 2 Cor. v. 5. for they cannot be laid in that glorious building, just as they came out of the quarry of depraved nature: Jewels of gold are not meet for swine, and far less Jewels of glory for unrenewed sinners. Beggars in their rags, are not meet for kings houses; nor sinners to enter into the King's palace, without the raiment of needle-work, Psal. xlv. 14, 15. What wise man would bring fishes out of the water to feed in his meadow; or send his oxen to feed in the sea? Even as little are the unregenerate meet for heaven, or is heaven meet for them. It would never be liked by them.

1. Therefore he looks on himself as a stranger on this earth, and his head is homeward, Heb. xi. 16. *They desire a better country, that is, an heavenly.* But the unregenerate man is the man of the earth, Psal. x. 18. written in the earth. Jer. xvii. 13. Now, home is home, be it never so homely; therefore he minds earthly things, Phil. iii. 19. There is a peculiar sweetness in our native soil, and hardly are men drawn to leave it, and dwell in a strange country. In no case does that prevail more than in this; for unrenewed men would quit their pretensions to heaven, were it not that they see they cannot make a better of it. (2.) There is nothing there of what they delight most in, as most agreeable to the carnal heart, Rev. xxi. 27. *And there shall in no wise enter into it, any thing that defileth.* When Mahomet gave out paradise to be a place of sensual delights, his religion was greedily embraced; for that is the heaven men naturally chuse. If the covetous man could get bags full of gold there, and the voluptuous man can promise himself his sensual delights there; they might be reconciled to heaven, and meet for it too: but since it is not so, tho' they may utter fair words about it, truly it has little of their hearts. (3.) Every corner there, is filled with that which, of all things, they have the least liking to; and that is holiness, true holiness, perfect holiness. Were one that abhors swine's flesh, bidden to a feast where all the dishes were of that sort of meat, but variously prepared; he would find fault with every dish at the table, notwithstanding all the art used to make them palatable. It is true, there is joy in heaven, but it is holy joy: there are pleasures in heaven, but they are holy pleasures: there are places to stand by in heaven, but it is holy ground. That holiness that casts up in every place, and in every thing there, would mar all to the unregenerate. (4.) Were they carried thither, they would not only change their place, which would be a great heart-break to them; but they would change their company too. Truly they would never like the company there, who care not for communion with GOD here; nor value the fellowship of his people, at least in the vitals of practical godliness. Many indeed mix themselves with the godly on earth, to procure a name to themselves, and to cover the naughtiness of their hearts: but that trade could not be managed there. (5.) They would never like the employment of heaven, they care so little for it now. The business

of the saints there, would be an intolerable burden to them, seeing it is not agreeable to their nature. To be taken up in beholding, admiring, & praising of him that sitteth upon the throne, and of the Lamb, would be work unsuitable, and therefore unsavoury to an unrenewed soul. *Lastly*, They would find this fault with it, that the whole is of everlasting continuance. This would be a killing ingredient in it to them. How would such as now account the sabbath-day a burden, brook the celebrating of an everlasting sabbath in the heavens?

Lastly, Regeneration is absolutely necessary to your being admitted into heaven, John iii. 3. No heaven without it. Though carnal men could digest all these things, which make heaven so unsuitable for them, yet GOD will never suffer them to come thither. Therefore born again ye must be; else ye shall never see heaven, ye shall perish eternally. For (1.) There is a bill of exclusion against you in the court of heaven, and against all your sort; *Except a man be born again, he cannot see the kingdom of God*, 1 John iii. 3. Here is a bar before you, that men and angels cannot remove. And to hope for heaven, over the belly of this peremptory sentence, is to hope GOD will recal his word, and sacrifice his truth and faithfulness to your safety; which is infinitely more than to hope the earth shall be forsaken for you, and the rock removed out of his place. (2.) There is no holiness without regeneration. It is the new man, which is created in true holiness, Eph. iv. 24. And no heaven without holiness; for, *Without holiness no man shall see the Lord*, Heb. xii. 14. Will the gates of pearl be opened, to let in dogs and swine? No; their place is without, Rev. xxii. 15. GOD will not admit such into the holy place of communion with him here; and will he admit them into the holiest of all hereafter? Will he take the children of the devil, and give them to sit with him in his throne? Or will he bring the unclean into the city, whose street is pure gold? Be not deceived, grace and glory are but two links of one chain, which GOD has joined, and no man shall put asunder. None are transplanted into the paradise above, but out of the nursery of grace below. If ye be unholy while in this world, ye will be forever miserable in the world to come. (3.) All the unregenerate are without CHRIST, and therefore having no hope while in that case, Eph. ii. 12. Will CHRIST prepare mansions of glory for them, that refuse to receive him into their hearts? Nay; rather, will he not laugh at their calamity, who now set at nought all his counsel? Prov. i. 25, 26. Lastly, There is an infallible connection betwixt a finally unregenerate state & damnation, rising from the nature of the things themselves;

this life. Depraved nature makes men meet to be partakers of the inheritance of the damned, in utter darkness. (1.) The heart of stone within thee is a sinking weight; as a stone naturally goes downward, so the hard stony heart tends downward to the bottomless pit. Ye are hardned against reproof; tho' ye are told your danger, yet you will not see it, ye will not believe it. But remember, that the conscience its being seared with a hot iron, is a sad presage of everlasting burnings. (2.) Your unfruitfulness under the means of grace, fits you for the ax of GOD's judgments, Mat. iii. 10. *Every tree that bringeth not forth good fruit, is hewn down and cast into the fire.* The withered branch is fuel for the fire, John xv. 6. Tremble at this ye despisers of the gospel; if ye be not thereby made meet for heaven, ye will be like the barren ground, bearing briers and thorns, nigh unto cursing, whose end is to be burned, Heb. vi. 8. (3.) The hellish disposition of mind, which discovers themselves in profanity of life, fit the guilty for the regions of horror. A profane life will have a miserable end, *They which do such things, shall not inherit the kingdom of God,* Gal. v. 19, 20, 21. Think on this, ye prayerless persons, ye mockers of religion, ye cursers and swearers, ye unclean and unjust persons, who have not so much as moral honesty to keep you from lying, cheating and stealing. What sort of a tree think ye it to be, upon which these fruits grow? Is it a tree of righteousness, which the LORD hath planted? Or is it not such an one as cumbers the ground, which GOD will pluck up for fuel to the fire of his wrath? (4.) Your being dead in sin makes you meet to be wrapt in flames of brimstone, as a winding sheet; and to be buried in the bottomless pit, as in a grave. Great was the cry in Egypt, when the first-born in each family was dead: but are there not many families, where all are dead together? Nay, many there are, who are twice dead, plucked up by the roots. Sometime, in their life, they have been rouzed by apprehensions of death, and its consequences; but now they are so far on in their way to the land of darkness, that they hardly ever have the least glimmering of light from heaven. (5.) The darkness of your minds presageth eternal darkness. O the horrible ignorance some are plagued with: while others who have got some rays of morning light into their heads, are utterly void of spiritual light in their hearts! If ye knew your case, ye would cry out, Oh darkness! darkness! darkness making way for the blackness of darkness for ever! The face-covering is upon you already, as condemned persons; so near are ye to everlasting darkness. It is only JESUS CHRIST who can stop the execution, pull the napkin off the face of the condemned malefactor, and put a pardon in his hand, Isa. xxv. 7. *And he will destroy in this mountain, the face of the covering cast over all people,* i. e. The face-covering cast over the condemned, as in Haman's case, Esther vii. 8. *As the word went out of the king's mouth, they covered Haman's face.* Lastly, The chains of darkness ye are bound with in the prison of your depraved state, Isa. lxi. 1. fits you to be cast into the burning fiery furnace. Ah miserable men! Sometimes their consciences stir within them, and they begin to think of amending their ways. But alas! they are in chains, they cannot do it. They are chained by the heart; their lusts cleave so fast to them, that they cannot, nay, they will not shake them off. Thus you see what affinity there is betwixt an unregenerate state, and the state of the damned, the state of absolute and irretrieveable misery; be convinced then, that ye must be born again: put a high value on the new birth, and eagerly desire it.

The text tells you, that the word is the seed, whereof the new creature is formed; therefore take heed to it and entertain it, for it is your life. Apply yourselves to the reading of the scripture. Ye that cannot read, cause others read it to you. Wait diligently on the preaching of the word, as by divine appointment, the special mean of conversion: *For it pleased God by the foolishness of preaching, to save them that believe,* 1 Cor. i. 21. Wherefore cast not yourselves out of CHRIST's way; reject not the means of grace, lest ye be found to judge yourselves unworthy of eternal life. Attend carefully to the word preached. Hear every sermon, as if you were hearing for eternity: and take heed, the fowls of the air pick not up this seed from you as it is sown. Give thyself wholly to it, 1 Tim. iv. 15. *Receive it not as the word of men, but as it is in truth the word of God.* 1 Thess. ii. 13. And hear it with application, looking on it as a message sent from heaven, to you in particular, tho' not to you only, Rev. iii. 22. *He that hath an ear let him hear, what the Spirit saith unto the churches.* Lay it up in your hearts, meditate upon it; and be not as the unclean beasts, that chew not the cud, but by earnest prayer beg the dew of heaven may fall on thy heart, that the seed may spring up there.

More particularly. (1.) Receive the testimony of the word of GOD, concerning the misery of an unregenerate state, the sinfulness thereof, and the absolute necessity of regeneration. (2.) Receive its testimony concerning God, what a holy and just one he is. (3.) Examine thy ways by it; namely, the thoughts of thy heart, the expressions of thy lips, and the tenor of thy life. Look back thro' the several periods of thy life, and see thy sins from the precepts of the word; and learn from its threatnings, what thou art liable to, on the account of these sins. (4.) View the corruption of thy nature, by the help of the same word of God; as a glass which represents our ugly face in a lively manner. Were these things deeply rooted in the heart, they might be the seed of that fear and sorrow, on account of thy soul's state, which are necessary to prepare and stir thee up to look after a Saviour. Fix your thoughts upon him offered to thee in the gospel, as fully suited to thy case; having, by his obedience to the death, perfectly satisfied the justice of God, and brought in everlasting righteousness. This may prove the seed of humiliation, desire, hope, and faith; and put thee on to stretch out the withered hand unto him at his command.

Let these things sink deeply into your hearts, and improve them diligently. Remember, whatever ye be, ye must be born again: else it had been better for you ye had never been born. Wherefore, if any of you shall live and die in an unregenerate state, ye will be inexcusable, having been fairly warned of your hazard.

HEAD II.
The Mystical Union betwixt CHRIST and Believers.

JOHN xv. 5. *I am the vine, ye are the branches.*

HAVING spoken of the change, made by regeneration, on all those that shall inherit eternal life, in opposition to their natural state, the state of degeneracy; I proceed to speak of the change made upon them, in their union with the LORD JESUS CHRIST, in opposition to their natural relative state, the state of misery. The doctrine of the saints union with CHRIST, is very plainly and fully insisted on, from the beginning of the 15th verse of this chapter; which is a part of our LORD's farewel sermon to his disciples. Sorrow had now filled their hearts; they were apt to say, Alas! what will become of us, when our Master is taken from our head? Who will then instruct us? Who will solve our doubts? How will we be supported under our difficulties and discouragements? How will we be able to live, without our wonted communications with him? Wherefore our Lord Jesus Christ seasonably teaches them the mystery of their union with him, comparing himself to the vine-stock, and them to the branches.

He compares, I say, (1.) himself to a vine-stock; *I am the vine*? He had been celebrating, with his disciples, the sacrament of his supper, that sign and seal of his people's union with himself; and had told them, he would drink no more of the fruit of the vine, till he should drink it new with them, in his Father's kingdom: and now he shews himself to be the vine, from whence the wine of their consolation should come. The vine hath less beauty than many other trees, but is exceeding fruitful; fitly representing the low condition our Lord was then in, yet bringing many sons to glory. But that which is chiefly aimed at, in his comparing himself to a vine, is to represent himself as the supporter and nourisher of his people, in whom they live, and bring forth fruit. (2.) He compares them to the branches; *Ye are the branches* of that vine. *Ye are the branches*, knit to, and growing on this stock; drawing all your life and sap from it. It is a beautiful comparison: As if he had said, I am as a vine; ye are as the branches of that vine. Now there are two sorts of branches, (1.) Natural branches, which at first spring out of the stock: These are the branches that are in the tree, and were never out of it. (2.) There are ingrafted branches, which are branches broken off from the tree that first gave their life; and put into another to grow upon it. Thus branches come to be on a tree, which originally were not on it. The branches mentioned in the text, are of the latter sort; branches broken off (as the word, in the original language, denotes) namely, from the tree that first gave them life. None of the children of men are natural branches of the second Adam, viz. Jesus Christ, the true Vine: they are all the natural branches of the first Adam, that degenerate vine: But the elect are, all of them, sooner or later, broken off from the natural stock, and ingrafted into Christ, the true Vine.

Doct. They who are in the state of grace, are ingrafted in, and united to, the Lord Jesus Christ. They are taken out of their natural stock, cut off from it; and are now ingrafted into Christ, as the new stock. In handling of this, I shall speak to the mystical union, (1.) More generally. (2.) More particularly.

A general View of the Mystical Union.

First, In the general, for understanding the union betwixt the Lord Jesus Christ, and his elect, who believe in him, and on him:

1. It is a spiritual union. Man and wife, by their marriage-union, become one flesh: CHRIST and true believers, by this union, become one spirit, 2 Cor. vi. 17. As one soul or spirit actuates both the head and the members in the natural body; so the one Spirit of GOD dwells in CHRIST and the Christian; for, *If any man have not the Spirit of Christ, he is none of his,* Rom. viii. 9. Corporal union is made by contract; so the stones in a building are united; but this is an union of another nature. Were it possible we could eat the flesh, and drink the blood of CHRIST, in a corporal and carnal manner, it would profit nothing, John vi. 63. It was not Mary's bearing him in her womb, but her believing on him, that made her a saint. Luke xi. 27, 28. *A certain woman---said unto him, Blessed is the womb that bare thee, and the paps which thou hast sucked. But he said, Yea, rather, blessed are they that hear the word of God, and keep it.*

2. It is a real union. Such is our weakness in our present state, so much are we immersed in sin, that we are prone to form in our fancy an image of every thing proposed to us; and as to whatsoever is denied us, we are apt to suspect it to be but a fiction, or what has no reality. But nothing is more real, than what is spiritual; as approaching nearest to the nature of him who is the fountain of all reality, namely, GOD himself. We do not see with our eyes, the union betwixt our own soul and body; neither can we represent it to ourselves truly, by imagination, as we do sensible things; yet the reality of it is not to be doubted. Faith is no fancy, but the substance of things hoped for, Heb. xi. 1. Neither is the union thereby made betwixt CHRIST and believers, imaginary, but most real; *For we are members of his body, of his flesh, and of his bones,* Eph. v. 30.

3. It is a most close and intimate union. Believers, regenerate persons, who fiduciously credit him, and rely on him, have put on CHRIST, Gal. iii. 27. If that be not enough, he is in them, John xvii. 23. formed in them, as the child in the mother's belly, Gal. iv. 19. He is the foundation, 1 Cor. iii. 11. They are the lively stones built upon him, 1 Pet. ii. 5. He is the head, and they the body, Eph. i. 22, 23. Nay, he liveth in them, as their very souls in their bodies, Gal. ii. 20. And, what is more than all this, they are one in the Father and the Son, as the Father is in CHRIST, and CHRIST in the Father, John xvii. 21. *That they all may be one, as thou, Father, art in me, and I in thee, they also may be one in us.*

4. Though it is not a mere legal union, yet it is an union sustained in law. CHRIST, as the cautioner, the elect as the principal debtors, are one, in the eye of the law. When the elect had run themselves, with the rest of mankind, in debt to

the justice of God; Christ became surety for them, and paid the debt. When they believe on him, they are united to him in a spiritual marriage-union; which takes effect so far, that what he did and suffered for them, is reckoned, in law, as if they had done and suffered for themselves. Hence they are said to be crucified with Jesus, Gal. ii. 20. Buried with him, Col. ii. 12. Yea, raised up together, namely with Christ, and made to sit together in heavenly places in Christ Jesus, Eph. ii. 6. In which places, saints on earth, of whom the Apostle there speaks, cannot be said to be sitting, but in the way of law-reckoning.

5. It is an indissolvable union: Once in Christ, ever in him. Having taken up his habitation in the heart, he never removes. None can untie this happy knot. Who will dissolve this union? Will he himself do it? No, he will not; we have his word for it; *I will not turn away from them,* Jer. xxxii. 40. But perhaps the sinner will do this mischief for himself; no, he shall not; *They shall not depart from me,* saith their God. Can devils do it? No, unless they be stronger than Christ, and his Father too: *Neither shall any man pluck them out of my hand,* saith our Lord, John x. 28. *And none is able to pluck them out of my Father's hand,* verse 39. But, what say you of death, which parts husband and wife; yea, separates the soul from the body? Will not death do it? No; the Apostle, Rom. viii. 38, 39. is persuaded, that either death, for as terrible as it is, nor life, for as desirable as it is, nor devils, those evil angels, nor the devil's persecuting agents, though they be principalities or powers on earth; nor evil things present, already lying on us, nor evil things to come on us; nor the height of worldly felicity, nor depth of worldly misery; nor any other creature, good or ill, shall be able to separate us from the love of God, which is in Christ Jesus our Lord. As death separated Christ's soul from his body, but could not separate either his soul or body from his divine nature; so though the saints should be separated from their nearest relations in the world, and from all their earthly enjoyments; yea, though their souls should be separate from their bodies, and their bodies separate in a thousand pieces, their bones scattered, as when one cutteth or cleaveth wood; yet soul and body, and every piece of the body, the smallest dust of it shall remain united to the Lord Christ; for even in death, they sleep in Jesus, 1 Thess. iv. 14. And he keepeth all their bones, Psal. xxxiv. 20. Union with Christ, is the grace wherein we stand, firm and stable, as mount Zion, which cannot be removed.

Lastly, It is a mysterious union. The gospel is a doctrine of mysteries. It discovers to us the substantial union of the three persons in one God-head, 1 John v. 7. *These three are one:* the hypostatical union of the divine and human natures, in the person of the LORD JESUS CHRIST: 1 Tim. iii. 16. *God was manifest in the flesh.* And the mystical union, betwixt CHRIST and believers, is a great mystery also. Eph. v. 32. O what mysteries are here! the Head in heaven, the members on earth, yet really united! CHRIST in the believer, living in him, walking in him: and the believer dwelling in GOD, putting on the LORD JESUS; eating his flesh, and drinking his blood! This makes the saints a mystery to the world; yea, a mystery to themselves.

SECONDLY, I come now more particularly to speak of this union with, and ingrafting into JESUS CHRIST. And, (1.) I shall consider the natural stock, which the branches are taken out of. (2.) The supernatural stock, they are ingrafted into. (3.) What branches are cut off the old stock, and put into the new. (4.) How it is done. And, lastly, The benefits flowing from this union and ingrafting.

Of the natural and supernatural Stocks, and the Branches, taken out of the former, and ingrafted into the latter.

1. Let us take a view of the stock, which the branches are taken out of. The two Adams, that is, Adam and CHRIST, are the two stocks; for the scripture speaks of these two, as if there had never been more men in the world than they, 1 Cor. xv. 45. 47. *The first man Adam was made a living soul, the last Adam was made a quickning Spirit.——The first man is of the earth, earthy; the second man is the Lord from heaven.* And the reason is, there were never any, that were not branches of one of these two; all men being either in the one stock or in the other: for in these two sorts all mankind stands divided, verse 48. *As is the earthy, such are they also that are earthy: and as is the heavenly, such are they also that are heavenly.* The first Adam, then, is the natural stock; on this stock are the branches found growing at first; which are afterwards cut off, and ingrafted into CHRIST. As for the fallen angels, as they had no relation to the first Adam, so they have none to the second.

There are four things to be remembered here, (1.) That all mankind, the man CHRIST excepted, are naturally branches of the first Adam, Rom. v. 12. *By one man sin entered into the world, and death by sin; and so death passed upon all men.*

(2.) The bond which knit us unto the natural stock, was the covenant of works. Adam being our natural root, was made the moral root also; being all his posterity, as representing them in the covenant of works. For, *By one man's disobedience many were made sinners*, Rom. v. 19. Now, there behoved to be a peculiar relation betwixt that one man and the many, as a foundation for imputing his sin to them. This relation did not arise from the mere natural bond betwixt him & us, as a father to his children; for so we are related to our immediate parents, whose sins are not thereupon imputed to us as Adam's sin is. It behoved then to arise from a moral bond betwixt Adam and us, the bond of a covenant, which could be no other than the covenant of works wherein we were united to him as branches to a stock. Hence JESUS CHRIST, tho' a son of Adam, Luke iii. 23. 38. was none of these branches; for seeing he came not of Adam, in virtue of the blessing of marriage, which was given before the fall, Gen. i. 28. *Be fruitful and multiply*, &c. but in virtue of a special promise made after the fall, Gen. iii. 15. *The seed of the woman shall bruise the serpent's head*: Adam could not represent him in a covenant made before his fall. (3.) As it is impossible for a branch to be in two stocks at once; so no man can be, at one and the same time, both in the first and second Adam. (4.) Hence it evidently follows, that all who are not ingrafted in JESUS CHRIST, are yet branches of the old stock; and so partake of the nature of the same. Now, as to the first Adam, our natural stock; Consider,

First, What a stock he was originally. He was a vine of the LORD's planting, a choice vine, a noble vine, wholly a right seed. There was a consultation of the Trinity, at the planting of this vine, Gen. i. 26. *Let us make man in our own image, after our own likeness*. There was no rottenness at the heart of it. There was sap and juice enough in it, to have nourished all the branches, to bring forth fruit unto GOD. My meaning is, Adam was made able perfectly to keep the commandments of GOD, which would have procured eternal life to himself, and to all his posterity; for seeing all die by Adam's disobedience; all should have had life, by his obedience, if he had stood. Consider,

Secondly, What that stock now is: Ah; most unlike to what it was, when planted by the author and fountain of all good. A blast from hell, and a bite with the venomous teeth of the old serpent, have made it a degenerate stock, a dead stock, nay, a killing stock.

1*st*, It is a degenerate naughty stock. Therefore the LORD GOD said to Adam, in that dismal day, *Where art thou?* Gen.

iii. 9. In what condition art thou now? How art thou turned into the degenerate plant of a strange vine, unto me? Or, Where wast thou? Why not in the place of meeting with me? Why so long acoming? What meaneth this fearful change, this hiding of thyself from me? Alas! the stock is degenerate, quite spoiled, become altogether naughty, and brings forth wild grapes. Converse with the devil is preferred to communion with God. Satan is believed, and God, who is truth itself, disbelieved. He who was the friend of God, is now in conspiracy against him. Darkness is come into the room of light; ignorance prevails in the mind, where divine knowledge shone; the will, sometime righteous or regular is now turned rebel against its LORD; and the whole man is in dreadful disorder.

Before I go further, let me stop and observe, Here is a mirror both for saints and sinners. Sinners, stand here and consider what you are: and saints learn ye, what once ye were. Ye sinners are branches of a degenerate stock. Fruit you may bear indeed; but now that your vine is the vine of Sodom, your grapes must of course be grapes of gall, Deut. xxxii. 32. The scripture speaks of two sorts of fruit, which grow on the branches upon the natural stock; and it is plain enough, they are of the nature of their degenerate stock. (1.) The wild grapes of wickedness, Isa. v. 2. These grow in abundance by influence from hell: See Gal. v. 19, 20, 21. At their gates are all manner of these fruits both new and old. Storms come from heaven to put them back; but they still grow. They are struck at with the sword of the Spirit, the word of GOD; conscience gives them many a secret blow; yet they thrive. (2.) Fruit to themselves, Hosea x. 1. What else are all the unrenewed man's acts of obedience, his reformation, sober deportment, his prayers, and good works? They are all done, chiefly for himself, not for the glory of GOD. These fruits are like the apples of Sodom, fair to look at, but fall to ashes, when handled and tried. Ye think ye have not only the leaves of a profession, but the fruits of a holy practice too; but if ye be not broken off from the old stock, and ingrafted in CHRIST JESUS, GOD accepts not, nor regards your fruits.

Here I must take occasion to tell you, there are five faults will be found in heaven, with your best fruits. (1.) Their bitterness; your clusters are bitter, Deut. xxxii. 31. There is a spirit of bitterness, wherewith some come before the LORD, in religious duties, living in malace and envy; and which some professors entertain against others, because they outshine them, by holiness of life, or because they are not of their opinion or way. This, wheresoever it reigns, is a fearful symtom of an unregenerate state. But I do not so much mean this, as that which is common to all the branches of the old stock; namely, the leaven of hypocrisy, Luke xii. 1. which sours and embitters every duty they perform. The wisdom, that is full of good fruits, is without hypocrisy. James iii. 17. (2.) Their ill savour. Their works are abominable, for themselves are corrupt, Psal. xiv. 1. They all savour of the old stock, not of the new: it is the peculiar privilige of the saints, that they are unto God a sweet savour of Christ, 2 Cor. ii. 15. The unregenerate man's fruits savour not of love to Christ, nor of the blood of Christ, nor of the inceuse of his intercession; and therefore will never be accepted of in heaven. (3.) Their unripeness. Their grape is an unripe grape, Job xv. 33. There is no influence on them from the Sun of righteousness, to bring them to perfection; they have the shape of fruit, but no more. The matter of duty is in them; but they want right principles and ends; their works are not wrought in God, John iii. 21. Their prayers drop from their lips, before their hearts be impregnate with the vital sap of the Spirit of supplication; their tears fall from their eyes, ere their hearts be truly softened; their feet turn to new paths and their way is altered; while yet their nature is not changed. (4.) Their lightness. Being weighed in the balances, they are found wanting, Dan. v. 27. For evidence whereof, you may observe, they do not humble the soul, but lift it up in pride. The good fruits of holiness bear down the branches they grow upon, making them to salute the ground, 1 Cor. xv. 10. *I laboured more abundantly than they all: yet not I, but the grace of God which was with me.* But the blasted fruits of unrenewed mens performance, hang lightly on branches towering up to heaven, Judges xvii. 13. *Now know I, that the Lord will do me good, seeing I have a Levite to my priest.* They look indeed so high, that God cannot behold them, *Wherefore have we fasted,* say they *and thou seest not!* Isa. lviii. 3. The more duties they do, and the better they seem to perform them, the less are they humbled, the more they are lifted up. This disposition of the sinner, is the exact reverse of what is to be found in the saint. To men, who neither are in Christ, nor are solicitous to be found in him, their duties are like windy bladders, wherewith they think to swim ashore to Immanuel's land; but these must needs break, & they consequently sink; because they take not Christ for the lifter up of their head, Psalm iii. 3. *Lastly,* They are not all manner of pleasant fruits, Cant. vii. 13. Christ as a King must be served with variety. Where God makes the heart his garden, he plants it as Solomon did his, with trees of all kinds of fruits, Eccl. ii. 5. And accordingly it brings forth the fruit of the Spirit in all goodness, Eph. v. 9. But the ungodly are not so; their obedience is never universal; there is always some one thing or other excepted. In one word, their fruits are fruits of an ill tree, that cannot be accepted in heaven.

2dly, Our natural stock is a dead stock, according to the threatning, Gen. ii. 17. *In the day thou eatest thereof, thou shalt surely die.* Our root now is rottenness, no marvel the blossom go up as dust. The stroke is gone to the heart; the sap is let out, and the tree is withered. The curse of the first covenant, like a hot thunder-bolt from heaven, has lighted on it, and ruined it. It is cursed now as the fig-tree. Mat. xxi. 19. *Let no fruit grow on thee, henceforth for ever.* Now it is good for nothing, but to cumber the ground, and furnish fuel for Tophet.

Let me inlarge a little here also. Every unrenewed man is a branch of a dead stock. When thou seest, O sinner, a dead stock of a tree, exhausted of all its sap, having branches on it in the same condition; look on it as a lively representation of thy soul's state. (1.) Where the stock is dead, the branches must needs be barren. Alas! the barrenness of many professors plainly discovers on what stock they are growing. It is easy to pretend to faith, but shew me thy faith without thy works, if thou canst, James ii. 17. (2.) A dead stock can convey no sap to the branches, to make them bring forth fruit. The covenant of works was the bond of our union with the natural stock, but now it is become weak through the flesh; that is, through the degeneracy and depravity of human nature, Rom. vii. 3. It is strong enough to command, and to bind heavy burdens on the shoulders of those who are not in CHRIST; but it affords no strength to bear them. The sap, once in the root, is now gone; and the law, like a merciless creditor, apprehends Adam's heirs, saying, Pay what thou owest; when alas! his effects are riotously spent. (3.) All pains and cost are lost on the tree, whose life is gone. In vain do men labour to get fruit on the branches, when there is no sap in the root. *First*, The gardener's pains are lost: ministers lose their labour on the branches of the old stock, while they continue on it. Many sermons are preached to no purpose; because there is no life to give sensation. Sleeping men may be awakened, but the dead cannot be raised without a miracle; even so, the dead sinner, must remain so, if he be not restored to life, by a miracle of grace.

Secondly, The influences of heaven are lost on such a tree: in vain doth the rain fall upon it; in vain is it laid open to the winter-cold and frosts. The LORD of the vineyard digs about many a dead soul, but it is not bettered, *Bruise the fool in a morter, his folly will not depart.* Tho' he meets with many crosses, yet he retains his lusts; let him be laid on a sick-bed, he will there lie like a sick beast, groaning under his pain, but not mourning for, nor turning from his sin. Let death itself stare him in the face; he will presumptuously maintain his hope, as if he would look the grim messenger out of countenance. Sometimes there are common operations of the divine Spirit performed on him; he is sent home with a trembling heart, & with arrows of conviction sticking in his soul; but at length he prevails against these things, and turns as secure as ever. *Thirdly,* Summer and winter are alike to the branches of the dead stock. When others about them are budding, blossoming, and bringing forth fruit, there is no change on them; the dead stock has no growing time at all. Perhaps it may be difficult to know in the winter what trees are dead, and what are alive; but the spring plainly discovers it. There are some seasons, wherein there is little life to be perceived, even among saints; yet times of reviving come at length. But even when the vine flourisheth, and the pomegranates bud forth, when saving grace is discovering itself, by its lively actings, wheresoever it is the branches on the old stock are withered: when the dry bones are coming together, bone to bone, among saints; the sinners bones are still lying about the grave's mouth. They are trees that cumber the ground, near to be cut down, and will be cut down for the fire, if GOD in his mercy prevent it not, by cutting them off from that stock, and ingrafting them into another.

Lastly, Our natural stock is a killing stock. If the stock die, how can the branches live? If the sap be gone from the root and heart, the branches must needs wither. *In Adam all die,* 1 Cor. xv. 22. The root died in Paradise; and all the branches in it, and with it. The root is impoisoned, thence the branches come to be infected; death is in the pot; and all that taste of the pulse or pottage are killed.

Know then, that every natural man is a branch of a killing stock. Our natural root not only gives us not life, but it has a killing power reaching all the branches thereof. There are four things, which the first Adam conveys to all his branches: and they are abiding in, and lying on such of them as are not ingrafted to CHRIST. *First,* A corrupt nature. He sinned, and his nature was thereby corrupted or depraved; and this corruption is conveyed to all his posterity. He was infected, and the contagion spread itself all over his seed. *Secondly,* Guilt; that is an obligation to punishment, Rom. v. 21 *By one man sin entered into the world, and death by sin: & so death passed upon all men, for that all have sinned.* The threatnings of the law, as cords of death, are twisted about the branches of the old stock, to draw them over the hedge into the fire. And till they be cut off from this stock by the pruning knife, the sword of vengeance hangs over their heads, to cut them down.——— *Thirdly,* This killing stock transmits the curse into the branches. The stock as the stock, for I speak not of Adam in his personal and private capacity, being cursed, so are the branches, Gal. 3. 10. *For as many as are of the works of the law, are under the curse.* This curse affects the whole man, and all that belongs to him, every thing he possesses; and worketh three ways. (1.) As poison, infecting; thus their blessings are cursed, Mal. ii. 2. Whatever the man enjoys, it can do him no good, but evil, being thus impoisoned by the curse. His prosperity in the world destroys him, Prov. i. 32. The ministry of the gospel is a savour of death unto death to him, 2 Cor. ii. 16. His seeming attainments in religion are cursed to him; his knowledge serves but to puff him up, and his duties to keep him back from CHRIST. (2.) It worketh as a moth, consuming and wasting by little and little, Hos. v. 12. *Therefore will I be unto Ephraim as a moth.* There is a worm at the root, consuming them by degrees. The curse pursued Saul, till it wormed him out of all his enjoyments, & out of the very shew he had of religion. Sometimes they decay as the fat of lambs, and melt away as the snow in a sun-shine. (3.) It acteth as a lion rampant, Hos. v. 14. *I will be unto Ephraim as a lion.* The LORD rains on them snares, fire and brimstone, and an horrible tempest, in such a manner, that they are hurried away with the stream. He teareth their enjoyments from them in his wrath, pursueth them with terrors, rents their souls from their bodies, and throws the deadned branch into the fire. Thus the curse devours like fire, which none can quench. *Lastly,* This killing stock transmits death to the branches upon it. Adam took the poisonous cup and drank it off; this occasioned death to himself and us. We came into the world spiritually dead, thereby obnoxious to eternal death, and absolutely liable to temporal death. This root is to us like the Scythian river, which they say, brings forth little bladders every day, out of which come certain small flies, which are bred in the morning, winged at noon, and dead at night; a very lively emblem of our mortal state.

Now, Sirs, is it not absolutely necessary to be broken off from this our natural stock? What will our fair leaves of a profession, or our fruits of duties avail, if we be still branches of the degenerate, dead and killing stock? But, alas! among the many questions tossed among us, few are taken up about these: Whether am I broken off from the old stock, or not? Whether am I ingrafted in CHRIST, or not? Ah! wherefore all this waste? Why is there so much noise about religion amongst many, who can give no good account of their having laid a good foundation, being mere strangers to experimental religion? I fear, if GOD do not, in mercy, timeously undermine the religion of many of us, and let us see we have none at all; our root will be found rottenous, and our blossom go up as dust in a dying hour. Therefore let us look to our state, that we be not found fools in our latter end.

II. Let us now view the supernatural stock, in which the branches, cut off from the natural stock, are ingrafted. JESUS CHRIST is sometimes called *the Branch*, Zech. ii. 8. So he is, in respect of his human nature; being a branch, and the top-branch of the house of David. Sometimes he is called a *Root*. Isa. xi. 10. We have both together, Rev. xxii. 16. *I am the root and the Offspring of David*: David's root, as GOD; and his offspring, as man. The text tells, that he is *the Vine*: that is, He, as a Mediator, is the vine-stock, whereof believers are the branches. As the sap comes from the earth into the root & stock, & from thence is diffused into the branches; so by CHRIST, as Mediator, divine life is conveyed from the fountain, unto these who are united to him by faith, John vi. 57. *As the living Father hath sent me, and I live by the Father; so he that eateth me, even he shall live by me*. Now CHRIST is Mediator, not as GOD only, as some have asserted; nor yet as man only, as the Papists generally hold: But he is Mediator, as God-man, Acts xx. 28. *The church of God, which he hath purchased with his blood*. Heb. ix. 14. *Christ, who thro' the eternal Spirit, offered himself, without spot to God*. The divine and human natures, have their distinct actings; yet a joint operation in this, discharging the office of a Mediator. This is illustrated by the similitude of a fiery sword, which at once cuts and burns; cutting it burneth, and burning it cutteth: the steel cuts and the fire burns. Wherefore CHRIST, God-man, is the stock, whereof believers are the branches: And they are united to whole CHRIST. They are united to him in his human nature, as being members of his body, of his flesh, and of his bones, Eph. v. 30. And they are united to him in his divine nature; for so the Apostle speaks of this union, Col. i. 27. *Christ in you, the hope of glory*. And by him they are united to the Father, and to the Holy Ghost, 1 John iv. 15. *Whosoever shall confess that Jesus is the Son of God, God dwelleth in him, and he in God*. Faith, the bond of this union, receives whole CHRIST, God-man; and so unites us to him as such.

Behold here, O believers, your high privilege! Ye were once branches of a degenerate stock, even as others; but ye are, by grace, become branches of the true Vine, John xv.

2. Ye are cut out of a dead and killing stock, and ingrafted in the last Adam, who was made a quickning spirit, 1 Cor. xv. 45. Your loss by the first Adam is made up, with great advantage, by your union with the second. Adam at his best estate, was but a shrub, in comparison with CHRIST the tree of life. He was but a servant; CHRIST is the Son, the Heir, and LORD of all things; the LORD from heaven. It cannot be denied, that grace was shone in the first covenant: but it is as far exceeded, by the grace of the second covenant, as the twilight is, by the light of the mid-day.

III. What branches are taken out of the natural stock, and grafted into this Vine? *Ans.* These are the elect, and none other. They, and they only, are grafted into CHRIST; and consequently, none but they are cut off from the killing stock. For them alone he interceeds, that they may be one in him & his Father, John xvii. 9. 23. Faith, the bond of this union, is given to none else; it is the faith of GOD's elect, Tit. i. 1. The LORD passeth by many branches growing on the natural stock, and cuts off only here one, and there one, and grafts them into the true Vine, according as free love hath determined. Oft does he pitch upon the most unlikely branch, leaving the top boughs; passing by the mighty, and the noble, and calling the weak, base, and despised, 1 Cor. i. 26, 27. Yea he often leaves the fair and smooth, and takes the rugged and knotty: *And such were some of you; but ye are washed,* &c. 1 Cor. vi. 11. If ye inquire why so? We find no other reason but because they were chosen in him, Eph. i. 4. *Predestinated to the adoption of children by Jesus Christ,* ver. 5. Thus are they gathered together in CHRIST, while the rest are left growing on their natural stock, to be afterwards bound up in bundles for the fire. Wherefore, to whomsoever the gospel may come in vain, it will have a blest effect on GOD's elect, Acts xiii. 48. *As many as were ordained to eternal life believed.* Where the LORD has much people, the gospel will have much success, sooner or latter. Such as are to be saved, will be added to the mystical body of CHRIST.

How the Branches are taken out of the Natural Stock and ingrafted into the Supernatural Stock.

IV. I am to shew how the branches are cut off from the natural stock, the first Adam, and grafted into the true Vine, the LORD JESUS CHRIST. Thanks to the Husbandman, not to the branch, that it is cut off from its natural stock, and ingrafted into a new one. The sinner, in his coming off from the first stock, is passive; and neither can, nor will come off from it of his own accord; but clings to it, till almighty power make him to fall off, John vi. 44. *No man can come unto me, except the Father, which hath sent me, draw him.* And, chap. v. 40. *Ye will not come unto me, that ye might have life.* The ingrafted branches are GOD's husbandry, 1 Cor. iii. 9. *The planting of the Lord,* Isa. lxi. 3. The ordinary means he makes use of in this work, is the ministry of the word, 1 Cor. iii. 9. *We are labourers together with God.* But the efficacy thereof is wholly from him, whatever the minister's part or piety be, ver. 7. *Neither is he that planteth any thing, neither he that watereth; but God that giveth the increase.* The Apostle preached to the Jews, yet the body of that people remained in infidelity, Rom. x. 16. *Who hath believed our report?* Yea, CHRIST himself who spoke as never man spoke, saith concerning the success of his own ministry *I have laboured in vain; I have spent my strength for nought,* Isa. xlix. The branches may be hacked by the preaching of the word; but the stroke will never go through, till it be carried home on them, by an omnipotent arm. However GOD's ordinary way is, *By the foolishness of preaching, to save them that believe,* 1 Cor. i. 21.

The cutting off of the branch from the natural stock, is performed by the pruning knife of the law, in the hand of the Spirit of GOD, Gal. ii. 19. *For I thro' the law, am dead to the law.* It is by the bond of the covenant of works, as I said before, that we are knit to our natural stock: and therefore, as a wife, unwilling to be put away, pleads and hangs by the marriage-tie; so do men by the covenant of works. They hold by it, like the man who held the ship with his hands; and when one hand was cut off, held it with the other; and when both were cut off, held it with his teeth. This will appear from a distinct view of the LORD's work on men, in bringing them off from the old stock; which I now offer in these following particulars.

First, When the Spirit of the LORD comes to deal with a person, to bring him to CHRIST; he finds him in Laodicea's case, in a sound sleep of security, dreaming of heaven, and the favour of GOD, tho' full of sin against the holy One of Israel, Rev. iii. 17. *Thou knowest not that thou art wretched, and miserable, and poor, and blind, and naked.* And therefore he darts in some beams of light into the dark soul, and lets the man see he is lost, if he turn not over a new leaf, and betake himself to a new course of life. Thus by the Spirit of the LORD, acting as a spirit of bondage, there is a criminal court erected in the man's breast; where he is arraigned, accused, and condemned, for breaking the law of God, convinced of sin and judgment, John xvi. 8. And now he can no longer sleep securely in his former course of life. This is the first stroke the branch gets, in order to cutting off.

Secondly. Hereupon the man forsakes his former profane courses; his lying, swearing, Sabbath-breaking, stealing, and such like practices; tho' they be dear to him as right eyes, he will rather quit them than ruin his soul. The ship is like to sink, and therefore he throweth his goods overboard, that he himself may not perish. And now he begins to bless himself in his heart, and look joyfully on his evidences for heaven; thinking himself a better servant to God than many others, Luke xviii. 11. *God, I thank thee, I am not as other men are, extortioners, unjust, adulterers,* &c. But he soon gets another stroke with the ax of the law, shewing him that it is only he that *doth* what is written in the law, who can be saved by it; and that his negative holiness is too scanty a cover from the storm of God's wrath: And thus, altho' his sins of commission only were heavy on him before; his sins of omission now crowd into his thoughts, attended with a train of law-curses and vengeance: And each of the ten commands discharges thunder-claps of wrath against him, for his omitting required duties.

Thirdly, Upon this, he turns to a positively holy course of life. He not only is not profane, but he performs religious duties: he prays, seeks the knowledge of the principles of religion, strictly observes the Lord's day, and like Herod, does many things, and hear sermons gladly. In one word, there is a great conformity in his outward conversation, to the letter of both tables of the law. And now there is so mighty a change upon the man, that his neighbours cannot miss to take notice of it. Hence he is cheerfully admitted by the godly into their society, as a praying person, and can confer with them about religious matters, yea, and about soul-exercise, which some are not acquainted with. And their good opinion of him confirms his good opinion of himself. This step in religion is fatal to many, who never get beyond it. But here the Lord reacheth the elect-branch a farther stroke. Conscience flies in the man's face, for some wrong steps in his conversation; the neglect of some duty or commission of some sin, which is a blot in his conversation: and then the flaming sword of the law appears again over his head: and the curse wrings in his ears, for him that continueth not in all things written in the law, to do them, Gal. iii. 10.

Fourthly, On this account he is obliged to seek another salve for his sore. He goes to GOD, confesseth his sins, seeks the pardon of it, promising to watch against it for the time to come; and so finds ease, and thinks he may very well take it, seeing the scripture saith, *If we confess our sins, he is faithful and just to forgive us our sins,* 1 John i. 9. not considering that he grasps at a privilege, which is theirs only who are ingrafted into CHRIST, and under the covenant of grace, and which the branches yet growing on the old stock, cannot plead. And here sometimes there are formal and express vows made against such and such sins, and binding to such and such duties. Thus many go on all their days, knowing no other religion but to do duties, and to confess, and pray for pardon of that wherein they fail, promising themselves eternal happiness, tho' they are utter strangers to CHRIST. Here many elect ones have been cast down, wounded, and many reprobates have been slain; while the wounds of neither of them have been deep enough, to cut them off from their natural stock. But the Spirit of the LORD gives yet a deeper stroke to the branch which is to be cut off; shewing him that, as yet, he is but an outside saint; and discovering to him the filthy lusts lodged in his heart, which he took no notice of before, Rom. vii. 9. *When the commandment came sin revived and I died.* Then he sees his heart a dunghill of hellish lusts; filled with covetousness, pride, malice, filthiness, and the like. Now, as soon as the door of the chambers of his imagery is thus opened to him, and he sees what they do there in the dark, his outside religion is blown up as insufficient; and he learns a new lesson in religion; namely, That he is not a Jew which is one outwardly, Rom. ii. 28.

Fifthly, Upon this he goes further, even to inside religion: sets to work more vigorously than ever; mourns over the evils of his heart, and strives to bear down the weeds he finds growing in that neglected garden. He labours to curb his pride and passion, and to banish speculative impurities; prays more fervently, hears attentively, and strives to get his heart affected in every religious duty he performs; and thus he comes to think himself not only an outside, but an inside Christian. Wonder not at this; for there is nothing in it beyond the power of nature, or what one may attain to under a vigorous influence of the covenant of works. Therefore another stroke yet deeper is reached: The law chargeth home on the man's conscience that he was a transgressor from the womb; that he came into the world a guilty creature; and that, in the time of his ignorance, and even since his eyes were opened, he has been guilty of many actual sins;

either altogether overlooked by him, or not sufficiently mourned over: For spiritual sores, not healed by the blood of CHRIST, but skinned over some other way, are easily ruffled, and as soon break out again. And therefore the law takes him by the throat, saying, *Pay what thou owest.*

Sixthly, Then the sinner says in his heart, *Have patience with me, and I will pay thee all:* and so falls to work to pacify an offended GOD, and to atone for these sins. He renews his repentance, such as it is; bears patiently the afflictions laid upon him; yea, he afflicts himself, denies himself the use of his lawful comforts, sighs deeply, mourns bitterly, cries with tears for a pardon, till he hath wrought up his heart to a conceit of having obtained it: having thus done penance for what is past, and resolving to be a good servant to GOD, and to hold on in outward and inward obedience, for the time to come. But the stroke must go nearer the heart yet, ere the branch fall off. The LORD discovers to him, in the glass of the law, how he sinneth in all he does, even when he does the best he can; and therefore the dreadful sound returns to his ears, Gal. iii. 10. *Cursed is every one that continueth not in all things,* &c. *When ye fasted and mourned,* saith the LORD, *did ye at all fast unto me, even to me?* Will muddy water make clean clothes? Will you satisfy for one sin with another? Did not your thoughts wander in such a duty? Were not your affections flat in another? Did not your heart give a whorish look to such an idol? And did it not rise in a fit of impatience under such an affliction? *Should I accept this of your hands? Cursed be the deceiver, which sacrificeth to the Lord a corrupt thing,* Mal. i. 13, 14. And thus he becomes so far broke off, that he sees he is not able to satisfy the demands of the law.

Seventhly, Hence, like a broken man, who finds he is not able to pay all his debts, he goes about to compound with his creditor. And being in pursuit of ease and comfort, he does what he can to fulfil the law; and wherein he fails, he looks that GOD will accept the will for the deed. Thus doing his duty, and having a will to do better, he cheats himself into a persuasion of the goodness of his state; and hereby thousands are ruined. But the elect get another stroke, which looseth their hold in this case. The doctrine of the law is born in on their consciences! demonstrating to them, that exact and perfect obedience is required by it, under pain of the curse; and that it is doing, and not wishing to do, which will avail. Wishing to do better will not answer the law's demands; and therefore the curse sounds again, Cursed is every one that continueth not to do them: that is, actually to do them. In vain is wishing then.

Eighthly, Being broken off from hopes of compounding with the law, he falls a-borrowing. He sees that all he can do to obey the law, and all his desires to be, and to do better, will not save his soul; therefore he goes to CHRIST, intreating, that his righteousness may make up what is wanting in his own, and cover all the defects of his doings and sufferings; that so GOD, for CHRIST's sake, may accept them, and thereupon be reconciled. Thus doing what he can to fulfil the law, and looking to CHRIST to make up all his defects, he comes at length again to sleep in a sound skin: Many persons are ruined this way. This was the error of the Galatians, which Paul in his epistle to them, disputes against. But the Spirit of GOD breaks off the sinner from this hold also, by bearing in on his conscience that great truth, Gal. iii. 12. *The law is not of faith; but the man that doth them shall live in them.* There is no mixing of the law and faith in this business; the sinner must hold by one of them, and let the other go; the way of the law and the way of faith, are so far different, that it is not possible for a sinner to walk in the one, but he must come off from the other: and if he be for doing, he must do all alone; CHRIST will not do a part for him, if he do not all. A garment pieced up of sundry sorts of righteousness, is not a garment meet for the court of heaven. Thus the man, who was in a dream, and thought he was eating, is awakened by the stroke, and behold his soul is faint; his heart sinks in him like a stone, while he finds he can neither bear his burden himself alone, nor can he get help under it.

Ninthly, What can one do, who must needs pay, and yet neither has as much of his own as will bring him out of debt, nor can he get as much to borrow; and to beg he is ashamed? What can such an one do, I say, but sell himself as the man under the law that was waxen poor? Lev. xxv. 47. Therefore the sinner, beat off from so many holds, goes about to make a bargain with CHRIST, and to sell himself to the Son of GOD, if I may so speak, solemnly promising and vowing, that he will be a servant to CHRIST, as long as he lives, if he will save his soul. And here oft-times the sinner makes a personal covenant with CHRIST, resigning himself to him on these terms; yea, and takes the sacrament to make the bargain sure. Hereupon the man's great care is, to obey CHRIST, keep his commands, and so fulfil his bargain. In this the soul finds a false, unsound peace, for a while; till the Spirit of the LORD fetch another stroke, to cut off the man from this refuge of lies likewise. And that happens in this manner: When he fails of the duties he engaged to, and falls again into the sin he covenanted against; it is powerfully carried home on his conscience, that his covenant is broken; so all his comfort goes, and terrors afresh seize on his soul, as one that has broken covenant with CHRIST; and commonly the man, to help himself, renews his covenant, but breaks again as before. And how is it possible it should be otherwise, seeing he is still upon the old stock? Thus the work of many, all their days, as to their souls, is nothing but a making and breaking such covenants over and over again.

Object. Some perhaps will say, Who liveth and sinneth not? Who is there that faileth not of the duties he is engaged to? If you reject this way as unsound, who then can be saved? *Ans.* True believers will be saved; namely, all who do by faith take hold of GOD's covenant. But this kind of covenant is **men's** own covenant, devised of their own heart; not GOD's covenant revealed in the gospel of his grace: and the making of it is nothing else, but the making of a covenant of works with CHRIST, confounding the law and the gospel; a covenant he will never subscribe to, though we should sign it with our heart's blood, Rom. iv. 14. 16. *For if they which are of the law be heirs, faith is made void, and the promise made of none effect.---Therefore it is of faith, that it might be by grace, to the end the promise might be sure to all the seed.* Chap. xi. 6. *And if by grace, then it is no more of works; otherwise grace is no more grace. But if it be of works, then it is no more grace: otherwise work is no more work.* GOD's covenant is everlasting: once in, never out of it again: **and** the mercies of it are sure mercies, Isa. lv. 3. But that covenant of yours is a tottering covenant, never sure, but broken every day. It is a mere servile covenant, giving CHRIST service for salvation: but GOD's covenant is a filial covenant, in which the sinner takes CHRIST, and his salvation freely offered, and so becomes a son, John i. 12. *But as many as received him, to them gave he power to become the sons of God;* and being become a son, he serves his Father, not that the inheritance may be his, but because it is his through JESUS CHRIST, see, Gal. iv. 24. and downward. To enter into that spurious covenant, is to buy CHRIST with money; but to take hold of God's covenant, is to buy of him without money and without price, Isa. lv. 1. that is to say, to beg of him. In that covenant men work for life; in GOD's covenant they come to CHRIST for life, and work from life. When a person under that covenant fails in his duty, all is gone, the covenant must be made over again; but under GOD's covenant, although the man fail in his duty, and for his failures fall under the discipline of the covenant, and lies under the weight of it, till such time as he has recourse to the blood of CHRIST for pardon, and renew his repentance, yet all that he trusted to for life, and salvation, namely, the righteousness of CHRIST still stands entire, and the covenant remains firm, see Rom. vii. 24, 25. and viii. 1.

Now, though some men spend their lives in making and breaking such covenants of their own, the terror upon the breaking of them wearing weaker and weaker by degrees, till at last it creates them little or no uneasiness; yet the man in whom the good work is carried on, till it be accomplished in cutting him off from the old stock, finds these covenants to be as rotten cords, broke at every touch; and the terror of GOD, being thereupon redoubled on his spirit, and the waters at every turn getting into his very soul, he is obliged to cease from catching hold of such covenants and to seek help some other way.

Tenthly, Therefore the man comes at length to beg at CHRIST's door for mercy; but yet he is a proud beggar, standing on his personal worth. For, as the Papists have mediators to plead for them, with the one only Mediator; so the branches of the old stock, have always something to produce, which they think may commend them to CHRIST, and engage him to take their cause in hand. They cannot think of coming to the spiritual market, without money in their hand. They are like persons, who have once had an estate of their own, but are reduced to extreme poverty, and forced to beg. When they come to beg, they still remember their former character; and though they have lost their substance, yet they retain much of their former spirit! therefore they cannot think they ought to be treated as ordinary beggars, but deserve a particular regard; and, if that be not given them, their spirits rise against him to whom they address themselves for supply. Thus God gives the unhumbled sinner many common mercies, and shuts him not up in the pit, according to his deserving; but all this is nothing in his eyes. He must be set down at the children's table, otherwise he reckons himself hardly dealt with, and wronged; for he is not yet brought, so low, as to think, GOD may be justified when he speaketh, against him, and clear from all iniquity, when he judgeth him according to his real demerit, Psal. li. 4. He thinks perhaps, that even before he was enlightned, he was better than many others; he considers his reformation of life, his repentance, the grief and tears his sin has cost him, his earnest desires after CHRIST, his prayers, and wrestlings for mercy: and useth all these now, as bribes for mercy, laying no small weight on them in his addresses to the throne of grace. But here the Spirit of the LORD shoots a sheaf of arrows into the man's heart, whereby his confidence in these things is sunk and destroyed; and instead of thinking himself better than many, he is made to see himself worse than any. The naughtiness of his reformation of life is discovered. His repentance appears to him no better than the repentance of Judas; his tears like Esau's, and his desires after CHRIST to be selfish and lothsome, like theirs who sought CHRIST because of the loaves, John vi. 26. His answer from GOD seems now to be, Away proud beggar, *How shall I put thee among the children?* He seems to look sternly on him, for his slighting of JESUS CHRIST by unbelief, which is a sin he scarce discerned before. But now at length, he beholds it in its crimson colours; and is pierced to the heart as with a thousand darts, while he sees how he has been going on blindly, sinning against the remedy of sin, & in the whole course of his life, trampling on the blood of the Son of GOD. And now he is, in his own eyes, the miserable object of law-vengeance, yea and gospel-vengeance too.

Eleventhly, The man being thus far humbled, will no more plead, he is worthy for whom CHRIST should do this thing; but, on the contrary, looks on himself as unworthy of Christ, & unworthy of the favour of GOD. We may compare him in this case, to the young man who followed CHRIST, having a linen cloth cast about his naked body; on whom, when the young men laid hold, he left the linen cloth, and fled from them naked, Mark xiv. 51, 52. Even so the man had been following Christ, in the thin & coldrife garment of his own personal worthiness; but by it, even by it, which he so much trusted to, the law catcheth hold of him, to make him prisoner; and then he is fain to leave it, and flees away naked; yet not to CHRIST, but from him. If you now tell him, he is welcome to come to CHRIST, if he will come to him; he is apt to say, Can such a vile and unworthy wretch as I, be welcome to the holy JESUS? If a plaister be applied to his wounded soul, it will not stick. He says, *Depart from me for I am a sinful man, O Lord*, Luke v. 8. No man needs speak to him of his repentance, for his comfort; he can quickly espy such faults in it, as makes it naught: nor of his tears, for he is assured, they have never come into the LORD's bottle: He disputes himself away from CHRIST, and concludes now that he has been such a slighter of CHRIST, and is such an unholy and vile creature, he cannot, he will not, he ought not to come to CHRIST; and that he must either be in better case, or else he will never believe. And hence he now makes his strongest efforts, to amend what was amiss in his way before; he prays more earnestly than ever, mourns more bitterly, strives against sin, in heart and life, more vigorously, and watcheth more diligently; if by any means he may, at length, be fit to come to CHRIST. One would think the man is well humbled now: But ah! devilish pride lurks under the veil of all this seeming humility. Like a kindly branch of the old stock, he adheres still, and will not submit to the righteousness of GOD, Rom. x. 3. He will not come to the market of free grace, without money. He is bidden to the marriage of the King's Son, where the bridegroom himself furnisheth all the guests with wedding-garments, stripping them of their own: but he will not come, because he wants a wedding-garment, howbeit he is very busy making one ready. This is sad work, and therefore he must have a deeper stroke yet, else he is ruined. This stroke is reached him with the ax of the law, in its irritating power. Thus the law girding the soul with cords of death, and holding it in with the rigorous commands of obedience, under the pain of the curse; and GOD, in his holy and wise conduct, withdrawing his restraining grace; corruption is irritated, lusts become violent, and the more they are striven against, the more they rage, like a furious horse checked with the bit. Then do corruptions set up their heads, which he never saw in himself before. Here oft-times atheism, blasphemy, and in one word, horrible things concerning GOD, terrible thoughts concerning the faith, arise in his breast; so that his heart is a very hell within him. Thus while he is sweeping the house of his heart, not yet watered with gospel-grace, these corruptions which lay quiet before in neglected corners, fly up and down in it like dust. He is as one who is mending a dam, and while he is repairing breaches in it, and strengthening every part of it, a mighty flood comes down, overturns his work, and drives all away before it, as well what was newly laid, as what was laid before; read Rom. vii. 8, 9, 10. 13. This is a stroke which goes to the heart; and by it, his hope of getting himself more fit to come to CHRIST, is cut off.

Lastly, Now the time is come, when the man, betwixt hope and despair, resolves to go to CHRIST as he is: and, therefore, like a dying man stretching himself, just before his breath goes out, he rallies the broken forces of his soul; tries to believe, and, in some sort, lays hold on JESUS CHRIST. And now the branch hangs on the old stock, by one single tack of a natural faith, produced by the natural vigour of one's own spirit, under a most pressing necessity, Psal. lxxviii. 34, 35. *When he slew them, then they sought him: and they returned and enquired early after God. And they remembered that God was their rock, and the high God their redeemer.* Hos. viii. 2. *Israel shall cry unto me, My God, we know thee.* But the LORD minding to perfect his work, fetches yet another stroke, whereby the branch falls quite off. The Spirit of God convincingly discovers to the sinner, his utter inability to do any thing that is good; and so he dieth. Rom. vii. 9. That voice powerfully strikes thro' his soul, *How can ye believe?* John v. 44. Thou canst no more believe, than thou canst reach up thine hand to heaven, and bring CHRIST down from thence. And thus, at length, he sees he can neither help himself, by working nor believing: and having no more to hang by, on the old stock, he therefore falls off. And while he is thus distressed, seeing himself like to be swept away with the flood of GOD's wrath; and yet unable so much as to stretch forth a hand, to lay hold of a twig of the tree of life growing on the banks of the river; he is taken up, and ingrafted into the true Vine, the LORD JESUS CHRIST giving him the spirit of faith.

By what has been said on this head, I design not to rack or distress tender consciences; for though there are but few such, at this day, yet GOD forbid I should offend any of CHRIST's little ones. But, alas; a dead sleep is fallen upon this generation; they will not be awakened, let us go as near the quick as we will: and therefore, I fear there is another sort of awakening abiding this sermon-proof generation, which shall make the ears of them that hear it to tingle. However, I would not have this to be looked upon as the sovereign GOD's stinted method of breaking off sinners from the old stock; but this I assert, as a certain truth, that all who are in CHRIST, have been broken off from all these several confidences; and that they who were never broken off from them, are yet in their natural stock. Nevertheless, if the house be pulled down, and the old foundation razed; it is all one, whether it was taken down stone by stone, or undermined, and all fell down together.

Now it is, that the branch is ingrafted in JESUS CHRIST. And, as the law, in the hand of the Spirit of GOD, was the instrument to cut off the branch from the natural stock, so the gospel, in the hand of the same Spirit, is the instrument used for ingrafting it into the supernatural stock, 1 John i. 3. *That which we have seen and heard, declare we unto you; that ye also may have fellowship with us: And truly our fellowship is with the Father, and with his Son, Jesus Christ.* See Isaiah lxi. 1, 2, 3. The gospel is a silver cord let down from heaven, to draw perishing sinners to land. And, though the preaching of the law prepares the way of the LORD, yet it is in the word of the gospel, that CHRIST and a sinner meet. Now, as in the natural grafting, the branch being taken up, is put into the stock; and being put into it, takes with it; and so they are united: even so in the spiritual ingrafting, CHRIST apprehends the sinner; and the sinner, being apprehended of CHRIST, apprehends him; and so they become one, Phil. iii. 12.

First, CHRIST apprehends the sinner by his Spirit, and draws him to himself, 1 Cor. xii. 13. *For by one Spirit, we are all baptized into one body.* The same Spirit, which is in the Mediator himself, he communicates to his elect in due time; never to depart from them, but to abide in them, as a principle of life. Thus he takes hold of them, by his own Spirit put into them; and so the withered branch gets life. The soul is now in the hands of the LORD of life, & possessed by the Spirit of life; how then can it but live? The man gets a ravishing sight of CHRIST'S excellency, in the glass of the gospel; He sees him a full, suitable, and willing Saviour: and gets a heart to take him for, and instead of all. The Spirit of faith furnisheth him with feet to come to CHRIST, and hands to receive him. What by nature he could not do, by grace he can; the holy Spirit working in him the work of faith with power.

Secondly, The sinner thus apprehended, apprehends CHRIST by faith, and so takes with the blessed stock, Eph. iii. 17. *That Christ may dwell in your hearts by faith.* The soul that before tried many ways of escape, but all in vain, doth now look again, with the eye of faith, which proves the healing look. As Aaron's rod laid up in the tabernacle, budded and brought forth buds, Num. xvii. 8. So the dead branch apprehended by the LORD of life, put into, and bound up with, the glorious quickning stock, by the Spirit of life, buds forth in actual believing on JESUS CHRIST, whereby this union is completed: *We having the same spirit of faith, believe*, 2 Cor. iv. 13. Thus the stock and the graft are united, CHRIST and the Christian are married: faith being the soul's consent to the spiritual marriage-covenant, which as it is proposed in the gospel to mankind sinners indefinitely, so it is demonstrated, attested, and brought home, to the man in particular, by the holy Spirit: and so he being joined to the LORD, is one spirit with him. Hereby a believer lives in and for CHRIST, and CHRIST lives in and for the believer, Gal. ii. 20. *I am crucified with Christ. Nevertheless I live: yet not I, but Christ liveth in me.* Hos. iii. 3. *Thou shalt not be for another man, so will I also be for thee.* The bonds then of this blessed union are, the Spirit on CHRIST'S part, and faith on the believer's part.

Now, both the souls and bodies of believers are united to CHRIST. *He that is joined to the Lord, is one spirit*, 1 Cor. vi. 17. The very bodies of believers have this honour put upon them, that they are the temples of the holy Ghost, ver. 19. And the members of CHRIST, ver. 15. When they sleep in the dust, they sleep in Jesus, 1 Thes. iv. 14. And it is in virtue of this union, they shall be raised up out of the dust again, Rom. viii. 11. *He shall quicken your mortal bodies by his Spirit, that dwelleth in you.* In token of this mystical union, the church of believers is called by the name of her Head and Husband, 1 Cor. xii. 12. *For as the body is one, and hath many members,—so also is Christ.*

Use. From what is said, we may draw these following *Inferences*.

1. The preaching of the law is most necessary. He that would ingraft, must needs use the snedding knife. Sinners have many shifts to keep them from CHRIST; many things by which they keep their hold of the natural stock: therefore they have need to be closely pursued, and hunted out of their skulking holes, and refuge of lies.

Yet, it is the gospel that crowns the work; the law makes nothing perfect. The law lays open the wound, but it is the gospel that heals. The law strips a man, wounds him, and leaves him half dead: The gospel binds up his wounds, pouring in wine and oil, to heal them. By the law we are broken off; but, it is by the gospel we are taken up, and implanted in CHRIST.

3. *If any man have not the Spirit of Christ, he is none of his,* Rom. viii. 9. We are told of a monster in nature, having two bodies differently animated, as appeared from contrary affections at one and the same time; but so united, that they were served with the self-same legs. Even so, however men may cleave to CHRIST, call themselves of the holy city, and stay themselves upon the GOD of Israel. Isa. xlviii. 2. And they may be bound up as branches in him, John xv. 2. by the outward ties of sacraments: yet, if the Spirit that dwells in CHRIST, dwell not in them, they are not one with him. There is a great difference betwixt adhesion and ingrafting. The ivy claps and twists itself about the oak, but it is not one with it, for it still grows on its own root; so, to allude to, Isa. iv. 1. many professors take hold of CHRIST and eat their own bread, and wear their own apparel, only they are called by his name. They stay themselves upon him, but grow upon their own root: they take him to support their hopes, but their delights are elsewhere.

4. The union betwixt CHRIST and his mystical members, is firm and indissolvable. Were it so that the believer only apprehended CHRIST, but CHRIST apprehended not him; we could promise little on the stability of such an union; it might quickly be dissolved: but, as the believer apprehends CHRIST by faith, so CHRIST apprehends him by his Spirit, and none shall pluck him out of his hand. Did the child

only keep hold of the nurse, it might at length weary and let go its hold, and so fall away: but if she have her arms about the child, it is in no hazard of falling away, even though it be not actually holden by her: so, whatever sinful intermissions may happen in the exercise of faith, yet the union remains sure, by reason of the constant indwelling of the Spirit. Blessed JESUS! all his saints are in thy hand, Deut. xxxiii. 3. It is observed by some, that the word *Abba* is the same, whether you read it forward or backward! Whatever the believer's case be, the LORD is still to him, *Abba Father*.

Lastly, They have an unsure hold of CHRIST, whom he has not apprehended by his Spirit. There are many half-marriages here, where the soul apprehends CHRIST, but is not apprehended of him. Hence many fall away, and never rise again: they let go their hold of CHRIST; and when that is gone, all is gone. These are the branches in CHRIST, that bear not fruit, which the husbandman taketh away, John xv. 2. *Quest.* How can that be? *Ans.* These branches are set in the stock, by a profession, or an unsound hypocritical faith; they are bound up with it, in the external use of the sacraments: but the stock and they are never knit; therefore they cannot bear fruit. And they need not be cut off, nor broken off; they are by the husbandman only taken away, or, as the word primarily signifies, lifted up; and so taken away, because there is nothing to hold them; they are indeed bound up with the stock, but they have never united with it.

Quest. How shall I know if I am apprehended of CHRIST? *Ans.* You may be satisfied in this inquiry, if you consider and apply these two things.

First, When CHRIST apprehends a man by his Spirit, he is so drawn, that he comes away to CHRIST with his whole heart; for true believing is believing with all the heart, Acts viii. 37. Our LORD'S followers are like these who followed Saul at first, men whose hearts GOD has touched, 1 Sam. x. 26. When the Spirit pours in overcoming grace, they pour out their hearts like water before him, Psal. lxii. 8. They flow unto him like a river, Isa. ii. 2. *All nations shall flow unto it*, namely, to the mountain of the LORD'S house. It denotes not only the abundance of converts, but the disposition of their souls, in coming to CHRIST: they come heartily and freely, as drawn with loving-kindness, Jer. xxxi. 3. *Thy people shall be willing in the day of thy power*, Psal. cx. 3. i. e. free, ready, open-hearted, giving themselves to thee as free-will offerings. When the bridegroom has the Bride's heart, it is a right marriage; but some give their hand to CHRIST, who give him not their heart. They that are only driven to CHRIST by terror, will surely leave him again, when that terror is gone. Terror may break a heart of stone, but the pieces into which it is broken, still continue to be stone; the terrors cannot soften it into a heart of flesh. Yet terror may begin the work, which love crowns: the strong wind, the earthquake, and the fire going before; the still small voice, in which the LORD is, may come after them. When the blessed JESUS is seeking sinners to match with him, they are bold and perverse, they will not speak with him, till he hath wounded them, made them captives, and bound them with the cords of death. When this is done, then it is he makes love to them, and wins their hearts. The LORD says, Hof. ii. 16.—20. that his chosen Israel shall be married unto himself. But, how will the bride's consent be won? Why, in the first place, he will bring her into the wilderness, as he did the people when he brought them out of Egypt, ver. 14. There she will be hardly dealt with, scorched with thirst, and bitten with serpents; and then he will speak comfortably to her, or, as the expression is, he will speak upon her heart. The sinner is first driven, and then drawn to CHRIST. It is with the soul as with Noah's dove; she was forced back again to the ark, because she could find nothing else to rest upon; but when she did return, she would have rested on the outside of it, if Noah had not put forth his hand and pulled her in, Gen. viii. 9. The LORD sends the avenger of blood in pursuit of the criminal, and he, with a sad heart leaves his own city: and with tears in his eyes, parts with his old acquaintance, because he dare not stay with them; and he flees for his life to the city of refuge. This is not at all his choice, it is forced work; necessity has no law. But when he comes to the gates, and sees the beauty of the place the excellency and loveliness of it charms him; and then he enters it with heart and good-will, saying, *This is my rest, and here will I stay*; and, as one said in another case, I had perished unless I had perished.

Secondly, When CHRIST apprehends a soul, the heart is disengaged from, and turned against sin. As in cutting off the branch from the old stock, the great idol, self is brought down, the man is powerfully taught to deny himself; so, in the apprehending of the sinner by his Spirit, that union is dissolved, which was betwixt the man and his lusts, while he was in the flesh, as the Apostle expresses it, Rom. viii. 5. the heart is loosed from them, though formerly as dear to him, as the members of his body, as his eyes, legs and arms; and, instead of taking pleasure in them, as sometimes he did, he longs to be rid of them. When the LORD JESUS comes to a soul, in the day of converting grace; he finds it like Jerusalem in the day of her nativity, Ezek. xvi. 4. with its naval not cut, drawing its fulsome nourishment and satisfaction from its lusts; but, he cuts off this communication, that he may set the soul on the breasts of his own consolations, and give it rest in himself. And thus the LORD wounds the head and heart of sin, and the soul comes to him saying, *Surely our fathers have inherited lies, vanity and things wherein there are no profit,* Jer. xvi. 19.

Of the benefits flowing to true Believers, from their union with Christ.

V. And *lastly,* I come to speak of the benefits flowing to true believers from their union with CHRIST. The chief of the particular benefits **believers** have by it, are justification, peace, adoption, sanctification, growth in grace, fruitfulness in good works, acceptance of these good works, establishment in a state of grace, support and a special conduct of providence about them. As for communion with CHRIST, it is such a benefit, as being the immediate consequent of union with him, comprehends all the rest as mediate ones. For look, as the branch, immediately upon its union with the stock, hath communion with the stock, in all that is in it; so the believer uniting with CHRIST, hath communion with him; in which he launcheth forth into an ocean of happiness, is led into a paradise of pleasures, and has a saving interest in the treasure hid in the field of the gospel, the unsearchable riches of CHRIST. As soon as the believer is united to CHRIST, CHRIST himself, in whom all fulness dwells, is his, Cant. ii. 16. *My beloved is mine, and I am his.* And, *How shall he not with him freely give us ALL things?* Rom. vii. 32. *Whether Paul, or Apollos, or Cephas, or the world, or life, or death, or things present, or things to come, ALL are yours,* 1 Cor. iii. 22. Thus communion with CHRIST is the great comprehensive blessing, necessarily flowing from our union with him. Let us now consider the particular benefits flowing from it, before-mentioned.

The *First* particular benefit, that a sinner hath by his union with CHRIST, is justification; for being united to CHRIST, he hath communion with him in his righteousness, 1 Cor. i. 30. *But of him are ye in Christ Jesus, who of God is made unto us wisdom and righteousness.* He stands no more condemned, but justified before GOD, as being in CHRIST, Rom. viii. 1. *There is therefore now no condemnation to them which are in Christ Jesus.* The branches hereof are pardon of sin, and personal acceptance.

1st, His sins are pardoned, the guilt of them is removed. The bond obliging him to pay his debt, is cancelled. GOD the Father takes the pen, dips it into the blood of his Son, crosseth the sinner's accounts, and blotteth them out of his debt-book. The sinner, out of CHRIST, is bound over to the wrath of GOD; he is under an obligation in law, to go to the prison of hell, and there to lie till he has paid the utmost farthing. This ariseth from the terrible sanction with which the law is fenced, which is no less than death, Gen. ii. 17. So that the sinner passing the bounds assigned him, is as Shimei in another case, a man of death, 1 Kings ii. 42. But now being united to CHRIST, GOD saith, *Deliver him from going down to the pit: I have found a ransom*, Job xxxiii. 24. The sentence of condemnation is reversed, the believer is absolved, and set beyond the reach of the condemning law. His sins, which sometimes were set before the LORD, Psalm xc. 8. so that they could not be hid, GOD now takes and casts them all behind his back, Isa. xxxvii. 17. Yea, he casts them into the depths of the sea, Micah vii. 19. What falls into a brook, may be got up again; but what is cast into the sea, cannot be recovered. Ay, but there are some shallow places in the sea; true, but their sins are not cast in there, but into the depths of the sea; and the depths of the sea are devouring depths, from whence they shall never come forth again. But what if they do not sink? He will cast them in with force; so that they shall go to the ground, and sink as lead in the mighty waters of the Redeemer's blood. They are not only forgiven, but forgotten, Jer. xxxi. 34. *I will forgive their iniquity, and I will remember their sins no more.* And though their after-sins do in themselves, deserve eternal wrath, and do actually make them liable to temporal strokes, and fatherly chastisements, according to the tenor of the covenant of grace, Psalm lxxxix. 30.----33. Yet they can never be actually liable to eternal wrath, or the curse of the law; for they are dead to the law in CHRIST, Rom. vii. 4. And they can never fall from their union with CHRIST, nor can they be in CHRIST, and yet under condemnation, Rom. viii. 1. *There is therefore now no condemnation to them which are in Christ Jesus.* This is an inference drawn from that doctrine of the believer's being dead to the law, delivered by the Apostle, chap. vii. 1----6. as is clear from chap. viii. 2, 3, 4. And in this respect, the justified man is the blessed man, unto whom the LORD imputeth not iniquity, Psalm xxxii. 2. As one who has no design to charge a debt on another, sets it not down in his count-book.

2dly, The believer is accepted as righteous in GOD's sight, 2 Cor. v. 21. For he is found in CHRIST, not having his own righteousness, but that which is through the faith of CHRIST, the righteousness which is of GOD by faith, Phil. iii. 9. He could never be accepted of GOD as righteous, upon the account of his own righteousness; because at best, it is but imperfect; and all righteousness, properly so called, which will abide a trial before the throne of GOD, is perfect. The very name of it implies perfection; for unless a work be perfectly conform to the law, it is not right but wrong; and so cannot make a man righteous before GOD, whose judgment is according to truth. Yet if justice demand a righteousness of one that is in CHRIST, upon which he may be accounted righteous before the LORD; *Surely shall such an one say, In the Lord have I righteousness*, Isa. xlv. 24. The law is fulfilled; its commands are obeyed, its sanction is satisfied. The believer's Cautioner has paid the debt. It was exacted, and he answered for it.

Thus the person united to CHRIST, is justified. You may conceive of the whole proceeding herein, in this manner. The avenger of blood pursuing the criminal, Christ, as the Saviour of lost sinners, doth by the Spirit apprehend him, and draw him to himself; and he by faith lays hold on CHRIST; so the LORD our righteousness, and the unrighteous creature unite. From this union with CHRIST, results a communion with him, in his unsearchable riches, and consequently, in his righteousness, that white raiment which he has for clothing of the naked, Rev. iii. 18. Thus the righteousness of CHRIST becomes his; and because it is his by unquestionable title, it is imputed to him; it is reckoned his, on the judgment of GOD, which is always according to the truth of the thing. And so the believing sinner having a righteousness which fully answers the demands of the law, he is pardoned and accepted as righteous. See Isa. xlv. 22. 24, 25. Rom. iii. 24. and chap. v. 1. Now he is a free man; who shall lay any thing to the charge of these whom GOD justifieth? Can justice lay any thing to their charge? No; for it is satisfied. Can the law? No, for it has got all its demands of them in JESUS CHRIST, Gal. ii. 26. *I am crucified with Christ*. What can the law require more, after it has wounded their Head; poured in wrath, in full measure, into their soul; and cut off their life, and brought it into the dust of death? In so far as it has done all this to JESUS CHRIST, who is their Head, Eph. i. 22. their Soul, Acts ii. 25. 27. and their Life? Col. iii. 4. What is become of the sinner's own hand-writing, which would prove the debt upon him? CHRIST has blotted it out Col. ii. 14. But, it may be justice may get its eye upon it again; no, *he took it out of the way*. But, O that it had been torn in pieces, may the sinner say: yea, so it is; the nails that pierced CHRIST's hands and feet, are driven through it, he nailed it. But what if the torn pieces be set together again? That cannot be, for he nailed it to his cross, and his cross was buried with him: but will never rise more, seeing CHRIST dieth no more. Where is the face-covering that was upon the condemned man? CHRIST has destroyed it, Isa. xxv. 7. Where is death, that stood before the sinner with a grim face, and an open mouth, ready to devour him? CHRIST has swallowed it up in victory, ver. 8. Glory, glory, glory to him, that thus loved us, and washed us from our sins in his own blood!

The second benefit flowing from the same spring of union with CHRIST, and coming by the way of justification, in Peace: peace with GOD, and peace of conscience, according to the measure of the sense the justified have of their peace with GOD, Rom. v. 1. *Therefore, being justified by faith, we have peace with God.* Chap. xiv. 27. *For the kingdom of God is not meat and drink, but righteousness and peace, and joy in the holy Ghost.* Whereas GOD was their enemy before, now he is reconciled to them in CHRIST: they are in a covenant of peace with him; and as Abraham was, so they are the friends of GOD. He is well pleased with them in his beloved Son. His word, which spoke terror to them formerly, now speaks peace, if they rightly take up its language. And there is love in all his dispensations towards them, which makes all work together for their good. Their consciences are purged of that guilt and filthiness that sometime lay upon them: his conscience-purifying blood streams through their souls, by virtue of their union with him Heb. ix. 14. *How much more shall the blood of Christ—purge your conscience from dead works, to serve the living God?* The bonds laid on their consciences, by the Spirit of GOD, acting as the spirit of bondage, are taken off, never more to be laid on by that hand, Rom. vii. 15. *For ye have not received the spirit of bondage again to fear.* Hereby the conscience is quieted, as soon as the soul becomes conscious of the application of that blood; which falls sooner or later, according to the measure of faith, and as the only wise GOD sees meet to time it. Unbelievers may have troubled consciences which they may get quieted again: but, alas! their consciences become peaceable, ere they become pure! so their peace is but the seed of greater horror and confusion. Carelessness may give ease for a while, to a sick conscience; men neglecting its wounds, they close again of their own accord, before the filthy matter is purged out. Many bury their guilt in the grave of an ill memory: conscience smarts a little; at length the man forgets his sin, and there is an end of it: But that it only an ease before death. Business, or the affairs of life, often give ease in this case. When Cain is banished from the presence of the LORD, he falls a-building of cities. When the evil spirit came upon Saul, he calls not for his Bible, nor for the priests to converse with him about his case; but for musick, to play it away. So many, when their consciences begin to be uneasy, they fill their heads and hands with business, to divert themselves, and to regain ease at any rate. Yea, some will sin, over the belly of their convictions; and so some get ease to their consciences, as Hazael gave to his master, by stifling him. Again, the performing of duties may give some ease to a disquieted conscience; and this is all that legal professors have recourse to, for quieting of their consciences. When conscience is wounded, they will pray, confess, mourn, and resolve to do so no more; and so they become whole again, without any application of the blood of CHRIST by faith. But they, whose consciences are rightly quieted, come for peace and purging to the blood of sprinkling. Sin is a sweet morsel, that makes GOD's elect sick souls, ere they get it vomited up. It leaves a sting behind it, which, some one time or other, will create them no little pain.

Elihu shews us both the case and cure, Job xxxiii. Behold the case one may be in, whom GOD has thoughts of love to! He darteth convictions into his conscience and makes them stick so fast, that he cannot rid himself of them, ver. 16 *He openeth the ears of men, and sealeth their instruction.* His very body sickens, ver. 19. *He is chastened also, with pain upon his bed; and the multitudes of his bones with strong pain.* He loseth his stomach, ver. 20. *His life abhorreth bread, and his soul dainty meat.* His body pines away, so that there is nothing on him but skin and bone, ver. 21. *His flesh is consumed away, that it cannot be seen; and his bones, that were not seen, stick out.* Though he is not prepared for death, he has no hopes of life, ver. 22. *His soul draweth near unto the grave, and,* which is the height of his misery, *his life to the destroyers.* He is looking every moment, when devils, these destroyers, Rom. ix. 11. these murderers, or man-slayers, John viii. 44. will come & carry away his soul to hell! O dreadful case! yet there is hope. GOD designs to keep back his soul from the pit, although he bring him forward to the brink of it, ver. 18. Now, see how the sick man is cured: The physician's art cannot prevail here: the disease lies more inward, than that his medicines can reach it. It is soul-trouble that has brought the body into this disorder, and therefore the remedies must be applied to the sick man's soul and conscience. The physician for this case, must be a spiritual phyfician; the remedies muſt be ſpiritual; a righteouſneſs, a ranſom, or atonement. Upon the application of theſe, the ſoul is cured, the conſcience is quieted, and the body recovers, ver. 23, 24, 25, 26. "If there be a meſſenger with him, an interpreter, one among a thouſand, to ſhew unto man his uprightneſs; then he is gracious unto him, and ſaith, Deliver him from going down to the pit, I have found a ranſom. His fleſh ſhall be freſher than a child's, he ſhall return to the days of his youth. He ſhall pray unto GOD, and he ſhall be favourable unto him, and he ſhall ſee his face with joy." The proper phyſician for this patient, is *a meſſenger, an interpreter*, ver. 23. that is, as ſome expoſitors, not without ground, underſtand it, the great phyſician JESUS CHRIST, whom Job had called his Redeemer, chap. xix. 25. He is *a meſſenger*, the meſſenger of the covenant of peace, Mal. iii. 1. who comes ſeaſonably to the ſick man. He is *an interpreter*, the great interpreter of GOD's counſels of love to ſinners, John i. 28. *One among a thouſand*, even the chief among ten thouſand, Cant. v. 10. One choſen out of the people, Pſal. lxxxix. 29. One to whom the LORD hath given the tongue of the learned, to ſpeak a word in ſeaſon to him that is weary, Iſa. l. 4. 5, 6. It is he that is with him, by his Spirit, now, to convince him of righteouſneſs; as he was with him before, to convince him of ſin and judgment, John xvi. 8. His work now, is to ſhew unto him his uprightneſs, or his righteouſneſs, *i. e.* the interpreter CHRIST his righteouſneſs; which is the only righteouſneſs ariſing from the paying of a ranſom, and upon which a ſinner is delivered from going down to the pit, ver. 24. And thus CHRIST is ſaid to declare GOD's name, Pſalm xxii. 22. and to preach righteouſneſs, Pſalm xl. 9. The phraſe is remarkable; it is not to ſhew unto *the man*, but *unto man*, his righteouſneſs; which not obſcurely intimates that he is more than a man, who ſhews, or declareth this righteouſneſs: Compare Amos iv. 13. *He that formeth the mountains, and createth the wind, and declareth unto man what is his thought.* There ſeems to be in it a ſweet alluſion to the firſt declaration of this righteouſneſs unto man, or as the word is, *unto Adam*, after the fall; while he lay under terror from apprehenſions of the wrath of GOD; which declaration was made by the Meſſenger, the interpreter, namely, the eternal Word of the Son of GOD, called, *The voice of the Lord God*, Gen. iii. 8. and by him appearing, probably, in human ſhape. Now, while by his Spirit, he is the Preacher or righteouſneſs to the man, it is ſuppoſed the man lays hold on the offered righteouſneſs; whereupon the ranſom is applied to him, and he is delivered from going down to the pit: for GOD hath a ranſom for him. This is intimate to him; GOD saith, *Deliver him.* ver. 24. Hereupon his conscience, being purged by the blood of atonement, is pacified, and sweetly quieted: *He shall pray unto God—and see his face with joy,* which before he beheld with horror, ver. 26. That is New-Testament language. *Having an High-Priest over the house of God, he shall draw near with a true heart, in full assurance of faith; having his heart sprinkled from an evil conscience,* Heb. x. 21. 22. But then, what becomes of the body, the weak and weary flesh? Why, *His flesh shall be fresher than a child's; he shall return to the days of his youth,* ver. 25. Yea, all *his bones,* which were chastened with strong pain, ver. 19. *shall say, Lord, who is like unto thee?* Psalm xxxv. 10.

A third benefit, flowing from union with CHRIST, is, Adoption. Believers, being united to CHRIST, become children of GOD, and members of the family of heaven. By their union with him, who is the Son of GOD by nature, they become the sons of GOD by grace, John i. 12. As when a branch is cut off from one tree, and grafted in the branch of another; the ingrafted branch, by means of its union with the adopting branch, as some not unfitly have called it, is made a branch of the same stock, with that into which it is ingrafted: so sinners being ingrafted into JESUS CHRIST, whose name is the Branch, his Father is their Father; his GOD their GOD, John xx. 12. And thus they, who are by nature children of the devil, become the children of GOD. They have the Spirit of adoption, Rom. viii. 15. namely, the Spirit of his Son, which bring them to GOD, as children to a father: to pour out their complaints in his bosom, and to seek necessary supply, Gal. iv. 6. *Because ye are sons, God hath sent forth the Spirit of his Son into your hearts, crying, Abba, Father.* Under all their weaknesses, they have fatherly pity and compassion shewn them, Psalm ciii. 13. *Like as a father pitieth his children, so the Lord pitieth them that fear him.* Although they were but foundlings, found in a desart land; yet now that to them belongs the adoption, he keeps them as the apple of his eye, Deut. xxxii. 10. Whosoever pursue them, they have a refuge, Prov. xiv. 26. *His children shall have a place of refuge.* In a time of common calamity, they have chambers for protection, where they may be hid, until the indignation be overpast, Isa. xxvi. 20. And he is not only their refuge for protection, but their portion for provision, in that refuge, Psalm cxlii. 5. *Thou art my refuge and my portion, in the land of the living.* They are provided for, for eternity, Heb. xi. 16. *He hath prepared for them a city.* And what he sees they have need of, for time they shall not want, Mat. vi. 31, 32. *Take no thought, saying, What shall we eat? Or, What shall we drink? Or, Wherewithal shall we be clothed? For your heavenly Father knoweth that ye have need of all these things.* Seasonable correction is likewise their privilege as sons: so they are not suffered to pass with their faults, as happens to others who are not children, but servants of the family, and will be turned out of doors for their miscarriages at length, Heb. xii. 7. *If ye endure chastening, God dealeth with you as with sons; for what son is he whom the Father chasteneth not?* They are heirs of, and shall inherit the promises, Heb. vi. 12. Nay, they are heirs of GOD, who himself is the portion of their inheritance, Psal. xvi. 5. and joint heirs with CHRIST, Rom. viii. 17. And because they are the children of the great King, and young heirs of glory, they have angels for their attendants who are sent forth to minister for them that shall be heirs of salvation, Heb. i. 14.

A Fourth benefit is Sanctification, 1 Cor. i. 30. *But of him are ye in Christ Jesus, who of God is made unto us wisdom and righteousness, and sanctification.* Being united to CHRIST they partake of his Spirit, which is the Spirit of holiness. There is a fulness of the Spirit in CHRIST, & it is not like the fulness of a vessel, which only retains what is poured into it; but it is the fulness of a fountain for diffusion and communication, which is always sending forth its water, and yet is always full. The Spirit of CHRIST, that spiritual sap which is in the stock, and from thence is communicate to the branches, is the Spirit of grace, Zech. xii. 10. And where the Spirit of grace dwells, there will be found a complication of all graces. Holiness is not one grace only, but all the graces of the Spirit; it is a constellation of graces; it is all the graces in their seed and root. And as the sap conveyed from the stock into the branch, goes through it, and through every part of it; so the Spirit of GOD sanctifies the whole man. The poison of sin was diffused through the whole spirit, soul and body of the whole man; and sanctifying grace pursues it into every corner, 1 Thess. v. 23. Every part of the man is sanctified, though no part is perfectly so. The truth we are sanctified by, is not held in the head, as in a prison; but runs, with its sanctifying influences, through heart and life. There are indeed some graces in every believer, which appear as top-branches above the rest; as meekness in Moses, patience in Job; but seeing there is in every child of GOD, a holy principle going along with the holy law, in all the parts thereof, loving, liking, and approving of it; as appears from their universal respect to the commands of GOD; it is evident they are endued with all the graces of the Spirit: because there can be no more in the effect, than there was in the cause.

Now, this sanctifying Spirit, whereof believers partake, is unto them, (1.) A Spirit of mortification. *Through the Spirit they mortify the deeds of the body*, Rom. viii. 13. Sin is crucified in them, Gal. v. 24. They are planted together, namely, with CHRIST, in the likeness of his death, which was a lingering death, Rom. vi. 5. Sin in the saint, though not quite dead, yet is dying. If it were dead, it would be taken down from the cross and buried out of his sight; but it hangs there as yet, working and struggling under its mortal wounds. Look, as when a tree has got such a stroke as reaches the heart of it, all the leaves and branches thereof begin to fade and decay; so, where the sanctifying Spirit comes and breaks the power of sin, there is a gradual ceasing from it, and dying to it, in the whole man, so, that he no longer lives in the flesh to the lusts of men. He does not make sin his trade and business; it is not his great design to seek himself, and to satisfy his corrupt inclinations; but he is for Immanuel's land, and is walking in the high-way to it, the way which is called, The way of holiness; though the wind from hell, that was on his back before, blows now full in his face, makes his travelling uneasy, and often drives him off the high-way. (2.) This Spirit is a Spirit of vivification to them; for he is the Spirit of life, and makes them live unto righteousness, Ezek. xxxvi. 27. *And I will put my Spirit within you, and cause you to walk in my statutes*. Those that have been planted together, with CHRIST, in the likeness of his death, shall be also in the likeness of his resurrection, Rom. vi. 5. At CHRIST's resurrection, when his soul was re-united with his body, every member of that blessed body was enabled again to perform the actions of life; so, the soul being influenced by the sanctifying Spirit of CHRIST, is enabled more and more, to perform all the actions of spiritual life. And as the whole of the law, and not some scraps of it only, is written on the holy heart; so believers are enabled to transcribe that law in their conversation. And although they cannot write one line of it without blots, yet GOD, for CHRIST's sake, accepts of the performances, in point of sanctification; they being disciples to his own Son, and led by his own Spirit.

This sanctifying Spirit communicated by the LORD JESUS to his members, is the spiritual nourishment the branches have from the Stock into which they are ingrafted, whereby the life of grace, given them in regeneration, is preserved, continued and actuated. It is the nourishment whereby the new creature liveth, and is nourished up towards perfection. Spirtual life needs to be fed, & must have supply of nourishment; and believers derive the same from CHRIST, whom the Father has constituted the head of influences to all his members, Col. ii. 19. *And not holding the head, from which all the body by joints & bands having nourishment ministred* or supplied, &c. Now, this supply is, *the supply of the Spirit of Jesus Christ*, Phil. i. 19. The saints feed richly, eating CHRIST's flesh, and drinking his blood, for their spiritual nourishment; yet our LORD himself teacheth us, that it is the Spirit that quickneth, even that Spirit who dwells in that blessed body, John vi. 63. The human nature is united to the divine nature, in the person of the Son, and so, like the bowl in Zechariah's candlestick, Zech. iv. lies at the fountain head, as the conveyance of influences, from the fountain of the Deity; and receives not the Spirit by measure, but ever hath a fulness of the Spirit by reason of that personal union. Hence, believers being united to the man CHRIST, as the seven lamps to the bowl, by their seven pipes, Zech. iv 2. His flesh is to them meat indeed, and his blood drink indeed; for, feeding on that blessed body, *i. e.* effectually applying CHRIST to their souls by faith, they partake more and more of that Spirit who dwelleth therein, to their spiritual nourishment. The holiness of GOD could never admit of an immediate union with the sinful creature, nor, consequently, an immediate communion with it; yet the creature could not live the life of grace, without communion with the fountain of life: Therefore, that the honour of GOD's holiness and the salvation of sinners, might jointly be provided for, the second Person of the glorious Trinity, took into a personal union with himself, a sinless human nature: that so this holy, harmless and undefiled humanity, might immediately receive a fulness of the Spirit, of which he might communicate to his members by his divine power and efficacy. And like as, if there was a tree, having its root in the earth, and its branches reaching to heaven, the vast distance betwixt the root and the branches, would not interrupt the communication betwixt the root and the top-branch; even so, the distance betwixt the man CHRIST, who is in heaven, and his members who are on earth, cannot hinder the communication betwixt them. What though the parts of mystical CHRIST, *viz.* the head and the members, are not contiguous, as joined together into the way of a corporal union? The union is not therefore the less real and effectual. Yea, our LORD himself shews us, that albeit we should eat his flesh in a corporal and carnal manner, yet it would profit nothing, John vi. 63. we would not be one whit holier thereby. But the members of CHRIST on earth, **are** united to their head in heaven, by the invisible bond of the self-same Spirit dwelling in both; in him as the head, and in them as the members; even as the wheels in Ezekiel's vision, were not contiguous to the living creatures, yet were united to them, by an invisible bond of one Spirit in both; so that when the living creatures went, the wheels went by that, and when the living creatures were lift up from the earth, the wheels were lift up, Ezek. i. 19. *For*, says the Prophet, *the spirit of the living creatures was in the wheels*, ver. 20.

Hence we may see the difference, betwixt true sanctification, and that shadow of it, which is to be found amongst some strict professors of Christianity, who yet are not true Christians, are not regenerate by the Spirit of CHRIST, and is of the same kind with what has appeared in many sober heathens. True sanctification is the result of the soul's union with the holy JESUS, the first and immediate receptacle of the sanctifying Spirit out of whose fulness his members do, by virtue of their union with him, receive sanctifying influences. The other is the mere product of the man's own spirit, which whatever it has, or seems to have of the matter of true holiness, yet does not arise from the supernatural principles, not to high aims and ends thereof; for as it comes from self, so it runs out into the dead sea of self again; and lies as wide of true holiness, as nature doth of grace. They who have this bastard holiness, are like common boat-men, who serve themselves with their own oars; whereas, the ship bound for Immanuel's land, sails by the blowings of the divine Spirit. How is it possible there should be true sanctification without CHRIST? Can there be true sanctification, without partaking of the Spirit of holiness? Can we partake of that Spirit, but by JESUS CHRIST, the way, the truth, and the life? The falling dew shall as soon make its way through the flinty rock, as influences of grace shall come from GOD to sinners, any other, but through him whom the Father has constituted the head of influences, Col. i. 19. *For it pleased the Father, that in him should all fulness dwell*; and cha. ii. 9. *And not holding the head, from which all the body by joints and bands having nourishment ministered and knit together, increaseth with the increase of God.* Hence see how it comes to pass, that many fall away from their seeming sanctification, and never recover; it is because they are not branches truly knit to the true vine. Meanwhile others recover from their decays, because of their union with the life-giving stock, by the quickening Spirit, 1 John ii. 19. *They went out from us, but they were not of us; for if they had been of us, they would no doubt have continued with us.*

A *Fifth* benefit is Growth in grace. *Having nourishment ministered, they increase with the increase of God,* Col. ii. 19. *The righteous shall flourish like the palmtree, he shall grow like a ceder in Lebanon,* Psalm xcii. 12. Grace is of growing nature; in the way to Zion they go from strength to strength. Though the holy man be at first a little child in grace, yet at length he becomes a young man, a father, 1 John ii. 13. Though he does but creep in the way to heaven sometimes, yet afterwards he walks, he runs, he mounts up with wings as eagles, Isa. xl. 31. If a branch grafted into a stock never grows, it is a plain evidence of its not having knit with the stock.

But some may perhaps say, If all true Christians be growing ones, what shall be said of these, who instead of growing, are going back? I answer, *First,* There is a great difference between the Christian's growing simply, and his growing at all times. All true Christians do grow, but I do not say, that they grow at all times. A tree that has life and nourishment, grows to its perfection; yet it is not always growing; it grows not in the winter. Christians also have their winters, wherein the influences of grace, necessary for growth, are ceased, Cant. a. v. *I sleep.* It is by faith, the believer derives gracious influence from CHRIST; like as each lamp in the candlestick, received oil from the bowl, by the pipe going betwixt them, Zech. iv. 9. Now if that pipe be stopt, if the saint's faith lies dormant and unactive, then all the rest of the graces will become dim and seem ready to be extinguished. In consequence whereof, depraved nature will gather strength, and become active. What then will become of the soul? Why, there is still one sure ground of hope. The saint's faith is not as the hypocrites, like a pipe laid short of the fountain, whereby there can be no conveyance: it still remains a bond of union betwixt CHRIST and the soul: and therefore, because CHRIST lives, the believer shall live also, John xiv. 19. The LORD JESUS puts in his hand by the hole of the door, and clears the means of conveyance; and then influences for growth flow, and the believer's graces look fresh and green again, Hos. xiv. 7. *They that dwell under his shadow, shall return: they shall revive as the corn, and grow as the vine.* In the worst of times, the saints have a principle of growth in them, 1 John iii. 9. *His seed remaineth in him.* And therefore after decays they revive again: namely, when the winter is over, and the Sun of righteousness returns to them, with his warm influences. Mud thrown into a pool, may lie there at ease; but if it be cast into a fountain, the spring will at length work it out, and run clear as formerly. *Secondly,* Christians may mistake their growth, and that two ways. (1.) By judging of their case according to their present feeling. They observe themselves and cannot percieve themselves to be growing; but there is no reason thence to conclude they are not growings, Mark iv. 27. *The seed springs and grows up, he knoweth not how.* Should one fix his eye ever so stedfastly, on the sun running his race, or on a growing tree, he would not perceive the sun moving, or the tree growing; but if he compare the tree as it now is, with what it was some years ago, and consider the place in the heavens, where the sun was in the morning, he will certainly percieve the tree has grown, and the sun has moved. In like manner may the Christian know, whether he be in a growing or declining state, by comparing his present with his former condition. (2.) Christians may mistake their case, by measuring their growth by the advances of the top only, not of the root. Though a man be not growing taller, he may be growing stronger. If a tree be taking with the ground fixing itself in the earth, and spreading out its roots, it is certainly growing, although it be nothing taller than formerly. So, albeit a Christian may want the sweet consolation and flashes of affection, which sometimes he has had, yet if he be growing in humility, self-denial, and sense of needy dependence on JESUS CHRIST, he is a growing Christian, Hos. xiv. 5. *I will be as the dew unto Israel, he shall cast forth his roots as Lebanon.*

Quest. But do hypocrites grow at all? And if so, how shall we distinguish betwixt their growth, and true Christian growth? *Ans.* To the first part of the question, Hypocrites do grow. The tares have their growth, as well as the wheat: And the seed that fell among thorns did spring up, Luke viii. 7. only it did bring no fruit to perfection, ver. 14. Yea, a true Christian may have a false growth. James and John seemed to grow in the grace of holy zeal, when their spirits grew so hot in the cause of CHRIST, that they would have had fired whole villages, for not receiving their LORD and Master, Luke ix. 54. *They said, Lord, wilt thou that we command fire to come down from heaven, to consume them, even as Elias did?* But it was indeed no such thing; And therefore he turned and rebuked them ver. 55. and said, *Ye know not what manner of spirit ye are of.* To the second part of the question, it is answered, That there is a peculiar beauty in true Christian growth, distinguishing it from all false growth; it is universal, regular, proportionable. It is a *growing up to him in all things, who is the head,* Eph. iv. 15. The growing Christian grows proportionably in all the parts of the new man. Under the kindly influences of the Son of righteousness, believers grow up as calves in the stall, Mal. iv. 2. Ye would think it a monstrous growth in these creatures, if ye saw their heads grow, and not their bodies; or if ye saw one leg grow, and another not; or if all the parts do not grow proportionably. Ay, but such is the growth of many in religion. They grow like rickety children who have a big head, but a slender body: they get more knowledge into their heads, but no more holiness into their hearts and lives: They grow very hot outwardly, but very cold inwardly; like men in a fit of the ague. They are more taken up about the externals of religion, than formerly; yet as great strangers to the power of godliness as ever. If a garden is watered with the hand, some of the plants will readily get much, some little, and some no water at all; and therefore some wither, while others are coming forward; but after a shower from the clouds, all come forward together. In like manner all the graces of the Spirit grow proportionably, by the special influences of divine grace. The branches ingrafted in CHRIST, growing aright, do grow in all the several ways of growth at once. They grow inward, growing into CHRIST, growing aright, do grow in all the several ways of growth at once. They grow inward, growing into CHRIST, Eph. iv. 15. uniting more closely with him; and cleaving more firmly to him, as the head of influences, which is the spring of all other true Christian growth. They grow outward, in good works in their life and conversation. They not only, with Naphtali, *give goodly words*; but, like Joseph, they are *fruitful boughs*. They grow upward, in heavenly-mindedness, and contempt of the word; for their conversation is in heaven, Philip. iii. 20. And, finally, they grow downward in humility and self-loathing. The branches of the largest growth in CHRIST, are, in their own eyes, less than the least of all saints, Eph. iii. 8. The chief of sinners, 1 Tim. i. 15. More brutish than any man, Prov. xxx. 2. They see they can do nothing, no not so much as to think any thing, as of themselves, 2 Cor. iii. 5. that they deserve nothing, being not worthy of the least of all the mercies shewed unto them, Genesis xxxii. 10. and that they are nothing, 2 Cor. xii. 2.

A sixth benefit is Fruitfulness. The branch ingrafted into CHRIST, is not barren, but brings forth fruit, John xv. 5. *He that abideth in me, and I in him, the same bringeth forth much fruit.* For that very end are souls married to CHRIST, that they may bring forth fruit unto GOD, Rom. vii. 4. They may be branches in CHRIST by profession, but not by real implantation, that are barren branches. Whosoever are united to CHRIST, bring forth the fruits of gospel-obedience and true holiness. Faith is always followed with good works. The believer is not only come out of the grave of his natural state, but he has put off his grave-clothes, namely, reigning

P

lusts, in the which he walked sometime like a ghost, being dead while he lived in them, Col. iii. 7, 8. For CHRIST has said of him, as of Lazarus, *Loose him, and let him go*. And now that he has put on CHRIST, he personates him, so to speak, as a beggar in borrowed robes, represents a king on the stage, walking as he also walked. Now the fruit of the Spirit in him is in all goodness, Eph. v. 9. The fruits of holiness will be found in the hearts, lips, and lives of those who are united to CHRIST. The hidden man of the **heart**, is not only a temple built for GOD and consecrated to him; but used and employed for him; where love, fear, trust, and all the other parts of unseen religion are exercised, Philip. iii. 3. *For we are of the circumcision which worship God in the Spirit*. The heart is no more the devil's common, where thoughts go free; for there even vain thoughts are hated, Psal. cxix. 113. But it is GOD's inclosure, hedged about as a garden for him, Cant. iv. 16. It is true, there are weeds of corruption there, because the ground is not yet perfectly healed: But the man, in the day of his new creation, is set to dress and keep it. A live-coal from the alter has touched his lips, and they are purified, Psal. xv. 1, 2, 3. *Lord, who shall abide in thy tabernacle? Who shall dwell in thy holy hill? He that speaketh the truth in his heart. He that backbiteth not with his tongue, nor taketh up a reproach against his neighbour*. There may be indeed a smooth tongue, where there is a false heart. The voice may be Jacob's, while the hands are Esau's. But, *If any man among you seem to be religious, and bridleth not his tongue, but deceiveth his own heart, that man's religion, is vain*, James i. 26. The power of godliness will rule over the tongue, though a world of iniquity. If one be a Galilean his speech will bewray him; he will not speak the language of Ashdod, but the language of Canaan. He will neither be dumb in religion, nor will his tongue walk at random, seeing to the double guard nature hath given the tongue, grace hath added a third. The fruits of holiness will be found in his outward conversation, for he hath clean hands, as well as a pure heart, Psal. xxiv. 4. He is a godly man, and religiously discharges the duties of the first table of the law: he is a righteous man, and honestly performs the duties of the second table. In his conversation he is a good Christian, and a good neighbour too. He carries it towards GOD, as if mens eyes were upon him; and towards men, believing GOD's eye to be upon him. These things which GOD hath joined in his law, he dare not, in his practice, put asunder.

Thus the branches of CHRIST are full of good fruits. And those fruits are a cluster of vital actions, whereof JESUS CHRIST is the principle and end; the principle, for he lives in them; and the life which they live, is by the faith of the Son of GOD, Gal. i. 20. The end, for they live to him; and to them to live, is CHRIST, Philip. i. 21. The duties of religion are, in the world, like fatherless children, in rags; some will not take them in, because they never loved them nor their Father; some take them in, because they may be serviceable to them; but the saints take them in for their Father's sake: that is, for CHRIST's sake; and they are lovely in their eyes, because they are like him. O! whence is the new life of the saints? Surely it could never have been hammered out of the natural powers of their souls, by the united force of all created power. In eternal barrenness should their womb have been shut up, but that being married to CHRIST, they bring forth fruit unto GOD, Rom. vii. 4.

If you ask me, How your nourishment, growth and fruitfulness may be forwarded? I offer these few advices. (1.) Make sure work, as to your knitting with the stock, by faith unfeigned: and beware of hypocrisy; a branch that is not sound at the heart, will certainly wither. The trees of the LORD's planting are trees of righteousness. Isa. lxi. 3. *So when others fade, they bring forth fruit.* Hypocrisy is a disease in the vitals of religion, which will consume all at length. It is a leak in the ship, that will certainly sink it. Sincerity of grace will make it lasting, be it never so weak: as the smallest twig, that is found at the heart, will draw nourishment from the stock, and grow, while the greatest bough that is rotten, can never recover, because it receives no nourishment. (2.) **Labour** to be stedfast in the truths and way of GOD. An unsettled and wavering judgment is a great enemy to Christian growth and fruitfulness, as the Apostle teaches. Eph. iv. 14, 15. *That we henceforth be no more children, toss'd to and fro, and carried about with every wind of doctrine. But speaking the truth in love, may grow up unto him in all things, which is the head, even Christ.* A rolling stone gathers no fog, and a wavering judgment makes a fruitless life. Though a tree be never so sound, yet how can it grow, or be fruitful, if we be still removing it out of one soil into another? (3.) Endeavour to cut off the suckers, as gardeners do, that their trees may thrive. These are unmortified lusts. Therefore *mortify your members that are upon the earth,* **Col.** iii. 5. When the Israelites got meat to their lusts, they got leanness to their souls. She that has many hungry children about her hand, and must be still putting into their mouths, will have much ado to get a bit put into her own. They must refuse the craving of inordinate affections, who would have their souls to prosper. *Lastly,* Improve for these ends, the ordinances of GOD. The courts of our GOD are the places, where the trees of righteousness flourish, Psal. xcii. 13. The waters of the sanctuary are the means appointed of GOD, to cause his people grow as willows by the water-courses. Therefore drink in with desire the sincere milk of the word, that ye may grow thereby, 1 Pet. ii. 2. Come to these wells of salvation, not to look at them only, but to draw water out of them. The sacrament of the LORD's supper is in a special manner appointed for these ends. It is not only a solemn public profession, and a seal of our union and communion with CHRIST, but it is a mean of most intimate communion with him, and strengthens our union with him; our faith, love, repentance, and other graces, 1 Cor. x. 26. *The cup of blessing which we bless, is it not the communion of the blood of Christ? The bread which we break, is it not the communion of the body of Christ?* And chap. xii. 13. *We have been all made to drink into one Spirit.* Give yourselves unto prayer; open your mouths, and he will fill them. By these means the branches in CHRIST may be further nourished, grow up and bring forth much fruit.

A *Seventh* benefit is, The acceptance of their fruits of holiness before the LORD. Though they be very imperfect, they are accepted, because they savour of CHRIST the blessed stock, which the branches grow upon; while the fruits of others are rejected of GOD, Gen. ii. 4, 5. *And the Lord had respect unto Abel, and to his offering: But unto Cain and his offering he had not respect.* Compare Heb. xi. 3. *By faith Abel offered unto God a more excellent sacrifice than Cain.* O how defective are the saints duties in the eye of the law! The believer himself espies many faults in his best performances, yet the LORD graciously receives them. There is no grace planted in the heart, but there is a weed of corruption hard by its side, while the saints are in this lower world. Their very sincerity is not without mixture of dissimulation or hypocrisy, Gal. ii. 13. Hence there are defects in the exercise of every grace, in the performance of every duty; depraved nature always drops something to stain their best works. There is still a mixture of darkness with their clearest light. Yet this does not mar their acceptance, Cant. vi. 10. *Who is she that looketh forth as the morning?* or as the dawning. Behold how CHRIST's spouse is esteemed and accepted of her LORD, even when she looks forth as the morning, whose beauty is mixed with the blackness of the night! When the morning was looking out, as the word is, Judges xix. 26. *i.e.* in the dawning of the day, as we read it. So the very dawning of grace, and good-will to CHRIST, grace peeping out from under a mass of darkness in believers, is pleasant and acceptable to him, as the break of day is to the weary traveller. Though the remains of unbelief make their hand of faith to shake, and tremble, yet the LORD is so well pleased with it, that he employs it to carry away pardons and supplies of grace, from the throne of grace, and the fountain of grace. His faith was effectual, who cried out, and said with tears, *Lord, I believe, help thou mine unbelief*, Mark ix. 24. Though the remains of sensual affections make the flame of their love weak and smoaky; he turns his eyes from the smoak, and beholds the flame, how fair it is, Cant. iv. 10. *How fair is thy love, my sister, my spouse!* The smell of their under-garments of inherent holiness, as imperfect as it is, is like the smell of Lebanon, ver. 11. and that because they are covered with their elder brother's clothes, which make the sons of GOD to smell as a field which the LORD hath blessed. Their good works are accepted; their cups of cold water given to a disciple, in the name of a disciple shall not want a reward. Though they cannot offer for the tabernacle, gold, silver, and brass, and onyx-stone, let them come forward with what they have; if it were but goats hair, it shall not be rejected; if it be but ram-skins, they shall be kindly accepted, for they are dyed red, dipt by faith in the Mediator's blood, and so presented unto GOD. A very ordinary work done in faith, and from faith, if it were but the building of a wall about the holy city, is a great work, Neh. vi. 3. If it were but the bestowing of a box of ointment on CHRIST, it shall never be forgotten, Matth. xxvi. 13. Even a cup of cold water only, given to one of CHRIST's little ones, in the name of a disciple, shall be rewarded, Mat. x. 42. Nay, not a good word for CHRIST, shall drop from their mouths, but it shall be registred in GOD's book of remembrance, Mal. iii. 16. Nor shall a tear drop from their eyes for him, but he will put it into his bottle, Psal. lvi. 8. Their will is accepted for the deed; their sorrow for the want of will, for the will itself, 2 Cor. 12. *For if there be first a willing mind, it is accepted according to that a man hath, and not according to that he hath not.* Their groanings, when they cannot well word their desires, are heard in heaven; **the meaning of these groans is well known there, and they will be returned like the dove with an olive branch of peace in her mouth,** see Rom. viii. 26, 27. Their mites are better than other mens talents. Their lisping and broken sentences, are more pleasant to their Father in heaven, than the most fluent and flourishing speeches of those that are not in CHRIST. Their voice is sweet, even when they are ashamed it should be heard; their countenance is comely even when they blush, and draw a vail over it, Can. ii. 14. The mediator takes their petitions, blots out some parts, rectifies others, and then presents them to the Father, in consequence whereof they pass in the court of heaven.

Every true Christian is a temple to GOD. If ye look for sacrifices, they are not wanting there; they offer the sacrifice of praise, and they do good; with such sacrifices GOD is well pleased, Heb. xiii. 15, 16. CHRIST himself is the alter that sanctifies the gift, ver. 10. But what comes of the skins and dung of their sacrifices? They are carried away without the camp. If we look for incense, it is there too. The graces of the Spirit are found in their hearts; and the Spirit of a crucified CHRIST fires them and puts them in exercise, like as the fire was brought from the altar of burnt-offering, to set the incense on flame; then they mount heaven-ward, like pillars of smoke, Cant. iii. 6. But the best of incense will leave ashes behind it; yes indeed; but as the priest took away the ashes of the incense in a golden dish, and threw them out; so our High-priest takes away the ashes and refuse of all the saints services, by his mediation in their behalf.

An *Eighth* benefit flowing from union with CHRIST, is Establishment. The Christian cannot fall away, but must persevere unto the end, John x. 28. *They shall never perish, neither shall any man pluck them out of my hand.* Indeed if a branch do not knit with the stock, it will fall away when shaking winds arise: but the branch knit to the stock stands fast, whatever winds blow. Sometimes a stormy wind of temptation blows from hell, and tosseth the branches in CHRIST the true vine, but their union with him, is their security, moved they may be, but removed they never can be; The LORD will, with the temptation, also make away to escape, 1 Cor. x. 13. Calms are never of any continuance; there is almost always some wind blowing; and therefore branches are rarely altogether at rest. But sometimes violent winds arise which threaten to rend them from off their stock. Even so it is with saints; they are daily put to it, to keep their ground against temptation: but sometimes the wind from hell riseth so high, and bloweth so furiously, that it makes even top-branches to sweep the ground; yet being knit to CHRIST their stock, they get up again in spite of the most violent efforts of the prince of the power of the air, Psal. xciv. 18. *When I said my foot slippeth, thy mercy, O Lord, held me up.* But the Christian improves by this trial; and is so far from being damaged, that he is benefited by it, in so far as it discovers what hold the soul has of CHRIST, and what hold CHRIST has of the soul. And look, as the wind in the bellows, which would blow out the candle, blows up the fire; even so it often comes to pass, that such temptations do enliven the true Christian, awakening the graces of the Spirit in him; and, by that mean, discovers both the reality, and the strength of grace in him. And hence, as Luther, that great man of GOD, saith, One Christian who hath had experience of temptation, is worth a thousand others.

Sometimes a stormy wind of trouble and persecution from the men of the world, blows upon the vine, *i. e.* mystical CHRIST; but union with the stock is a sufficient security to the branches. In a time of the church's peace and outward prosperity, while the angels hold the winds that they blow not; there are a great many branches taken up, and put into the stock, which never knit with it, nor live by it, though they be bound up with it, by the bonds of external ordinances. Now these may stand a while on the stock, and stand with great ease while the calm lasts: But when once the storms arise, and the winds blow, they will begin to fall off, one after another; and the higher the wind riseth, the greater will the number be that falls. Yea some strong boughs of that sort, when they fall, will by their weight, carry others of their **own kind**, quite down to the earth with them, and will bruise and press down some true branches in such a manner, that they would also fall off, were it not for their being knit to the stock: in virtue whereof they get up their heads again, and cannot fall off, because of that fast hold the stock has of them. Then it is that many branches, sometime high and eminent, are found lying on the earth withered, and fit to be gathered up and cast into the fire, Matth. xiii. 6. *And when the sun was up, they were scorched; and because they had no root, they withered away.* John xv. 6. *If a man* **abide** *not in me, he is cast forth as a branch, and is withered, and men gather them, and cast them into the fire, and they are burned.* But however violently the winds blow, none of the truly ingrafted branches, that are knit with the stock, are found missing, when the storm is changed into a calm, John xvii. 12. *Those that thou gavest me, I have kept, and none of them is lost.* The least twig growing in CHRIST shall stand it out, and subsist; when the tallest cedars growing on their own root, shall be laid flat on the ground, Rom. viii. 35,---39. *Who shall separate us from the* ‡ *of Christ? Shall tribulation, or distress, or persecution, or famine, or nakedness, or peril,* **or** *sword?* However severely Israel be sifted, yet shall not the least grain, or as it is in the original language, a little stone fall upon the earth, Amos ix. 9. It is an allusion to the sifting of fine pebble stones from among heaps of dust and sand; though the sand and dust fall to the ground, be blown away with the wind, and trampled under foot, yet there shall not fall on the earth so much as a little stone, such is the exactness of the sieve, and care of the sifter. There is nothing more ready to fall on the earth than a stone; yet if professors of religion be lively stones built on CHRIST the chief cornerstone; altho' they be little stones, they shall not fall to the earth, whatever storm beat upon them, see 1 Pet. ii. 4, 5, 6. All the good grain in the church of CHRIST is of this kind; they are stones in respect of solidity, and lively stones in respect of activity. If men be solid, substantial Christians, they will not be like chaff tossed to and fro with every wind; having so much of the liveliness, that they have nothing of the stone; and if they be lively Christians, whose spirit will stir in them, as Paul's did when he saw the city wholly given to idolatry, Acts xvii. 16. they will not be like stones to be turned over hither and thither, cut and carved, according to the lusts of men; having so much of the stone, as leaves nothing of liveliness in them.

Our GOD's house is a great house, wherein are not only vessels of gold, but also of earth, 2 Tim. ii. 20. Both these are apt to contract filthiness; and therefore when GOD brings trouble upon the church, he hath an eye to both. As for the vessels of gold they are not destroyed, but purged by a fiery trial in the furnace of affliction, as goldsmiths purge their gold, Isa. i. 25. *And I will turn my hand upon thee, and purely purge away thy dross.* But destruction is to the vessels of earth; they shall be broken in shivers, as a potter's vessel, ver. 28. *And the destruction, or breaking of the transgressors, and of the sinners, shall be together.* It seems to be an allusion to that law, for breaking the vessels of earth, when unclean; while vessels of wood, and consequently vessels of gold, were only to be rinsed, Lev. xv. 12.

A *Ninth* benefit is Support. If thou be a branch ingrafted in CHRIST, the root beareth thee. The believer leans on CHRIST; as a weak woman in a journey, leaning upon her beloved husband, Cant. viii. 5. He stays himself upon him, as a feeble old man stays himself on his staff, Isa. l. 10. He rolls himself on him, as one rolls a burden he is not able to walk under, off his own back, upon another who is able to bear it, Psalm. xxii. 8. *Marg.* There are many weights to hang upon, and press down the branches in CHRIST the true Vine. But ye know, whatever weights hang on branches, the stock bears all; it bears the branch, and the weight that is upon it too.

1*st*. CHRIST supports believers in him, under a weight of outward troubles. That is a large promise, Isa. xliii. 2. *When thou passest through the waters, I will be with thee: and through the rivers, they shall not overflow thee.* See how David was supported under a heavy load, 1 Sam. xxx. 6. His city Ziklag was burnt, his wives were taken captives, his men spoke of stoning him; nothing was left him but his GOD and his faith: but, by his faith, he encouraged himself in his

GOD. The LORD comes and lays his cross on his people's shoulders; it presseth them down: they are like to sink under it, and therefore cry, *Master, save us; we perish!* But he supports them under their burden; he bears them up, and they bear their cross. Thus the Christian having a weight of outward troubles upon him, goes lightly under his burden, having withal the everlasting arms underneath him. The Christian has a spring of comfort, which he cannot lose; and therefore **never** wants something to support him. **If one** have **all his** riches in money, robbers may take these away; and then what has he more? But though the landed man be robbed of his money, yet his lands remain for his support. They that build their comfort on worldly goods, may quickly be comfortless; but they that are united to CHRIST, shall find comfort, when all the streams of worldly enjoyments are dried up, Job, vi. 13. *Is not my help in me? And is wisdom driven quite from me?* As if he had said, Though my substance is gone; though my servants, my children, my health, and soundness of body, are all gone; yet my grace is not gone too. Though the Sabeans have driven away my oxen and asses, and the Chaldeans have driven away my camels; they have not driven away my faith and my hope too; these are yet in me, they are not driven from me; so that by them I can fetch comfort from heaven, when I can have none from earth.

2*ly*, CHRIST supports his people under a weight of inward troubles and discouragements. Many times heart and flesh fail them, but then GOD is the strength of their heart, Psal. lxxiii. 26. They may have a weight of guilt pressing them. This is a load that will make their back to stoop, and their spirits to sink; but he takes it off, and puts a pardon in their hand, while they cast their burden on him. CHRIST takes the soul, as one marries a widow, under a burden of debt: And so, when the creditors come to CHRIST's spouse, she carries them to her Husband, confesseth the debt, declares she is not able to pay, and lays all over upon him. The Christian sometimes, through **carelessness**, loseth his discharge: he cannot find it; however he search for it. The law takes that opportunity, and bends up a process against him for a debt paid already. GOD hides his face, and the soul is distressed. Many arrows go through the heart now; many long accounts are laid before the man, which he reads and acknowledges. Often does he see the officers coming to apprehend him, and the prison-door open to receive him. What else keeps him from sinking utterly under discouragements in this case, but that the everlasting **arms** of a Mediator are underneath him, and that he relies upon the great Cautioner? Further, they may have a weight of strong lusts pressing them. They have a body of death upon them. Death is a weight, that presseth the soul out of the body. A leg or an arm of death, if I may so speak, would be a terrible load! One lively lust will sometimes lie so heavy on a child of GOD, that he can no more remove it, than a child could throw a giant from off him. How then are they supported under a whole body of death? Why, their support is from the root that bears them, from the everlasting arm that is underneath them; His grace is sufficient for them, 2 Cor. xiii. 9. The great stay of the believer is not the grace of GOD within him, that is a well, whose streams sometimes run dry; but it is the grace of GOD without him, the grace that is in JESUS CHRIST; which is an ever-flowing fountain, to which the believer can never come a miss. For the Apostle tells us in the same verse, it is *the power of Christ*:— *Most gladly, therefore* saith he, *will I rather glory in my infirmities, that the power of Christ may rest upon me, or tabernacle above me*; as the cloud of glory did on the Israelites, which GOD spread for a covering, or shelter to them in the wilderness, Psal. cv. 39. compare Isa. iv. 5. 6. So that the believer, in this combat, like the eagle, first flies aloft, by faith, and then comes down on the pray, Psal. xxxiv. 5. *They looked on him, & were lightened*. And, finally, they have a weight of weakness and wants upon them, but they cast over that burden on the LORD, their strength, and he sustains them, Psal. lv. 22. With all their wants and weaknesses, they are cast upon him: as the poor, weak and naked babe, coming out of the womb, is cast into the lap of one appointed to take care of it, Psal. xxii. 10. Though they be destitute, as a shrub in the wilderness, which the foot of every beast may tread down, the LORD will regard them, Psal. cii. 17. It is no marvel, the weakest plant may be safe in a garden; but our LORD JESUS CHRIST is a hedge for protection, to his weak and destitute ones, even in a wilderness.

Object. But if the saints be supported, how is it that they fall so often under temptation and discouragements? *Ans.* (1.) However long they fall, they never fall off; and that is a great matter. They are kept by the power of GOD, through faith unto salvation, 1 Pet. i. 5. Hypocrites may so fall, so as to fall off, and fall into the pit, as a bucket falls into a well, when the chain breaks. But though the child of GOD may fall, and that so low as the water goes over his head; yet there is still a bond of union betwixt CHRIST and him; the chain is not broken; he will not go to the ground, he will be drawn up again, Luke xxii. 31, 32. *And the Lord said, Simon, Simon, Satan hath desired to have you, that he may sift you as wheat;* but I *have prayed for thee, that thy faith fail not.* (2.) The falls of the saints flow from their not improving their union with CHRIST their not making use of him by faith, for staying or bearing them up, Psal. xxvi. 13. *I had fainted, unless I had believed.* While the nurse holds the child in her arms, it cannot fall to the ground; yet, if the unwary child hold not by her, it may fall backwards in her arms, to its great hurt. Thus David's fall broke his bones, Psalm li. 8. but it did not break the bond of union betwixt CHRIST and him; The holy Spirit, the bond of that union, was not taken from him, ver. 11.

The last benefit I shall name, is, The special care of the husbandman, John xv. 1. 2. *I am the true vine, and my Father is the husbandman.——Every branch that beareth fruit, he purgeth it, that it may bring forth more fruit.* Believers, by virtue of their union with CHRIST, are the object of GOD's special care and providence. Mystical CHRIST is GOD's vine; other societies in the world, are but wild olive-trees. The men of the world, are but GOD's out-field; the saints are his vineyard, which he has a special propriety in, and a special concern for, Ca. viii. 12. *My vineyard, which is mine is before me.* He that slumbers not, nor sleeps, is the keeper of it; he doth keep it, lest any hurt, he will keep it night and day; he in whose hand is the dew of heaven, will water it every moment, Isa. xxvii. 3 He dresseth and purgeth it, in order to further fruitfulness, John xv. 2. He cuts off the luxuriant twigs, that mar the fruitfulness of the branch. This is done, especially, by the word, and by the cross of afflictions. The saints need the ministry of the word, as much as the vineyard needeth one to dress and prune the vines, 1 Cor. iii. 9. *We are labourers together with God.——Ye are God's husbandry, ye are God's building.* And they need the cross too, 1 Pet. i. 6.

And therefore, if we should reckon the cross amongst the benefits flowing to believers from their union with CHRIST, I judge, we should not reckon it a miss. Sure I am, in their sufferings, they suffer with him, Rom. viii. 17. And the assurances they have of the cross, have rather, the nature of a promise, as of a threatning, Psal. lxxxix. 30, 31, 32, 33. *If his children forsake my law——then will I visit their transgression with the rod, and their iniquity with stripes. Nevertheless, my loving-kindness will I not utterly take from him: nor suffer my faithfulness to fail.* This looks like a tutor's engaging to a dying father, to take care of the children left upon him; and to give them both nurture and admonition, for their good. The covenant of grace does truly beat the spears of affliction into pruning hooks, to them that are in CHRIST, Isa. xxvii. 9. *By this therefore shall the iniquity of Jacob be purged, and* this is all the fruit, to take away his sin. Why then should we be angry with the cross? Why should we be frighted at it? The believer must take up his cross, and follow his leader, the LORD JESUS CHRIST. He must take up his ilk-day's cross, Luke ix. 23. *If any man will come after me, let him deny himself, and take up his cross daily.* Yea, he must take up his holy-day's cross too, Lam. ii. 22. *Thou hast called, as in a solemn day, my terrors round about.* The church of the Jews had, of a long time, many a pleasing meeting at the temple, on solemn days, for the worship of GOD; but they got a solemnity of another nature, when GOD called together, about the temple and city, the Chaldean army that burnt the temple and laid Jerusalem on heaps. And now, that the church of GOD is yet militant in this lower region, how can it be but the clouds will return after the rain? But the cross of CHRIST, which name the saints troubles do bear, is a kindly name to the believer. It is a cross indeed, but not to the believer's graces, but to his corruptions. The hypocrite's seeming graces may indeed breathe out their last on a cross, as those of the stony-ground hearers did, Mat. xiii. 6. *And when the sun*, of persecution, ver. 26, *was up, they were scorched: And because they had not root, they withered away.* But never did one of the real graces in a believer die upon the cross yet. Nay, as the candle shines brightest in the night, and the fire burns fiercest in intense frost; so the believer's graces are, ordinarily, most vigorous in a time of trouble.

There is a certain pleasure and sweetness in the cross, to them who have their senses exercised to discern, and to find it out. There is a certain sweetness in one's seeing himself upon his trials for heaven, and standing candidate for glory. There is a pleasure in travelling over these mountains, where the Christian can see the prints of CHRIST's own feet, and the footsteps of the flock, who have been there before him. How pleasant is it to a saint, in the exercise of grace, to see how a good GOD crosseth his corrupt inclinations, and prevents his folly! How sweet it is to behold these thieves upon the cross! How refined a pleasure is there in observing how GOD draws away provision from unruly lusts, and so pincheth them, that the Christian may get them governed? Of a truth, there is a Paradise within his thorn-hedge. Many a time the people of GOD are in bonds, which are never loosed, till they be bound with cords of affliction. GOD takes them, and throws them into a fiery furnace, that burns off their bonds; and then, like the three children, Dan. iii. 25. they are loose, walking in the midst of the fire. GOD gives his children a portion, with one bitter ingredient; If that will not work upon them, he will put in a second, a third, and so on, as there is need, that they may work together, for their good, Rom. viii. 28. With cross-winds he hastens them to the harbour. They are often found in such ways, as that the cross is the happiest foot they can meet with: and well may they salute it, as David did Abigail, saying, *Blessed be the Lord God of Israel, who hath sent thee this day to meet me*, 1 Sam. xxv. 32. Worldly things are often such a load to the Christian, that he moves but very slowly heaven-ward. GOD sends a wind of trouble that blows the burden off the man's back: and then he walks more speedily on his way; after GOD hath drawn some guilded earth from him, that was drawing his heart away from GOD, Zeph. iii. 12. *I will also leave in the midst of thee, an afflicted and poor people, and they shall trust in the name of the Lord*. It was an observe of an heathen moralist, "That no history makes mention of any man, who hath been made better by riches." I doubt if our modern histories can supply the defect of ancient histories in this point. But sure I am, many have been the worse of riches; thousands have been hugged to death, in the embraces of a smiling world: and many good men have got wounds from outward prosperity, that behoved to be cured by the cross. I remember to have read of one, who having an imposthume in his breast, had in vain used the help of physicians; but being wounded with a sword, the imposthume broke; and his life was saved by that accident, which threatened immediate death. Often have spiritual imposthumes gathered in the breasts of GOD's people, in time of outward prosperity, and been thus broken and discussed by the cross. It is kindly for believers to be healed by stripes; although they are usually so weak, as to cry out for fear, at the sight of the pruning-hook, as if it were the destroying ax; and to think the LORD is coming to kill them, when he is indeed coming to cure them.

I shall now conclude, addressing myself in a few words, first to saints, and next to sinners.

I. To you that are saints, I say,

First, Strive to obtain and keep up actual communion and fellowship with JESUS CHRIST; that is, to be still deriving fresh supplies of grace, from the fountain thereof in him by faith; and making suitable returns of them in the exercise of grace and holy obedience. Beware of estrangement betwixt CHRIST and your souls. If it has got in already which seems to be the case of many in this day, endeavour to get it removed. There are multitudes in the world that slight CHRIST, though ye should not slight him: many have turned their backs on him, that sometimes looked fair for heaven. The warm sun of outward peace and prosperity, has caused some to cast their cloak of religion from them, who held it fast, when the wind of trouble was blowing upon them; and will ye also go away? John vi. 67. The greatest ingratitude is stampt on your slighting of communion with CHRIST, Jer. ii. 31. *Have I been a wilderness unto Israel; a land of darkness; Wherefore say my people, We are Lords: we will come no more unto thee?* Oh! beloved, is this your kindness to your friend? It is unbecoming any wife, to slight converse with her husband; but her especially, who was taken from a prison or a dung-bill, as ye were, by our LORD. But remember, I pray you, this is a very ill-chosen time to live at a distance from GOD: it is a time in which divine providence frowns upon the land we live in; the clouds of wrath are gathering, and are thick above our heads! It is not a time for you to be out of your chambers, Isa. xxvi. 20. They that now are walking most closely with GOD, may have enough ado to stand, when the trial comes; how hard will it be for others, than who are like to be surprised with troubles, when guilt is lying on their consciences unremoved. To be awakened out of a sound sleep and cast into a raging sea, as Jonah was, will be a fearful trial. To feel trouble before we see it coming, to be past hope, before we have any fear, is a very sad case. Wherefore break down your idols of jealousy, mortify these lusts, these irregular appetites and desires, that have stolen away your hearts, and lest you, like Samson without his hair, and say, *I will go and return to my first husband; for then it was better with me than now*, Hos. ii. 7.

Secondly, Walk as becomes those that are united to CHRIST. Evidence your union with him, by walking as he also walked, 1 John ii. 6. If ye be brought from under the power of darkness, let your light shine before men. Shine as lights in the world, holding forth the word of life, as the lanthorn holds the candle, which being in it, shines through it, Philip. ii. 15, 16. Now that ye profess CHRIST to be in you, let his image shine forth in your conversation, and remember the business of your lives is, to prove by practical arguments what ye profess.

1. You know the character of a wife: *She that is married, careth how she may please her husband:* Go you and do likewise: *Walk worthy of the Lord, unto all pleasing,* Col. l. 10. This is the great business of life; you must please him, tho' it should displease all the world. What he hates, must be hateful to you, because he hates it. Whatever lusts come in suit of your hearts, deny them, seeing the grace of GOD hat appeared, teaching so to do, and you are joined to the LORD. Let him be a covering to your eyes; for you have not your choice to make, it is made already: and you must not dishon-

our your Head. A man takes care of his feet, for that, if he catch cold there, it flies up to his head: *Shall I then take the members of Christ, and make them the members of an harlot? God forbid,* says the Apostle, 2 Cor. vi. 15. Wilt thou take that heart of thine, which is CHRIST's dwelling-place, and lodge his enemies there? Wilt thou take that body, which is his temple, and defile it, by using the members thereof, as the instruments of sin?

2. Be careful to bring forth fruit, and much fruit. The branch well laden with fruit, is the glory of the Vine, and of the Husbandman too, John xv. 8. *Herein is my Father glorified, that ye bear much fruit; so shall ye be my disciples.* A barren tree stands safer in a wood, than an orchard: And branches in CHRIST, that bring not forth fruit, will be taken away and cast into the fire.

3. Be heavenly minded, and maintain a holy contempt of the world. Ye are united to CHRIST; he is your Head and Husband, and is in heaven; Wherefore your hearts should be there also, Col iii. 1. *If ye then be risen with Christ, seek those things which are above, where Christ sitteth at the right hand of God.* Let the serpent's seed go on their belly, and eat the dust of this earth: but let the members of Christ be ashamed to bow down and feed with them.

4. Live and act dependently, depending by faith on JESUS CHRIST. That which grows on its own root, is a tree not a branch. It is of the nature of a branch, to depend on the stock for all, and to derive all its sap from thence. Depend on him for life, light, strength, and all spiritual benefits, Gal. ii. 20. *I live; yet not I, but Christ liveth in me. And the life which I now live in the flesh, I live by the faith of the Son of God.* For this cause, in the mystical union, strength is united to weakness, life to death, and heaven to earth; that weakness, death and earth, may mount up on borrowed wings. Depend on him for temporal benefits also, Mat. vi. 2. *Give us this day, our daily bread.* If we have trusted him with our eternal concerns, let us be ashamed to distrust him in the matter of our provision in the world.

Lastly, Be of a meek disposition, and an uniting temper with the fellow-members of CHRIST's body, as being united to the meek JESUS, the blessed centre of union. There is a prophecy to this purpose, concerning the kingdom of CHRIST, Isa. ii. 6. *The wolf shall dwell with the lamb; and the leopard shall lie down with the kid.* It is an allusion to the beasts in Noah's ark. The beasts of prey, that were wont to kill and devour others, when once they came into the ark, lay down in peace with them; the lamb was in no hazard by the wolf there; nor the kid by the leopard. There was a beautiful accomplishment of it in the primitive church, Acts iv. 32. *And the multitude of them that believed, were of one heart, and of one soul.* And this prevails in all the members of CHRIST, according to the measure of the grace of GOD in them. Man is born naked; he comes naked into this world, as if GOD designed him for the picture of peace; and surely when he is born again, he comes not into the new world of grace, with claws to tear, a sword to wound, and a fire in his hand, to burn up his fellow-members in CHRIST, because they cannot see with his light. O! It is sad to see CHRIST's lillies as thorns in one another's sides; CHRIST's lambs devouring one-another like lions; and GOD's diamonds cutting one-another; yet it must be remembered, that sin is no proper cement for the members of CHRIST, though Herod and Pontius Pilate may be made friends that way. The **Apostle's** rule is plain, Heb. xii. 14. *Follow peace with all men, and holiness.* To follow peace no further than our humour, credit, and such-like things will allow us, is too short: to pursue it further than holiness, that is, conformity to the divine will, allows us, is too far. Peace is precious, yet it may be bought too dear: wherefore we must rather want it, than purchase it, at the expence of truth or holiness: But otherwise it cannot be over-dear bought; and it will always be precious in the eys of the sons of peace.

II. And now, sinners, what shall I say to you? I have given you some view of the privileges of these in the state of grace: ye have seen them afar off. But, alas! they are not yours, because ye are not CHRIST's. The sinfulness of an unregenerate state is yours; and the misery of it is yours also: but, ye have neither part nor lot in this matter. The guilt of all your sins lies upon you: ye have no part in the righteousness of CHRIST. There is no peace to you! no peace with GOD, no true peace of conscience; for ye have no saving interest in the great Peace-maker. Ye are none of GOD's family: the adoption we spoke of, belongs not to you. Ye have no part in the Spirit of sanctification; and, in one word, ye have no inheritance among them that are sanctified. All I can say to you in this matter, is, that the case is not desperate, they may yet be yours, Rev. iii. 20. *Behold! I stand at the door and knock: if any man hear my voice, and open the door, I will come in to him, and will sup with him, and he with me.* Heaven is proposing an union with earth still, the potter is making suit to his own clay, and the gates of the city of refuge are not yet closed. O! that we could compel you to come in.

STATE IV.

NAMELY,

The Eternal State; or, State of consummate Happiness, or Misery.

HEAD I.

OF DEATH.

JOB xxx. 23.

For I know, that thou wilt bring me to death, and to the house appointed for all living.

I COME now to discourse of man's eternal state, into which he enters by death. Of this entrance Job takes a solemn, serious view, in the words of the text, which contain a general truth, and a particular application of it. The general truth is supposed; namely, that all men must, by death, remove out of this world; they must die. But whither must they go? They must go to the house appointed for all living; to the grave, that darksome, gloomy, solitary house, in the land of forgetfulness. Wheresoever the body is laid up till the resurrection, thither, as to a dwelling-house, death brings us home. While we are in the body, we are but in a lodging-house: in an inn, on our way homeward. When we come to our grave, we come to our home, our long home, Eccl. xii. 5. All living must be inhabitants of this house, good and bad, old and young. Man's life is a stream running into death's devouring deeps. They, who now live in palaces, must quit them, and go home to this house; and they, who have not where to lay their heads, shall thus have a house at length. It is appointed for all, by him, whose counsel shall stand. This appointment cannot be shifted; it is a law which mortals cannot transgress. Job's application of this general truth to himself, is expressed in these words; *I know that thou wilt bring me to death,* &c. He knew, that he behoved to meet with death; that his soul and body behoved to part; that GOD, who had set the tryst, would certainly see it kept. Sometimes Job was envying death to come to him, and carry

Q

him home to its house; yea, he was in hazard of running to it before the time, Job vii. 15. *My soul chooseth strangling and death, rather than my life.* But here he considers GOD would bring him to it; yea, bring him back to it, as the word imports. Whereby he seems to intimate, that we have no life in this world, but as runaways from death, which stretcheth out its cold arms, to receive us from the womb; but though we do thus narrowly escape its clutches, we cannot escape long; we will be brought back again to it. Job knew this, he had laid his account with it, and was looking for it.

DOCTRINE, *All must die.*

Although this Doctrine be confirmed by the experience of all former generations, ever since Abel entred into the house appointed for all living; and though the living know that they shall die, yet it is needful to discourse of the certainty of death, that it may be impressed on the mind, and duly considered.

Wherefore consider *First*, There is an unalterable statute of death, under which men are concluded. *It is appointed unto men once to die,* Heb. ix. 27. It is laid up for them, as **parents** lay up for their children; they may look for it, and cannot miss it, seeing GOD has designed and reserved it for them. There is no peradventure in it; we must needs die, 2 Sam. xiv. 14. Though some men will not hear of death, yet every man must see death, Psalm lxxxix. 48. Death is a champion all must grapple with; we must enter the lists with it, and it will have the mastery, Eccles. viii. 8. *There is no man that hath power over the spirit, to retain the spirit; neither hath he power in the day of wrath.* They indeed who are found alive at CHRIST's coming, shall all be changed, 1 Cor. xv. 51. But **that** change will be equivalent to death, will answer the purposes of it. All other persons must go the common road, the way of all flesh. *Secondly,* Let us consult daily observation. Every man seeth that wise men die, likewise the fool and brutish person, Psal. xlix. 15. There is room enough on this earth for us, notwithstanding of the multitudes that were upon it before us; they are gone to make room for us, as we must depart to leave room for others. It is long since death began to transport men into another world, and vast shoals and multitudes are gone thither already; yet the trade is going on still; death is carrying off new inhabitants daily, to the house appointed for all living. Who could ever hear the grave say, It is enough? Long it has been getting, but still it asketh. This world is like a great fair or market, where some are coming in, others going out; while the as-family that is in it, is confused; and the more part know not wherefore they are come together; or, like a town situate on the road, to a great city, through which some travellers are past, some are passing, while others are only coming in, Eccl. i. 4. *Our generation passeth away, and another generation cometh; but the earth abideth for ever.* Death is an inexorable, irresistible messenger, who cannot be diverted from executing his orders, by the force of the mighty, the bribes of the rich, nor the intreaties of the poor. It doth not reverence the hoary head, nor pity the harmless babe. The bold and daring cannot out-brave it; nor can the faint-hearted obtain a discharge in this war. *Thirdly,* The human body consists of perishing principles, Gen. iii. 19. *Dust thou art, and unto dust shalt thou return.* The strongest are but brittle earthen vessels, easily broken in shivers. The soul is but meanly housed, while in this mortal body, which is not a house of stone, but a house of clay; the mud-walls cannot but moulder away, especially seeing the foundation is not on a rock, but in the dust; they are crushed before the moth, though this insect be so tender, that the gentle touch of a finger will dispatch it, Job iv. 19. These principles are like gun-powder; a very small spark, lighting on them, will set them on fire, and blow up the house. The stone of a raisin, or a hair in milk, have choaked men, and laid the house of clay in the dust. If we consider the frame and structure of our bodies, how fearfully and wonderfully we are made; and on how regular and exact a motion of the fluids, and balance of humors, our life depends; and that death has as many doors to enter in by, as the body hath pores; and if we compare the soul and body together, we may justly reckon, there is somewhat more astonishing in our life, then in our death; and, that it is more strange, to see dust walking up and down on the dust, than lying down in it. Though the lamp of our life be not violently blown out, yet the flame must go out at length, for want of oil. And what are those distempers and diseases, we are liable to, but death's harbingers, that come to prepare its way? They meet us, as soon as we set our foot on earth, to tell us at our entry, that we do but come into the world to go out again. Howbeit, some are snatched away in a moment, without being warned by sickness or disease. *Fourthly,* We have sinful souls, and therefore have dying bodies; death follows sin as the shadow follows the body. The wicked must die, by virtue of the threatning of the covenant of works, Gen. ii. 17. *In the day that thou eatest thereof, thou shalt surely die.* And the godly must die too; that, as death entred by sin, sin may go out by death. CHRIST has taken away the sting of death as to them, albeit he has not as yet removed death itself.

Wherefore though it fasten on them, as the viper did on Paul's hand, it shall do them no harm; but because the leprosy of sin is in the walls of the house, it must be broken down, and all the materials thereof carried forth. *Lastly*, Man's life in this world, according to the scripture account of it, is but a few degrees removed from death. The scripture represents it as a vain and empty thing, short in its continuance, and swift in its passing away.

First, Man's life is a vain and empty thing, while it is: it vanisheth away, and lo! it is not, Job. viii. 6. *My days are vanity*. If ye suspect afflicted Job of partiality in this matter, hear the wise and prosperous Solomon's character of the days of his life, Eccl. viii. 15. *All things have I seen, in the days of my vanity*, i. e. my vain days. Moses, who was a very active man, compares our days to a sleep, Psalm xc. 5. *They are as asleep*, which is not noticed, till it be ended. The resemblance is pat: few men have right apprehensions of life, until death awaken them; then we begin to know we were living. *We spend our years as a tale that is told*, ver. 9. When an idle tale is a telling, it may affect a little, but when it is ended, it is forgot; and so is man forgotten, when the fable of his life is ended. It is as a dream, or vision of the night, in which there is nothing solid; when one awakes, all evanisheth, Job xx. 8. *He shall fly away as a dream, and shall not be found; yea he shall be chased away as a vision of the night*. It is but a vain show or image, Psal. xxxix. 6. *Surely every man walketh in a vain show*. Man in this world, is but, as it were, a walking statue; his life is but an image of life: there is so much of death in it.

If we look on our life, in the several periods of it, we will find it a heap of vanities. *Childhood and youth are vanity*, Eccles. xi. 10. We come into the world, the most helpless of all animals; young birds and beasts can do something for themselves, but infant man is altogether unable to help himself. Our childhood is spent in pitiful trifling pleasures, which become the scorn of our own after-thoughts. Youth is a flower that soon withereth, a blossom that quickly falls off; it is a space of time in which we are rash, foolish, and inconsiderate, pleasing ourselves with a variety of vanities, and swimming, as it were, through a flood of them. But ere we are aware, it is past, and we are in middle age, encompassed with a thick cloud of cares, through which we must grope; and finding ourselves beset with pricking thorns of difficulties, through them we must force our way, to accomplish the projects and contrivances of our riper thoughts. And the more we solace ourselves in any earthly enjoyment we attain to, the more bitterness do we find in parting with it. Then comes old age, attended with its own train of infirmities, labour and sorrow, Psal. xc. 10. and sets us down next door to the grave. In a word, *All flesh is grass*, Isaiah xl. 6. Every stage, or period in life, is vanity. *Man at his best state*, his middle age, when the heat of youth is spent, and the sorrows of old age have not yet overtaken him, *is altogether vanity*, Psalm xxxix. 5. Death carries off some in the bud of childhood, others in the blossom of youth, and others when they are come to their fruit; few are left standing, till like ripe corn, they forsake the ground: all die one time or other.

Secondly, Man's life is a short thing; it is not only a vanity, but a short-lived vanity. Consider, *First*, How the life of man is reckoned in the Scripture. It was indeed some times reckoned by hundreds of years; but no man ever arrived at a thousand: which yet bears no proportion to eternity. Now, hundreds are brought down to scores: three score and ten, or four score, is its utmost length, Psal. xc. 10. But few men arrive at that length of life. Death does but rarely wait, till men be bowing down, by reason of age, to meet the grave. Yet, as if years were too big a word, for such a small thing as the life of man on earth; we find it counted by months, Job xiv. 5. *The number of his months are with thee.* Our course, like that of the moon, is run in a little time; we are always waxing or waning, till we disappear. But frequently it is reckoned by days: and these but few, Job xiv. 1. *Man that is born of a woman, is of few days.* Nay, it it but one day in scripture account! and that a hireling's day, who will precisely observe when his day ends and give over his work, ver. 6. *Till he shall accomplish as an hireling his day.* Yea, the scripture brings it down to the shortest space of time, and calls it a moment, 2 Cor. iv. 17. *Our light affliction*, though it last all our life long, *is but for a moment.* But elsewhere it is brought down to yet a lower pitch, farther than which, one cannot carry it, Psalm xxxix. 5. *Mine age is as nothing before thee.* Agreeable to this, Solomon tells us, Eccle. iii. 2. *There is a time to be born, and a time to die;* but makes no mention of a time to live; as if our life were but a skip from the womb to the grave. Secondly, Consider the various similitudes by which the Scripture represents the brevity, or shortness, of man's life. Hear Hezekiah, Isa. xxxviii. 12. *Mine age is departed, and is removed from me as a shepherd's tent. I have cut off, like a weaver, my life.* The shepherd's tent is soon removed, for the flocks must not feed long in one place; such is a man's life on this earth, quickly gone. It is a web he is incessantly working; he is not idle so much as one moment; in a short time it is wrought, and then it is cut off. Every breathing is a thread in this web; and when the last breath is drown, the web is woven out, he expires: and then it is cut off, he breaths no more. Man is like grass, and like a flower, Isa. xl. 6. *All flesh*, even the strongest and most healthy, *is grass, and all the goodliness thereof, is as the flower of the field.* The grass is flourishing in the morning, but in the evening, being cut down by the mowers, it is withered; so man sometimes is walking up and down at ease in the morning; and, in the evening, is lying a corpse, being knocked down by a sudden stroke, with one or other of death's weapons. The flower, which is but a weak and tender thing, of short continuance, where-ever it grows: but, observe, man is not compared to the flower of the garden, but to the flower of the field, which the foot of every beast may tread down at any time. Thus is our life liable to a thousand accidents, every day; any of which may cut us off. But though we should escape all these, yet, at length, this grass withereth, this flower fadeth of itself. It is carried off, as the cloud is consumed, and vanisheth away, Job vii. 9. It looks big, as the morning cloud, which promiseth great things, and raiseth the expectations of the husbandman; but the sun is seen, and the cloud is scattered; death comes, and man evanisheth. The apostle James proposeth the question, *What is your life?* Hear his own answer; *It is even a vapour, that appeareth for a little time, and then vanisheth away,* Chap. iv. 14. It is frail, uncertain, and lasteth not. It is as smoak, which goes out of the chimney, as if it would darken the face of the heavens; but quickly is scattered and appears no more; thus goeth man's life, and where is he? It is a wind, Job vii. 7. *O remember that my life is wind.* It is but a passing blast, a short puff, a wind that passeth away, and cometh not again, Psalm lxxviii. 39. Our breath is in our nostrils, as it were always upon the wing to depart; ever passing and repassing, like a traveller, until it go away for good and all, not to return till the heavens be no more.

Lastly, Man's life is a swift thing; not only a passing but a flying vanity. Have you **not observed** how swiftly a shadow hath run along the ground, in a cloudy and windy day, suddenly darkening the places beautified before, with the beams of the sun, but as suddenly disappearing? Such is the life of man on the earth, for he fleeth as a shadow, and continueth not, Job xiv. 2. A weaver's shuttle is very swift in its motion; in a moment it is thrown from one side of the web to the other; yet our days are swifter than a weaver's shuttle, chap. vii. 6. How quickly is man tossed through time into eternity! See how Job describes the swiftness of the time of life: *Now my days are swifter than a post: they flee away, they see no good. They are hasted away as the swift ships, as* *the eagle that hasteth to the prey*, chap ix. 25, 26. He compares his days with a post, a foot-post, a runner who runs speedily to carry tidings, and will make no stay. But though the post were like Ahimaaz, who over-ran Cushi, our days would be swifter than he, for they flee away, like a man fleeing for his life, before the pursuing enemy; he runs with his utmost vigour, yet our days run as fast as he. Howbeit that is not all. Even he who is fleeing for life, cannot run always; he must needs sometimes stand still, lie down, or run in somewhere, as Sisery did into Jael's tent, to refresh himself; but our time never halts. Therefore it is compared to ships, which can sail night and day without intermission, till they be at their port; and swift ships, ships of desire, in which men quickly arrive at the desired haven; or ships of pleasure, that sail more swiftly than ships of burden. Yet the wind failing, the ship's course is marred; but our time always runs with a rapid course. Therefore it is compared to the eagle flying; not with his ordinary flight, for that is not sufficient to represent the swiftness of our days; but when he flies upon his prey, which is with an extraordinary swiftness. And thus, even thus, our days fly away.

Having thus discoursed of death, let us improve it, in discerning the vanity of the world; in bearing up, with Christian contentment, and patience, under all troubles and difficulties in it; in mortifying our lusts; in cleaving unto the LORD with purpose of heart on all hazards; and in preparing for death's approach.

And *First*, Let us hence, as in a looking-glass, behold the vanity of the world, and of all these things in it, which men so much value and esteem, and therefore set their hearts upon. The rich and poor are equally intent upon this world; they bow the knee to it, yet it is but a clay god; they court the bulky vanity, and run keenly to catch the shadow; the rich man is hugged to death in its embraces; and the poor man wearies himself in the fruitless pursuit. What wonder if the world's smiles overcome us, when we pursue it so eagerly, even while it frowns upon us? But look into the grave, O man, consider and be wise; listen to the doctrine of death, and learn, (1.) That hold as fast as thou canst, thou shalt be forced to let go thy hold of the world at length. Though thou load thyself with the fruits of this earth, yet all shall fall off when thou comest to creep into thy hole, the house under ground, appointed for all living. When death comes, thou must bid an eternal farewell to thy enjoyments in this world; thou must leave thy goods to another; and whose shall those things be which thou hast provided? Luke xii. 20. (2.) Thy portion of these things shall be very little ere long. If thou lie down on the grass, and stretch thyself at full length, and observe the print of thy body when thou risest, thou mayest see, how much of this earth will fall to thy share at last. It may be thou shalt get a coffin, and a winding-sheet; but thou art not sure of that: Many who have had abundance of wealth yet have not had so much when they took up their new house in the land of silence. But however that be, more ye cannot expect. It was a mortifying lesson, Saladine, when dying, gave to his soldiers: He called for his standard-bearer, and ordered him to take his winding-sheet upon his pike, and go out to the camp with it, and tell them, That of all his conquests, victories and triumphs, he had nothing now left him, but that piece of linen to wrap his body in for burial. *Lastly*, This world is a false friend, who leaves a man in time of greatest need, and flees from him when he has most ado. When thou art lying on a death-bed, all thy friends and relations cannot rescue thee; all thy substance cannot ransom thee; nor procure thee a reprieve for one day, nay, not for one hour. Yea, the more thou possessest of this world's goods, thy sorrow at death is like to be the greater; for though one may live more commodiously in a palace, than in a cottage, yet he may die more easily in the cottage, where he has very little to make him fond of life.

Secondly, It may serve as a storehouse for Christian-contentment and patience under worldly losses and crosses. A close application of the doctrine of death, is an excellent remedy against fretting; and gives some ease to a rankled heart. When Job had sustained very great losses, he sat down contented, with this meditation, Job i. 21. *Naked came I out of my mother's womb, and naked shall I return thither; The Lord gave, and the Lord hath taken away, blessed be the name of the Lord.* When providence brings a mortality or murrain among your cattle, how ready are you to fret and complain! But the serious consideration of your own death, to which you have a notable help from such providential occurrences, may be of use to silence your complaints, and quiet your rankled spirits. Look to the house appointed for all living, and learn, (1.) That ye must abide a sorer thrust, than the loss of worldly goods. Do not cry out for a thrust in the leg or arm, for ere long there will be a home-thrust at the heart. You may lose your dearest relations; the wife may lose her husband, and the husband his wife; the parents may lose their dear children, and the children their parents. But if any of these trials happen to you, remember you must lose your own life at last; and wherefore doth a living man complain? Lam. iii. 39. It is always profitable to consider, under affliction, how our case might have been worse than it is.

Whatever be consumed, or taken from us, it is of the LORD's mercies that we ourselves are not consumed, ver. 22. (2.) It is but for a short space of time we are to be in this world. It is but little our necessities require in this short space of time; when death comes, we will stand in need of none of these things. Why should men rack their heads with cares, how to provide for to-morrow: while they know not if they shall need any thing to-morrow? Though a man's provision, for his journey be near spent, he is not disquieted, if he think he is near home: are you working with candle-light, and is there little of your candle left? It may be there is as little sand in your glass: and if so, ye have little use for it. (3.) Ye have matters of greater weight that challenge your care. Death is at the door, beware you lose not your souls. If blood break out at one part of the body, they use to open a vein in another part of it, to turn the stream of blood and so to stop it. Thus the Spirit of GOD sometimes cures men of sorrow for earthly things, by opening the heart-vein to bleed for sin. Did we pursue heavenly things the more vigorously that our affairs in this life prosper not; we should thereby gain a double advantage; our worldly sorrow would be diverted, and our best treasure increased. (4.) Crosses of this nature will not last long. The world's smiles and frowns will be quickly buried together in everlasting forgetfulness. Its smiles go away as the foam on the water, and its frowns are as a passing stitch in a man's side. Time flies away with swift wings, and carries our earthly comforts, and crosses too along with it; neither of them will accompany us into the house appointed for all living; *There the wicked cease from troubling, and there the weary are at rest. There the prisoners rest together, they hear not the voice of the oppressor. The small and great are there, and the servant is free from his master,* Job iii. 17, 18, 19. Cast your eyes on eternity, and ye will see, affliction here is but for a moment. The truth is, our time is so very short, that it will not allow either our joys or griefs, to come to perfection. Wherefore, let them that weep, be as though they weeped not; and they that rejoice, as though they rejoiced not; &c. 1 Cor. vii. 29, 30, 31. (5.) Death will put all men on a level. The king and the beggar must dwell in one house, when they come to their journey's end: though their entertainment by the way be very different. *The small and the great are there,* Job iii. 19. We are in this world as on a stage; it is no great matter whether a man act the part of a prince or a peasant; for when they have acted their parts, they must both get behind the curtain, and appear no more. *Lastly,* If thou be not in CHRIST, whatever thy afflictions now be, troubles a thousand times worse, are abiding thee in another world.

Death will turn thy crosses into pure, unmixed curses; and then how gladly wouldst thou return to thy former afflicted state, and purchase it at any rate, were there any possibility of such a return. If thou be in Christ, thou mayst well bear thy cross. Death will put an end to all thy troubles. If a man on a journey be not well accommodated where he lodgeth only for a night, he will not trouble himself about the matter because he is not to stay there; it is not his home. Ye are on the road to eternity; let it not disquiet you, that you meet with some hardships in the inn of this world. Fret not, because it is not so well with you as with some others. One man travels with a cane in his hand; his fellow-traveller, perhaps, has but a common stick, or staff; either of them will serve the turn. It is no great matter which of them be yours; both will be laid aside, when you come to your journey's end.

Thirdly, It may serve for a Bridle, to curb all manner of Lusts, particularly those conversant about the body. A serious visit made to cold death, and that solitary mansion, the grave, might be of good use to repress them.

1st. It may be of use to cause men remit of their inordinate care for the body: which is to many the bane of their souls. Often do these questions, *What shall we eat? What shall we drink? And wherewithal shall we be clothed?* leave no room for another of more importance, viz. *Wherefore shall I come before the Lord?* The soul is put to the rack, to answer these mean questions, in favour of the body, while its own eternal interests are neglected. But ah! why are men so busy to repair the ruinous cottage, leaving the inhabitant **to bleed to** death of his wounds, unheeded, unregarded! Why **so much** care for the body, to the neglecting of the concerns of the immortal soul? O! be not so anxious for what can only serve your bodies; **since, ere long,** the clods of cold earth will serve for back and belly too.

2ly, It may abate your pride on account of bodily endowments, which vain man is apt to glory in. Value not yourselves on the blossom of youth; for while ye are in your blooming years, ye are but ripening for a grave; and death gives the fatal stroke, without asking any body's age. Glory not in your strength, it will quickly be gone; the time will soon be, when you shall not be able to turn yourselves on a bed, and you must be carried by your grieving friends to your long home. And what signifies your healthful constitution? Death does not always enter in soonest, where it beats loudest to knock at the door, but makes as great dispatch with some in a few hours, as with others in many years. Value not yourselves on your beauty, which shall consume in the grave, Psalm xlix. 14. Remember the change death makes on the fairest face, Job xiv. 20. *Thou changest his countenance, and sendeth him away.* Death makes the greatest beauty so loathsome, that it must be buried out of sight. Could a looking-glass be used in the house appointed for all living; it would be a terror to those, who now look oftner into their glasses, than into their Bibles. And what though the body be gorgeously arrayed? The finest clothes are but badges of our sin and shame; and, in a little time will be exchanged for a winding-sheet, when the body will become a feast to the worms.

3dly, It may be a mighty check upon sensuality and fleshly lusts, 1 Pet. ii. 11. *I beseech you, as strangers and pilgrims, abstain from fleshly lusts, which war against the soul.* It is hard to cause wet wood take fire; and when the fire doth take hold of it, it is soon extinguished. Sensuality makes men unfit for divine communications, and is an effectual means to quench the Spirit. Intemperance in eating and drinking, carries on the ruin of soul and body at once; and hastens death, while it makes the man most unfit for it. Therefore, take heed to yourselves, lest at any time your hearts be overcharged with surfeiting and drunkness, and so that day come upon you unawares, Luke xxi. 34. But O! how often is the soul struck through with a dart, in gratifying the senses! At these doors, destruction enters in. Therefore Job made a covenant with his eyes, Chap. xxxi. 1. *The mouth of a strange woman is a deep pit; he that is abhorred of the Lord, shall fall therein,* Prov. xxii. 14. *Let him that standeth, take heed lest he fall.* Beware of lasciviousness; study modesty in your apparel, words and actions. The ravens of the valley of death will, at length, pick out the wanton eye; The obscene, filthy tongue will, at length, be quiet, in the land of silence! And grim death, embracing the body in its cold arms, will effactually allay the heat of all fleshly lusts.

Lastly, In a word, it may check our earthly mindedness; and at once knock down the lust of the flesh, the lust of the eyes, and the pride of life. Ah! if we must die, why are we thus? Why so fond of temporal things; so anxious to get them, so eager in the embraces of them, so mightily touched with the loss of them? Let me, upon a view of the house appointed for all living, bespeak the worldling in the words of Solomon, Prov xxiii. 5. *Wilt thou set thine eyes upon that which is not? For riches certainly make themselves wings, they flee away as an eagle towards heaven.* Riches, and all worldly things, are but a fair nothing: they are that which is not,

They are not what they seem to be: they are all but gilded vanities, that deceive the eye. Comparatively, they are not; there is infinitely more of nothingness and not being, than of being and reality in the best of them. What is the world, and all that is in it, but a fashion, or fair show, such as men make on a stage, a passing show? 1 Cor. vii. 31. Royal pomp is but a gaudy show, or appearance in GOD's account, Acts xxv. 23. The best name they get is *good things*; but, observe it, they are only the wicked man's good things, Luke xvi. 25.—*Thou in thy life-time receivedst thy good things* says Abraham, in the parable, to the rich man in hell. And well may the men of the world, call these things their goods; for there is no other good in them, about them, nor attending them. Now, wilt thou set thine eyes upon empty shows and fancies? Wilt thou cause thine eyes to fly on them, as the word is? Shall mens hearts fly out at their eyes upon them, as a ravenous bird on its prey? If they do, let them know, that, at length these shall fly as fast away from them, as ever their eyes flew upon them: like a flock of fair-feathered birds, that settle on a fool's ground; the which, when he runs to catch them as his own, do immediately take wing, fly away, and, sitting down on his neighbour's ground, elude his expectation, Luke xii. 20. *Thou fool, this night thy soul shall be required of thee: then whose shall these things be?* Though you do not make wings to them as many do; they make themselves wings, and fly away; not as a tame house-bird, which may be catched again; nor as an hawk, that will show where she is by her bells, and be called again with the lure; but as an eagle, which quickly flies out of sight, and cannot be recalled. Forbear thou to behold these things, O mortal! there is no reason thou shouldst set thine eyes upon them. This world is a great inn, in the road to eternity, to which thou art travelling. Thou art attended by these things, as servants belonging to the inn, where thou lodgest; they wait upon thee, while thou art there, and when thou goest away, they will convoy thee to the door. But they are not thine; they will not go away with thee; but return to wait on other strangers, as they did on thee.

Fifthly, It may serve as a spring of Christian resolution, to cleave to CHRIST, adhere to his truths, and continue in his ways; whatever he may suffer for so doing. It would much allay the fear of man, that bringeth a snare: *Who art thou, that thou shouldst be afraid of a man that shall die?* Isa. li. 12. Look on persecutors as pieces of brittle clay, that shall be dashed to pieces; for then shall ye despise them as foes that are mortal; whose terrors to others, in the land of the living, shall quickly die with themselves. The serious consideration of the shortness of our time, and the certainty of death, will teach us, that all the advantage we can make by our apostacy, in time of trial, is not worth the while; it is not worth the going out of the way to get it; and what we refuse to forego, for CHRIST's sake, may quickly be taken from us by death. But, we can never lose it so honourably, as for the cause of CHRIST and his gospel: for what glory is it, that ye give up what ye have in the world; when GOD takes it away from you by death, whether you will or not? This consideration may teach us to undervalue life itself, and chuse to forego it rather than to sin. The worst that men can do, is to take away that life, which we cannot long keep, though all the world should conspire to help us to retain to the Spirit. And if we refuse to offer it up to GOD, when he calls for it, in defence of his honour, he can take it from us another way; as it fared with him, who could not burn for CHRIST, but was afterwards burnt by an accidental fire in his house.

Lastly, It may serve for a spur, to incite us to prepare for death. Consider, (1.) Your eternal state will be according to the state in which you die; death will open the doors of heaven or hell to you. As the tree falls so it shall lie through eternity. If the infant be dead-born, the whole world will not raise it to life again; and if one die out of CHRIST, in an unregenerate state, there is no more hope of him for ever. (2.) Seriously consider what it is to go into another world; a world of spirits, wherewith we are very ill acquainted. How frightful is converse with spirits to poor mortals in this life! And, how dreadful is the case, when men are hurried away into another world, not knowing but devils may be their companions for ever! Let us then give all diligence, to make and advance our acquaintance with the LORD of that world. (3.) It is but a short time ye have to prepare for death, therefore now or never; seeing the time assigned for preparation, **will soon** be over, Eccles. ix 10. *Whatsoever thy hand findeth to do, do it with thy might: for there is no work, nor device, nor knowledge, nor wisdom in the grave, whither thou goest.* **How** can we be idle, having so great a work to do, and so little time to do it in? But, if the time be short, the work of preparation for death, though hard work, will not last long. The shadows of the evening make the labourer work chearfully; knowing the time to be at hand, when he shall be called in from his labour. (4.) Much of our time is over already; and the youngest of us all cannot assure himself, that there is as much of his time to come, as is past. Our life in the world, is but a short preface to long eternity; and much of the tale is told. Oh! shall we not double our diligence, when so much of our time is spent, and so little of our great work is done? (3.) The present time is flying away; and we cannot bring back time past, it hath taken an eternal farewell of us; there is no kindling the fire again, that is burnt to ashes. The time to come is not ours; and we have no assurance of a share in it, when it comes. We have nothing we can call ours, but the present moment; and that is flying away; How soon our time may be at an end, we know not. Die we must, but who can tell us when? If death kept one set time for all, we are in no hazard of a surprise; but daily observation shews us, there is no such thing. Now the flying shadow of our life, allows no time for loitering. The rivers run speedily into the sea, from whence they came; but not so speedily as man to the dust, from whence he came. The stream of time is the swiftest current, and quickly runs out to eternity. *Lastly*, If once death carry us off, there is no coming back again to mend our matters, Job xiv. 14. *If a man die, shall he live again?* Dying is a thing we cannot get a trial of; it is what we can do only once, Heb. ix. 27. *It is appointed unto men* ONCE *to die*. And that which can be but once done, and yet is of so much importance, that our all depends on having it done right, we have need to use the utmost diligence, that we may do it well. Therefore prepare for death, and do it timeously.

If ye who are unregenerate, ask me, What ye shall do, to prepare for death, that ye may die safely? I answer, I have told you already, what must be done. And that is, your nature and state must be changed; ye must be born again: ye must be united to JESUS CHRIST by faith. And till this is done, ye are not capable of other directions, which belong to one's dying comfortably, whereof we may discourse afterwards in due place.

HEAD II.

The Difference betwixt the Righteous and the Wicked in their Death.

PROVERBS xiv. 32.

The Wicked is driven away in his Wickedness; But the Righteous hath hope in his Death.

THIS text looks like the cloud betwixt the Israelites and Egyptians; having a dark side towards the latter, and a bright side towards the former. It represents death like Pharaoh's jaylor, bringing the chief butler and the chief baker out of one prison; the one to be restored to his office, and the other to be led to execution. It shows the difference betwixt the godly and ungodly in their death; who as they act a very different part in life, so, in death, have a vastly different exit.

First, As to the death of a wicked man; here is, (1.) The manner of his passing out of the world, He is driven away; namely, in his death, as is clear from the opposite clause. He is forcibly thrust out of his place in this world, driven away as chaff before the wind. (2.) The state he passeth away in. He dies in a sinful and hopeless state. *First*, In a sinful state; he is driven away in his wickedness. He lived in it, and he dies in it: his filthy garments of sin, in which he wrapt up himself in his life, are his prison-garments in which he shall lie rapt up for ever. *Secondly*, In a hopeless state; *But the Righteous hath hope in his death*: which plainly imports the hopelessness of the wicked in their death. Whereby it is not meant, that no wicked man shall have any hope at all, when he is a-dying, but shall die in despair. No; sometimes it is so indeed, but frequently it is otherwise; foolish virgins may, and often do hope to the last breath. But the wicked man has no solid hope; and as for the delusive hopes he entertains himself with, death will root them up, and he shall be forever irretrievably miserable.

Secondly, As to the death of a righteous man; he hath hope in his death. This is ushered in with a *but*, importing a removal of these dreadful circumstances, with which the wicked man is attended, who is driven away in his wickedness; but the godly are not so. Not so, (1.) In the manner of their passing out of the world. The righteous is not driven away as chaff before the wind, but led away as a bride to the marriage-chamber, carried away by the angels into Abraham's bosom, Luke xvi. 22. (2.) Not so as to their state, when passing out of this life. The righteous man dies, (1.) Not in a sinful, but in a holy state. He goes not away in his sin, but out of it. In his life he was putting off the old man, changing his prison garments; and now the remaining rags of them are removed, and he is adorned with robes of glory. (2.) Not in a hopeless, but a hopeful state. He hath hope in his death; he has the grace of hope, and the well-founded expectation of better things, than ever he had in this world; and though the stream of his hope at death may run shallow; yet he has still as much of it, as makes him venture his eternal interests upon the LORD JESUS CHRIST.

Doctrine I.

The Wicked dying, are driven away in their Wickedness, and in a hopeless State.

In speaking to this doctrine, (1.) I shall shew how, and in what sense, the wicked are driven away in their wickedness, at death. (2.) I shall discover the hopelessness of their state at death. And *Lastly*, Apply the whole.

I. How, and in what sense the wicked are driven away in their wickedness. In discoursing of this matter, I shall briefly inquire, (1.) What is meant by their being driven away. (2.) Whence they shall be driven, and whither. (3.) In what respects they may be said, to be driven away in their wickedness. But, before I proceed, let me advertise you, that you are mistaken if you think, that no persons are to be called wicked, but they who are avowedly vitious and prophane, as if the devil could dwell in none but those whose name is Legion. In scripture-account, all who are not righteous, in the manner hereafter explained, are reckoned wicked. And therefore the text divides the whole world into two sorts, the righteous, and the wicked; and ye will see the same thing in that other text, Mal. iii. 18. *Then shall ye return, and discern between the righteous and the wicked.* Wherefore, if ye be not righteous, ye are wicked. If ye have not an imputed righteousness, and also an implanted righteousness, or holiness; if ye be yet in your natural state, unregenerated, not united to CHRIST by faith; howsoever moral, and blameless in the eyes of men, your conversation may be, ye are the wicked, who shall be driven away in their wickedness, if death find you in that state. Now,

FIRST, As to the meaning of this phrase *driven away*, there are three things in it; the wicked shall be taken away suddenly, violently, and irresistibly.

First, Unrenewed men shall be taken away suddenly at death. Not that all wicked men die suddenly; nor that they are all wicked, who die so: GOD forbid! But, (1.) Death commonly comes upon them unexpected, and so surpriseth them; as the deluge came surprisingly on the old world, tho' they were forewarned of it long before it came: as travail cometh on a woman with child, with surprising suddenness: although looked for and expected, 1 Thess. v. 3. Death seizeth them, as a creditor doth his debtor, to hale him to prison, Psalm lv. 15. and that when they are not aware. Death comes in as a thief at the window, and finds them full of busy thoughts about this life, which that very day perish. (2.) Death always seizeth them unprepared for it; the old house falls down about their ears, before they have another

a moment to destruction, and makes a most dismal change; the man, for the most part never knows where he is, till in hell he lift up his eyes, Luke xvi. 23. The floods of wrath suddenly overwhelm his soul, and ere he is aware, he is plunged in the bottomless pit.

Secondly, The unrenewed man is taken away out of the world violently. Driving is a violent action; he is chased out of the world, Job xviii. 18. Fain would he stay if he could; but death drags him away like a malefactor to the execution. He sought no other portion, than the profits and pleasures of this world, he hath no other, he really desires no other; how can he then go away out of it, if he were not driven.

Quest. But may not a wicked man be willing to die? *Ans.* He may indeed be willing to die; but, observe, it is only in one of three cases. (1.) In a fit of passion, by reason of some trouble that he is impatient to be rid of. Thus many persons when their passion has got the better of their reason, and when, on that account, they are most unfit to die, will be ready to cry, O to be gone! but should their desire be granted, and death come at their call, they would quickly shew they were not in earnest; and that if they go, they must be driven away against their wills. (2.) When they are brim-full of despair, they may be willing to die. Thus Saul murdered himself; and Spira wished to be in hell, that he might know the uttermost of what he believed, he was to suffer. In this manner men may seek after death, while it flies from them. But fearful is the violence these do undergo, whom the terrors of GOD do thus drive. (3.) When they are dreaming of happiness after death. Foolish virgins, under the power of delusion, as to their state, may be willing to die, having no fear of lying down in sorrow. How many are there, who can give no scripture-ground for their hope, who yet have no bands in their death! Many are driven to darkness sleeping; they go off like lambs, who would roar like lions, did they know but what place they are going to; though the chariot, in which they are, drive furiously to the depths of hell, yet they fear not, because they are fast asleep.

Lastly, The unregenerate man is taken away irresistibly. He must go, though sore against his will. Death will take no refusal, nor admit of any delay, though the man has not lived half his days, according to his own computation. If he will not draw, it will break him. If he will not come forth, it will pull the house down about his ears, for there he must not stay. Although the physician help, friends groan, the wife and the children cry, and the man himself use his utmost efforts to retain the spirit, his soul is required of him; yield he must, and go where he shall never more see light.

SECONDLY, Let us consider whence they are driven, and whither. When the wicked die, (1.) They are driven out of this world, where they sinned, into the other world, where they must be judged, and receive their particular sentence, Heb. ix. 27. *It is appointed unto men once to die but after this the judgment.* They shall no more return to their beloved earth. Though their hearts are wedded to their earthly enjoyments, they must leave them; they can carry nothing hence. How sorrowful must their departure be, when they have nothing in view, so good as that which they leave behind them! (2.) They are driven out of the society of the saints on earth, into the society of the damned in hell, Luke xvi. 22, 23. *The rich man also died, and was buried. And in hell he lift up his eyes.* What a multitude of the devil's goats do now take place among CHRIST's sheep! but at death they shall be led forth with the workers of iniquity, Psalm cxxv. 5. There is a mixed multitude in this world, but no mixture in the other; each party is there set by themselves. Though hypocrites grow here as tares among the wheat, death will root them up; and they shall be bound in bundles for the fire. (3.) They are driven out of time into eternity. While time lasts with them, there is hope; but when time goes, all hope goes with it. Precious time is now lavishly spent; it lies so heavy upon the hands of many, that they think themselves obliged to take several ways to drive away time. But beware of being at a loss what to do in life; improve time for eternity, whilst you have it: for ere long death will drive it from you, and you from it, so as ye shall never meet again. (4.) They are driven out of their specious pretences to piety. Death strips them of the splendid robes of a fair profession, with which some of them were adorned, and turns them off the stage, in the rags of a wicked heart and life. The word hypocrite, properly signifies a stage-player, who appears to be what indeed he is not. This world is the stage on which these children of the devil personate the children of GOD. Their shew of religion is the player's coat, under which one must look, who will judge of them aright. Now death turns them out of their coat, and then they appear in their native dress: it unveils them, and takes off their mask. There are none in the other world, who pretend to be better than they really are. Depraved nature acts in the regions of horror, unalloyed, and undisguised. *Lastly,* They are driven way from all means of grace; and are set beyond the line, quite out of all prospect of mercy. There is no more an opportunity to buy oil for the lamp; it is gone out at death, and can never be lighted again. There may be offers of mercy and peace made after they are gone: but they are to others, not to them; there are no such offers in the place, to which they are driven: these offers are only made in that place, from which they are driven.

LASTLY, In what respect may they be said to be driven away in their wickedness? *Ans.* (1.) In respect of their being driven away in their sinful, unconverted state. Having lived enemies to GOD, they die in a state of enmity to him; for none are brought into the eternal state of consummate happiness, but by the way of the state of grace, or begun recovery in this life. The child that is dead in the womb, is born dead, and is cast out of the womb into the grave; so he who is dead while he liveth, or is spiritually dead, is cast forth of the womb of time, in the same state of death into the pit of utter misery. O miserable death, to die in the gall of bitterness and bond of iniquity! it had been incomparably better for such as die thus, that they had never been born. (2.) In regard they die sinning, acting wickedly against GOD, in contradiction to the divine law; for they can do nothing but sin while they live. So death takes them in the very act of sinning; violently draws them from the embraces of their lusts, and drives them away to the tribunal to receive their sentence. It is a remarkable expression, Job xxxvi. 14. *They die in youth*: the marginal reading is, *their soul dieth in youth*: their lusts being lively, their desires vigorous, and expectations big, as is common in youth. *And their life is among the unclean:* or, *and the company*, or herd, *of them dieth among the Sodomites*,—i. e. is taken away in the heat of their sin and wickedness, as the Sodomites were, Gen. xix. Luke vii. 28, 29. (3.) In as much as they are driven away, loaded with the guilt of all their sins; this is the winding-sheet, that shall lie down with them in the dust, Job xx. 11. Their works follow them into the other world; they go away with the yoke of their transgressions wreathed about their necks. Guilt is a bad companion in life, but how terrible will it be in death! it lies now, perhaps, like cold brimstone on their benum'd consciences; but when death opens the way for sparks of divine vengeance, like fire, to fall upon it, it will make dreadful flames in the conscience, in which the soul will be, as it were wrapt up forever. *Lastly*, The wicked are driven away in their wickedness, in so far as they die under the absolute power of their wickedness. While there is hope, there is some restraint on the worst of men; and those moral endowments, which GOD gives to a number of men, for the benefit of mankind in this life, are so many allays and restraints upon the impetuous wickedness of human nature. But all hope being cut off, and these gifts withdrawn, the wickedness of the wicked, will then arrive at its perfection. As the seeds of grace sown in the hearts of the elect, come to their full maturity at death: so, wicked and hellish dispositions, in the reprobate, come then to their highest pitch. Their prayers to GOD will then be turned to horrible curses; and their praises to hideous blasphemies, Mat. xxii. 13. *There shall be weeping, and gnashing of teeth.* This gives a dismal, but genuine view of the state of the wicked, in another world.

II. I shall discover the hopelessness of the state of unrenewed men, at death. It appears to be very hopeless, if we consider these four things.

First, Death cuts off all their hopes and prospects of peace and pleasure in this life, Luke xii. 19, 20. *Soul, thou hast much goods laid up for many years; take thine ease, eat, drink and be merry. But God said unto him, Thou fool, this night thy soul shall be required of thee; then whose shall those things be, which thou hast provided?* They look for great matters in this world; they hope to increase their wealth, to see their families prosper, and to live at ease: but death comes like a stormy wind, and shakes off all their fond hopes, like green fruit from off a tree: *When he is about to fill his belly, God shall cast the fury of his wrath upon him,* Job xx. 23. He may begin a web of contrivances, for advancing his worldly interest; but, before he gets it wrought out, death comes, and cuts it out: *His breath goeth forth, he returneth to his earth: in that very day his thoughts perish,* Psalm cxlvi. 4.

Secondly, When death comes, they have no solid grounds, to hope, for eternal happiness: *For what is the hope of the hypocrite, though he hath gained, when God taketh away his soul?* Job xxvii. 8. Whatever hopes they fondly entertain, they are not founded on GOD's word, which is the only sure ground of hope: If they knew their own case, they would see themselves only happy in a dream. And indeed what hope can they have? The law is plain against them, and condemns them. The curses of it, these cords of death, are about them already. The Saviour, whom they slighted, is now their Judge; and their Judge is their enemy. How then can they hope? They have bolted the door of mercy against themselves, by their unbelief. They have despised the remedy, and therefore must die without mercy. They have no saving interest in JESUS CHRIST, the only channel of conveyance, in which mercy flows: and therefore they can never taste of it. The sword of justice guards the door of mercy, so as none can eater in, but the members of the mystical body of CHRIST, over whose heads is a covert of atoning blood, the Mediator's blood. These indeed may pass without harm, for justice has nothing to require of them. But others cannot pass, since they are not in CHRIST: death comes to them with the sting in it, the sting of unpardoned guilt. It is armed against them with all the force the sanction of a holy law can give it, 1 Cor. xv. 56. *The sting of death is sin, and the strength of sin is the law.* When that law was given on Sinai, the whole mount quaked greatly, Exod. xix. 18. When the Redeemer was making satisfaction for the elect's breaking of it, the earth did quake, and the rocks rent, Matth. xxvii. 51. What possible ground of hope then is there to the wicked man, when death comes upon him, armed with the force of this law? How can he escape that fire, which burnt unto the midst of heaven? Deut. iv. 11. How shall he be able to stand in that smoke, that ascended as the smoke of a furnace? Exod. xix. 18. How will he endure the terrible thunders and lightnings, ver 16. and dwell in the darkness, clouds and thick darkness? Deut. iv. 11. All these resemblances heaped together, do but faintly represent the fearful tempest of wrath and indignation, which shall pursue the wicked to the lowest hell; and for ever abide on them, who are driven to darkness at death.

Thirdly, Death roots up their delusive hopes of eternal happiness: then it is, their covenant with death, and agreement with hell, is broken. They are awakned out of their golden dreams, and at length lift up their eyes, Job viii. 14. *Whose hope shall be cut off, and whose trust shall be a spider's web.* They trust all shall be well with them after death: but this their trust, is but a web woven out of their own bowels, with a great deal of art and industry. They wrap themselves up in this their hope, as the spider wraps herself in her web. But it is but a weak and slender defence; for however it may withstand the threatnings of the word of GOD; death, that besom of destruction, will sweep them and it both away, so as there shall not be the least shred of it left them; but he, who this moment will not let his hope go, shall next moment be utterly hopeless. Death overturns the house, built on the sand: it leaves no man under the power of delusion.

Lastly, Death makes their state absolutely, and for ever hopeless. Matters cannot be retrieved and amended after death. For (1.) Time once gone, can never be recalled. If cries or tears, price or pains, could bring time back again; the wicked man might have hope in his death. But tears of blood will not prevail; nor will his roaring for millions of ages, cause it to return. The sun will not stand still, until the sluggard awake and enter on his journey: and when once it is gone down, he needs not expect the night to be turned into day for his sake; he must lodge through the long night of eternity, where his time left him. (2.) There is no returning to this life, to amend what is amiss: it is a state of probation and trial, which terminates at death; and therefore we cannot return to it again: it is but once we thus live, and once we die. Death carries the wicked man to his own place, Acts i. 25. This life is our working-day; and death closeth our day and our work together. We may readily imagine the wicked might have some hope in their death; if, after death has opened their eyes, they could return to life, and have but the trial of one Sabbath, one offer of CHRIST, one day, or but one hour more, to make up their peace with GOD; But, *man lieth down, and riseth not till the heavens be no more; they shall not awake, nor be raised out of their sleep,* Job xiv. 12. *Lastly,* In the other world, men have no access to get their ruined state and condition retrieved, if they never so fain would: *For there is no work, nor device, nor knowledge, nor wisdom in the grave, whither thou goest,* Eccles. ix. 10. Now, a man may flee from the wrath to come; now, he may get into a refuge: but when once death has done its work, the door is shut; there are no more offers of mercy, no more pardons: where the tree is fallen, there it must lie.

Let what has been said, be carefully pondered: And, that it may be of use, let me exhort you,

First, To take heed that ye entertain no hopes of heaven, but what are built on a solid foundation. Tremble to think what fair hopes of happiness death sweeps away, like cobwebs! How the hopes of many are cut off, when they seem to themselves to be on the very threshold of heaven! How, in the moment they expected to be carried by angels into Abraham's bosom, into the regions of bliss and peace; they are carried by devils, into the society of the damned in hell; into the place of torment, and regions of horror! I beseech you to beware, (1.) Of a hope built up, where the ground was never cleared. The wise builder digged deep, Luke vi. 48. Were your hopes of heaven never shaken; but ye have had good hopes all your days? Alas for it! you may see the mystery of your case explained, Luke xi. 21. *When a strong man, armed, keepeth his palace, his goods are in peace.* But if they have been shaken, take heed lest there have only been breaches been made in the old building, which you have but repaired again, by ways and means of your own. I assure you, your hope, howsoever fair a building it is, is not to trust to, unless your old hopes have been razed, and you have laid foundation quite new. (2.) Beware of that hope, which looks brisk in the dark; but looseth all its lustre, when it is set in the light of GOD's word; when it is examined and tried by the touchstone of divine revelation, John iii. 20, 21. *For every one that doth evil, hateth the light; neither cometh to the light, lest his deeds should be reproved. But he that doth the truth, cometh to the light, that his deeds may be made manifest, that they are wrought in God.* That hope, which cannot abide Scripture-trial, but sinks, when searched into by sacred truth, is a delusion, and not a true hope; for GOD's word is always a friend to the graces of GOD's Spirit, and an enemy to delusion. (3.) Beware of that hope, which stands without being supported by Scripture-evidences. Alas! many are big with hopes, who cannot give, because they really have not any Scripture grounds for them. Thou hopest, that all shall be well with thee, after death: but what word of GOD is it, on which thou hast been caused to hope? Psalm cxix. 49. What Scripture evidence hast thou, to prove that thy hope is not the hope of the hypocrite? What hast thou, after impartial self-examination, as in the sight of GOD, found in thyself, which the word of GOD determins to be a sure evidence of his right to eternal life, who is possessed of it? Numbers of men are ruined with such hopes, as stand unsupported by Scripture-evidence. Men are fond and tenacious of these hopes; but death will throw them down, and leave the self-deceiver hopeless. Lastly, Beware of that hope of heaven, which doth not prepare and dispose you for heaven, which never makes your soul more holy, 1 John iii. 3. *Every man that hath this hope in him, purifieth himself, even as he is pure.* The hope of the most part of men, is rather a hope to be free of pain and torment in another life, than a hope of true happiness, the nature whereof is not understood and discerned; and therefore it slakes down in sloth and indolence, and does not excite to mortification and a heavenly life. So far are they from hoping aright for heaven, that they must own, if they speak their genuine sentiments, removing out of this world into any other place whatsoever, is rather their fear than their hope. The glory of the heavenly city does not at all draw their hearts upwards towards it; nor do they lift up their heads with joy, in the prospect of arriving at it. If they had the true hope of the marriage-day, they would, as the bride, the Lamb's wife, be making themselves ready for it, Rev. xix. 7. But their hopes are produced by their sloth, and their sloth is nourished by their hopes. Oh! Sirs, as ye would not be driven away hopeless in your death, beware of these hopes. Raze them now, and build on a new foundadation; left death leave not one stone upon another, and ye never be able to hope any more.

Secondly, Hasten, O sinners, out of your wickedness, out of your sinful state, and out of your wicked life; if ye would not at death, be driven away in your wickedness. Remember the fatal end of the wicked man, as the text represents it. I know there is a great difference in the death of the wicked, in respect of some circumstances; but all of them, in their death, agree in this, that they are driven away in their wickedness. Some of them die resolutely, as if they scorned to be afraid. Some in raging despair; so filled with horror, that they cry out, as if they were already in hell; others in sullen despondency, opprest with fears; insomuch, that their hearts are sunk within them, upon the remembrance of misspent time, and the view they have of eternity; having neither head nor heart, to do any thing for their own relief. And others die stupid; they lived like beasts, and they die like beasts; without any concern on their spirits, about their eternal state. They groan, under their bodily distress, but have no sense of the danger of their souls. One may, with almost as much prospect of success, speak to a stone, as to speak to them: vain is the attempt to teach them; nothing that can be said, moves them. To discourse to them, either of the joys of heaven, or the torments of hell, is to blow on a rock, or beat the air. Some die like the foolish virgins, dreaming of heaven; their foreheads are steeled against the fears of hell, with presumptuous hopes of heaven. Their business, who would be useful to them, is not to answer doubts about the case of their souls; but to dispute them out of their false hopes. But which way soever the unconverted man dies, he is driven away in his wickedness. O dreadful case! Oh, let the consideration of so horrible a departure out of this world, move you to betake yourselves to JESUS CHRIST, as an all-sufficient Saviour, an Almighty Redeemer. Let it prevail to drive you out of your wickedness to holiness of heart and life. Though you reckon it pleasant to live in wickedness; you cannot but own it is bitter to die in it. And if you leave it not in time, you shall go in your wickedness to hell, the proper place of it, that it may be set there on its own base. For when you are passing out of this world, all your sins, from the eldest to the youngest of them, will swarm about you, hang upon you, accompany you to the other world, and as so many furies, surround you there for ever.

Lastly, O be concerned for others, especially for your relations, that they may not continue in their sinful natural state, but be brought into a state of salvation; lest they be driven away in their wickedness at death. What would ye not do, to prevent any of your friends dying an untimely and violent death? But alas! do not ye see them in hazard of being driven away in their wickedness? Is not death approaching them, even the youngest of them? And are they not strangers to true Christianity, remaining in that state in which they came into the world? Oh; make haste to pluck the brand out of the fire, before it be burnt to ashes. The death of relations often leaves a sting, in the hearts of these they leave behind them; for that they do not do for their souls, as they had opportunity; and that now the opportunity is forever taken out of their hands.

Doctrine II.

The State of the Godly in Death, is a hopeful State.

We have seen the dark side of the cloud looking towards ungodly men, passing out of the world; let us now take a view of the bright side of it, shining on the godly, as they are entring upon their eternal state. In discoursing this subject, I shall confirm this doctrine, answer an objection against it, and then make some practical improvement of the whole.

For Confirmation, let it be observed, that although the passage out of this world by death, have a frightful aspect to poor mortals, and to miscarry in it must needs be of fatal consequence, yet the following circumstances make the state of the godly in their death, happy and hopeful.

First, They have a trusty good friend before them in the other world? JESUS CHRIST their best friend, is LORD of that land to which death carries them. When Joseph sent for his father to come down to Egypt, telling him, GOD had made him LORD over all Egypt,——and when Jacob saw the waggons Joseph had sent to carry him, the spirit of Jacob revived, Gen. xlv. 9. 27. he frankly resolves to undertake the journey. I think, when the LORD calls a godly man out of this world, he sends him such glad tidings, and such a kind invitation into the other world, that if he had faith to believe it, his spirit must revive, when he sees the waggon of death, which comes to carry him thither. It is true indeed, he has a weighty trial to undergo; *After death the judgment*. But the case of the godly is altogether hopeful; for the LORD of the land is their husband, and their husband is their judge; *The Father hath committed all judgment unto the Son*, John v. 22. And surely the case of the wife is hopeful, when her own husband is her judge, even such a husband as hates putting away. No husband is so loving and so tender of his spouse as the LORD CHRIST is of his. One would think, it would be a very bad land, which a wife would not willingly go to, where her husband is the ruler and judge. Moreover, their Judge is their Advocate, 1 John ii. 1. *We have an advocate with the Father, Jesus Christ the righteous.* And therefore they need not fear their being put back & falling into condemnation. What can be more favourable? Can they think, that he who pleads their cause, will himself pass sentence against them? Yet further, their Advocate is the Redeemer; they are redeemed with the precious blood of CHRIST, 1 Pet. i. 18, 19. So when he pleads for them, he is pleading his own cause. Though an advocate may be careless of the interests of one who employs him, surely he will do his utmost to defend his own right; which he hath purchased with his money; and shall not their Advocate defend the purchase of his own blood? But more than all that, their Redeemer is their head, and they are his members, Eph. v. 23. 30. Though one were so silly as to let his own purchase go, without standing up to defend his right, yet surely will not quit a limb of his own body. Is not their case then hopeful in death, who are so closely linked and allied to the LORD of the other world, who hath the keys of hell and death.

Secondly, They shall have a safe passage to another world. They must indeed go through the valley of the shadow of death, but though it be in itself a dark and shady vale, it shall be a valley of hope to them; they shall not be driven through it, but walk through it, as men in perfect safety, who fear no evil, Psal. xxiii. 4. Why should they fear? They have the LORD of the land's safe conduct, his pass sealed with his own **blood**, namely, the blessed covenant, which is the saint's death-bed comfort, 2 Sam. xxiii. 5. *Although my house be not so with God, yet he hath made with me an everlasting COVENANT, ordered in all things and sure: for this is all my salvation, and all my desire, although he cause it not to grow.* Who then can harm them? It is safe riding in CHRIST's chariot, Cant. iii. 9. both through life and death. They have good and honorable attendants, a guard, even a guard of angels. These encamp about them in the time of their life; and surely will not leave them in the day of their death. These happy ministring spirits are attendants on their LORD's bride, and will doubtless convey her safe home to his house. When friends in mournful mood stand by the saint's bed-side, waiting to see him draw his last breath; his soul is waited for of holy angels, to be carried by them into Abraham's bosom,

Luke xvi. 22. The Captain of the faint's falvation is the captain of this holy guard, he was their guide even unto death, and he will be their guide through it too. Pfalm xxiii. 4. *Yea, though I walk through the valley of the shadow of death, I will fear no evil; for thou art with me.* They may without fear pafs that river, being confident it fhall not overflow them; and may walk through that fire, being fure they fhall not be burnt by it.

Death can do them no harm. It cannot even hurt their bodies; for though it feparate the foul from the body, it cannot feparate the body from the LORD CHRIST. Even death is to them but fleep, in JESUS, 1 Theff. iv. 14. They continue members of CHRIST, though in a grave. Their duft is precious duft, laid up in a grave, as in their LORD's cabinet. They lie in a grave mellowing; as precious fruit laid up to be brought forth to him at the refurrection. The hufbandman has corn in his barn, and corn lying in the ground; the latter is more precious to him than the former; becaufe he looks to get it returned with increafe. Even fo the dead bodies of the faints are valued by their Saviour; they are fown in corruption, to be raifed in incorruption; fown in difhonor, raifed in glory, 1 Cor. xv. 42, 43. It cannot hurt their fouls. It is with the fouls of the faints at death, as with Paul and his company in their voyage, whereof we have the hiftory, Acts xxvii. the fhip was broken in pieces, but the paffengers got all fafe to land. When the dying faint's fpeech is laid, his eyes fet, and his laft breath drawn, the foul gets fafe away into the heavenly paradife, leaving the body to return to its earth, but in the joyful hope of a re-union at its glorious refurrection. How can death hurt the godly? it is a foiled enemy; if it caft them down, it is only that they may rife up more **glorious.** *Our Saviour Jefus Chrift hath abolifhed* DEATH, 2 Tim. i. 10. The foul and life of it is gone; it is but a walking fhade that may fright but cannot hurt faints; it is only the fhadow of death to them, it is not the thing itfelf; their dying is but as dying, or fomewhat like dying. The Apoftle tells us, *It is Chrift that died*, Rom. viii. 34. Stephen, the firft Chriftian martyr, though ftoned to death, yet but fell afleep, Acts viii. 34. Certainly the nature of death is quite changed with refpect to the faints. It is not to them, what it was to JESUS CHRIST their head: It is not to the invenomed ruinating thing, wrapt up in the fanction of the firft covenant, Gen. ii. 19. *In the day thou eateft thereof, thou fhalt furely die.* It comes to the godly without its fting; they may meet it with that falutation, *O death where is thy fting?* Is this Mara? Is this bitter death? It went out full into the world, when the firft Adam opened the door to it; but the second Adam hath brought it again empty to his own people. I feel a sting, may the dying saint say; yet it is but a bee-sting, stinging only through the skin; but O death, where is thy sting, thine old sting, the serpent's sting, that stings to the heart and soul? The sting of death is Sin; but that is taken away. If death arrest the saint, and carry him before the Judge, to answer for the debt he contracted, the debt will be found paid by the glorious Cautioner; and he has the discharge to show. The thorn of guilt is pulled out of the man's conscience, and his name is blotted out of the black roll, and written among the living in Jerusalem. It is true, it is a great journey to go through the valley of the shadow of death; but the saint's burden is taken away from off his back, his iniquity is pardoned, he may walk at ease, *No lion shall be there, nor any ravenous beast*; the redeemed may walk at leisure there free from all apprehensions of danger.

Lastly, They shall have a joyful entrance into the other world. Their arrival in the regions of bliss, will be celebrated with rapturous hymns of praise to their glorious redeemer. A dying day is a good day to a godly man. Yea, it is his best day; it is better to him than his birth-day, or than the most joyous day he ever had on earth. *A good name*, says the wise man, *is better than precious ointment: and the day of death, than the day of one's birth*, Eccl. vii. 1. The notion of the immortality of the soul, and of future happiness, which obtained among some Pagan nations, had wonderful effects on them. Some of them when they mourned for the dead, did it in women's apparel; that being moved with the indecency of the garb, they might the sooner lay aside their mourning. Others buried them without any lamentation or mourning, but had a sacrifice, and a feast for friends upon that occasion. Some were wont to mourn at births, and rejoice at burials. But the practice of some Indian nations is yet more strange, of whom it is reported, That upon the husband's decease, his several wives were in use to contend, before the judges, which of them was the best beloved wife; and she, in whose favour it was determined, with a cheerful countenance, threw herself into the flames prepared for her husband's corpse, was burned with it, and reckoned happy, while the rest lived in grief, and were accounted miserable. But, howsoever lame notions of a future state, assisted by pride, affectation of applause, apprehensions of difficulties in this life, and such like principles, proper to depraved human nature, may influence rude, uncultivated minds, when strengthened by the arts of hell: O! what solid joy and consolation may they have who are true Christians, being in CHRIST, who hath brought life and immortality to light by the gospel! 2 Tim. i. 10. Death is one of these *all things*, that work together for good, to them that love God, Rom. viii. 28. When the body dies, the soul is perfected; the body of death goes off at the death of the body. What harm did the jaylor to Pharaoh's butler, when he opened the prison door to him, and let him out? Is the bird in worse case, when at liberty, than when confined in a cage? Thus, and no worse, are the souls of the saints treated by death. It comes to the godly man, as Haman came to Mordecai with the royal apparel and the horse, Esth. iv. 11. with commission to do them honour, howsoever aukwardly it be performed: I question not but Haman performed the ceremony with a very ill mein, a pale face, a down-look, and a cloudy countenance, and like one who came to hang him, rather than to honour him. But he, whom the king delighted to honour, behoved to be honoured; and Haman, Mordecai's grand enemy, must be the man employed to put this honour upon him. Glory, glory, glory, blessing and praise to our Redeemer or Saviour, our Mediator, by whose death, grim, devouring death, is made to do such an office to those, whom it might otherwise have hurried away in their wickedness, to utter and eternal destruction! a dying day is, in itself, a joyful day to the godly, it is their redemption-day, when the captives are delivered, when the prisoners are set free. It is the day of the pilgrims coming home from their pilgrimage; the day in which the heirs of glory return from their travels to their own country, and their Father's house; and enter into actual possession of the glorious inheritance. It is their marriage-day; now is the time of espousals; but then the marriage is consummate, and a marriage-feast begun, which has no period. If so, **is not the state of the godly in death a hopeful state?**

OBJECT. But if the state of the godly in their death be so hopeful, how cometh it to pass that many of them when dying, are full of fears, and have little hope? ANSW. It must be owned, that saints do not all die in one and the same manner; there is a diversity among them, as well as among the wicked; yet the worst case of a dying saint, is indeed a hopeful one. Some die triumphantly, in a full assurance of faith, *The time of my departure is at hand. I have fought a good fight, I have finished my course, I have kept the faith. Henceforth there is laid up for me a crown of righteousness*, 2 Tim. iv. 6, 7, 8. They get a taste of the joys of heaven, while here on earth, and begin the songs of Zion, while yet in a strange land.

Others die in a solid fiducial dependence on their LORD and Saviour; though they cannot sing triumphantly, yet they can and will say the LORD is their GOD. Though they cannot triumph over death, with old Simeon, having CHRIST in his arms, and saying, *Lord, now lettest thou thy servant depart in peace, according to thy word; For mine eyes have seen thy salvation,* Luke ii. 29, 30. yet they can say with dying Jacob, *I have waited for thy salvation, O Lord,* Gen. xlix. 18. His left hand is under their head to support them; though his right hand doth not embrace them; they firmly believe, though they are not filled with joy in believing. They can plead the covenant, and hang by the promise, although their house is not so with GOD, as they could wish. But the dying-day of some saints may be like that day mentioned, Zech. xiv. 7. not day, nor night. They may die under great doubts and fears; setting, as it were, in a cloud, and going to heaven in a mist. They may go mourning without the sun, and never put off their spirit of heaviness, till death strip them of it. They may be carried to heaven through the confines of hell; and may be pursued by the devouring lion, even to the very gates of the new Jerusalem, and may be compared to a ship almost wrecked in sight of the harbor, which yet gets safe into her port, 1 Cor. iii. 15. *If any man's work shall be burnt, he shall suffer loss; but he himself shall be saved, yet so as by fire.* There is safety amidst their fears, but danger in the wicked's strongest confidence: and there is a blessed seed of gladness in their greatest sorrows; *Light is sown for the righteous, and gladness for the upright in heart,* Psalm xcvii. 11.

Now, saints are liable to such perplexity in their death, because, though they be Christians indeed, yet they are men of like passions with others; and death is a frightful object in itself, whatever dress it appear in; the stern countenance, with which it looks at mortals, can hardly miss of causing them to shrink. Moreover, the saints are of all men the most jealous of themselves. They think of eternity, and of a tribunal, more deeply than others do; with them, it is a more serious thing to die, than the rest of mankind are aware of. They know the deceits of the heart, the subtilties of depraved human nature, better than others do. And therefore they may have much ado to keep up hope on a death-bed; while others pass off quietly, like sheep to the slaughter; the rather that Satan, who useth all his art to support the hopes of the hypocrite, will do his utmost to mar the peace, and increase the fears of the saint. Finally, the bad frame of spirit, and ill condition, in which death sometimes seizeth a true Christian, may cause this perplexity. By his being in the state of grace, he is indeed always habitually prepared for death, and his dying safely is insured; but there is more requisite to his actual preparation, and dying comfortably: his spirit must be in good condition too.

Wherefore there are three cases, in which death cannot but be very uncomfortable to the child of GOD. (1.) If it seize him at a time when a guilt of some particular sin unrepented of, is lying on his conscience: and death comes on that very account, to take him out of the land of the living; as was the case of many of the Corinthian believers, 1 Cor. xi. 30. *For this cause*, namely, of unworthy communicating, *many are weak and sickly among you, and many sleep*. If a person is surprised with the approach of death, while lying under the guilt of some unpardoned sin, it cannot but cause a mighty consternation. (2.) When death catches him napping. The mighty cry must be frightful to sleeping virgins. The man who lies in a ruinous house, and awakens not till the timber begins to crack, and the stones to drop down about his ears, may indeed get out of it safely, but not without fears of being crushed by its fall. When a Christian has been going on in a course of security and backsliding, and awakens not till death comes to his bed-side; it is no marvel if he get a fearful awakening. *Lastly*, When he has lost sight of his saving interest in CHRIST, and cannot produce evidences of his title to heaven. It is hard to meet death without some evidence of a title to eternal life at hand; hard to go through the dark valley, without the candle of the LORD shining upon the head. It is a terrible adventure to launch out into eternity, when a man can make no better of it, than a leap in the dark, not knowing where he shall light, whether in heaven or hell.

Nevertheless, the state of the saints, in their death, is always in itself hopeful. The presumptuous hopes of the ungodly, in their death, cannot make their state hopeful; neither can the hopelessness of a saint, make his state hopeless; for GOD judgeth according to the truth of the thing, not according to mens opinion about it. Howbeit the saints can no more be altogether without hope, than they can be altogether without faith. Their faith may be very weak, but it fails not; and their hope very low, yet they will, and do, hope to the end. Even while the godly seem to be carried away with the streams of doubts and fears, there remains still as much hope as determines them to lay hold on the tree of life, that grows on the banks of the river, Jonah ii. 4. *Then I said, I am cast out of thy sight: yet I will look again toward thy holy temple.*

USE. This speaks comfort to the godly against the fear of death. A godly man may be called a happy man, before his death; because, whatever befal him in life, he shall certainly be happy at death. You who are in CHRIST, who are true Christians, have hope in your end; and such hope as may comfort you against all those fears, which arise from the consideration of a dying hour. This I shall branch out, in answering some cases briefly.

Case 1. The prospect of death, will some of the saints say, is uneasy to me, not knowing what shall become of my family, when I am gone. *Ans.* The righteous hath hope in his death, as to his family, as well as to himself. Although you have little for the present, to live upon; which has been the case of many of GOD's chosen ones, 1 Cor. iv. 11. *We,* i. e. the Apostles, *both hunger and thirst, and are naked, and are buffeted, and have no certain dwelling-place.* And though you have nothing to leave them, as was the case of that son of the prophet's, who did fear the LORD, and yet died in debt, which he was unable to pay; as his poor widow represents, 2 Kings iv. 1. yet you have a good friend to leave them to; a covenanted GOD, to whom you may confidently commit them, Jer. xlix. 11. *Leave thy fatherless children, I will preserve them alive; and let thy widows trust in me.* The world can bear witness of signal settlements made upon the children of providence; such as, by their pious parents, have been cast upon GOD's providential care. It has been often remarked, that they wanted neither provision nor education. Moses is an eminent instance of this. He, albeit he was an out-cast infant, Exod. ii. 3. yet was learned in all the wisdom of the Egyptians, Acts vii. 22. and became king in Jeshurun, Deut. xxxiii. 5. O! may we not be ashamed, that we do not securely trust him with the concerns of our families, to whom, as our Saviour and Redeemer, we have committed our eternal interests.

Case 2. Death will take us away from our dear friends; yea, we shall not see the LORD in the land of the living, in the blessed ordinances. *Ans.* It will take you to your best friend, the LORD CHRIST. And the friends you leave behind you, if they be indeed persons of worth, you will meet them again, when they come to heaven; and you will never be separated any more. If death take you away from the temple below, it will carry you to the temple above. It will indeed take you from the streams, but it will set you down by the fountain. If it put out your candle, it will carry you where there is no night, where there is an eternal day.

Case 3. I have so much ado, in time of health, to satisfy myself, as to my interest in CHRIST, about my being a real Christian, a regenerate man; that I judge it is almost impossible I should die comfortably. *Ans.* If it is thus with you, then double your diligence, to make your calling and election sure. Endeavour to grow in knowledge, & walk closely with GOD. Be diligent in self-examination; and pray earnestly for the holy Spirit, whereby you may know the things freely given you of GOD. If you are enabled by the power and Spirit of CHRIST, thus diligently to prosecute your spiritual concerns; though the time of your life be neither day or night, yet, at evening time, it may be light. Many weak Christians indulge doubts and fears about their spiritual state, as if they placed, at least, some part of religion in this imprudent practice; but towards the period of life, they are forced to think and act in another manner. The traveller, who reckons he has time to spare, may stand still, debating with himself, whether this or the other be the right way; but when the sun begins to set, he is forced to lay aside his scruples, and resolutely to go forward on the road he judges to be the right one, lest he lie all night in the open fields. Thus some Christians, who perplex themselves much, throughout the course of their lives, with jealous doubts and fears, content themselves, when they come to die, with such evidences of the safety of their state, as they could not be satisfied with before; and, by disputing less against themselves, and believing more, court the peace they formerly rejected, and gain it too.

Case 4. I am under a sad decay, in respect of my spiritual condition. *Ans.* Bodily consumptions may make death easy, but it is not so in spiritual decays. I will not say, that a godly man cannot be in such a case, when he dies; but I believe it is rarely so. Ordinarily, I suppose, a cry comes to awaken sleepy virgins, before death come. Samson is set to grind in the prison, until his locks grow again. David and Solomon fell under great spritual decays; but, before they died, they recovered their spiritual strength and vigour. However, bestir ye yourselves without delay, to strengthen the things that remain; your fright will be the less, that ye awake from spiritual sleep, ere death come to your bed-side: and you ought to lose no time, seeing you know not how soon death may seize you.

Case 5. It is terrible to think of the other world, that world of spirits, which I have so little acquaintance with. *Ans.* Thy best friend is LORD of that other world. Abraham's bosom is kindly, even to those who never saw his face. After death thy soul becomes capable of converse with the blessed inhabitants of that other world. The spirits of just men made perfect, were once such as thy spirit now is. And as for the angels, howsoever they be of a superior nature, in the rank of beings, yet our nature is dignified above theirs, in the man-

CHRIST: and they are, all of them, thy LORD's servants, and so thy fellow-servants.

Case 6. The pangs of death are terrible. *Ans.* Yet not so terrible as pangs of conscience, caused by a piercing sense of guilt, and apprehensions of divine wrath, with which I suppose thee to be not altogether unacquainted. But who would not endure bodily sickness, that the soul may become sound, and every whit whole? Each pang of death will set sin a step nearer the door; and with the last breath, the body of sin will breath out its last. The pains of death will not last long; and the LORD thy GOD will not leave, but support thee under them.

Case 7. But I am like to be cut off in the midst of my days. *Ans.* Do not complain, you will be the sooner at home:— You have thereby the advantage of your fellow-labourers, who were at work before you in the vineyard. GOD, in the course of his providence, hides some early in the grave, that they may be taken away from the evil to come. An early removal out of this world, prevents much sin and misery; and they have no ground of complaint, who get the residue of their years in Immanuel's land. Surely thou shalt live as long as thou hast work cut out for thee, by the great Master, to be done for him in this world; and when that is at an end, it is high time to be gone.

Case 8. I am afraid of sudden death. *Ans.* Thou may indeed die so. Good Eli died suddenly, 1 Sam. iv. 18. Yet death found him watching, ver. 13. *Watch therefore, for ye know not what hour the Lord doth come.* Mat. xxv. 42. But be not afraid, it is an unexpressible comfort, that death, come when it will, can never catch thee out of CHRIST; and therefore can never seize thee, as a jailor, to hurry thee into the prison of hell. Sudden death may hasten and facilitate thy passage to heaven, but can do thee no prejudice.

Case 9. I am afraid it may be my lot to die wanting the exercise of my reason. *Ans.* I make no question but a child of GOD, a true Christian, may die in this case. But what harm? There is no hazard in it, as to his eternal state: a disease, at death, may divest him of his reason, but not of his religion. When a man, going a long voyage, has put his affairs in order, and put all his goods aboard; he himself may be carried aboard the ship sleeping; all is safe with him, although he knows not where he is, till he awaken in the ship. Even so the godly man, who dies in this case, may die uncomfortably, but not unsafely.

Case 10. I am naturally timorous, and the very thoughts of death are terrible to me. *Ans.* The less you think on death, the thoughts of it will be the more frightful: but make it familiar to you by **frequent meditations** upon it, and you may thereby allay yours. Look at the white and bright side of the cloud: take faith's view of the city that hath foundations: so shall you see hope in your death. Be duly affected with the body of sin and death, and frequent interruptions of your communion with God, and with the glory which dwells on the other side of death; this will contribute much to remove slavish fear.

It is pity saints should be so fond of life as they often are: they ought always to be in good terms with death. When matters are duly considered, it might well be expected every child of God, every regenerate man, should generously profess concerning this life, what Job did, Chap. vii. 16. *I lothe it; I would not live always.* In order to gain their hearts to this desirable temper, I offer the following additional considerations.

First, Consider the sinfulness that attends life in this world. While ye live here, ye sin, and see others sinning. Ye breathe infectious air. Ye live in a pest house. Is it at all strange to lothe such a life? (1.) Your own pilgrim's sores are running on you. Doth not the sin of your nature make you groan daily? Are you not sensible, that though the cure be begun, it is yet far from being perfected? Has not the leprosy got into the walls of the house, which cannot be removed without pulling it down? Is not your nature so vitiate, that no less than the separation of the soul from the body can root out the disease? Have you not your sores without, as well as your sickness within? Do ye not leave marks of your pollution, on whatsoever passes through your hands? Are not all your actions tainted and blemished with defects and imperfections? Who else then should be much in love with life, but such whose sickness is their health, and who glory in their shame? (2.) The loathsome sores of others are always before your eyes, go where you will. The follies and wickedness of men are every-where conspicuous, and make but an unpleasant scene. The sinful world is but an unsightly company, a disagreeable croud, in which the most loathsome are the most numerous. (3.) Are not your own sores oft-times breaking out again, after healing? Frequent relapses may well cause us remit of our fondness for this life. To be ever struggling, and anon falling into the mire again, makes weary work. Do ye never wish for cold death, thereby effectually to cool the heat of these lusts, which so often take fire again: even after a flood of godly sorrow has gone over them? (4.) Do not ye sometimes infect others, and others infect you? There is no society in the world, in which every member of it doth not sometimes lay a stumbling-block before the rest. The best carry about with them the tinder of a corrupt nature, which they cannot be rid of, while they live; and which is liable to be kindled at all times, and in all places; yea, they are apt to inflame others, and become the occasions of sinning. Certainly these things are apt to imbitter this life to the saints.

Secondly, Consider the misery and trouble, that attend it. Rest is desirable, but it is not to be found on this side of the grave. Worldly troubles attend all men in this life. This world is a sea of trouble, where one wave rolls upon another. They who fancy themselves beyond the reach of trouble, are mistaken; no state, no stage of life, is exempted from it.——— The crowned head is surrounded with thorny cares. Honour many times paves the way to deep disgrace: *Riches* (for the most part) *are kept to the hurt of the owners.* The fairest rose wants not prickles; and the heaviest cross is sometimes found wrapt up in the greatest earthly comfort. Spiritual troubles attend the saints in this life. They are like travellers travelling in a cloudy night, in which the moon sometimes breaks out from under one cloud, but quickly hides her head again under another: no wonder they long to be at their journey's end. The sudden alterations the best frame of spirit is liable to, the perplexing doubts, confounding fears, short-lived joys, and long running sorrows, which have a certain affinity with the present life, must needs create in the saints a desire to be with CHRIST, which is best of all.

Lastly, Consider the great imperfections attending this life. While the soul is lodged in this cottage of clay, the necessities of the body are many; it is always craving. The mud walls must be repaired and patched up daily, till the clay cottage fall down for good & all. Eating, drinking, sleeping, and the like, are, in themselves, but mean employments for a rational creature; and will be reputed such by the heaven-born soul. They are badges of imperfection, and, as such, unpleasant to the mind, aspiring unto that life and immortality, which is brought to light through the gospel: and would be very grievous, if this state of things were of long continuance. Doth not the gracious soul often find itself yoked with the body, as with a companion in travel, unable to keep pace with it? When the spirit is willing, the flesh is weak. When the soul would mount upward, the body is as a clog upon it, and as a stone tied to the foot of a bird, attempting to fly.——— The truth is, O believer! thy soul in this body is, at best, but like a diamond in a ring, where much of it is obscured: it is far sunk in the vile clay, till relieved by death.

I conclude this subject with a few directions how to prepare for death, so as we may die comfortably. I speak not here of habitual preparation for death, which a true Christian, in virtue of his gracious state, never wants, from the time he is born again and united to CHRIST: but of actual preparation or readiness, in respect of his circumstantiate case, frame, and disposition of mind and spirit; the want of which, makes even a saint very unfit to die.

First, Let it be your constant care, to keep a clean conscience; a conscience void of offence toward GOD, and toward man, Acts xxiv. 17. Beware of a standing controversy betwixt GOD and you, on the account of some iniquity regarded in the heart. When an honest man is about to leave his country, and not to return, he settles accompts with those he had dealings with, and lays down methods for paying his debts timeously; lest he be reckoned a bankrupt, and be attacked by an officer, when he is going off. Guilt lying on the conscience is a fountain of fears; and will readily sting severely, when death stares the criminal in the face. Hence it is, that many even of GOD's children, when a-dying, are made to wish passionately, and desire eagerly that they may live to do, what they ought to have done before that time. Wherefore, walk closely with GOD, be diligent, strict and exact in your course; beware of a loose, careless, and irregular conversation: as ye would not lay up for yourselves, anguish and bitterness of spirit, in a dying hour. And because, through the infirmity cleaving to us, in our present state of imperfection, in many things we offend all, renew your repentance daily, and be ever washing in the Redeemer's blood. As long as ye are in the world, ye will need to wash your feet, John xiii. 10. that is, to make application to the blood of CHRIST, anew, for purging your consciences from the guilt of daily miscarriages. Let death find you at the fountain; and if so, it will find you ready to answer its call.

Secondly, Be always watchful, waiting for your change; like unto men that wait for their LORD, that when he cometh and knocketh, they may open unto him immediately, Luke xxi. 36. Beware of slumbering and sleeping, while the bridegroom tarries. To be awakned out of spiritual slumber, by a surprising call to pass into another world, is a very frightful thing: but he who is daily waiting for the coming of his LORD, shall comfortably receive the grim messenger, while he beholds him ushering in Him, of whom he may confidently say, *This is my God, I have waited for him*. The way to die comfortably, is to die daily. Be often essaying, as it were, to die. Bring yourselves familiarly acquainted with death, by making many visits to the grave, in serious meditations upon it. This was Job's practice, Chap. xvii. 13, 14. *I have made my bed in the darkness.* Go then and do likewise; and when death comes, thou shalt have nothing ado but to lie down. *I have said to corruption, thou art my father; to the worm, thou art my mother and my sister.* Do thou say so too; and thou wilt be the fitter to go home to their house. Be frequently reflecting upon your conduct, and considering what course of life you wish to be found in, when death arrests you; and act accordingly. When you do the duties of your station in life, or are employed in acts of worship, think with yourselves, that, it may be, this is the last opportunity; and therefore act as if you was never to do more of that kind. When you lie down at night, compose your spirits as if you was not to awake, till the heavens be no more. And when you awake in the morning, consider that new day as your last! and live accordingly. Surely that night cometh, of which you will never see the morning, or that morning of which you will never see the night. But which of your mornings or nights will be such, you know not.

Thirdly, Employ yourselves much in weaning your hearts from the world. The man who is making ready to go abroad, busies himself in taking leave of his friends. Let the mantle of earthly enjoyments hang loose about you, that it may be easily dropt, when death comes to carry you away into another. Moderate your affections towards your lawful comforts of life: and let not your hearts be too much taken with them. The traveller acts unwisely, who suffers himself to be so allured with the conveniences of the inn where he lodgeth, as to make his necessary departure from it grievous. Feed with fear, and walk through the world as pilgrims and strangers. Like as, when the corn is forsaking the ground, it is ready for the sickle; when the fruit is ripe, it falls off the tree easily; so when a Christian's heart is truly weaned from the world, he is prepared for death, and it will be the more easy to him. A heart disengaged from the world is an heavenly one; and then are we ready for heaven, when our **heart** is there before us, Mat. vi. 21.

Fourthly, Be diligent in gathering and laying up evidences of your title to heaven, for your support and comfort at the hour of death. The neglect hereof mars the joy and consolation, which some Christians might otherwise have at their death. Wherefore examine yourselves frequently, as to your spiritual state; that evidences, which lie hid and unobserved, may be brought to light and taken notice of. And if you would manage this work successfully, make solemn work of it. Set apart some time for it. And after earnest prayer to God, through Jesus Christ, for the enlightening influences of the Holy Spirit, whereby ye may be enabled to understand his own word, to discern his own will in your souls; sift yourselves before the tribunal of your consciences, that ye may judge yourselves in this weighty matter.

In the first place, let the marks of a regenerate state be fixed, from the LORD's word: and have recourse to some particular text for that purpose, such as Prov. viii. 17. *I love them that love me.* Compare, Luke xiv. 26. *If any man come to me, and hate not his father and mother, and wife and children, and brethren, and sisters, yea, and his own life also, he cannot be my disciple.* Psal. cxix. 6. *Then shall I not be ashamed, when I have respect unto all thy commandments.* Psalm xviii. 23. *I was also upright before him; and I kept myself from mine iniquity.* Compare Rom. vii. 22, 23. *For I delight in the law of God, after the inward man; but I see another law in my members, warring against the law of my mind,* &c. 1 John iii. 3. *And every man that hath this hope in him, purifieth himself, even as he is pure.* Matth v. 3. *Blessed are the poor in spirit, for theirs is the kingdom of heaven.* Phil. iii. 3. *For we are the circumcision which worship,* or serve *God in the spirit, and rejoice in Christ Jesus, and have no confidence in the flesh.* The sum of the evidences arising from these texts, lies here. A real Christian is one who loves GOD for himself, as well as for his benefits, and that with a supreme love, above all persons and things: he has an awful and impartial regard to GOD's commands; he opposeth and wrestleth against that sin, which of all others most easily besets him; he approveth and loveth the holy law, even in that very point, wherein it strikes against his most beloved lust; his hope of heaven engageth him in the study of universal holiness; in the which he aims at perfection, though he cannot reach it in this life; he serves the LORD, not only in acts of worship, but in the whole of his conversation; and as to both, is spiritual in the principle, motives, aims, and ends of his service; yet he sees nothing in himself to trust to before the LORD: CHRIST and his fulness is the stay of his soul: and his confidence is cut off from all that is not CHRIST, or in CHRIST, in point of justification, or acceptance with GOD, and in point of sanctification too. Every one in whom these characters are found, has a title to heaven, according to the word. It is convenient and profitable to mark such texts for this special use, as they occur, while you read the scriptures, or hear sermons. The marks of a regenerate state thus fixed; in the next place, impartially search and try your own hearts thereby, as in the sight of GOD, with dependence on him for spiritual discerning, that ye may know whether they be in you or not. And when ye find them, form the conclusion deliberately and distinctly; namely, that therefore you are regenerate, and have a title to heaven. This you may gather evidences. But be sure to have recourse to GOD in CHRIST by earnest prayer, for the testimony of the Spirit, whose office is to bear witness with our spirit, that we are the children of God, Rom. viii. 16. Moreover carefully observe the course and method of Providence towards you; and likewise how your soul is affected under the same, in the various steps thereof; compare both with scripture-doctrines, promises, threatnings, and examples, so shall ye perceive, if the LORD deals with you as he useth to do unto those that love his name: and if you be going forth by the footsteps of the flock, this may afford you comfortable evidence. Walk tenderly and circumspectly; and the LORD will manifest himself to you, according to his promise, John xiv. 21. *He that hath my commandments and keepeth them, he it is that loveth me; and he that loveth me, shall be loved of my Father: and I will love him, and will manifest myself to him.* But it is in vain to think on successful self-examination, if ye be loose and irregular in your conversation.

Lastly, Dispatch the work of your day and generation with speed and diligence. *David, after he had served his own generation by the will of God, fell on sleep*, Acts xiii. 36. GOD has allotted us certain pieces of work of this kind, which ought to be dispatched before the time of working be over, Eccl. ix. 10. *Whatsoever thy hand findeth to do, do it with thy might; for there is no work, nor knowledge, nor wisdom in the grave, whither thou goest.* Gal. vi. 10. *As we have therefore opportunity, let us do good unto all men, especially unto them who are of the houshold of faith.* If a passenger, after he is got on ship-board, and the ship is getting under sail, remember that he has omitted to dispatch a piece of necessary business when he was ashore, it must needs be uneasy to him; even so reflection in a dying hour, upon neglected seasons, and lost opportunities, cannot fail to disquiet a Christian. Wherefore, whatever is incumbent upon thee to do for GOD's honour, and the good of others either as the duty of thy station, or by special opportunity put into thy hand, perform it seasonably, if thou wouldst die comfortably.

HEAD III.

The RESURRECTION.

John v. 28, 29.

Marvel not at this: For the hour is coming in the which all that are in their graves, shall hear his voice: And shall come forth; they that have done good unto the resurrection of life, and they that have done evil unto the resurrection of damnation.

THESE words are part of the defence our LORD JESUS CHRIST makes for himself, when persecuted by the Jews for curing the impotent man and ordering him to carry away his bed on the Sabbath; and for vindicating his conduct, when accused by them of having thereby profaned that day. On this occasion he professeth himself not only LORD of the Sabbath, but also LORD of life and death; declaring in the words of the text, the resurrection of the dead to be brought to pass by his power. This he introduceth with these words, as with a solemn preface, *Marvel not at this*, i. e. at this strange discourse of mine: do not wonder to hear me, whose appearance is so very mean in your eyes, talk at this rate; for the day is coming, in which the dead shall be raised by my power.

Observe in this text, (1.) The doctrine of the resurrection asserted, *All that are in the graves, shall hear his voice, and shall come forth.* The dead bodies which are reduced to dust, shall revive, and evidence life by hearing and moving. (2.) The author of it, JESUS CHRIST, *the Son of man*, ver. 27. The dead shall hear his voice and be raised thereby. (3.) The number that shall be raised, *All that are in the graves*, i. e. all the dead bodies of men, howsoever differently disposed of, as it were, in different kinds of graves; or all the dead, good or bad. They are not all buried in graves, properly so called; some are burnt to ashes, some drowned, and buried in the bellies of fishes; yea some devoured by man-eaters called Cannibals; but wheresoever the matter or substance, of which the body was composed, is to be found, thence they shall come forth. (4.) The great distinction that shall be made betwixt the godly and the wicked. They shall indeed both rise again in the resurrection. None of the godly will be missing; though perhaps they either had no burial, or a very obscure one: and all the wicked shall come forth; their vaulted tombs shall hold them no longer than the voice is uttered. But the former shall have a joyful resurrection to life, while the latter have a dreadful resurrection to damnation. *Lastly*, The set time of this great event: There is an hour, or certain fixed period of time, appointed of GOD for it. We are not told when that hour will be, but that it is coming; for this, among other reasons, that we may always be ready.

DOCTRINE.

There shall be a Resurrection of the Dead.

In discoursing of this subject I shall, *First*, Shew the certainty of the resurrection. *Secondly*, I shall enquire into the nature of it: And *Lastly*, Make some practical improvement of the whole.

I. In shewing the certainty of the resurrection, I shall evince (1.) That GOD can raise the dead. And, (2.) That he will do it; which are the two grounds or topics laid down by CHRIST himself, when disputing with the Sadducees, Mat. xxii. 29. *Jesus answered and said unto them, Ye do err, not knowing the scriptures, nor the power of God.*

First, Seeing GOD is Almighty, surely he can raise the dead. We have instances of this powerful work of GOD, both in the Old and New Testament. The son of the widow in Sarepta, was raised from the dead, 1 Kings xvii. 22. The Shunamite's son 2 Kings iv. 36. And the man cast into the sepulchre of Elisha, chap. xiii. 21. In which we may observe a gradation, the second of these miraculous events being more illustrious than the first, and the third than the second. The first of these persons was raised when he was but newly dead; the prophet Elijah who raised him, being present at his decease. The second, when he had him lain dead a considerable time; namely, while his mother travelled from Shunem to mount Carmel, reckoned about the distance of sixteen miles and returned from thence to her house with Elisha who raised him. The last, not till they were burying him, and the corpse was cast into the prophet's grave. In like manner in the New Testament, Jairus' daughter, Mark v. 41. And Dorcas, (Acts ix. 40.) were both raised to life, when lately dead; the widow's son in Nain, when they were carrying him out to bury him, Luke vii. 11. 15. And Lazarus, when stinking in the grave, John xi. 39. 44.

Can men make curious glasses out of ashes, reduce flowers into ashes, and raise them again out of these ashes, restoring them to their former beauty; and cannot the great Creator who made all things of nothing, raise man's body, after it is reduced into dust? If it be objected, How can men's bodies be raised up again after they are dissolved into dust, and the ashes of many generations are mingled together? Scripture and not reason furnish the answer. *With men it is impossible, but not with God.* It is absurd for men to deny that GOD can do a thing, because they see not how it may be done. How small a portion do we know of his ways! how absolutely incapable are we of conceiving distinctly of the external of almighty power, and much more of comprehending its actings and the method of procedure! I question not, but many illiterate men are as great infidels to many chymical experiments as some learned men are to the doctrine of the resurrection: and as these last are ready to deride the former, so the LORD will have them in derision. What a mystery was it to the Indians, that the Europeans could, by a piece of paper, converse together, at the distance of some hundreds of miles? And how much were they astonished to see them with their guns, produce as it were, thunder and lightning in a moment, and at pleasure kill men afar off? Shall some men do such things as are wonders in the eyes of others, because they cannot comprehend them: and shall men confine the infinite power of GOD, within the narrow boundaries of their own shallow capacities, in a matter no ways contrary to reason? An inferior nature has but a very imperfect conception of the power of a superior. Brutes do not conceive of the actings of reason in men; & men have but lame notions of the power of angels; how low and inadequate a conception then, must a finite nature have of the power of that which is infinite! though we cannot conceive how GOD acts, yet we ought to believe he can do above what we can think or can conceive of.

Wherefore, let the bodies of men be laid in the grave; let them rot there, and be resolved into the most minute particles; or let them be burnt, and the ashes cast into rivers, or thrown up into the air, to be scattered by the wind; let the dust of a thousand generations be mingled, and the streams of the dead bodies wander to and fro in the air; let birds or wild beasts eat the dead bodies, or the fishes of the sea devour them, so that the parts of human bodies, thus destroyed pass into substantial parts of birds, beasts, or fishes; or what is more than that, let man-eaters, who themselves must die, and rise again, devour human bodies, and let others devour them again; and then let our modern Sadducees propose the question in these cases, as the ancient Sadducees did, in the case of the woman, who had been married to seven husbands successively, Mat. xxii. 28. We answer as our blessed LORD and Saviour did, ver. 26. *Ye do err not knowing the scriptures nor the power of God.* We believe GOD to be omniscient, and omnipotent, infinite in knowledge and in power; and hence, agreeable to the dictates of reason, we conclude the possibility of the resurrection, even in the cases supposed.

Material things may change their forms and shapes, may be resolved into the principles of which they are formed; but they are not annihilated, or reduced to nothing; nor can they be so, by any created power. GOD is omniscient, his understanding is infinite, therefore he knows all things whatsoever; what they were, at any time, what they are, and where they are to be found. Though the country-man, who comes into the apothecary shop, cannot find out the drug he wants, yet the apothecary himself knows what he has in his shop, whence it came, and where it is to be found. And in a mingle of many different seeds, the expert gardner can distinguish betwixt seed and seed: Why then may not omniscience distinguish betwixt dust and dust? Can he who knows all things to perfection, be liable to any mistake about his own creatures? Whoso believes an infinite understanding, must needs own, that no mass of dust is so jumbled together, but GOD perfectly comprehends, and infallibly knows how the most minute particle, and every one of them, is to be matched. And therefore he knows where the particles of each dead body are, whether in the earth, sea, or air, how confused soever they lie. And particularly, he knows where to find the primitive substance of the man-eater; however evaporated or reduced, as it were, into air or vapour, by sweat or perspiration; and how to separate the parts of the body that was eaten, from the body of the eater, howsoever incorporate, or made one body with it; and so understands, not only how, but whence, he is to bring back the primitive substance of the man-eater to its proper place; and also to separate from the man-eater's body, that part of the devoured body which goes into its substance; and is indeed but a very small part of it. It is certain, the bodies of men, as of all other animals, or living creatures, are in a continual flux; they grow, and are sustained by daily food, so small a part whereof becomes nourishment, that the most part is evacuate. And it is reckoned that, at least as much of the food is evacuate insensibly by perspiration, as is voided by other perceptible ways. Yea, the nourishing part of the food, when assimilate, and thereby become a part of the body, is evacuate by perspiration thro' the pores of the skin, and again supplied by the use of the food; yet the body is still reckoned one, and the same body. Whence we may conclude, that it is not essential to the resurrection of the body, that every particle of the matter, which at any time was part of a human body, should be restored to it, when it is raised up from death to life. Were it so, the bodies of men would become of so huge a size, that they would bear no resemblance of the persons. It is sufficient to denominate it the same body that died, when it is risen again; if the body that is raised, be formed in its former proportions of the same particles of matter, which at any time were its constituent parts, howsoever it be refined; like as, we reckon it is the same body that was pined away by long sickness, which becomes fat and fair again after recovery.

Now, to this infinite understanding, join infinite power, whereby he is able to subdue all things unto himself; and this glorious great work appears most reasonable. If omniscience discover every little particle of dust, where it is, & how it is to be matched; cannot omnipotence bring them, and join them together in their order? Can the watch-maker take up the several pieces of a watch, lying in a confused heap before him, and set each in its proper place; and cannot GOD put the human body in order, after its dissolution? Did he speak this world into being, out of nothing; and can he not form man's body, out of its pre-existent matter? If he calleth those things, which be not, as tho' they were; surely he can call things that are dissolved, to be as they were, before the compound was resolved into its parts and principles: Wherefore, GOD can raise the dead. And, *Wherefore should it be thought a thing incredible with you, that God should raise the dead?* Acts xxvi. 8.

Secondly, GOD will do it. He not only can do it, but he certainly will do it, because he has said it. Our text is very full to this purpose: *All that are in their graves, shall hear his voice: and shall come forth: they that have done good, unto the resurrection of life; and they that have done evil, unto the resurrection of damnation.* These words relate to, and are an explanation of, that part of Daniel's prophecy, Dan. xii. 2. *And many of them that sleep in the dust of the earth, shall awake; some to everlasting life, and some to shame and everlasting contempt.* The which appears to have been calculated to confront the doctrine of the Sadducees; which the holy Ghost knew was to be at a great height in the Jewish church, under the persecution of Antiochus. There are many other texts in the Old and New Testaments, that might here be adduced; such as Acts xxiv. 15. *And have hope towards God, which they themselves also allow, that there shall be a resurrection of the dead, of the just and unjust.* And, Job xix. 26, 27. *And though, after my skin, worms destroy this body, yet in my flesh shall I see God: whom I shall see for myself, and mine eyes shall behold, and not another: though my reins be consumed within me.* But I need not multiply testimonies, in a matter so clearly and frequently taught in sacred scripture. Our LORD and Saviour himself proves it, against the Sadducees, in that remarkable text, Luke xx. 37, 38. *Now that the dead are raised, even Moses shewed at the bush, when he calleth the Lord, the God of Abraham, and the God of Isaac, and the God of Jacob: For he is not a God of the dead, but of the living; for all live unto him.* These holy patriarchs were now dead; nevertheless, the LORD JEHOVAH is called their GOD, namely, in virtue of the covenant of grace, and in the sense thereof; in which sense, the phrase comprehends all blessedness, as that which, by the covenant, is secured to them who are in it, Heb. xi. 16. *God is not ashamed to be called their God, for he hath prepared for them a city.* He is not called the GOD of their souls only; but *their God,* the GOD of their persons, souls and bodies; the which, by virtue of his truth and faithfulness, must have its full effect: Now it cannot have its full effect on the dead, who, in as far as they are dead, are far from all blessedness; but on the living, who alone are capable of it; therefore, since GOD is still called *their God,* they are living in respect of GOD, although their bodies are yet in the grave; for in respect of him, who by his power can restore them to life, and in his covenant has declared his will and purpose so to do, and whose promise cannot fail, they all are to be reckoned to live; and, consistent with the covenant, their death is but a sleep, out of which, in virtue of the same covenant, securing all blessedness to their persons, their whole man, they must and shall certainly be awakned. The apostle Paul proves the resurrection at large, 1 Cor. xv. and shews it to be a fundamental article, the denial whereof is subversive of Christianity, ver. 13, 14. *If there be no resurrection of the dead, then is Christ not risen. And if Christ be not risen, then is our preaching vain, and your faith is also vain.*

To assist us in conceiving of it, the scripture gives us types of the resurrection of the dead; as the dry bones living, Ezek. xxxvii. Jonah's coming out of the whale's belly, Mat. xii. 40. And nature affords us emblems and resemblances of it; as the sun's setting and rising again; night and day, winter and summer, sleeping and awaking; swallows in winter, lying void of all appearance of life, in ruinous buildings, and subterraneous caverns, and reviving again in the spring season; the seeds dying under the clod, and thereafter springing up again: all which, and the like, may justly be admitted, as designed by the GOD of nature, though not for proofs, yet for memorials, of the resurrection; whereof we have assurance from the scripture, 1 Cor. xv. 36. *Thou fool, that which thou sowest is not quickned except it die.*

II. I shall enquire into the nature of the resurrection, shewing, 1st, Who shall be raised. 2dly, What shall be raised. 3dly, How the dead shall be raised.

First, Who shall be raised? Our text tells us who they are; namely, All that are in the graves; *i. e.* all mankind, who are dead. As for those persons who shall be found alive at the second coming of CHRIST; they shall not die, and soon thereafter be raised again: but such a change shall suddenly pass upon them, as shall be to them instead of dying and rising again; so that their bodies shall become like to those bodies which are raised out of the graves, 1 Cor. xv. 51, 52. *We shall not all sleep, but we shall all be changed; in a moment, in the twinkling of an eye.* Hence those who are to be judged at the great day, are distinguished into quick and dead, Acts x. 42. All the dead shall arise, whether godly or wicked, just or unjust, Acts xxiv. 15. old or young; the whole race of mankind, even those who never saw the sun, but died in their mother's belly, Rev. xx. 12. *And I saw the dead, small and great, stand before God.* The sea and earth shall give up their dead, without reserve, none shall be kept back.

Secondly, What shall be raised? The bodies of mankind. A man is said to die, when the soul is separated from the body, and returns unto GOD who gave it, Eccl. xii. 7. But it is the body only which is laid in the grave, and can be properly said to be raised; wherefore the resurrection is, strictly speaking, competent to the body only. Moreover, it is the same body that dies, which shall rise again. At the resurrection, men shall not appear with other bodies for substance, than these which they now have, and which are laid down in the grave: but with the self-same bodies endowed with other qualities. The very notion of a resurrection implies this: since nothing can be said to rise again, but that which falls. But to illustrate it a little. *First*, it is plain from Scripture-testimony: The Apostle tells, it is this mortal which must put on immortality, 1 Cor. xv. 53. and that CHRIST shall change our vile body, that it may be fashioned like unto his glorious body, Philip. iii. 21. Death, in Scripture-language, is a sleep, and the resurrection an awaking out of that sleep, Job xiv. 12. which shews the body rising up, to be the self-same that died. *Secondly*, The equity of the divine procedure, both with respect to the godly and the wicked, evinces this. It is not reckoned equal among men, that one do the work, and another get the reward. Though the glorifying of the bodies of saints, is not, properly speaking, and in a strict sense, the reward of their services or sufferings on earth; yet this is evident, that it is not at all agreeable to the manner of the divine dispensation, that one body serve him, and another be glorified; that one fight, and another receive the crown. How can it be imagined, that the temples of the holy Ghost, as these bodies of believets are termed, 1 Cor. vi. 19. should always lie in rubbish; and others be reared up in their stead: That these members of CHRIST, ver. 15. shall perish utterly, and other bodies come in their room? Nay, surely as these bodies of the saints now bear a part in glorifying GOD, and some of them suffer in his cause; so they shall partake of the glory that is to be revealed. And these bodies of the wicked, which are laid in the dust, shall be raised again; that the same body, which sinned, may suffer. Shall one body sin here, and another suffer in hell for that sin? Shall that body, which was the soul's companion in sin, lie for ever hid in the dust; and another body, which did not act any part in sinning, be its companion in torment? No, no; it is that body, which now takes up all their thoughts to provide for its back and belly, that shall be raised up to suffer in hell. It is that tongue that is now swearing, lying tongue, which will need water to cool it, in eternal flames. These same feet, that now stand in the way of sinners, and carry men in their ungodly courses, shall stand in the burning lake. And these now covetous and lascivious eyes, shall take part in the fire and smoke of the pit.

Thirdly, How the dead shall be raised. The same JESUS, who was crucified without the gate of Jerusalem, shall at the last day, to the conviction of all, be declared both LORD and CHRIST: appearing as Judge of the world, attended with his mighty angels, 2 Thess. i. 7. He shall descend from heaven with a shout, with the voice of the arch-angel, and with the trump of GOD, 1 Thess. iv. 16. The trumpet shall sound, and the dead shall be raised, and those who are alive, changed, 1 Cor. xv. 52. Whether this shout, voice, and trumpet, do denote some audible voice, or only the workings of divine power, for the raising of the dead, and other awful purposes of that day, though the former seems probable, I will not positively determine. There is no question but this coming of the Judge of the world will be in greater majesty and terror, than we can conceive; yet that awful grandeur, majesty and state, which was displayed at the giving of the law, viz. thunders heard, lightnings and a thick cloud upon the mount seen; the LORD descending in fire, the whole mount quaking greatly, and the voice of the trumpet waxing louder, and louder, Exod. xix. 16, 18, 19. may help forward a becoming thought of it. However, the sound of the trumpet shall be heard all the world over; it shall reach to the depths of the sea, and into the bowels of the earth. At this loud alarm, bones shall come together, bone to his bone; the scattered dust of all the dead shall be gathered together, dust to his dust; neither shall one thrust er, they shall walk every one in his path; and meeting together again, shall make up that very same body, which crumbled into dust in the grave. And at the same alarming voice, shall every soul come again into its own body, never more to be separated. The dead can stay no longer in their graves, but must bid an eternal farewel to their long homes: They hear his voice, and must come forth, and receive their final sentence.

Now, as there is a great difference betwixt the godly and the wicked in their life, and in their death; so will there be also in their resurrection.

The godly shall be raised up out of their graves, by virtue of the Spirit of CHRIST, the blessed bond of their union with him, Rom. viii. 11. *He that raised up Christ from the dead, shall also quicken your mortal bodies, by his Spirit that dwelleth in you.* JESUS CHRIST arose from the dead, as the first-fruits of them that slept, 1 Cor. xv. 20. So they that are CHRIST's shall follow at his coming, ver. 23. The mystical Head having got above the waters of death, he cannot but bring forth the members after him, in due time.

They shall come forth with inexpressible joy; for then shall that passage of scripture, which, in its immediate scope respected the Babylonish captivity, be fully accomplished in its extensive spiritual view, Isa. xxvi. 19. *Awake and sing, ye that dwell in the dust.* As a bride, adorned for her husband, goes forth of her bed-chamber unto the marriage; so shall the saints go forth of their graves, unto the marriage of the Lamb. Joseph had a joyful out-going from the prison, Daniel from the lion's den, and Jonah from the whale's belly; yet those are but faint representations of the saints out-going from the grave at the resurrection. Then shall they sing the song of Moses and of the Lamb, in highest strains; death being quite swallowed up in victory. They had, while in this life, sometimes sung, by faith, the triumphant song over death and the grave, *O death, where is thy sting? O grave, where is thy victory?* 1 Cor. xv. 55. But when they sing the same, from sight and sense; the black band of doubts and fears, which frequently disturbed them, and disquieted their minds, is forever cashiered.

May we not suppose the soul and body of every saint, as in mutual embraces, to rejoice in each other, and triumph in their happy meeting again? And may not one imagine the body to address the soul thus? "O my soul, have we got together again, after so long a separation! art thou come back into thine old habitation, never more to remove! O joyful meeting! how unlike is our present state to what our case was, when a separation was made betwixt us at death!

now is our mourning turned into joy; the light and gladness sometimes sow'n, are now sprung up, and there is perpetual spring in Immanuel's land. Blessed be the day, in which I was united to thee, whose chief care was to get CHRIST in us the hope of glory, and to make me a temple for his Holy Spirit. O blessed soul, which, in the time of our pilgrimage, kept thine eye on the land afar off, but now near at hand! thou tookest me up into secret places, and there madst me bow these knees before the LORD, that I might bear a part in our humiliations before him; and now is the due time, and I am lifted up. Thou didst employ this tongue, in confessions, petitions and thanksgivings, which henceforth shall be employed in praising for evermore. Thou madst these (sometimes) weeping eyes sow that seed of tears, which is now sprung up in joy that shall never end. I was happily beat down by thee, and kept in subjection; while others pampered their flesh, and made their bellies their gods, to their own destruction: and, now I gloriously arise, to take my place in the mansions of glory, whilst they are dragged out of their graves, to be cast into fiery flames. Now, my soul, thou shalt complain no more of a sick and pained body, thou shalt be no more clogged with weak and weary flesh; I shall now hold pace with thee in the praises of our GOD forevermore." And may not the soul say? "O happy day in which I return to dwell in that blessed body, which was, and is, and will be forever a member of CHRIST, a temple of the Holy Spirit! now shall I be eternally knit to thee; the silver cord shall never be loosed more; death shall never make another separation betwixt us. Arise then, my body, and come away; and let these eyes, which served to weep over my sins, behold now with joy, the face of our glorious Redeemer; Lo! this is our GOD, and we have waited for him. Let these ears, which served to hear the word of life, in the temple below, come now and hear the hallelujahs in the temple above. Let these feet, that carried me to the congregation of saints on earth, take their place now among these who stand by. And let that tongue, which confessed CHRIST before men, and used to be still dropping something to his commendation, join the choir of the upper house in his praises for evermore. Thou shalt fast no more, but keep an everlasting feast; thou shalt weep no more, neither shall thy countenance be overclouded; but thou shalt shine forever, as a star in the firmament. We took part together in the fight, come now, let us go together to receive and wear the crown."

But, on the other hand, the wicked shall be raised by the power of CHRIST, as a just Judge, who is to render vengeance to his enemies. The same divine power which shut up their souls in hell, and kept their bodies in a grave, as in a prison, shall bring them forth, that soul and body together may receive the dreadful sentence of eternal damnation, and be shut up together in the prison of hell!

They shall come forth of their graves, with unspeakable horror and consternation. They shall be dragged forth as so many malefactors out of a dungeon, to be led to execution; crying to the mountains and to the rocks, to fall on them, and hide them from the face of the Lamb. Fearful was the cry in Egypt, that night the destroying angel went through, and slew their first-born. Dreadful were the shouts, at the earth opening her mouth, and swallowing up Dathan and Abiram, and all that appertained to them. What hideous crying then must there be, when at the sound of the last trumpet, the earth and sea shall open their mouths, and cast forth all the wicked world, delivering them up to the dreadful Judge? How will they cry, roar, and tear themselves! how will the jovial companions weep and howl, and curse one-another! how will the earth be filled with their doleful shrieks and lamentations, while they are pulled out like sheep for the slaughter? They who, while they lived in the world, were profane debauchees, covetous, worldlings, or formal hypocrites, shall then, in anguish of mind, wring their hands, beat their breasts, and bitterly lament their case; roaring forth their complaints, and calling themselves beasts, fools and mad-men, for having acted so mad a part in this life, and not having believed what they then see!

They were driven away in their wickedness at death; and now all their sins rise with them, and like so many serpents, twist themselves about their wretched souls, and bodies too, which have now a frightful meeting after a long separation.

Then we may suppose the miserable body thus to accost the soul: "Hast thou again found me, O mine enemy, my worst enemy! savage soul! more cruel than a thousand tygers! Cursed be the day that ever we met! O that I had remained a lifeless lump, rotten in the belly of my mother; and had never received sense, life, nor motion. O that I had rather been the body of a toad or serpent, than thy body; for then I had lain still, and had not seen this terrible day! If I behoved to be thine, O that I had been thy ass, or one of thy dogs, rather than thy body; for then wouldst thou have taken more true care of me, than thou didst. O cruel kindness! hast thou thus hugged me to death, thus nourished me to the slaughter? Is this the effect of thy tenderness for me? Is this what I am to reap of thy pains and concern about me? What do riches and pleasure avail now, when this fearful reckoning is come, of which thou hadst fair warning? O cruel grave, why didst thou not close thy mouth upon me forever? Why didst thou not hold fast thy prisoner? Why hast thou shaken me out, while I lay still, and was at rest? Cursed soul, wherefore didst thou not abide in thy place, wrapt up in flames of fire? Wherefore art thou come back to take me also down to the bars of the pit? Thou madst me an instrument of unrighteousness, and now I must be thrown into the fire! This tongue was by thee employed in mocking at religion, cursing, swearing, lying, backbiting, and boasting; and with-held from glorifying GOD; and now it must not have so much as a drop of water to cool it in the flames. Thou didst withdraw mine ears from hearing the sermons which gave warning of this day. Thou foundest ways and means to stop them from attending to seasonable exhortations, admonitions and reproofs: But why didst thou not stop them from hearing the sound of this dreadful trumpet? Why dost thou not now reve and fly away on the wings of imagination, thereby, as it were, transporting me, during these frightful transactions, as thou was wont to do, when I was set down at sermons, communions, prayers, and godly conferences; that I might now have as little sense of the one, as I formerly had of the other? But ah! I must burn forever, for thy love to thy lusts, thy profanity, thy sensuality, thy unbelief and hypocrisy!"

But may not the soul answer; "Wretched and vile carcase, am I now driven back into thee! O that thou hadst lain forever rotting in thy grave! Had I not torment enough before? Must I be knit to thee again, that, being joined together, as two dry sticks for the fire, the wrath of GOD may the more keenly burn us up? It was by caring for you, I lost myself. It was your back and your belly, and the gratifying of your senses, which ruined me. How often was I ensnared by your ears? How often betrayed by your eyes? It was to spare you, that I neglected so many precious opportunities of making peace with GOD, loitered away Sabbaths, lived in the neglect of prayer, went to the house of mirth, rather than to the house of mourning; and that I chused to deny CHRIST, and forsake his cause and interests in the world; and so am fallen a sacrifice to your cursed ease. When at any time my conscience began to awake, and I was setting myself to think of my sins, and the misery I have felt since we parted, and now feel; it was you that diverted me from these thoughts, and drew me off to make provision for thee, O wretched flesh. By your silken cords of fleshly lusts I was drawn to destruction over the belly of my light and conscience; but now they are turned into iron chains, with which I am to be held under wrath for ever more. Ah, wretched profits! ah cursed plea-tures! for which I must lie forever in utter darkness." But no complaints will then avail. O that men were wise, that they understood this, that they would consider their latter end!

As to the Qualities with which the bodies of the saints shall be endowed at the resurrection, the Apostle tells us, they shall be raised incorruptible, glorious, powerful, and spiritual, 1 Cor. xv. 42, 43, 44. *It is sown in corruption, it is raised in incorruption. It is sown in dishonour, it is raised in glory. It is sown in weakness, it is raised in power. It is sown a natural body, it is raised a spiritual body.*

First, The bodies of the saints shall be raised incorruptible. They are now, as the bodies of others, a very mass of corruption, full of the seeds of diseases and death; and when dead, become so nauseous, even to their dearest friends, that they must be buried out of their sight, in a grave, there to rot, and be consumed: yea, loathsome sores and diseases, make some of them very unsightly, even while alive. But, at the resurrection, they leave all the seeds of corruption behind them, in the grave; and rise incorruptible, incapable of the least indisposition, sickness, or sore, and much more of dying. External violences, and inward causes of pain, shall for ever cease; they shall feel it no more; yea, they shall have an everlasting youth and vigour, being no more subject to the decays which age produces in this life.

Secondly, They shall be glorious bodies; not only beautiful, comely, and well-proportioned, but full of splendor and brightness. The most beautiful face, and best proportioned body, that now appears in the world, is not to be named, in comparison with the body of the meanest saint at the resurrection; for then shall the righteous shine forth as the sun, Mat. xiii. 43. If there was a dazzling glory on Moses' face, when he came down from the mount; and if Stephen's face was as it had been the face of an angel, when he stood before the council; how much more shall the faces of the saints be beautified and glorious, full of sweet agreeable majesty, when they have put off all corruption and shine as the sun? But observe, this beauty of the saints, is not restricted to their faces; but diffuses itself through their whole bodies: For the whole body is raised in glory, and shall be fashioned like unto their LORD and Saviour's glorious body; in whose transfiguration not only did his face shine as the sun, but also his raiment was white as the light, Mat. xvii. 2.—— Whatever defects, or deformities, the bodies of the saints had, when laid in the grave, occasioned by accidents in life, or arising from secret causes in their formation in the womb, they shall rise out of the grave free of all these. But suppose the marks of the LORD JESUS, the scars or prints of the wounds and bruises some of the saints received while on earth, for his sake, should remain in their bodies after the resurrection; like as the print of the nails remained in the Lord Jesus' body, after his resurrection; these marks will rather be badges of distinction, and add to their glory, than detract from their beauty. But howsoever that be, surely Isaac's eyes shall not then be dim, nor will Jacob halt; Leah shall not be tender-eyed, nor Mephibosheth lame of his legs. For as the goldsmith melts down the old crazy vessel, and casts it over again into a new mould, bringing it forth with a new lustre; so shall the vile body which lay dissolved in the grave, come forth at the resurrection in perfect beauty and comely proportion.

Thirdly, They shall be powerful and strong bodies. The strongest men on earth, being frail and mortal, may justly be reckoned weak and feeble; in regard their strength, howsoever great, is quickly worn out and consumed. Many of the saints, now, have bodies weaker than others; but the feeble among them, to allude to Zech. xii. 8. at that day, shall be as David; and the house of David shall be as God. A grave divine says, That one shall be stronger at the resurrection, than an hundred, yea, than thousands are now. Certainly great, and vastly great, must the strength of glorified bodies be, seeing they shall bear up under an exceeding and eternal weight of glory. The mortal body is not at all adapted to such a state. Do transports of joy occasion death, as well as excessive grief does? And can it bear up under a weight of glory? Can it subsist in union with a soul filled with heaven's raptures? Surely no. The mortal body would sink under that load, and such a fill would make the earthen pitcher to fly all in pieces. The Scripture has plainly told us, That flesh and blood (namely, in their present frail state, though it were the flesh and blood of a giant) cannot inherit the kingdom of God, 1 Cor. xv. 50. How strong must the bodily eyes be, which, to the soul's eternal comfort, shall behold the dazzling glory and splendor of the new Jerusalem; and stedfastly look at the transcendent glory and brightness of the man Christ; the Lamb, who is the light of that city, the inhabitants whereof shall shine as the sun? The Lord of heaven doth now, in mercy, hold back the face of his throne, and spreadeth his cloud upon it, that mortals may not be confounded with the rays of glory, which shine forth from it, Job xxvi. 9. But then the vail shall be removed, and they made able to behold it, to their unspeakable joy. How strong must their bodies be, who shall not rest night nor day; but be, without intermission, for ever employed in the heavenly temple, in singing and proclaiming the praises of God, with out weariness, which is a weakness incident to the frail mortal, but incompetent to the glorified body!

Lastly, They shall be spiritual bodies. Not that they shall be changed into spirits; but they shall be spiritual, in respect of their spirit-like qualities and endowments. The body shall be absolutely subservient to the soul, subject to it, and influenced by it; and therefore, no more a clog to its activity, nor the animal appetites a snare to it. There will be no need to beat it down, nor to drag it to the service of GOD. The soul, in this life, is so much influenced by the body, that, in Scripture-style, it is said to be carnal: but then, the body shall be spiritual, readily serving the soul in the business of heaven; and in that only, as if it had no more relation to earth than a spirit. It will have no further need of the now necessary supports of life, namely, food and raiment, and the like: *They shall hunger no more, neither thirst any more*, Rev. vii. 16. *For in the resurrection, they neither marry, nor are given in marriage; but are as the angels of God in heaven.*—— Then shall the saints be strong without meat or drink; warm without cloaths; ever in perfect health, without medicines; and ever fresh and vigorous, though they shall never sleep, but serve him night and day in his temple, Rev. vii. 15. They will need none of these things, more than spirits do. They will be nimble and active, as spirits, and of a most refined constitution. The body, that is now lumpish and heavy, shall then be most sprightly. No such thing as melancholy shall be found, to make the heart heavy, and the spirits flag and sink. Where the carcase is, there shall the saints, as so many eagles, be gathered together. I shall not further dip into this matter, the day will declare it.

As to the qualities of the bodies of the wicked, at the resurrection, I find the Scripture speaks but little of them. Whatever they may need, they shall not get a drop of water to cool their tongues, Luke xvi. 24, 25. Whatever may be said of their weakness, it is certain they will be continued forever in life; that they may be ever dying; they shall bear up, howsoever unwillingly, under the load of GOD's wrath, and shall not faint away under it: *The smoak of their torment ascendeth up forever and ever. And they have no rest day nor night.* Surely they shall not partake of the glory and beauty of the saints: All their glory dies with them, and shall never rise again.—— Daniel tells us, they shall awake to shame, and everlasting contempt, Chap. xii. 2. Shame follows sin, as the shadow followeth the body; but the wicked, in this world, walk in the dark, and often under a disguise; nevertheless, when the Judge comes, in flaming fire, at the last day, they will be brought to the light; their mask will be taken off, and the shame of their nakedness will clearly appear to themselves and others, and fill their faces with confusion. Their shame will be too deep for blushes; for all faces shall gather blackness, at that day, when they shall go forth of their graves, as malefactors out of their prisons, to execution; for their resurrection is the resurrection of damnation. The greatest beauties, who now pride themselves in their comeliness of body, not regarding their deformed souls, will then appear with ghastly countenances, a grim and death-like visage. Their looks will be frightful; and they will be horrible spectacles, coming forth of their graves like infernal furies out of the pit. They shall rise also to everlasting contempt. They shall then be the most contemptible creatures, filled with contempt from God, as vessels of dishonour, whatever honourable uses they have been employed to, in this world; and filled also with contempt from men. They will be most despicable in the eyes of the saints, even of those saints who gave them honour here, either for their high station, the gifts of God in them, or because they were of the same human nature with themselves. But then shall their bodies be as so many lothsome carcases, which they shall go forth and look upon with abhorrence; yea, they shall be an abhorring unto all flesh, Isa. lxvi. 24. The word here rendered an abhorring, is the same which in the other text is rendered contempt; and Isaiah and Daniel point at one and the same thing, namely, the lothsomeness of the wicked at the resurrection. They will be lothsome in the eyes of one another. The unclean wretches were never so lovely to each other, as then they will be lothsome; dear companions in sin will then be an abhorring, each one to his fellow; and the wicked, great and honourable men, shall be no more regarded by their wicked subjects, their servants, their slaves, than the mire in the streets.

Use I. Of comfort to the people of God. The doctrine of the resurrection is a spring of consolation and joy unto you. Think on it, O believers, when ye are in the house of mourning, for the loss of your godly relations or friends, that ye sorrow not, even as others which have no hope; for ye will meet again, 1 Thess. iv. 13, 14. They are but lain down, to rest in their beds for a little while, Isa. lvii. 2. but in the morning of the resurrection they will awake again, and come forth out of their graves. The vessel of honour was but coarse, it had much alloy of base metal in it; it was too weak, too dim and inglorious, for the upper house, whatever lustre it had in the lower one. It was crackt, it was polluted; and therefore it behoved to be melted down, that it may be refined and fashioned more gloriously. Do but wait a while, and you shall see it come forth out of the furnace of earth, vying with the stars in brightness; nay, as the sun when he goeth forth in his might. Have you laid your infant children in the grave? You will see them again. Your GOD calls himself the GOD of your seed, which, according to our Saviour's exposition, secures the glorious resurrection of the body. Wherefore let the covenant you embraced for yourself and your babes now in the dust, comfort your hearts, in the joyful expectation, that by virtue thereof, they shall be raised up in glory; and that, as being no more infants of days, but brought to a full and perfect stature, as is generally supposed. Be not discouraged by reason of a weak and sickly body; there is a day coming, when thou shalt be every whit whole. At the resurrection, Timothy shall be no more liable to his often infirmities; his body, that was weak and sickly, even in youth, shall be raised in power: Lazarus shall be whole & sound, his body being raised incorruptible. And although perhaps thy weakness will not allow thee now, to go one furlong to meet the LORD in the public ordinances, yet the day cometh, when thy body shall be no more a clog to thee, but thou shalt meet the LORD in the air, 1 Thess. iv. 17. It will be with the saints coming up from the grave, as with the Israelites, when they came out of Egypt, Ps. cv. 37. *There was not one feeble person among their tribes.* Hast thou an uncomely, or deformed body? There is a glory within, which will then set all right without, according to the desire of thine heart. It shall rise a glorious, beautiful, handsome, well-proportioned body. Its uncomeliness, or deformities may go with it to the grave, but they shall not come back with it. O that these who are now so desirous to be beautiful and handsome, would not be too hasty to effect it with their foolish and sinful arts; but wait and study the heavenly art of beautifying the body, by endeavouring now to become all glorious within, with the graces of GOD's Spirit! this would at length make them admirable and everlasting beauties. Thou must indeed, O believer, grapple with death, and shalt get the first fall; but thou shalt rise again, and come off victorious at last. Thou must go down to the grave, but though it be thy long home, it will not be thine everlasting home. Thou wilt not hear the voice of thy friends there, but thou shalt hear the voice of CHRIST there. Thou mayst be carried thither with mourning, but shalt come up from it rejoicing. Thy friends indeed will leave thee there, but thy GOD will not. What GOD said to Jacob concerning his going down to Egypt, Gen. xlvi. 3, 4. he says to thee, anent thy going down to the grave, *Fear not to go down---I will go down with thee,---and I will surely bring thee up again.* O solid comfort! O glorious hope! Wherefore comfort yourselves, and one another with these words, 1 Thess. iv. 18.

Use II. Of terror to all unregenerate men. Ye who are yet in your natural state, look at this piece of the eternal state; and consider what will be your part in it, if ye be not in time brought into the state of grace. Think, O sinner, on that day, when the trumpet shall sound; at the voice of which, the bars of the pit shall be broken asunder, the doors of the grave shall fly open, the devouring depths of the sea shall throw up their dead, the earth cast forth hers, and death every-where, in the excess of astonishment, shall let go its prisoners; and thy wretched soul and body shall be re-united, to be sisted before the tribunal of God. Then if thou hast a thousand worlds at thy disposal, thou wouldst gladly give them all away, upon condition thou mightest lie still in thy grave, with the hundreth part of that case, wherewith thou hast sometimes lain at home, on the Lord's day; or, if that cannot be obtained, that thou mightest be but a spectator of the transactions of that day, as thou hast been at some solemn occasions, and rich gospel-feasts; or, if even that is not to be purchased, that a mountain or a rock might fall on thee, and cover thee from the face of the Lamb. Ah! how are men bewitched, thus to trifle away the precious time of life, in, almost, as little concern about death, as if they were like the beasts that perish; some will be telling where their corpse must be laid, while yet they have not seriously considered whether their graves shall be their beds, where they shall awake with joy in the morning of the resurrection; or their prisons, out of which they shall be brought to receive the fearful sentence. Remember now is your seed-time, and as ye sow, ye shall reap. God's seed-time begins at death: and at the resurrection, the bodies of the wicked, that were full of sins, that lie down with them in the dust, Job xx. 11. shall spring up again, sinful, wretched, and vile. Your bodies, which are now instruments of sin, the Lord will lay aside for the fire, at death, and bring them forth for the fire, at the resurrection. That body, which is not now employed in God's service, but is abused by uncleanness and lasciviousness, will then be brought forth in all its vileness, thenceforth to lodge with unclean spirits. The body of the drunkard shall then stagger by reason of the wine of the wrath of God, poured out to him, and poured into him, without mixture. These who now please themselves in their revellings, will reel to and fro at another rate; when, instead of their songs and music, they shall hear the sound of the last trumpet. Many toil their bodies for worldly gain, who will be loth to distress them for the benefit of their souls;

by labour unreasonably hard, they will quite disfit themselves for the service of GOD; and when they have done, will reckon it a very good reason for shifting duty, that they are already tired out with other business; but the day cometh when they will be made to abide a yet greater stress. They will go several miles for back and belly, who will not go half the way for the good of their immortal souls; they will be sickly and unable on the LORD's day, who will be tolerably well all the rest of the week. But when that trumpet sounds, the dead shall find their feet, and none shall be missing in that great congregation. When the bodies of the saints shine as the sun, fearful will the looks of their persecutors be. Fearful will their condition be, who sometimes shut up the saints in nasty prisons, stigmatized, burned them to ashes, hanged them, and stuck up their heads and hands in public places, to fright others from the ways of righteousness which they suffered for. Many faces now fair, will then gather blackness. They shall be no more admired and caressed for that beauty, which has a worm at the root, that will cause it to issue in loathsomeness and deformity. Ah! what is that beauty, under which there lurks a monstrous, deformed, and graceless heart? What but a sorry paint, a slight varnish; which will leave the body so much the more ugly, before that flaming-fire, in which the Judge shall be revealed from heaven, taking vengeance on them that know not GOD, and that obey not the gospel, 2 Thess. i. 7, 8. They shall be stript of all their ornaments, and not have a rag to cover their nakedness; but their carcases shall be an abhorring to all flesh, and serve as a foil to set off the beauty and glory of the righteous and make it appear the brighter.

Now is the time to secure for yourselves, a part in the resurrection of the just. The which if ye would do, unite with JESUS CHRIST by faith, rising spiritualy from sin, and glorifying GOD with your bodies. He is the resurrection and the life, John xi. 25 If your bodies be members of CHRIST, temples of the Holy Ghost, they shall certainly arise in glory. Get into this ark now, and ye shall come forth with joy into the new world. Rise from your sins; cast away these grave-cloaths, putting off your former lusts. How can one imagine, that those who continue dead while they live, shall come forth, at the last day, unto the resurrection of life? But that will be the privilege of all those, who having first consecrated their souls and bodies to the LORD, by faith, do glorify him with their bodies, as well as their souls; living and acting to him, and for him, yea, and suffering for him too, when he calls them to it.

HEAD IV.

The General JUDGMENT.

MATTHEW xxv. 31, 32, 33, 34. 41. 46.

When the Son of Man shall come in his glory, and all the holy angels with him, then shall he sit upon the throne of his glory. And before him shall be gathered all nations, and he shall separate them one from another; as a shepherd divideth his sheep from the goats.
And he shall set the sheep on his right hand, but the goats on the left. Then shall the King say unto them on his right hand, Come ye blessed, &c.
— Unto them on the left hand, Depart from me ye cursed, &c. And these shall go away into everlasting punishment; but the righteous into life eternal.

THE dead being raised, and these, found alive at the coming of the Judge, changed, follows the general judgment, plainly and awfully described in this portion of scripture; in which we shall take notice of the following particulars. (1.) The coming of the Judge, *When the Son of man shall come in his glory, &c.* The Judge is JESUS CHRIST, *the Son of man*; the same, by whose almighty power, as he is GOD, the dead will be raised. He is also called *the King*, ver. 34. The judging of the world being an act of the Royal Mediator's kingly office. He will come *in glory*; glorious in his own Person, and having a glorious retinue, even *all the holy angels with him*, to minister unto him at this great solemnity. (2.) The Judge's mounting the tribunal. He is a King, and therefore it is a throne, a glorious throne, *He shall sit upon the throne of his glory*, ver. 31. (3.) The compearance of the parties. These are *all nations*; all and every one, small and great, of whatsoever nation, who ever were, are, or shall be on the face of the earth; all shall be gathered before him; sisted before his tribunal. (4.) The sorting of them. He shall separate the elect sheep and reprobate goats, setting each party by themselves; as a shepherd who feeds his sheep and goats together all the day, separates them at night, ver. 32. The godly he will set on his right hand, as the most honourable place; the wicked on the left, ver. 33. Yet so as they shall be both before him, ver. 32. It seems to be an allusion to a custom in the Jewish courts, in which, one sat at the right hand of the Judge, who wrote the sentence of absolution; another at their left, who wrote the sentence of condemnation. (5.) The sentencing of the parties, and that according to their works; the righteous being absolved, and the wicked condemned, ver. 34. 41. *Lastly*, The execution of both sentences, in the driving away of the wicked into hell, and carrying the godly into heaven, ver. 46.

DOCTRINE.

There shall be a general Judgment.

This doctrine I shall, (1.) confirm, (2.) explain, & (3.) apply.

I. For confirmation of this great truth, that there shall be a general judgment.

First, It is evident from plain scripture-testimonies. The world has in all its ages been told of it. Enoch before the flood taught it in his prophecy, related, Jude 14, 15. "Behold the LORD cometh with ten thousand of his saints, to execute judgment upon all," &c. Daniel describes it, chap. vii. 9, 10. "I beheld till the thrones were cast down, and the Ancient of days, did sit, whose garments was white as snow, and the hair of his head like pure wool; his throne was like the fiery flame, and his wheels as burning fire. A fiery stream issued and came forth from before him; thousand thousands stood before him; the judgment was set, and the books were opened." The apostle is very express, Acts xvii. 31. "He hath appointed a day in the which he will judge the world in righteousness, by that man whom he hath ordained." See Mat. xvi. 27. 2 Cor. v. 10. 2 Thess. i. 7, 8, 9, 10. Rev. xx. 11,---15. GOD has not only said it, but he has sworn it, Rom. xiv. 10, 11. *We must all stand before the judgment-seat of Christ. For it is written, As I live faith the Lord, every knee shall bow to me, and every tongue shall confess to God.* So that the truth of GOD is most solemnly plighted for it.

Secondly, The rectoral justice and goodness of GOD, the sovereign Ruler of the world, do necessarily require it, inasmuch as they require its being well with the righteous, and ill with the wicked. Howbeit, we often now see wickedness exalted, while truth and righteousness fall in the streets; piety oppressed, while profanity and irreligion do triumph. This is so very ordinary, that every one who sincerely embraceth the way of holiness, must and doth lay his account with the loss of all he has, which the world can take away from him, Luke xiv. 26. *If any man come to me and hate not his father and mother, and wife and children, and brethren and sisters, yea, and his own life also, he cannot be my disciple.* But it is inconsistent with the justice and goodness of God, that the affairs of men should always continue in this state, which they appear in from one generation to another, but that every man be rewarded according to his works; and since that is not done in this life, there must be a judgment to come, *Seeing it is righteous with God, to recompence tribulation to them that trouble you; and to you who are troubled, rest with us, when the Lord Jesus shall be revealed from heaven*, 2 Thess. i. 6, 7. There will be a day, in which the tables will be turned; and the wicked shall be called to an account for all their sins, and suffer the due punishment of them; and the pious shall be the prosperous: for, as the Apostle argues for the happy resurrection of the saints, *If in this life only we have hope in Christ, we are of all men most miserable*, 1 Cor. xv. 19. It is true, God sometimes punisheth the wicked in this life, that men may know, he is a God that judgeth in the earth; but yet much wickedness remains unpunished, and undiscovered, to be a pledge of the judgment to come. If none of the wicked were punished here, they would conclude that God had utterly forsaken the earth; if all of them were punished in this life, men would be apt to think, there is no after-reckoning. Therefore, in the wisdom of God, some are punished now, and some not. Sometimes the Lord smites sinners, in the very act of sin, to shew unto the world, that he is witness to all their wickedness, and will call them to an account for it. Sometimes he delays long, ere he strike; that he may discover to the world, that he forgets not mens ill deeds, though he does not presently punish them. Besides all this, the sins of many do outlive them; and the impure fountain, by them opened, runs long after they are dead and gone. As in the case of Jeroboam the first king of the ten tribes; whose sin did run on all along unto the end of that unhappy kingdom, 2 Kings xvii. 22, 23. *The children of Israel walked in all the sins of Jeroboam, which he did; they departed not from them; Until the Lord removed Israel out of his sight.*

Thirdly, The resurrection of Christ is a certain proof, that there shall be a day of judgment. This argument Paul useth to convince the Athenians; says he, *He hath given assurance to all men, in that he hath raised him from the dead*, Acts xvii. 31. The Judge is already named, his patent written and sealed, yea and read before all men, in his rising again from the dead. Hereby God hath given assurance of it, or *offered faith*, Marg. He hath by raising Christ from the dead, exhibited his credentials as Judge of the world. When, in the days of his humiliation, he was set before a tribunal, arraigned, accused, and condemned of men; he plainly told them of this judgment, and that he himself would be the Judge, Matth. xxvi. 64. *Hereafter shall ye see the Son of man sitting on the right hand of power, and coming in the clouds of heaven.* And now that he was raised from the dead, though condemned as a blasphemer on this very head, is it not an undeniable proof from heaven, of the truth of what he asserted? Moreover, this was one of the great ends of CHRIST's death and resurrection: *For to this end Christ both died, and rose, and revived, that he might be the Lord* (i. e. The Lord Judge, as is evident from the context) *both of the dead and of the living,* Rom. xiv. 9.

Lastly, Every man bears about with him a witness to this, within his own breast, Rom. ii. 15. *Which shew the work of the law written in their hearts, their conscience also bearing witness, and their thoughts the mean while accusing, or else excusing one another.* There is a tribunal erected within every man, where conscience is accuser, witness, and judge, binding over the sinner to the judgment of GOD. This fills the most profligate wretches with horror, and inwardly stings them, upon the commission of some atrocious crime; in effect summoning them to answer for it, before the Judge of the quick and dead. And this it doth, even when the crime is secret, and hid from the eyes of the world. It reacheth those, whom the laws of men cannot reach, because of their power or craft. When men have fled from the judgment of their fellow-creatures, yet go where they will, conscience, as the supreme Judge's officer, still keeps hold of them, reserving them in its chains to the judgment of the great day. And whether they escape punishment from men, or fall by the hand of public justice, when they perceive death's approach, they hear from within of this after-reckoning: being constrained to hearken thereto, in these the most serious minutes of their life. If there be some, in whom nothing of this doth appear, we have no more ground thence to conclude against it, than we have to conclude, that because some men do not groan, therefore they have no pain; or, that dying is a mere jest, because there have been, who have seemed to make little else of it. A good face may be put upon an ill conscience; and the more hopeless mens case is, they reckon it the more their interest to make no reflections on their state and case. But every one, who will consult himself seriously, shall find in himself the witness to the judgment to come. Even the Heathens wanted not a notion of it, though mixed with fictions of their own. Hence, though some of the Athenians, when they heard of the resurrection of the dead, mocked, Acts xvii. 32. yet there is no account of their mocking, when they heard of the general judgment. ver.

II. For explication, the following particulars may serve to give some view of the nature and transactions of that great day.

First, GOD shall Judge the world by JESUS CHRIST; *He will judge the world in righteousness, by that Man whom he hath ordained*, Acts xvii. 31. The Psalmist tells us, that *God is Judge himself*, Psalm l. 6. The holy blessed Trinity, Father, Son, and holy Ghost, is Judge in respect of judicial authority, dominion, and power; but the Son incarnate is the Judge, in respect of dispensation, and special exercise of that power. The judgment shall be exercised or performed by him, as the royal Mediator; for he has a delegated power of judgment from the Father, as his Servant, his King, whom he hath set upon his holy hill of Zion, Psalm ii. 6. and to whom he hath committed all judgment, John v. 22. This is a part of the Mediator's exaltation, given him, in consequence of his voluntary humiliation, Philip. ii. 8, 9, 10. *He humbled himself, and became obedient unto death, even the death of the cross. Wherefore God hath highly exalted him, and given him a name, which is above every name*, i. e. power and authority over all, to wit, *That at*, or *in, the name of Jesus*, not the name of JESUS, that is not the name above every name, being common to others, as to Justus, Col. iv. 11. and Joshua, Heb. iv. 8. *every knee shall bow*. The which is explained by the Apostle himself, of standing before the judgment seat of CHRIST, Rom. xiv. 10, 11. So he who was judged and condemned of men, shall be the Judge of men and angels.

Secondly, JESUS CHRIST, the Judge, descending from heaven into the ear, 1 Thes. iv. 16. shall *come in the clouds of heaven, with power and great glory*, Matth. xxiv. 30. This his coming, will be a mighty surprise to the world, which will be found in deep security; foolish virgins sleeping, and the wise slumbering. There will then be much luxury and debauchery in the world, little sobriety and watchfulness; a great throng of business, but a great scarcity of faith and holiness; *As it was in the days of Noah, so also shall it be in the days of the Son of man: They did eat, they drank, they married wives, they were given in marriage, until the day that Noah entered into the ark; and the flood came and destroyed them all. Likewise, also, as it was in the days of Lot; they did eat, they drank, they bought, they sold, they planted, they builded---- Even thus shall it be, in the day when the Son of man is revealed*, Luke xvii. 26, 27, 28, 30. The coming of the Judge will surprise some at markets, buying and selling; others at table, eating and drinking, and making merry; others busy with their new plantings; some building new houses; nay, some's wedding-day, will be their own and the world's judgment day. But the Judge cometh! the markets are marred: the buyer throws away what he has bought; the seller casts down his money; they are raised from the table, and their mirth is extinguished in a moment; tho' the tree be set in the earth, the gardener may not stay to cast the earth about it; the workmen throw away their tools, when the house is but half built, and the owner regards it no more; the bridegroom, bride, and guests, must leave the wedding-feast, and appear before the tribunal; for, *Behold he cometh with clouds, and every eye shall see him*, Rev. i. 7. He shall come most gloriously; for he will *come in the glory of his Father with the holy angels*, Mark viii. 38. When he came in the flesh, to die for sinners, he laid aside the robes of his glory, and was despised and rejected of men; but when he comes again, to judge the world, such shall be his visible glory and majesty, that it shall cast an eternal veil over all earthly glory, and fill his greatest enemies with fear and dread. Never had prince, or potentate in the world, such a glorious train, as will accompany this Judge! All the holy angels shall come with him, for his honour and service. Then he, who was led to the cross with a band of soldiers, will be gloriously attended to the place of judgment, by (not a multitude of the heavenly host, but) the whole host of angels: *All his holy angels*, says the text.

Thirdly, At the coming of the Judge, the summons is given to the parties, by the sound of the last trumpet; at which the dead are raised, and those found alive, changed: of which before, 1 Thess. iv. 16, 17. O loud trumpet! that shall be heard at once, in all corners of the earth, and of the sea! O wonderful voice, that will not only disturb those who sleep in the dust; but effectually awaken, rouze them out of their sleep and raise them from death! Were trumpets sounding now, drums beating, furious soldiers crying and killing men, women and children running and shrieking, the wounded groaning and dying; those who are in the graves, would have no more disturbance, than if the world were in most profound peace. Yea, were stormy winds casting down the lofty oaks, the seas roaring and swallowing up the ships, the most dreadful thunders going along the heavens, lightnings every-where flashing, the earth quaking, trembling, opening, and swallowing up whole cities, and burying multitudes at once; the dead would still enjoy a perfect repose, and sleep soundly in the dust, tho' their own dust should be thrown out of its place. But at the sound of this trumpet, they shall all awake. The morning is come, they can sleep no longer; the time of the dead, that they must be judged; they must get out of their graves, and appear before the Judge.

Fourthly, The Judge shall sit down on the tribunal, *He shall sit on the throne of his glory*. Sometime he stood before a tribunal on earth, and was condemned as a malefactor: then shall he sit on his own tribunal, and judge the world. Sometime he hung upon a cross, covered with shame; then he shall sit on a throne of glory. What this throne shall be, whether a bright cloud, or what else, I shall not enquire: Our eyes will give an answer to that question at length. John saw a great white throne, Rev. xx. 11. *His throne*, says Daniel, *was like the fiery flame, and his wheels as burning fire*, chap. vii. 9. Whatever it be, doubtless it shall be a throne, glorious beyond expression; and, in comparison with which, the most glorious throne on the earth, is but a seat on a dung-hill; and the sight of it will equally surprise kings, who sit on thrones in this life, and beggars, who sat in dung-hills. It will be a throne, for stateliness and glory, suited to the quality of him who shall sit on it. Never had a judge such a throne, and never had a throne such a judge on it.

Leaving the discovery of the nature of the throne, until that day, it concerns us more nearly to consider what a Judge will sit upon it; a point in which we are not left to uncertain conjectures. The Judge on the throne will be (1.) A visible Judge, visible to our bodily eyes, Rev. i. 7. *Every eye shall see him*. When GOD gave the law on mount Sinai, the people saw no similitude, only they heard a voice; but when he calls the world to an account, how they have observed his law; the man CHRIST being judge, we shall see our Judge with our eyes, either to our eternal comfort or confusion, according to the entertainment we give him now. That very body which was crucified without the gates of Jerusalem, betwixt two thieves, shall then be seen on the throne, shining in glory. We now see him symbolically in the sacrament of his supper; the saints see him by the eye of faith: then, all shall see him with these eyes now in their heads. (2.) A judge, having full authority and power, to render unto every one according to his works. CHRIST, as GOD, hath authority of himself; and, as Mediator, he hath a judicial power and authority, which his Father has invested him with, according to the covenant betwixt the Father and the Son, for the redemption of sinners. And his divine glory will be a light, by which all men shall see clearly to read his commission for this great and honourable employment. All power is given unto him, in heaven and in earth, Mat. xxviii. 18. He hath the keys of hell and of death, Rev. i. 18. There can be no appeal from this tribunal; sentence once past there, must stand forever; there is no reversing of it. All appeals are from an inferior court to a superior one; but when GOD gives sentence against a man, where can he find a higher court, to bring his process to? This judgment is the Mediator's judgment, and therefore the last judgment. If the Intercessor be against us, who can be for us? If CHRIST condemn us, who will absolve us? (3.) A Judge of infinite wisdom. His eyes will pierce into, and clearly difcern, the moft intricate cafes. His omnifcience qualifies him for judging of the moft retired thoughts as well as of words and works. The moft fubtle finner fhall not be able to outwit him, nor, by any artful management, to palliate the crime. He is the fearcher of hearts, to whom nothing can be hid or perplexed, but all things are naked and open unto his eyes, Heb. iv. 13. (4.) A moft juft Judge; a Judge of perfect integrity. He is the righteous Judge, 2 Tim. iv. 8. And his throne, a great white throne, Rev. xx. 11. From whence no judgment fhall proceed, but what is moft pure and fpotlefs. The Thebans painted juftice blind, and without hands; for judges ought not to refpect perfons, nor take bribes. The Areopagites judged in the dark, that they might not regard who fpoke, but what was fpoken. With the Judge on this throne, there will be no refpect of perfons; he will neither regard the perfons of the rich, nor of the poor, but juft judgment fhall go forth in every one's caufe. *Laftly*, An omnipotent Judge, able to put his fentence in execution. The united force of devils and wicked men, will be altogether unable to withftand him. They cannot retard the execution of the fentence againft them, one moment; far lefs can they ftop it altogether. Thoufand thoufands of angels minifter unto him, Dan. vii. 10. And, by the breath of his mouth, he can drive the curfed herd whither he pleafeth.

Fifthly, The parties fhall compear. Thefe are men and devils. Although thefe laft, the fallen angels, were, from the firft moment of their finning, fubjected to the wrath of GOD, and were caft down to hell; and wherefoever they go, they carry their hell about with them; yet, it is evident, that they are referved unto judgment, 2 Pet. ii. 14. namely, unto the judgment of the great day, Jude 6. And then they fhall be folemnly and publicly judged, 1 Cor. vi. 3. *Know ye not, that we fhall judge angels?* At that day, they fhall anfwer for their trade of finning, and tempting to fin, which they have been carrying on from the beginning. Then many a hellifh brat, which Satan has laid down at the faint's door, but not adopted by them, fhall be laid at the door of the true father of them, that is, the devil. And he fhall receive the due reward of all the difhonour done to GOD, and of all the mifchief he has done to men. Thofe wicked fpirits, now in chains, tho' not in fuch ftrait cuftody, but that they go about, like roaring lions, feeking whom they may devour, fhall then receive their final fentence, and be fhut up in their den, namely, in the prifon of hell; where they fhall be held in extreme and unfpeakable torment thro' all eternity, Rev. xx. 10. *And the devil, that deceived them, was caft into the lake of fire and brimftone, where the beaft and the falfe prophet are; and fhall be tormented day and night, for ever and ever.* In profpect of which, the devils said to CHRIST, *Art thou come hither to torment us before the time?* Mat. viii. 29.

But what we are chiefly concerned to take notice of, in the case of men in that day. All men must compear before this tribunal: all, of each sex, and of every age, quality and condition; the great and small, noble and ignoble; none are excepted. Adam and Eve, with all their sons and daughters; every one who has had, or, to the end of the world, shall have, a living soul united to a body, will make up this great congregation. Even those who refused to come to the throne of grace, shall be forced to the bar of justice; for there can be no hiding from the all-seeing Judge, no flying from him who is present every where, no resisting him who is armed with almighty power. *We must all stand before the judgment-seat of Christ*, 2 Cor. v. 10. *Before him shall be gathered all nations*, says the text. This is to be done by the ministry of angels. By them shall the elect be gathered, Mark xiii. 27. *Then shall he send his angels, and shall gather together his elect from the four winds.* And they also shall gather the reprobate, Mat. xiii. 40, 41. *So shall it be in the end of this world, The Son of man shall send forth his angels, and they shall gather out of his kingdom all things that offend, and them which do iniquity.* From all corners of the world, shall the inhabitants thereof be gathered unto the place, where he shall set his throne for judgment.

Sixthly, There shall be a separation made betwixt the righteous and the wicked; the fair company of the elect sheep being set on CHRIST's right hand, and the reprobate goats on his left. There is no necessity to wait for this separation, till the trial be over; since the parties do rise out of their graves, with plain outward marks of distinction, as was cleared before. The separation seems to be effected by that double gathering before-mentioned: the one of the elect, Mark xiii. 27. the other of them that do iniquity, Mat. xiii. 41. The elect being caught up together in the clouds, meet the LORD in the air, 1 Thes. iv. 17. and so are set on his right hand; and the reprobate left on the earth, Mat. xxv. 40. upon the Judge's left hand. Here is now a total separation of two parties, who were always opposite to each other, in their principles, aims, and manner of life; who, when together, were a burden the one to the other, under which the one groaned, and the other raged; but now they are freely parted, never to come together any more. The iron and clay, alluded to Dan. ii. 41. 42. which could never mix, are quite separated: the one being drawn up in the air, by the attractive virtue of the stone cut out of the mountain, namely JESUS CHRIST; the other left upon its earth to be trod under foot.

Now let us look to the right hand, and there we will see a glorious company of saints shining as so many stars in their orbs; and with a cheerful countenance, beholding him who sitteth upon the throne. Here will be two wonderful sights, which the world used not to see. (1.) A great congregation of saints, in which not so much as one hypocrite. There was a bloody Cain in Adam's family, a cursed Ham in Noah's family, in the ark; a treacherous Judas in Christ's own family, but in that company shall be none but sealed ones, members of Christ, having all one Father; and this is a sight reserved for that day. (2.) All the godly upon one side. Seldom or never do the saints on earth make such a harmony, but there are some jarring strings among them. It is not to be expected, that men who see but in part, though they be going to one city, will agree as to every step in the way; no, we need not look for it, in this state of imperfection. But at that day, Paul and Barnabas shall meet in peace and unity, though once the contention was so sharp between them, that they departed asunder, the one from the other, Acts xv. 39. There shall be no more divisions, no more separate standing, among those who belong to Christ. All the godly of the different parties, shall then be upon one side; seeing, whatever were their differences in lesser things, while in the world, yet even then, they met and **concentred** all in one Lord Jesus Christ, by a true and lively faith, and in the one way of holiness or practical godliness. And the naughty hypocrites, of whatsoever party, shall be led forth with the workers of iniquity.

Look to the left hand, and there you will see the cursed goats, all the wicked ones, from Cain to the last ungodly person who shall be in the world, gathered together into one most miserable congregation. There are many assemblies of the wicked now; then there shall be but one. But all of them shall be present there, brought together as one herd for the slaughter, bellowing and roaring, weeping and howling for the miseries come on them. And remember thou shalt not be a mere spectator, to look at these two so different companies; but must thyself take thy place in one of the two, and shalt share with the company, whatever hand it be upon. These who now abhor no society so much, as that of the saints, would then be glad to be allowed to get in among them, though it were but to lie among their feet. But then not one tare shall be found with the wheat; he will thoroughly purge his floor. Many of the right-hand men of this world, will be left-hand men in that day. Many who must have the door and the right hand of these, who are better than they, if the righteous be more excellent than his neighbour, shall then be turned to the left hand, as most despicable wretches. O how terrible will the separation be to the ungodly! how dreadful will this gathering them together into one company be; what they will not believe, they will then see, namely, that but few are saved. They think it enough now, to be neighbour-like, and can securely follow the multitude; but the multitude on the left hand will yield them no comfort. How will it sting the ungodly Christian, to see himself set on the same hand with Turks and Pagans! how will it gall men to find themselves standing, profane Protestants with idolatrous Papists; praying people with their profane neighbours, who mocked at religious exercises; formal professors, strangers to the new birth and the power of godliness, with persecutors! now there are many opposite societies in the world, but then all the ungodly shall be in one society. And how dreadful will the faces of companions in sin be to one another they there; what doleful shrieks, when the whore-monger and his whore shall meet; when the drunkards, who have had many a jovial day together, shall see one another in the face; when the husband and wife, the parents and children, the Master and servants, and neighbours, who have been snares & stumbling-blocks to one another, to the ruin of their own souls, and those of their relatives, shall meet again in that miserable society! Then will there be curses instead of salutations; and tearing of themselves, and raging against one-another, instead of the wonted embraces.

Seventhly, The parties shall be tried. The Trial cannot be difficult, in regard the Judge is omniscient, and nothing can be hid from him. But, that his righteous judgment may be evident to all, he will set the hidden things of darkness in clearest light at that trial, 1 Cor. iv. 5.

Men shall be tried, *First*, Upon their works; for, *God shall bring every work into Judgment, with every secret thing, whether it be good or whether it be evil*, Eccl. xii. 14. The Judge will try every man's conversation, and set his deeds done in the body, with all the circumstances thereof, in a true light. Then will many actions commended and applauded of men, as good and just, be discovered to have been evil, and abominable, in the sight of God; and many works, now condemned by the world, will be approven and commended by the great Judge, as good and just. Secret things will be brought to light; and what was hid from the view of the world, shall be laid open. Wickedness, which hath kept its lurking place in spite of all human search, will then be brought forth to the glory of God, and the confusion of impenitent sinners who hid it. The world appears now very vile, in the eyes of those who are exercised to godliness; but it will then appear a thousand times more vile, when that, which is done of men in secret, comes to be discovered. Every good action shall then be remembered; and the hidden religion and good works, most industriously concealed by the saints, from the eyes of men, shall no more be hid; for though the LORD will not allow men to proclaim every man his own goodness, yet he himself will do it in due time. *Secondly*, Their words shall be judged, Mat. xii. 37. *For by thy words thou shalt be justified, and by thy words thou shalt be condemned.* Not a word spoken for GOD, and his cause in the world, from love to himself, shall be forgotten. They are all kept in remembrance, and shall be brought forth as evidences of faith, and of an interest in CHRIST, Mat. iii. 16, 17. *Then they that feared the Lord, spake often one to another, and the Lord hearkned and heard it; and a book of remembrance was written before him. And they shall be mine, saith the Lord of hosts, in that day when I make up my jewels.* And the tongue, which did run at random, shall then confess to GOD; and the speaker shall find it to have been followed, and every word noted that dropped from his unsanctified lips. *Every idle word that men shall speak, they shall give account thereof in the day of judgment*, Mat. xii. 36. And if they shall give account of idle words, that is, words spoken to no good purpose, neither to GOD's glory, one's own, or one's neighbour's good: how much more shall mens wicked words, their sinful oaths, curses, lies, filthy communications, and bitter words be called over again that day? The tongues of many shall then fall upon themselves and ruin them. *Thirdly*, Mens thoughts shall be brought into judgment; the Judge will make manifest the counsel of the hearts, 1 Cor. iv. 5. Tho'ts go free from man's judgment, but not from the judgment of the heart-searching GOD, who knows mens thoughts, without the help of signs to discern them by. The secret springs of mens actions, will then be brought to light; and the sins, that never came further than the heart, will then be laid open. O what a figure will man's corrupt nature make, when his inside is turned out, and all his speculative impurities are exposed! the rottenness that is within many a whited sepulchre, the speculative filthiness and wantonness, murder and malignity, now lurking in the hearts of men, as in the chamber of imagery, will then be discovered; and what good was in the hearts of any, shall no more lie concealed. If it was in their hearts to build a house to the LORD, they shall hear, that they did well that it was in their heart.

This trial will be righteous and impartial, accurate and searching, clear and evident. The Judge is the righteous Judge, and he will do right to every one. He has a just balance for good and evil actions, and for honest and false hearts. The fig-leaf cover of hypocrisy will then be blown aside and the hypocrite's nakedness will appear; as when the LORD came to judge Adam and Eve, in the cool, or, as the word is, in the *wind*, of the day, Gen. iii. 8. The fire, which tries things most exquisitely, shall try every man's work, of what sort it is, 1 Cor. iii. 13. Man's judgment is oft-times perplexed & confused: but here the whole process shall be clear and evident, as written with a sunbeam. It shall be clear to the judge, to whom no case can be intricate; to the parties, who shall be convinced, Jude 15. And the multitudes on both sides, shall see the judge is clear when he judgeth; for then the heavens shall declare his righteousness, in the audience of all the world; and so it shall be universally known, Psalm l. 6.

On these accounts it is, that this trial is held out in the Scripture, under the notion of opening of books; and men are said to be judged out of those things written in the books, Rev. xx. 12. The Judge of the world, who infallibly knoweth all things, hath no need of books to be laid before him, to prevent mistake in any point of law or fact; but the expression points at his proceeding, as most nice, accurate, just, and well grounded, in every step of it. Now, there are four books that shall be opened in that day.

First, The book of GOD's remembrance or omniscience, Mal. iii. 19. This is an exact record of every man's state, thoughts, words, and deeds, good or evil; it is, as it were, a day-book, in which the LORD puts down all that passeth in mens hearts, lips, and lives; and it is a-filling up every day that one lives. In it are recorded men's sins and good works, secret and open, with all their circumstances. Here are registred all their privileges, mercies temporal and spiritual, sometime laid to their hand; the checks, admonitions, & rebukes, given by teachers, neighbours, afflictions, & mens own consciences; every thing in its due order. This book will serve only as a libel, in respect of the ungodly; but it will be for another use in respect of the godly, namely, for a memorial of their good. The opening of it, is the Judge's bringing to light what is written in it: the reading, as it were, of the libel and memorial, respectively, in their hearing.

Secondly, The book of conscience will be opened, and shall be as a thousand witnesses to prove the fact, Rom. ii. 15. *Which shew the work of the law written in their hearts, their conscience also bearing witness*. Conscience is a censor going with every man whithersoever he goes, taking an account of his deeds done in the body, and, as it were, noting them in a book; the which being opened, will be found a double of the former, so far as it relates to one's own state and case. Much is written in it, which cannot be read now; the writing of conscience being, in many cases, like to that which is made with the juice of lemons, not to be read, till it be held before the fire; but then men shall read it clearly and distinctly; the fire which is to try every man's work, will make the book of conscience legible in every ry point. Though the book be sealed now, the conscience blind, dum and deaf, the seals will then be broken, and the book opened. There shall be no more a weak or misinformed conscience among those on the right hand or those on the left. There shall not be a silent conscience, and far less a seared conscience among all the ungodly crew; but their consciences shall be most quick sighted, and most lively, in that day. None shall then call good evil, or evil good. Ignorance of what sin is, and what things are sins, will have no place among them; and the subtle reasonings of men, in favour of their lusts, will then be for ever baffled by their own consciences. None shall have the favour, if I may so speak, of lying under the soft cover of delusion; but they shall all be convicted by their conscience. Nill they, will they, they shall look on this book, read and be confounded, and stand speechless, knowing that nothing is charged upon them by mistake; since this is a book, which was always in their own custody. Thus shall the Judge make every man see himself in the glass of his own conscience, which will make quick work.

Thirdly, The book of the Law shall be opened. This book is the standard and rule, by which is known what is right, and what is wrong; as also, what sentence is to be passed accordingly, on those who are under it. As to the opening of this book, in its statutory part, which shews what is sin, and what is duty; it falls in with the opening of the book of conscience. For conscience is set, by the sovereign Lawgiver, in every man's breast, to be his private teacher, to shew him the law, and his private pastor, to make application of the same; and, at that day, it will be perfectly fit for its office; so that the conscience, which is most stupid now, shall then read to the man, most accurate, but dreadful lectures on the law. But what seems, mainly at least, pointed at, by the opening of this book, is the opening of that part of it, which determines the reward of mens works. Now, the law promised life, upon perfect obedience; but none can be found on the right hand, or on the left, who will pretend to that, when once the book of conscience is opened, it threateneth death upon disobedience, and will effectually bring it upon all under its dominion. And this part of the book of the law, determining the reward of mens works, is opened, only to shew what must be the portion of the ungodly, and that there they may read their sentence before it be pronounced. But it is not opened for the sentence of the saints; for no sentence, absolving a sinner, could ever be drawn out of it. The law promiseth life, not as it is a rule of actions, but as a covenant of works; and therefore innocent man could not have demanded life upon his obedience, till the law was reduced into the form of a covenant, as was shewn before. But the saints having been, in this life, brought under a new covenant, namely, the covenant of grace, were dead to the law, as a covenant of works, and it was dead to them. Wherefore, as they shall not have any fears of death from it, so they can have no hopes of life from it, since they are not under the law, but under grace, Rom. vi. 14. But, for their sentence, another book is opened; of which in the next place.

Thus the Book of the Law is opened, for the sentence against all those on the left hand; and by it they will clearly see the justice of the judgment against them, and how the Judge proceeds therein, according to law. Nevertheless, there will be this difference, namely, that these who had only the natural law, and lived not under any special revelation, shall be judged by that law of nature they had in their hearts: which law bears, *That they who commit such things, as they will stand convicted of, are worthy of death,* Rom. i. 32. But these, who had the written law, to whom the word of GOD came, as it has sounded in the visible church, shall be judged by that written law. So says the Apostle, Rom. ii. 12. *For, as many as have sinned without* (the written) *law, shall perish without* (the written) *law: And as many as have sinned in the law* (i. e. under the written law) *shall be judged by the* (written) *law.*

Lastly, Another book shall be opened, which is the book of life Rev. xx. 12. In this the names of all the elect are written, as CHRIST said to his disciples, Luke x. 20. *Your names are written in heaven.* This book contains GOD's gracious and unchangeable purpose, to bring all the elect to eternal life; and that, in order thereto, they be redeemed by the blood of his Son, effectually called, justified, adopted, sanctified, and raised up by him at the last day without sin. It is now lodged in the Mediator's hand, as the book of the manner of the kingdom; and having perfected the work the Father gave them to do, he shall, on the great day, produce and open the book, and present the persons therein named, faultless before the presence of his glory, Jude 24. *Not having spot or wrinkle, or any such thing,* Eph. v. 27. None of them all, who are named in the book, shall be missing. They shall be found qualified, according to the order of the book, redeemed, called, justified, sanctified, raised up without spot; what remains then, but that, according to the same book, they obtain the great end, namely, everlasting life. This may be gathered from that precious promise, Rev. iii. 5. *He that overcometh, the same shall be clothed in white raiment,* being raised in glory, *and I will not blot out his name out of the book of life. But I will confess his name* (it shall be, as it were, read out among the rest of GOD's elect) *before my Father, and before his angels.* Here is now the ground of the saints absoluture, the ground of the blessed sentence they shall receive. The book of life being opened, it will be known to all, **who** are elected, and who are not. Thus far of the Trial of the parties.

Eighthly, Then shall the Judge pronounce that blessed sentence on the saints, *Come ye blessed of my Father, inherit the kingdom prepared for you from the foundation of the world*, Mat. xxv. 34. It is most probable, the man CHRIST will pronounce it with an audible voice; which not only all the saints, but all the wicked likewise, shall hear and understand. Who can conceive the inexpressible joy, with which these happy ones shall hear these words? Who can imagine that fulness **of joy**, which shall be poured into their hearts, with these words reaching their ears? And who can conceive how much of hell shall break into the hearts of all the ungodly crew, by these words of heaven? It is certain this sentence shall be pronounced, before the sentence of damnation, Mat. xxv. 34. 41. *Then shall the King say unto them on his right hand, Come ye blessed, &c.—Then shall he say also to them on the left hand, Depart from me, ye cursed,* &c. There is no need of this order, that the saints may, without fear, &c. hear the other sentence on the reprobate; they who are raised in glory, caught up to meet the LORD in the air, presented without spot, and whose souls, for the far greater part of them, have been so long in heaven before, shall not be capable of any such fear. But hereby they will be orderly brought in, to sit in judgment, as CHRIST's assessors, against the ungodly; whose torment will be aggravated by it. It will be a hell to them, to be kept out of hell, till they see the doors of heaven opened to receive the saints, who once dwelt in the same country, parish, or town, and sat under the same ministry with themselves. Thus will they see heaven afar off, to make their hell the hotter. Like that unbelieving lord, 2 Kings vii. 19, 20. they shall see the plenty with their eyes, but shall not eat thereof. Every word of the blessed sentence, shall be like an envenomed arrow shot into their hearts, while they see what they have lost, and from thence gather what they are to expect.

This sentence passeth on the saints according to their works, Rev. xx. 12. But not for their works, nor for their faith neither, **as if** eternal life were merited by them. The sentence itself overthrows this absurd conceit. The kingdom they are called to, was prepared for them, from the foundation of the world; not left to be merited by themselves, who were but of yesterday. They inherit it as sons, but procure it not to themselves, as servants do the reward of their work. They were redeemed by the blood of CHRIST, and clothed with his spotless righteousness, which is the proper cause of the sentence. They were also qualified for heaven, by the sanctification of his Spirit; and hence it is according to their works; so that the ungodly world shall see now, that the Judge of the quick and dead does good to them, who were good. Therefore it is added to the sentence, *For I was an hungered, and ye gave me meat,* &c. ver. 35, 36. which doth not denote the ground, but the evidence of their right to heaven; as if a judge should say, he absolves a man pursued for debt, for the witnesses depone, that it is paid already. So the Apostle says, 1 Cor. x. 5. *But with many of them God was not well pleased, for they were overthrown in the wilderness.* Their overthrow in the wilderness was not the ground of GOD's displeasure with them, but an evidence of it. And thus our LORD teacheth us the necessary connexion betwixt glory and good works, namely, works evangelically good; works having a respect to JESUS CHRIST, and done out of faith in him, and love to him, without which they will not be regarded in that day. And the saints will so far be judged according to such works, that the degrees of glory amongst them shall be according to these works; for it is an eternal truth, *He that soweth sparingly, shall reap sparingly,* 2 Cor. ix. 6.

Thus shall the good works of the godly have a glorious, not a gratuitous reward; a reward of grace, not of debt; which will fill them with wonder at the riches of free grace, and the LORD's condescending to take any notice, especially such public notice, of their poor, worthless works. The which seems to be the import of what they are said to answer, *Saying, Lord, when saw we thee an hungered,* &c. ver. 37, 38, 39. And may they not justly wonder, to see themselves set down to the marriage-supper of the Lamb, in consequence of a dinner or supper, a little meat or drink, such as they had, which they gave to an hungry or thirsty member of CHRIST, for his sake? Oh plentiful harvest following upon the seed of good works! rivers of pleasure springing up from, perhaps, a cup of cold water given to a disciple, in the name of a disciple! eternal mansions of glory rising out of a night's lodging given to a saint, who was a stranger! everlasting robes of glory given in exchange of a new coat, or, it may be, an old one, bestowed on some saint, who had not necessary clothing! a visit to a sick saint, repaid by CHRIST himself, coming in the glory of his Father, with all his holy angels! a visit made to a poor prisoner, for the cause of CHRIST, repaid with a visit from the Judge of all, taking away the visitant with him to the palace of heaven, there to be ever with himself! these things will be matter of everlasting wonder, and should stir up all, to sow liberally in time, while the seed-time of good works doth last. But it is CHRIST's stamp on good works, that puts a value on them, in the eye of a gracious GOD; which seems to be the import of our LORD's reply, ver. 40. *In as much as ye have done it, unto one of the least of these my brethren, ye have done it unto me.*

IX. Now the saints having received their own sentence, they shall judge the world, 1 Cor. vi. 2. This was not fulfilled, when the empire became Christians, and Christians were made magistrates. No, the Psalmist tells us, *This honour have all the saints*, Psal. cxlix. 9. And the Apostle in the forecited place, adds, *And if the world shall be judged by you, are ye unworthy to judge the smallest matters?* Ver. 3. *Know ye not that we shall judge angels?* Being called, they come to receive their kingdom, in the view of angels and men; they go as it were, from the bar to the throne, *To him that overcometh, will I grant to sit with me on my throne*, Rev. iii. 21. They shall not only judge the world, in CHRIST their head, by way of communion with him; by their works compared with these of the ungodly; or, by way of testimony against them; but they shall be assessors to JESUS CHRIST the Judge, giving their voice against them, consenting to his judgment as just, and saying Amen, to the doom pronounced against all the ungodly; as is said of the saints upon the judgment of the great whore, Rev. xix. 1, 2. *Hallelujah, for true and righteous are his judgments*. Thus the upright shall have dominion over them, in the morning of the resurrection, Psa. xlix. 14. Then, and not till then shall that be fully accomplished, which ye may read, Ps. cxlix. 6, 7, 8, 9. *Let the high praises of God be in their mouth, and a two-edged sword in their hand, to execute vengeance upon the heathen, and punishments upon the people,—this honour have all his saints*. O! what a strange turn of affairs, will appear here! what an astonishing sight will it be, to see wicked churchmen and statesmen, standing as criminals before the saints, whom sometimes they condemned as heretics, rebels and traitors! to see men of riches and power, stand pale-faced before these whom they oppressed! to see the mocker stand trembling before those whom he mocked, the worldly-wise man before those whom he accounted fools! then shall the despised faces of the saints, be dreadful faces to the wicked; and those who sometimes were the song of the drunkards, shall then be a terror to them. All wrongs must be righted at length, and every one set in his proper place.

Tenthly, The Judge shall pronounce the sentence of damnation on all the ungodly multitude. *Then shall he say also unto them on the left hand, Depart from me, ye cursed, into everlasting fire, prepared for the devil and his angels*, ver. 41. Fearful doom! and that from the same mouth, from whence proceeded the sentence of absolution before. It was an aggravation of the misery of the Jews, when their city was destroyed, that they were ruined by one who was accounted the darling of the world. O! what an aggravation of the misery of the wicked will it be, that he shall pronounce this sentence also! to hear the curse from mount Zion, must needs be most terrible. To be damned by him, who came to save sinners, must be double damnation. But thus it shall be. The Lamb of GOD shall roar, as a lion, against them! he shall excommunicate, and cast them out of his presence for ever, by a sentence from the throne, saying, *Depart, from me, ye cursed.* He shall adjudge them to everlasting fire, and the society of devils for evermore. And this sentence also, we suppose, shall be pronounced with an audible voice, by the man CHRIST. And all the saints shall say, *Hallelujah, true and righteous are his judgments.* None were so compassionate as the saints, when on earth, during the time of GOD's patience. But now that time is at an end, their compassion on the ungodly is swallowed up in joy, in the Mediator's glory, and his executing of just judgment, by which his enemies are made his footstool. Tho' sometimes the righteous man did weep in secret places for their pride, and because they would not hear; yet, then, *He shall rejoice, when he seeth the vengeance he shall wash his feet in the blood of the wicked,* Psa. lviii. 10. No pity shall then be shewn to them, from their nearest relations. The godly wife shall applaud the justice of the Judge, in the condemnation of her ungodly husband; the godly husband shall say Amen to the damnation of her who lay in his bosom: the godly parents shall say, Hallelujah, at the passing of the sentence against their ungodly child; and the godly child shall, from his heart, approve the damnation of his wicked parents, the father who begat him, and the mother who bore him. The sentence is just: they are judged *according to their works,* Rev. xx. 12.

There is no wrong done them; *For I was hungry,* saith our LORD, *and ye gave me no meat; I was thirsty, and ye gave me no drink; I was a stranger, and ye took me not in; naked, and ye clothed me not; sick, and in prison, and ye visited me not,* ver. 42, 43. These are not only evidences of their ungodly and cursed state, but most proper causes and grounds of their condemnation; for tho' good works do not merit salvation, yet evil works merit damnation. Sins of one kind only, namely, of omission, are here mentioned; not that these alone shall then be discovered, for the opening of the books lay all open, but because these, tho' there were no more, are sufficient to damn unpardoned sinners. And if men shall be condemned for sins of omission, much more for sins of commission. The omission of works of charity and mercy, is condescended on particularly, to stop the mouths of the wicked; for it is most just, that he have judgment without mercy, that hath shewed no mercy, Jam. ii. 13. The mentioning of the omission of acts of charity and mercy towards the distressed members of CHRIST, intimates, that it is the judgment of those who have heard of CHRIST in the gospel, that is principally intended here, in this portion of scripture; and that the slighting of CHRIST, will be the great cause of the ruin of those who hear the gospel; but the enmity of the hearts of the wicked against himself, is discovered by the entertainment they now give to his members.

In vain will they say, *When saw we thee an hungred, or a-thirst?* &c. ver. 44. For the LORD reckons, and will reckon, the world's unkindness to his people, unkindness to himself: *In as much as ye did it not to one of the least of these, ye did it not to me,* ver. 45. O meat and drink unhappily spared, when a member of CHRIST was in need of it! O wretched neglect, that the stranger saint was not taken in! it had been better for them, they had quitted their own room, and their own bed, than he had wanted lodging. O cursed clothing, may the wicked say, that was in my house, locked up in my chest, or hanging in my wardrobe, and was not brought out to clothe such a-one! O that I had stripped myself, rather than he had gone away without cloathing! Cursed business, that diverted me from visiting a sick saint! O that I had rather watched whole nights with him! Wretch that I was! why did I sit at ease in my house, when he was in prison, and not visit him? But now the tables are turned; CHRIST's servants shall eat, but I shall be hungry; his servants shall drink, but I shall be thirsty; they rejoice but I am ashamed, Isa. lxv. 13. They are taken in, but I am cast out, and bid depart; they are clothed with robes of glory, but I walk naked and they see my shame, Rev. xvi. 15. They are now raised up on high, beyond the reach of sickness or pain; but I must now lie down in sorrow, Isa. l. 11. Now shall they go to the palace of heaven, but I must go to the prison of hell.

But if our LORD thus resents mens' neglecting to help his people under these, and the like distresses; what may they expect, who are the authors and instruments of them? If they shall be fed with wrath, who fed them not when they were hungry; what shall become of those, who robbed and spoiled them, and took their own bread away from them? What a full cup of wrath shall be the portion of those who were so far from giving them meat or drink, when hungry or thirsty, that they made it a crime for others to entertain them, and made themselves drunk with their blood! they must lodge with devils for evermore, who took not in the LORD's people, when strangers; then, what a lodging shall those have, who drave them out of their own houses, out of their native land, and made them strangers? Men will be condemned for not clothing them, when naked; then, how heavy must the sentence of those be, who have stript them, and made them go without cloathing? Surely, if not visiting of them in sickness, or in a prison, shall be so severely punished; they shall not escape a most heavy doom, who have cast them into prisons, and have put them under such hardships, as have impaired their health, brought sickness on them, and cut their days in prison, or out of prison.

To put a face upon such wicked practices, men will pretend to retain an honour for CHRIST and religion, while they thus treat his members, walking in his ways, and keeping the truth. They are here represented to say, *When saw we thee an hungred, or a-thirst, or a stranger, or naked, or sick, or in prison, and did not minister unto thee?* ver. 44. As if they should say, Our bread, drink, lodging, clothing, and visits, were indeed refused, but not to CHRIST; but to a set of men, of a bad character; men who turned the world upside down, Acts xvii. 6. who troubled Israel, 2 Kings xviii. 17. an humorous and fantastic sort of people, having laws diverse from all people; factious and rebellious, they did not keep the king's laws, and therefore a very dangerous set of men; it was not for the king's profit to suffer them, Esther iii. 8. But altho' men cast iniquity upon the godly, and give them ill names, that they may treat them as criminals; all these pretences will avail them nothing, in the great day, before the righteous Judge, nor before their own consciences neither; but the real ground of their enmity against the saints, will be found, to their own conviction, to be their enmity against CHRIST himself. This seems to be the import of the objection of the damned, ver. 44. and of the answer to it, ver. 45. *In as much as ye did it not to one of the least of these, ye did it not to me.*

Lastly, Sentence being past on both parties, follows the full execution of the same, ver. 46. *And these shall go away into everlasting punishment, but the righteous into life eternal.* The damned shall get no reprieve, but go to their place without delay; they shall be driven away from the judgment-seat into hell; and the saints shall enter into the king's palace, Ps. xlv. 15. namely, into heaven the seat of the blessed. But our LORD CHRIST, and his glorious company, shall keep the field that day, and see the backs of all their enemies; for the damned go off first.

In this day of the LORD, the great day, shall be the general conflagration, by which those visible heavens, the earth and sea shall pass away. Not that they shall be annihilated, or reduced to nothing, that is not the operation of fire; but they shall be dissolved, and purged by that fire, from all the effects of sin, or of the curse, upon them; and then renewed, and made more glorious and stable. Of this conflagration, the Apostle Peter speaks, 2 Pet. iii. 10. *But the day of the Lord will come, as a thief in the night; in the which the heavens shall pass away with a great noise, and the elements shall melt with fervent heat; the earth also, and the works that are therein shall be burnt up.* See also ver. 7. 12. And of the renewing of the world, he adds, ver. 13. *Neverthe-*

we, according to his promise, look for new heavens, and a new earth, wherein dwelleth righteousness.

It seems most agreeable to the scriptures, and to the nature of the thing, to conceive this conflagration to follow after the general judgment; sentence being past on both parties before it. And I judge it probable, that it will fall in with the putting of the sentence in execution against the damned; so as they shall, according to their sentence, depart, and the heavens and the earth pass away, together and at once, at that furious rebuke from the throne, driving away the damned out of the world, in this fire, to the everlasting fire prepared for the devil and his angels. Even as, in the deluge, with which the Apostle Peter compares the conflagration or burning of the world, 2 Pet. iii. 6, 7. the world itself, and the wicked upon it, perished together; the same water which destroyed the earth, sweeping away the inhabitants. For it is not likely, that the wicked shall at all stand on the new earth, wherein dwelleth righteousness, 2 Pet. iii. 13. and as for this earth, it shall flee away, which seems to denote a very quick dispatch, and it shall flee from his face, who sits on the throne, Rev. xx. 11. *And I saw a great white throne, and him that sat on it, from whose face the earth and the heavens fled away.* The execution of the sentence on the wicked, is also thus expressed: They shall be punished with everlasting destruction from the presence, or from the face of the LORD, 2 Thess. i. 9. The original word is the same in both texts, the which being compared, seem to say, that these creatures abused by the wicked, being left to stand, as witnesses against them in the judgment, are, after sentence past on their abusers, made to pass away with them from the face of the Judge. It is true, the fleeing away of the earth and heaven is narrated, Rev. xx. 11. before the judgment; but that will not prove its going before the judgment, more than the narrating of the judgment, ver. 12. before the resurrection, ver. 13. will prove the judgment to be before it. Further, it is remarkable, in the execution of the sentence, Rev. xx. 14, 15. that not only the reprobate are cast into the lake, but death and hell, are cast into it likewise; all effects of sin, and of the curse, are removed out of the world, for which very cause shall the conflagration be, and they are confined to the place of the damned. Besides all this, it is evident the end of the world is by the conflagration; and the Apostle tells us, 1 Cor. xv. 24, 25. that, *Then cometh the end, when he shall have delivered up the kingdom to God, even the Father: when he shall have put down all rule, and all authority, and power. For he must reign, till he hath put all enemies under his feet.* The which last, as it must be done before the end; so it seems not to be done, but by putting the sentence in execution, past in the day of judgment, against the wicked.

Now, if the burning of Sodom and Gomorrah, that are set forth for an example, Jude 7. was so dreadful; how terrible will that day be, when the whole world shall be at once in flames! how will wretched worldlings look, when their darling world shall be all set on fire? Then shall strong castles, and towering palaces, with all their rich furniture, go up together in one flame with the lowest cottages. What heart can fully conceive the terror of that day to the wicked, when the whole fabric of heaven and earth, shall at once be dissolved by that fire! when that miserable company shall be driven from the tribunal to the pit, with fire within them, and fire without them, and on every hand of them; fire before & behind them, awaiting them in the lake, whither this fire, for ought appears, may follow them!

As for the particular place of this judgment, though some point us to the valley of Jehoshaphat for it, yet our LORD, who knew it, being asked the question by his disciples, *Where Lord?* told them only, *Wheresoever the body is, thither will the eagles be gathered together,* Luke xvii. 37. After which answer, it is too much for men to renew the question. As for the time when it shall be; in vain do men search for what the LORD has purposely kept secret, Acts i. 8. *It is not for you to know the times or the seasons, which the Father has put in his own power.* The Apostle Paul, after having very plainly described the second coming of CHRIST, 1 Thes. iv. 16, 17. adds, chap. v. 2. *But of the times and seasons, brethren, ye have no need that I write unto you. For yourselves know perfectly, that the day of the Lord so cometh, as a thief in the night.* Nevertheless, some in several ages, have made very bold with the time; and several particular years, which are now past, have been given out to the world, for the time of the end, by men who have pried into the secrets of GOD. Time has proclaimed to the world their rashness and folly; and it is likely, they will be no more happy in their conjectures, whose determinate time is yet to come. Let us rest in that he cometh. GOD hath kept the day hid from us, that we may be every day ready for it, Mat. xxv. 13. *Watch therefore, for ye know neither the day nor the hour, wherein the Son of man cometh.* And let us remember, that the last day of our life will determine our state, in the last day of the world; and as we die, so shall we be judged.

I shall now shut up this subject, with some application of what has been said.

USE I. Of comfort to all the saints. Here is abundance of consolation to all who are in the state of grace. Whatever be your afflictions in the world, this day will make up all your losses. *Though you have lain among the pots, yet shall ye be as the wings of a dove covered with silver, and her feathers with yellow gold,* Psalm lxviii. 13. Though the world reproach, judge and condemn you, the Judge will at that day absolve you, and bring forth your righteousness as the light. The world's fools, will then appear to have been the only wise men who were in it. Though the cross be heavy, you may well bear it in expectation of the crown of righteousness, which the righteous Judge will then give you. If the world do despise you, and treat you with the utmost contempt, regard it not; the day cometh wherein you shall sit with CHRIST in his throne. Be not discouraged, by reason of manifold temptations; but resist the devil, in confidence of a full and complete victory; for you shall judge the tempter at last. Though you have had wrestling now with the body of sin and death; yet ye shall get all your enemies under your feet at length, and be presented faultless before the presence of his glory. Let not the terror of that day dispirit you, when you think upon it; let these who have slighted the Judge, and continue enemies to him, and to the way of holiness, droop and hang down their heads, when they think of his coming; but lift ye up your heads with joy, for the last day will be your best day. The Judge is your Head and Husband, your Redeemer, and your Advocate. Ye must appear before the judgment-seat, but ye shall not come into condemnation, John v. 24. His coming will not be against you, but for you. He came in the flesh, to remove the lawful impediments of the spiritual marriage, by his death; he came in the gospel to you, to espouse you to himself; he will come, at the last day, to solemnize the marriage, and take the bride home to his Father's house. *Even so come Lord Jesus.*

USE II. Of Terror to all unbelievers. This may serve to awaken a secure generation, a world lying in wickedness, as if they were never to be called to an account for it; and slighting the Mediator, as if he were not to judge them. Ah! how few have the lively impressions of the judgment to come! most men live, as if what is said of it, from the word, were but idle tales. The profane lives of many, speak the thoughts of it to be far from their hearts, and in very deed make a mock of it before the world, saying in effect, Where is the promise of his coming? The hypocrisy of others, who blind the eyes of the world with a splendid profession, being in appearance CHRIST's sheep, while they are indeed the devil's goats, is an evidence, that the great separation of the sheep from the goats, is very little laid to heart. How do many indulge in secret wickedness, of which they would be ashamed before witnesses; not considering that their most secret thoughts and actions will, at that day, be discovered, before the great congregation! how eagerly are mens hearts set on the world, as if it were to be their everlasting habitation! the solemn assemblies, and public ordinances, wherein the Judge is upon a transaction of peace with the criminals, are undervalued; mens hearts will swim like feathers in the waters of the sanctuary, that will sink, like stones, to the bottom, in cares of this life; they will be very serious in trifles of this world, and trifle in the most serious and weighty things of another world. But O! consider the day that is approaching, in which CHRIST shall come to judgment; the world shall be summoned, by the sound of the last trumpet, to compear before his tribunal. The Judge shall sit on his throne, and all nations shall be sisted before him; the separation shall be made betwixt the godly and the wicked, the books opened, and the dead judged out of them; one party shall be adjudged to everlasting life, and the other to everlasting fire, according to their works.

It would be a sight of admirable curiosity, if thou couldst wrap up thyself in some dark cloud, or hide thyself in the cleft of some high rock, from whence thou mightest espy wicked kings, princes, judges, and great ones of the earth, rising out of their marble tombs, and brought to the bar, to answer for all their cruelty, injustice, oppression, and profanity, without any marks of distinction, but what their wickedness puts upon them: profane, unholy and unfaithful churchmen, pursued with the curses of the ruined people, from their graves to the judgment-seat, and charged with the blood of souls, to whom they gave no faithful warning; mighty men standing trembling before the Judge, unable to recover their wonted boldness, to out-wit him with their subtilties, or defend themselves by their strength; delicate women cast forth of their graves, as abominable branches, dragged to the tribunal, to answer for their ungodly lives; the ignorant, suddenly taught in the law, to their cost; and the learned declared, before the world, fools and laborious triflers; the atheist convinced, the hypocrite unmasked; and the profane, at long run, turned serious about his eternal state: secret murders, adulteries, thefts, cheats, and other works of darkness, which scorned all human search, discovered and laid open before the world, with their most minute circumstances; no regard had to the rich, no pity shewn to the poor; the scales of the world turned; oppressed and despised piety set on high; and prosperous wickedness at last brought low; all, not found in CHRIST, arraigned, convicted, and condemned without respect of persons, and driven from the tribunal to the pit; while these found in him, at that day being absolved before the world, go with him into heaven. Nay, but thou canst not so escape. Thyself, whosoever thou art, not being in CHRIST, must bear a part in this tragical and frightful action.

Sinner, that same LORD CHRIST, whom thou now despisest, whom thou woundest through the sides of his messengers, and before whom thou dost prefer thy lusts, will be thy Judge. And a neglected Saviour will be a severe Judge. O! what mountain, what rock wilt thou get to fall on thee, and hide thee from the face of him that sitteth on the throne? Thou hast now a rock within thee, a heart of adamant, so that thou canst count the darts of the world as stubble, and laugh at the shaking of the spear; but that rock will rent, at the sight of the Judge! that hard heart will then break, and thou shalt weep and wail, when weeping and wailing will be to no purpose. Death's bands will fall off; the grave will vomit thee out; and the mountains shall skip from thee; and the rocks refuse to grind thee to powder. How will these cursed eyes abide the sight of the Judge! Behold he cometh! where is the profane swearers, who tore his wounds? the wretched worldling, now abandoned of his god? the formal hypocrite, who kissed him, and betrayed him? the despiser of the gospel, who sent him away in his messengers groaning, profaned his ordinances, and trampled under foot his precious blood? O, murderer, the slain Man is thy Judge! There is he whom thou didst so maltreat! Behold the neglected Lamb of GOD, appearing as a lion against thee! How will thine heart endure the darts of his fiery looks! That rocky heart now kept out against him, shall then be blown up! that face, which refuseth to blush now, shall then gather blackness! arrows of wrath shall pierce, where arrows of conviction cannot enter now. What wilt thou answer him, when he riseth up, and chargeth thee with thy unbelief and impenitency? Wilt thou say, thou wast not warned? Conscience within thee, will give thee the lie; the secret groans and weariness of those, who warned thee, will witness the contrary. If a child or a fool did tell you, that your house were on fire, you would immediately run to quench it; but, in matters of eternal concern, men will first fill their hearts with prejudices against the messengers, and then cast their message behind their backs. But these silly shifts and pretences will not avail, in the day of the LORD. How will these cursed ears, now deaf to the call of the gospel, inviting sinners, to come to CHRIST, hear the fearful sentence, *Depart from me, ye cursed, into everlasting fire, prepared for the devil and his angels?* No sleepy hearer shall be there; no man's heart will then wander; their hearts and eyes will then be fixed on their misery, which they will not now believe. O that we knew in this our day, the things that belong to our peace.

Lastly, Be exhorted to believe this great truth; and believe it so, as you may prepare for the judgment betimes. Set up a secret tribunal in your own breasts, and often call yourselves to an account there. Make the Judge your friend in time, by closing with him in the offer of the gospel; and give all diligence, that ye may be found in CHRIST, at that day. Cast off the works of darkness, and live, as believing you are, at all times, and in all places, under the eye of your Judge, who will bring every work into judgment, with every secret thing. Be fruitful in good works, knowing that as ye sow, ye shall reap. Study piety towards GOD, righteousness and charity towards men. Lay up in store plenty of works of charity and mercy, towards them who are in distress, especially such as are of the houshold of faith, that they may be produced that day as evidences, that ye belong to CHRIST. Shut not up your bowels of mercy, now, towards the needy; lest ye, then, find no mercy. Take heed, that in all your works, ye be single and sincere; aiming, in them all, at the glory of your LORD, a testimony of your love to him, and obedience to his command. Leave it to hypocrites, who have their reward, to proclaim every man his own goodness, and to sound a trumpet, when they do their alms. It is a base and unchristian spirit, which cannot have satisfaction in a good work, unless it be exposed to the view of others; it is utterly unworthy of one, who believes that the last trumpet shall call together the whole world; before whom the Judge himself shall publish works truly good, how secretly soever they were done. Live in a believing expectation of the coming of the LORD. Let your loins be always girt, and your lamps burning; so when he comes, whether in the last day of your life, or in the last day of the world, ye shall be able to say with joy, *Lo, this is our God, and we have waited for him.*

HEAD V.

The Kingdom of HEAVEN.

MATTHEW xxv. 34:

Then shall the King say unto them on his right hand, Come ye blessed of my Father, inherit the kingdom prepared for you from the foundation of the world.

HAVING, from this portion of Scripture, which the text is a part of, discoursed of the general judgment; and being to speak of the everlasting happiness of the saints, and the everlasting misery of the wicked, from the respective sentences to be pronounced upon them, in the great day; I shall take them in the order wherein they lie before us; the rather that, a sentence is first past upon the righteous, so the execution thereof is first begun, though possibly the other may be fully executed before it be compleated.

The words of the text contain the joyful sentence itself, together with an historical introduction thereto, which gives us an account of the Judge pronouncing the sentence; the King, JESUS CHRIST; the parties on whom it is given, *them on his right hand*; and the time when, *then*, as soon as the trial is over. Of these I have spoken already. It is the sentence itself we are now to consider, *Come, ye blessed of my Father*, &c. Stand a-back, O ye profane goats; have away all unregenerate souls, not united to JESUS CHRIST; this is not for you. Come, O ye saints, brought out of your natural state, into the state of grace; behold here the state of glory awaiting you. Here is glory let down to us in words and syllables; a looking-glass in which you may see your everlasting happiness; a scheme, or draught, of CHRIST's Father's house, wherein there are many mansions.

This glorious sentence bears two things. (1.) The complete happiness to which the saints are adjudged, *the kingdom*. (2.) Their solemn admission to it, *Come ye blessed of my Father, inherit*, &c. *First*, Their complete happiness is a kingdom. A kingdom is the top of worldly felicity; there is nothing on earth greater than a kingdom; therefore the hidden weight of glory in heaven, is held forth to us under that notion. But it is not an ordinary kingdom, it is *the kingdom*; the kingdom of heaven, surpassing all the kingdoms of the earth in glory, honour, profit and pleasure, infinitely more than they do in these excel the low and inglorious condition of a beggar in rags and on a dunghill. *Secondly*, There is a solemn admission of the saints into this their kingdom, *Come ye, inherit the kingdom*. In the view of angels, men and devils, they are invested with royalty, and solemnly inaugurated before the whole world by JESUS CHRIST the heir of all things, who hath all power in heaven and in earth. Their right to the kingdom is solemnly recognized and owned; They are admitted to it, as undoubted heirs of the kingdom, to possess it by inheritance or lot, as the word properly signifies; because of old, inheritances were designed by lot, as Canaan to Israel, GOD's first-born, as they are called, Exod. iv. 22. And because this kingdom is the Father's kingdom, therefore they are openly acknowledged in their admission to it, to be the blessed of CHRIST's Father; the which blessing was given them long before this sentence, but is now solemnly recognized and confirmed to them by the Mediator, in his Father's name. It is observable, he says not, Ye blessed of *the* Father; but ye blessed of *my* Father; to shew us, that all blessings are derived upon us from the Father, the fountain of blessing, as he is the GOD and Father of our LORD JESUS CHRIST, through whom we are blessed, Eph. i. 3. And finally, they are admitted to this kingdom, as that which was prepared for them from the foundation of the world, in God's eternal purpose, before they, or any of them were; that all the world may see eternal life to be the free gift of God.

DOCTRINE,

The Saints shall be made completely happy, in the Possession of the Kingdom of Heaven.

Two things I shall here inquire into, (1.) The nature of this kingdom. (2.) The admission of the saints thereto. And then I shall make practical improvement of the whole.

First, As to the nature of the kingdom of heaven, our knowledge of it is very imperfect! for, *Eye hath not seen, nor ear heard, neither have entered into the heart of man, the things which God hath prepared for them that love him,* 1 Cor. ii. 9. As, by familiar resemblances, parents instruct their little children concerning things, of which otherwise they can have no tolerable notion; so our gracious God, in contemplation of our weakness, is pleased to represent to us heaven's happiness, under similitudes taken from earthly things, glorious in the eyes of men; since naked discoveries of the heavenly glory, divested of earthly resemblances, would be too bright for our weak eyes, and in them we would but lose ourselves. Wherefore now, one can but speak as a child of these things, which the day will fully discover.

The state of glory is represented under the notion of a *kingdom*; a kingdom among men, being that in which the greatest number of earthly good things doth concenter. Now every saint shall, as a king, inherit a kingdom. All Christ's subjects shall be kings, each one with his crown upon his head; not that the great King shall divest himself of his royalty, but he will make all his children partakers of his kingdom.

I. The saints shall have kingly power and authority given. Our Lord gives not empty titles to his favourites; he makes them kings indeed. The dominion of the saints will be a dominion far exceeding that of the greatest monarch ever was in earth. They will be absolute masters over sin, that sometime had dominion over them. They will have a complete rule over their own spirits; an entire management of all their affections and inclinations which now create them so much molestation; the turbulent root of corrupt affections, shall be forever expelled out of that kingdom, and never be able any more to give them the least disturbance. They shall have power over the nations, the ungodly of all nations, and shall rule them with a rod of iron, Rev. ii. 26, 27. The whole world of the wicked shall be broken before them; Satan shall be bruised under their feet, Rom. xvi. 20. He shall never be able to fasten a temptation on them any more: but he will be judged by them; and in their sight cast, with the reprobate crew, into the lake of fire and brimstone. So shall they rule over their oppressors. Having fought the good fight, and got the victory, CHRIST will entertain them as Joshua did his captains, causing them come near, and put their feet upon the necks of kings, Josh. x. 24.

II. They shall have the Ensigns of Royalty. For a throne, CHRIST will grant them to sit with him on his throne, Rev. iii. 12. They will be advanced to the highest honour and dignity they are capable of; and, in the enjoyment of it, they will have an eternal undisturbed repose, after all the tossings they meet with in the world, in their way to the throne. For a crown, they shall receive a crown of glory, that fadeth not away, 1 Pet. v. 4. Not a crown of flowers, as subjects, being conquerors, or victors, sometimes have got; such a crown quickly fades; but their crown never fadeth. Not a crown of gold, such as earthly kings do wear; even a crown of gold is often stained, and can never make them happy who wear it. But it shall be a crown of glory. A crown of glory is a crown of life, Rev. ii. 10. that life which knows no end; a crown which death can never make to fall off one's head. It must be an abiding crown; for it is a crown of righteousness, 2 Tim. iv. 8. It was purchased for them by CHRIST's righteousness, which is imputed to them; they are qualified for it by inherent righteousness; GOD's righteousness or faithfulness secures it to them. They shall have a sceptre, a rod of iron, Rev. ii. 27. terrible to all the wicked world. And a sword too, a two-edged sword in their hand, to execute vengeance upon the heathen, and punishment upon the people, Psalm cxlix. 6, 7. They shall have royal apparel. The royal robes in this kingdom are white robes, Rev. iii. 4. *They shall walk with me in white.* And these last do, in a very particular manner, point at the inconceivable glory of the state of the saints in heaven.

The LORD is pleased often to represent unto us the glorious state of the saints, under the notion of their being clothed in white garments. It is promised to the overcomer, that he shall be clothed in white raiment, Rev. iii. 5. The elders about the throne are clothed in white raiment, chap. iv. 4. The multitude before the throne are clothed with white robes, chap. vii. 9. arrayed in white robes, ver. 13. made white in the blood of the Lamb, ver. 14. I own, the last two testimonies adduced, do respect the state of the saints on earth; but withal the terms are borrowed from the state of the church in heaven. All garments, properly so called, being badges of sin and shame, shall be laid aside by the saints, when they come to their state of glory. But if we consider on what occasions white garments were wont to be put on, we shall find much of heaven under them.

First, The Romans, when they manumitted their bond-servants, gave them a white garment, as a badge of their freedom. So shall the saints that day get on white robes; for it is the day of the glorious liberty of the children of GOD, Rom. viii. 21. the day of the redemption of their body, ver. 23. They shall no more see the house of bondage, nor lie any more among the pots. If we compare the state of the saints on earth, with that of the wicked, it is indeed a state of freedom; whereas the other is a state of slavery; but in comparison with their state in heaven, it is but a servitude. A saint on earth is indeed a young prince, and heir to the crown; but his motto may be, *I serve*, for he differeth nothing from a servant, though he be lord of all, Gal. iv. 1. What are the groans of a saint, the sordid and base work he is sometimes found employed in, the black and tattered garments he walks in, but badges of this comparative servitude? But from the day the saints come to the crown, they receive their compleat freedom, and serve no more. They shall be fully freed from sin, which of all evils is the worst, both in itself, and in their apprehensions too: How great then must that freedom be, when these Egyptians whom they see to-day, they shall see them no more again forever? They shall be free from all temptation to sin; Satan can have no access to tempt them any more, by himself, nor by his agents. A full answer will then be given to that petition they have so often repeated, *Lead us not into temptation.* No hissing serpent can come into the paradise above; no snare nor trap can be laid there, to catch the feet of the saints; they may walk there fearlessly, for they can be in no hazard, there are no lions dens, no mountains of the leopards there. They shall be set beyond the possibility of sinning, for they shall be confirmed in goodness. It will be the consummate freedom of their will to be unalterably determined to good. And they shall be freed from all the effects of sin; *There shall be no more death, neither sorrow, nor crying, neither shall there be any more pain*, Rev. xxi. 4. What kingdom is like unto this? Death makes its way now into a palace, as easily as into a cottage; sorrow fills the heart of one who wears a crown on his head; royal robes are no fence against pain, and crying by reason of pain. But in this kingdom no misery can have place. All reproaches shall be wiped off; and never shall a tear drop any more from their eyes. They shall not complain of desertions again; the LORD will never hide his face from them: but the Sun of righteousness shining upon them in his meridian brightness, will dispel all clouds, and give them an everlasting day, without the least mixture of darkness. A deluge of wrath, after a fearful thunder-clap from the throne, will sweep away the wicked from before the judgment-seat, into the lake of fire; but they are, in the first place, like Noah brought into the ark, and out of harm's way.

Secondly, White raiment hath been a token of purity. Therefore the Lamb's wife is arrayed in fine linen, clean and white, Rev. xix. 8. And those who stood before the throne, washed their robes, and made them white in the blood of the Lamb, chap. vii. 14. The saints shall then put on the robes of perfect purity, and shine in spotless holiness, like the sun in his strength, without the least cloud to intercept his light. Absolute innocence shall then be restored, and every appearance of sin banished far from his kingdom. The guilt of sin, and the reigning power of it, are now taken away in the saints; nevertheless sin dwelleth in them, Rom. vii. 20. But then it shall be no more in them; the corrupt nature will be quite removed; that root of bitterness will be plucked up, and no vestiges of it left in their souls; their nature shall be altogether pure and sinless. There shall be no more darkness in their minds; but the understanding of every saint, when he is come to his kingdom, will be as a globe of pure and unmixed light. There shall not be the least aversion to good, or inclination to evil, in their wills; but they will be brought to a perfect conformity to the will of God, blest with angelical purity, and fixed therein. Their affections shall not be liable to the least disorder or irregularity; it will cost them no trouble to keep them right; they will get such a set of purity, as they can never lose. They will be so refined from all earthly dross, as never to savour more of any thing but heaven. Were it possible they should be set again amidst the ensnaring objects of an evil world, they should walk among them without the least defilement; as the sun shines on the dunghill, yet untainted, and as the angels preserved their purity in the midst of Sodom. Their graces shall then be perfected, and all the imperfections now cleaving to them, done away. There will be no more ground for complaints of weakness of grace; none in that kingdom shall complain of an ill heart, or a corrupt nature. *It doth not yet appear what we shall be, but----when he shall appear, we shall be like him*, 1 John iii. 2.

Thirdly, Among the Jews, those who desired to be admitted into the priestly office, being tried, and found to be of the priest's line, and without blemish, were clothed in white, and enrolled among the priests. This seems to be alluded to, Rev. iii. 5. *He that overcometh---the saints shall be clothed in white raiment, and I will not blot out his name out of the book of life.* The saints are not kings only, but priests also; for they are a

Royal Priesthood, 1 Pet. ii. 9. They will be priests upon their thrones. They are judicially found descended from the great High-Priest of their profession, begotten of him by his Spirit, of the incorruptible seed of the word, and without blemish; so the trial being over, they are admitted to be priests in the temple above, that they may dwell in the house of the LORD for ever. There is nothing upon earth more glorious than a kingdom, nothing more venerable than the priesthood; and both meet together in the glorified state of the saints. The general assembly of the first-born, Heb. xii. 23. whose is the priesthood and the double portion, appearing in their white robes of glory, will be a reverend and glorious company. That day will shew them to be the persons, whom the LORD has chosen out of all the tribes of the earth, to be near unto him, and to enter into his temple, even into his holy place. Their priesthood, begun on earth, shall be brought to its perfection, while they shall be employed in offering the sacrifice of praise to GOD and the Lamb, for ever and ever. They got not their portion, in the earth, with the rest of the tribes; but the LORD himself was their portion, and will be their double portion, thro' the ages of eternity.

Fourthly, They were wont to wear white raiment, in a time of triumph; to the which also there seems to be an allusion, Rev. iii. 5. *He that overcometh, the same shall be clothed in white raiment.* And what is heaven but an everlasting triumph! None get thither, but such as fight, and overcome too. Though Canaan was given to the Israelites, as an inheritance, they behoved to conquer it, ere they could be possessors of it. The saints, in this world, are in the field of battle often in red garments, rolled in blood; but the day approacheth, in which they shall stand before the throne, and before the Lamb, clothed with white robes, and palms in their hands, Rev. vii. 9. having obtained a complete victory over all their enemies. The palm was used as a sign of victory! because that tree, oppressed with weights, yielded not, but rather shooteth upwards. And palm-trees were carved on the doors of the most holy place, 1-Kings vi. 32. which was a special type of heaven; for heaven is the place, which the saints are received into, as conquerors.

Behold the joy and peace of the saints, in their white robes! The joy arising from the view of past dangers, and of riches and honours gained at the very door of death, do most sensibly touch one's heart; and this will be an ingredient in the everlasting happiness of the saints, which could have had no place, in the heaven of innocent Adam, and his sinless offspring, supposing him to have stood. Surely the glorified saints will not forget the entertainment they met with in the world: it will be for the glory of GOD to remember it, and also for the heightening of their joy. The Sicilian king, by birth a son of a potter, acted a wise part, in that he would be served at his table, with earthern vessels; the which could not but put an additional sweetness in his meals, not to be relished by one born air to the crown. Can ever meat be so sweet to any as to the hungry man? Or can any have such a relish of plenty, as he who has been under pinching straits? The more difficulties the saints have passed through, in their way to heaven, the place will be the sweeter to them, when they come at it. Every happy stroke, struck in the spiritual warfare, will be a jewel in their crown of glory. Each victory obtained against sin, Satan, and the world, will raise their triumphant joy the higher. The remembrance of the cross will sweeten the crown; and the memory of their travel through the wilderness, will put an additional verdure on the fields of glory, while they walk through them, minding the day, when they went mourning without the sun.

And now that they appear triumphing in white robes, it is a sign they have obtained an honourable peace; such a peace as their enemies can disturb no more. So every thing peculiarly adapted to their militant condition is laid aside. The sword is laid down: and they betake themselves to the pen of a ready writer, to commemorate the praises of him, by whom they overcame. Public ordinances, preaching, sacraments, shall be honourably laid aside; there is no temple there, Rev. xix. 22. Sometimes these were sweet to them; but the travellers being all got home, the inns, appointed for their entertainment by the way, are shut up; the candles are put out, when the sun is risen; and the tabernacle, used in the wilderness, is folded up, when the temple of glory is come in its room. Many of the saints duties will then be laid aside; as one gives his staff out of his hand, when he is come to the end of his journey. Praying shall then be turned to praising; and, there being no sin to confess, no wants to seek the supply of; confession and petition shall be swallowed in everlasting thanksgiving. There will be no mourning in heaven; they have sown in tears, the reaping time of joy is come, and GOD shall wipe away all tears from their eyes, Rev. xxi. 4. No need of mortification there; and self-examination is then at an end. They will not need to watch any more, the danger is over. Patience has had its perfect work, and there is no use for it there. Faith is turned into sight, and hope is swallowed up in the ocean of sensible and full enjoyment. All the rebels are subdued, the saints quietly set on their throne; and so the forces, needful in the time of the spiritual warfare, are disbanded; and they carry on their triumph in profoundest peace.

Lastly, White garments were worn on festival days, in token of joy. And so shall the saints be clothed in white raiment; for they shall keep an everlasting Sabbath to the LORD, Heb. iv. 9. *There remaineth therefore a rest, or keeping of a Sabbath, to the people of God.* The Sabbath, in the esteem of saints, is the queen of days; and they shall have an endless *Sabbatism* in the kingdom of heaven; so shall their garments be always white. They will have an eternal *rest*, with an uninterrupted joy; for heaven is not a resting place where men may sleep out an eternity, there they rest not day nor night; but their work is their rest and continual recreation, and toil and weariness have no place there. They rest there in GOD, who is the centre of their souls. Here they find the complement, or satisfaction of all their desires; having the full enjoyment of GOD, and uninterrupted communion with him. This is the point, unto the which till the soul come, it will always be restless: but, that point reached, it rests; for he is the last end, and the soul can go no farther. It cannot understand, will, nor desire more; but in him it has what is commensurable to its boundless desires. This is the happy end of all the labours of the saints; their toil and sorrows issue in a joyful rest. The Chaldeans measuring the natural day, put the day first, and the night last: but the Jews counted the night first, and the day last. Even so, the wicked begin with a day of rest and pleasure, but end with a night of everlasting toil and sorrow; but GOD's people have their gloomy night first, and then comes their day of eternal rest. The which, Abraham, in the parable, observed to the rich man in hell, Luke xvi. 25. *Son, remember that thou in thy life-time receivedst thy good things, and likewise Lazarus evil things; but now he is comforted, and thou art tormented.*

III. If one enquires where the kingdom of the saints lies? It is not in this world; it lies in a better country, that is, an heavenly, Heb. xi. 16, a country better than the best of this world, namely, the heavenly Canaan, Immanuel's land, where nothing is wanting to complete the happiness of the inhabitants. This is the happy country, blest with a perpetual spring, and which yieldeth all things, for necessity, conveniency and delight. There men shall eat angel's food; they shall be entertained with the hidden manna, Rev. ii. 17. without being set to the painful gathering of it. They will be fed to the full, with the product of the land falling into their mouths, without the least toil to them. That land enjoys an everlasting day, for there is no night there, Rev. xxi. 25. An eternal sun-shine beautifies this better country, but there is no scorching heat there. No clouds shall be seen there for ever; yet it is not a land of drought; the trees of the LORD's planting, are set by the rivers of water, and shall never want moisture; for they will have an eternal supply of the Spirit, by JESUS CHRIST, from his Father. This is the country from whence our LORD came, and whither he is gone again; the country which all the holy patriarchs and prophets had their eye upon, while on earth; and which all the saints, who have gone before us, have fought their way to; and unto which, the martyrs have joyfully swimmed, through a sea of blood. This earth is the place of the saints pilgrimage: that is their country, where they find their everlasting rest.

IV. The Royal City is that great city, the holy Jerusalem, described at large, Rev. xxi. 10, &c. It is true, some learned divines place this city in the earth, but the particulars of the description seem to me to favour those most, who point us to the other world for it. The saints shall reign in that city, whose wall is of jasper, ver. 16. and the foundations of the wall garnished with all manner of precious stones, ver. 19. and the street of pure gold, ver. 21. so that their feet shall be set on that, which the men of this world set their hearts upon. This is the city GOD has prepared for them, Heb. xi. 16. A city that hath foundations, ver. 10. A continuing city, chap. xiii. 14. which shall stand and flourish, when all the cities of the world are laid in ashes; and which shall not be moved, when the foundations of the world are overturned. It is a city that never changeth its inhabitants; none of them shall ever be removed out of it; for life and immortality reign there, and no death can enter into it. It is blessed with a perfect and perpetual peace, and can never be in the least disturbed. Nothing from without can annoy it; the gates therefore are not shut at all by day, and there is no night there, Rev. xxi. 25. There can nothing from within trouble it. No want of provision there; no scarcity; no discord among the inhabitants. Whatever contentions are among the saints now, no vestige of their former jarrings shall remain there. Love to GOD, and to one another, shall be perfected: and these of them who stood at great distance here, will joyfully embrace and delight in one-another there.

V. The Royal Palace is CHRIST's Father's house; in which are many mansions, John xiv. 2. There shall the saints dwell for ever. This is the house prepared for all the heirs of glory, even these of them who dwell in the meanest cottage now, or have not where to lay their heads. As our LORD calls his saints to a kingdom, he will provide them a house suitable to the dignity he puts upon them. Heaven will be a convenient, spacious, and glorious house, for those whom the King delighteth to honour. Never was a house purchased at so dear a rate as this, being the purchase of the Mediator's blood! And no less could it be afforded for to them. Never was there so much ado, to fit inhabitants for a house. The saints were, by nature, utterly unfit for this house; and human art and industry could not make them meet for it. But the Father gives the designed inhabitants to his Son, to be by him redeemed; the Son pays the price of their redemption, even his own precious blood; that, with the allowance of justice, they may have access to the house; and the holy Spirit sanctifies them by his grace; that they may be meet to come in thither, where no unclean thing can enter. And no marvel, for it is the King's palace, they enter into, Psalm xlv. 15. The house of the kingdom, where the great King keeps his court; where he has his throne, and shews forth his glory, in a singular manner, beyond what mortals can conceive.

VI. Paradise is their Palace-garden. *This day shalt thou be with me in Paradise*, said our Saviour to the penitent thief on the cross, Luke xxiii. 43. Heaven is a Paradise for pleasure and delight; where there is both wood and water: *A pure river, of water of life, clear as crystal, proceeding out of the throne of God, and of the Lamb; and of either side of the river, the tree of life, which bears twelve manner of fruits, and yields her fruit every month*, Rev. xxii. 1, 2. How happy might innocent Adam have been in the earthly Paradise, where there was nothing wanting for necessity nor delight! Eden was the most pleasant spot of the uncorrupted earth, and Paradise the most pleasant spot of Eden; but what is earth in comparison of heaven? The glorified saints are advanced to the heavenly Paradise. There they shall not only see, but eat of the tree of life, which is in the midst of the Paradise of GOD, Rev. ii. 7. They shall behold the Mediator's glory, and be satisfied with his goodness. No flaming sword will be there, to keep the way of that tree of life; but they shall freely eat of it, and live for ever. And they shall drink of the river of pleasures, Psalm xxxvi. 8. these sweetest and purest pleasures, the which Immanuel's land doth afford; and shall swim in an ocean of unmixed delight for evermore.

VII. They shall have Royal Treasures, sufficient to support the dignity they are advanced unto. Since the street of the royal city is pure gold, and the twelve gates thereof are twelve pearls; their treasure must be of that which is better than gold or pearl. It is an eternal weight of glory, 2 Cor. iv. 17. O precious treasure! a treasure not liable to insensible corruption, by moths or rust; a treasure which none can steal from them, Matth. vi. 20. Never did any kingdom afford such a precious treasure, nor a treasure of such variety; for, *He that overcometh, shall inherit all things*, Rev. xxi. 7. No treasures on earth are stored with all things; if they were all put together in one, there would be far more valuable things wanting in

one, there would be far more valuable things wanting in that one, than found in it. This then is the peculiar treasure of these kings, who inherit the kingdom of heaven. They shall want nothing, that may contribute to their full satisfaction. Now they are rich in hope; but then they will have their riches in hand. Now all things are theirs in respect of right; then all shall be theirs in possession. They may go forver through Immanuel's land, and behold the glory and riches thereof, with the satisfying thought, that all they see is their own. It is pity these should ever be uneasy under the want of earthly good things, who may be sure, they shall inherit all things at length.

VIII. Albeit there is no material **Temple** therein, no mediate serving of GOD, in the use of ordinances, as here on earth; yet, as for this kingdom, *The Lord God Almighty, and the Lamb, are the Temple of it*, Rev. xxi. 22. As the Temple was the glory of Canaan, so will the celestial temple be the glory of heaven. The saints shall be brought in thither as a royal Priesthood, to dwell in the house of the LORD for ever; for JESUS CHRIST will then make every saint a pillar in the temple of GOD, and he shall go no more out, Rev. iii. 12. as the Priests and Levites did, in their courses, go out of the material temple. There the saints shall have the cloud of glory, the divine presence, with most intimate, uninterrupted communion with GOD; there they shall have JESUS CHRIST as the true ark, wherein the fiery law shall be for ever hid from their eyes; and the mercy-seat, from which nothing shall be breathed, but everlasting peace and good-will towards them: the cherubims, the society of holy angels, who shall join with them in eternal admiration of the mystery of CHRIST: the golden candlestick, with its seven lamps; for the glory of GOD doth lighten it, and the Lamb is the light thereof, Rev. xxi. 23. The incense-altar, in the intercession of CHRIST, who ever liveth to make intercession for them, Heb. vii. 25. eternally exhibiting the merits of his death and sufferings, and efficaciously willing for ever, that these, whom the Father hath given him, be with him; and the shew-bread table, in the perpetual feast, they shall have together, in the enjoyment of GOD. This leads me more particularly to consider,

IX. The Society in this kingdom. What would royal power and authority, ensigns of royalty, richest treasures, and all other advantages of a kingdom, avail without comfortable society? Some crowned heads have had but a sorry life through the want of it; their palaces have been but unto them as prisons, and their badges of honour, as chains on a prisoner; while hated of all, they had none they could trust in, or whom they could have comfortable fellowship with. But the chief part of heaven's happiness, lies in the blessed society the saints shall have there. For clearing of which, consider these few things:

First, The society of the Saints, among themselves, will be no small part of heaven's happiness. The communion of saints on earth, is highly prized by all those who are travelling through the world unto Zion; and companions in sin can never have such true pleasure and delight in one another as sometime the Lord's people have in praying together, and conversing about these things, which the world is a stranger to. Here the saints are but few in company, at best; and some of them are so polled, as they seem to themselves to dwell alone; having no access to such, as they could freely unbosom themselves to, in the matter of their spiritual case. They sigh and say, *Wo is me, for I am as when they have gathered the summer-fruits---there is no cluster to eat---the good man is perished out of the earth*, Mic. vii. 1, 2. But in the general assembly of the first-born in heaven, none of all the saints, who ever were, or will be on the earth, shall be missing. They will be all of them together in one place, all possess one kingdom, and all sit down together to the marriage-supper of the Lamb. Here, the best of the saints want not their sinful imperfections, making their society less comfortable; but there they shall be perfect, without spot or wrinkle, or any such thing, Eph. v. 27. And all natural, as well as sinful imperfections are then done away; *They shall shine as the brightness of the firmament*, Dan. xii. 3.

There we will see Adam and Eve in the heavenly paradise, freely eating of the tree of life; Abraham, Isaac and Jacob, and all the holy patriarchs, no more wandering from land to land, but come to their everlasting rest; all the prophets feeding their eyes on the glory of him, of whose coming they prophesied; the twelve Apostles of the Lamb, sitting on their twelve thrones; all the holy martyrs in their long white robes with their crowns on their heads; the godly kings advanced to a kingdom which cannot be moved; and them that turn many to righteousness, shining as the stars for ever and ever. There will we see our godly friends, relations and acquaintances, pillars in the temple of God, to go no more out from us. And it is more than probable, that the saints will know one another in heaven; that, at least, they will know their friends, relatives, and these they were acquainted with on earth, and such as have been most eminent in the church; howbeit that knowledge will be purged from all earthly thoughts and affections. This seems to be included in that perfection of happiness, to which the saints shall be advanced there. If Adam knew who and what Eve was at first sight, when the Lord God brought her to him, Gen. ii. 23, 24. why should one question, but husbands and wives, parents and children, will know each other in glory?

If the Thessalonians, converted by Paul's ministry, shall be his crown of rejoicing, in the presence of our LORD JESUS CHRIST, at his coming, 1 Thes. ii. 19. Why may not one conclude, that ministers shall know their people, and people their ministers in heaven? And if the disciples, on the mount of transfiguration, knew Moses and Elias, whom they had never seen before, Mat. xvii. 19. we have ground to think, we shall know them too, and such as they, when we come to heaven. The communion of saints shall be most intimate there; they shall sit down with Abraham, Isaac, and Jacob, in the kingdom of heaven, Mat. viii. 11. Lazarus was carried by the angels into Abraham's bosom, Luke xvi. 23. which denotes most intimate and familiar society. And though diversity of tongues shall cease, 1 Cor. xiii. 8. I make no question, but there will be an use of speech in heaven; and that the saints will glorify GOD in their bodies there, as well as in their spirits, speaking forth his praises with an audible voice. (As for the language, we shall understand what it is, when we come thither.) When Paul was caught up to the third heaven, the seat of the blessed, he heard there unspeakable words, which it is not lawful for a man to utter, 2 Cor. xii. 4. Moses and Elias, on the mount with CHRIST, talked with him, Mat. xvii. 3. and spake of his decease which he should accomplish at Jerusalem, Luke ix. 31.

Secondly, The saints will have the society of all the holy angels there. An innumerable company of angels shall be companions to them in their glorified state. Happy were the shepherds, who heard the song of the heavenly host, when CHRIST was born; but thrice happy they, who shall join their voices with theirs, in the choir of saints and angels in heaven, when he shall be glorified in all, who shall be about him there. Then shall we be brought acquainted with the blessed spirits, who never sinned. How bright will these morning-stars shine in the holy place! they were ministering spirits to the heirs of salvation, loved them for their LORD and Master's sake; encamped round about them, to preserve them from danger; how joyfully will they welcome them to their everlasting habitations; and rejoice to see them come at length to their kingdom, as the tutor doth the prosperity of his pupils? The saints shall be no more afraid of them, as sometime they were wont to be; they shall then have put off mortality, and infirmities of the flesh, and be themselves, as the angels of GOD, fit to entertain communion and fellowship with these shining ones. And both being brought under one head, the LORD JESUS CHRIST; they shall join in the praises of GOD, and of the Lamb, *Saying, with a loud voice, Worthy is the Lamb that was slain,* &c. Rev. v 11,12. Whether the angels shall, as some think, assume airy bodies, that they may be seen by the bodily eyes of the saints, and be in nearer capacity to converse with them, I know not; but as they want not ways of converse amongst themselves, we have reason to think, that conversation betwixt them and the saints, shall not be for ever blocked up.

Lastly, They shall have society with the LORD himself in heaven, glorious communion with GOD and CHRIST, which is the perfection of happiness. I chuse to speak of communion with GOD, and the man CHRIST, together; because as we derive our grace from the Lamb, so we will derive our glory from him too; the man CHRIST being, if I may be allowed the expression, the centre of the divine glory in heaven, from whence it is diffused unto all the saints. This seems to be taught us by these scriptures, which express heaven's happiness by being with CHRIST. Luke xxiii. 43. *This day shalt thou be with me in paradise.* John xxvii. 24. *Father, I will that these also, whom thou hast given me, be with me.* And remarkable to this purpose is what follows, *that they may behold my glory.* 1 Thess. iv. 17. *So shall we ever be with the Lord,* viz. the LORD CHRIST, whom we shall meet in the air. This also seems to be the import of these scriptures, wherein GOD and the Lamb, the slain Saviour, are jointly spoken of, in the point of the happiness of the saints in heaven, Rev. vii. 17. *For the Lamb which is in the midst of the throne, shall feed them, and shall lead them unto living fountains of waters; and God shall wipe away all tears from their eyes.* Chap. xxi. 3. *Behold the tabernacle of God is with men, and he will dwell with them,* viz. as in a tabernacle, so the word signifies, that is, in the flesh of CHRIST, compare John i. 14. and 22. *The Lord God Almighty, and the Lamb are the temple of it.* Here lies the chief happiness of the saints in heaven, that without which they could never be happy, though lodged in that glorious place, and blessed with the society of angels there. What I will venture to say of it, shall be comprised in three things.

1st, The saints in heaven shall have the glorious presence of GOD, and of the Lamb; *God himself shall be with them,* Rev. xxi. 3. and they shall be ever with the LORD. GOD is every-where present, in respect of his essence; the saints militant have his special gracious presence; but in heaven they have his glorious presence. There they are brought near to the throne of the great King, and stand before him, where he shews his inconceivable glory. There they have the tabernacle of GOD, on which the cloud of glory rests, the all glorious human nature of CHRIST, wherein the fulness of the Godhead dwells, not vailed as in the days of his humiliation, but shining through that blessed flesh, that all the saints may behold his glory, and making that body more glorious than a thousand suns; so that the city has no need of the sun, nor of the moon, but the glory of

God doth lighten it, and the Lamb is *the light thereof*, properly, *the candle thereof*, Rev. xxi. 23. *i. e.* The Lamb is the luminary, or luminous body, which gives light to the city; as the sun and moon now give light to the world, or as a candle lightens a dark room; and the light proceeding from that glorious luminary, for the city is the glory of God. Sometime that candle burnt very dim, it was hid under a bushel, in the time of his humiliation; but that, now and then, it darted out some rays of this light, which dazzled the eyes of the spectators; but now it is set on high, in the city of God, where it shines, and shall shine forever, in perfection of glory. It was sometimes laid aside, as a stone disallowed of the builders; but now it is, and for ever will be, the light or luminary of that city; and that, like unto a stone most precious, even like a jasper stone clear as crystal, ver. 11.

Who can conceive the happiness of the saints, in the presence-chamber of the great King, where he sits in his chair of state, making his glory eminently to appear in the man Christ? His gracious presence makes a mighty change upon the saints in this world; his glorious presence in heaven then must needs screw up their graces to their perfection, and elevate their capacities. The saints do experience, that the presence of God now with them in his grace, can make a little heaven of a sort of hell; how great then must the glory of heaven be, by his presence there in his glory! If a candle, in some sort, beautifies a cottage or prison, how will the shining sun beautify a palace or paradise! The gracious presence of God made a wilderness lightsome to Moses, the valley of the shadow of death to David, a fiery furnace to the three children: What a ravishing beauty shall then arise from the sun of righteousness, shining in his meridian brightness, on the street of the city laid with pure gold? The glorious presence of God in heaven, will put a glory on the saints themselves. The pleasant garden hath no beauty, when the darkness of the night sits down on it; but the shining sun puts a glory on the blackest mountains; so these who are now as bottles in the smoak, when set in the glorious presence of God, will be glorious both in soul and body.

edly, The saints in heaven shall have the full enjoyment of God and of the Lamb. This is it that perfectly satisfies the rational creature; and here is the saints everlasting rest. This will make up all their wants, and fill the desires of their souls, which, after all here obtained, still cry, *Give, give*, not without some anxiety; because, though they do enjoy God, yet they do not enjoy him fully. As to the way and manner of this enjoyment, our Lord tells us, John xvii. 3. *This is life eternal, that they may know thee, the only true God, and Jesus Christ, whom thou hast sent.* Now, there are two ways, how a declable object is known most perfectly and satisfyingly; the one is by sight, the other by experience: sight satisfies the understanding, and experience satisfies the will. Accordingly one may say, that the saints enjoy GOD, and the Lamb, in heaven, (1.) By an intuitive knowledge. (2.) By an experimental knowledge, both of them perfect, I mean, in respect of the capacity of the creature; for, otherwise, a creature's perfect knowledge of an infinite Being is impossible. The saints below, enjoy GOD, in that knowledge they have of him by report, from his holy word, which they believe: they see him likewise, darkly, in the glass of ordinances, which do, as it were, represent the bridegroom's picture, or shadow, while he is absent; they have also some experimental knowledge of him, they taste that GOD is good, and that the LORD is gracious. But the saints above shall not need a good report of the King, they shall see himself; therefore faith ceaseth; they will behold his own face; therefore ordinances are no more; there is no need of a glass; they shall drink, and drink abundantly of that whereof they have tasted; and so hope ceaseth, for they are at the utmost bounds of their desires.

1. The saints in heaven shall enjoy GOD and the Lamb, by sight; and that in a most perfect manner, 1 Cor. xiii. 12. *For now we see, through a glass, darkly; but then face to face.* Here our sight is but mediate, as by a glass; in which we see not things themselves, but the images of things; but there we shall have an immediate view of GOD and the Lamb. Here our knowledge is but obscure; there it shall be clear, without the least mixture of darkness. The LORD doth now converse with his saints, through the lattesses of ordinances; but then shall they be in the presence-chamber with him. There is a vail now on the glorious face, as to us; but when we come to the upper house, that vail, through which some rays of beauty are now darted, will be found entirely taken off; and then shall glorious excellencies and perfections, not seen in him by mortals, be clearly discovered, for we shall see his face, Rev. xxii. 4. The phrase seems to be borrowed from the honour put on some in the courts of monarchs, to be attendants on the king's person. We read, Jer. liii. 25. of seven men of them that were (Heb. *Seers of the king's face,* i. e. as we read it) near the king's person. O unspeakable glory! the great king keeps his court in heaven; and the saints shall all be his courtiers, ever near the King's person, seeing his face: *The throne of God, and of the Lamb shall be in it; and his servants shall serve him, and they shall see his face,* Rev. xxii. 3, 4.

(1.) They shall see JESUS CHRIST with their bodily eyes, since he will never lay aside the human nature. They will always behold that glorious blessed body, which is personally united to the divine nature, and exalted far above principalities and powers, and every name that is named. There we will see, with our eyes, that very body which was born of Mary at Bethlehem, and crucified at Jerusalem betwixt two thieves; that blessed head that was crowned with thorns; the face that was spit upon; the hands and feet that were nailed to the cross; all shining with unconceivable glory. The glory of the Man CHRIST, will attract the eyes of all the saints; and he will be for ever admired in all them that believe, 2 Thes. i. 10. Were each star in the heavens, shining as the sun in its meridian brightness, and the light of the sun so increased, as the stars, in that case, should bear the same proportion to the sun in point of light, that they do now; it might possibly be some faint resemblance of the glory of the Man CHRIST, in comparison with that of the saints; for though the saints shall shine forth as the sun; yet not they, but the Lamb, shall be the light of the city. The wise men fell down, and worshipped him, when they saw him a young child, with Mary his mother, in the house. But O! what a ravishing sight will it be, to see him in his kingdom, on his throne, at the Father's right hand! *The Word was made flesh*, John i. 14. and the glory of GOD shall shine through that flesh, and the joys of heaven spring out from it, unto the saints, who shall see and enjoy GOD, in CHRIST. For since the union betwixt CHRIST and the saints, is never dissolved, but they continue his members for ever; and the members cannot draw their life, but from their Head; seeing that which is dependent on the head, as to vital influence, is no member: therefore JESUS CHRIST will remain the everlasting bond of union betwixt GOD and the saints; from whence their eternal life shall spring, John xvii. 2, 3. 22, 23. *Thou hast given him power over all flesh, that he should give eternal life to as many as thou hast given him. And this is life eternal, that they might know thee, the only true God, &c. And the glory which thou gavest me, I have given them, that they may be one, even as we are one; I in them, and thou in me, that they may be made perfect in one.* Wherefore, the immediate enjoyment of GOD in heaven, is to be understood in respect of the laying aside of word and sacraments, and such external means as we enjoy GOD by, in this world; but not as if the saints should then cast off their dependence on their Head, for vital influences; nay, *The Lamb, which is in the midst of the throne, shall feed them; and shall lead them unto living fountains of waters*, Rev. vii. 17.

Now, when we shall behold him, who died for us, that we might live for evermore, whose matchless love made him swim through the read sea of GOD's wrath, to make a path in the midst of it for us, by which we might pass safely to Canaan's land; then we will see what a glorious one he was, who suffered all this for us; what entertainment he had in the upper house; what hallelujahs of angels could not hinder him to hear the groans of a perishing multitude on earth, and to come down for their help; and what a glory he laid aside for us. Then will we be more able to comprehend, with all saints, what is the breadth, and length, and depth, and heighth: and to know the love of CHRIST, which passeth knowledge, Eph. iii. 19. When the saints shall remember, that the waters of wrath he was plunged into, are the wells of salvation, from whence they draw all their joy; that they have got the cup of salvation, in exchange of the cup of wrath his Father gave him to drink, which his sinless human nature shivered at; how will their hearts leap within them, burn with seraphic love, like coals of juniper, and the arch of heaven ring with their songs of salvation? The Jews, celebrating the feast of tabernacles, which was the most joyful of all their feasts, and lasted seven days, went once every day about the altar, singing hosanna, with their myrtle, palm, and willow branches in their hand, the two former signs of victory, the last of chastity, in the mean time bending their boughs towards the altar. When the saints are presented as a chaste virgin to CHRIST, and, as conquerors, have got their palms in their hands, how joyfully will they compass the altar evermore; and sing their hosannas, or rather their hallelujahs, about it, bending their palms towards it, acknowledging themselves to owe all unto the Lamb that was slain, and redeemed them with his blood! And to this agrees what John saw, Rev. vii. 9, 10. *A great multitude----stood before the throne, and before the Lamb, clothed with white robes, and palms in their hands; and cried with a loud voice, saying, Salvation to our God, which sitteth upon the throne, and unto the Lamb.*

(2.) They shall see GOD, Matt. v. 8. They will be happy in seeing the Father, Son, and Holy Ghost, not with their bodily eyes, in respect of which GOD is invisible, 1 Tim. i. 17. but, with the eyes of their understanding; being blest with the most perfect, full, and clear knowledge of GOD and divine things, which the creature is capable of. This is called *the beatific vision*, and is the perfection of the Understanding, the utmost term thereof. It is but an obscure delineation of the glory of GOD, that mortals can have on earth; a sight, as it were, of his back-part, Exod. xxxiii. 23. But there they will see his face, Rev. xxii. 4. They shall see him in the fulness of his glory, and behold him fixedly; whereas it is but a passing view they can have of him here, Exod. xxxiv. 6. There is a vast difference betwixt the sight of a king in his night-clothes, quickly passing by us; and a fixed leisure view of him sitting on his throne, in his royal robes, his crown on his head, and his sceptre in his hand: such a difference will there be, between the greatest manifestation of GOD that ever a saint had on earth, and the display of his glory, that shall be seen in heaven. There the saints shall eternally, without interruption, feed their eyes upon him, and be ever viewing his glorious perfections. And as their bodily eyes shall be strengthened and fitted, to behold the glorious majesty of the Man CHRIST; as eagles gaze on the sun, without being blinded thereby; so their minds shall have such an elevation, as will fit them to see GOD in his glory. Their capacities shall be enlarged, according to the measure in which he shall be pleased to communicate himself unto them, for their compleat happiness.

This blissful sight of GOD, being quite above our present capacities, we must needs be much in the dark about it. But it seems to be something else, than the sight of that glory, which we will see with our bodily eyes, in the saints and in the man CHRIST, or any other splendor or refulgence from the Godhead whatsoever; for no created thing can be our chief good and happiness, or fully satisfy our souls; and it is plain, that these things are somewhat different from GOD himself. Therefore, I conceive, that the souls of the saints shall see GOD himself; for the scriptures teach us, that we shall see face to face, and know even as we are known, 1 Cor. xiii. 12. And that we shall see him as he is, 1 John iii. 2. Howbeit, the saints can never have an adequate conception of GOD; they cannot comprehend that which is infinite. They may touch the mountain, but cannot grasp it in their arms. They cannot with one glance of their eye behold what grows on every side; but the divine perfections will be an unbounded field, in which the glorified shall walk eternally, seeing more and more of GOD; since they can never come to the end of that which is infinite. They may bring their vessels to this ocean every moment, and fill them with new waters. What a ravishing sight would it be, to see all the perfections, and lovely qualities, that are scattered here and there among the creatures, gathered together into one! but even such a sight would be infinitely below this blissful sight the saints shall have in heaven. For they shall see GOD, in whom all these perfections shall eminently appear, with infinitely more; whereof there is no vestige to be found in the creature. In him shall they see every thing desirable, and nothing but what is desirable.

Then shall they be perfectly satisfied, as to the love of GOD towards them, which they are now ready to question on every turn. They will be no more set to persuade themselves of it, by marks, signs and testimonies: they will have an intuitive knowledge of it. They shall, with the profoundest reverence be it spoken, look into the heart of GOD, and there see the love he bore to them from all eternity, and the love and good-will he will bear to them for evermore. The glorified shall have a most clear and distinct understanding of divine truths, for, *in his light we shall see light*, Psalm xxxvi. 9. The light of glory will be a compleat commentary on the Bible, and loose all the hard and knotty questions in divinity. There is no joy on earth, comparable to that which ariseth from the discovery of truth; no discovery of truth comparable to the discovery of scripture-truth, made by the Spirit of the LORD unto the soul. *I rejoice at thy word*, says the Psalmist, *as one that findeth great spoil*, Psal. cxix. 162. Yet it is but an imperfect discovery we have of it while here. How ravishing then will it be, to see the opening of the whole treasure, hid in that field! they shall also be let into the understanding of the works of GOD. The beauty in the works of creation and providence, will then be seen in a due light. Natural knowledge will be brought to perfection by the light of glory. The web of providence concerning the church, and all men whatsoever, will then be cut out, and laid before the eyes of the saints, and it will appear a most beautiful mixture; so as they shall say together, on the view of it, He hath done all things well. But, in a special manner, the work of redemption, shall be the eternal wonder of the saints, and they will admire and praise the glorious contrivance forever. Then shall they get a full view of its suitableness to the divine perfections, and to the case of sinners: and clearly read the covenant, that past betwixt the Father and the Son, from all eternity, touching their salvation. They shall forever wonder and praise, and praise and wonder at the mysteries of wisdom and love, goodness and holiness, mercy and justice, appearing in the glorious device. Their souls shall be eternally satisfied with the sight of GOD himself, and of their election by the Father, their redemption by the Son, and application thereof to them by the holy Spirit.

2. The saints in heaven shall enjoy GOD in CHRIST by experimental knowledge, which is, when the object itself is given and possessed. This is the participation of the divine goodness in full measure, which is the perfection of the will, and utmost term thereof. *The Lamb shall lead them unto living fountains of waters*, Rev. vii. 17. These are no other but GOD himself, the fountain of living waters, who will fully and freely communicate himself unto them. He will pour out of his goodness eternally into their souls; and then shall they have a most lively sensation, in the innermost part of their souls, of all that goodness they heard of, and believed to be in him; and of what they see in him by the light of glory. This will be an everlasting practical exposition of that word, which men and angels cannot sufficiently unfold, viz. GOD shall----*be their God*, Rev. xi. 3. GOD will communicate himself unto them fully; they

will be no more set to taste of the streams of divine goodness in ordinances, as they were wont, but shall drink at the fountain-head. They will be no more entertained with fine sips and drops, but filled with all the fulness of God. And this will be the entertainment of every saint; for, though in created things what is given to one, is with-held from another, yet an infinite good can fully communicate itself to all, and fill all. These who are heirs of GOD, the great heritage, shall then enter into a full possession of their inheritances; and the LORD will open his treasures of goodness unto them, that their enjoyment may be full. They shall not be stinted to any measure; but the enjoyment shall go, as far as their enlarged capacities can reach. As a narrow vessel cannot contain the ocean, so neither can the finite creature comprehend an infinite good; but no measure shall be set to the enjoyment, but what ariseth from the capacity of the creature. So that, although there be degrees of glory, yet all shall be filled, and have what they can hold; though some would be capable to hold more than others, there will be no want to any of them, all shall be fully satisfied, and perfectly blessed in the full enjoyment of divine goodness, according to their enlarged capacities. As when bottles of different sizes are filled, some contain more, others less; yet all of them have what they can contain. The glorified shall have all, in GOD, for the satisfaction of all their desires. No created thing can afford satisfaction to all our desires; clothes may warm us, but they cannot feed us; the light is comfortable, but cannot nourish us.—But in GOD we shall have all our desires, and we shall desire nothing without him. They shall be the happy ones, that desire nothing but what is truly desirable; and withal have all they desire. GOD will be all in all to the saints; he will be their life, health, riches, honour, peace, and all good things. He will communicate himself freely to them; the door of access to him shall never be shut again, for one moment. They may, when they will, take of the fruits of the tree of life, for they will find it on each side of the river, Rev. xxii. 2. There will be no vail betwixt GOD and them, to be drawn aside; but his fulness shall ever stand open to them. No door to knock at, in heaven; no asking to go before receiving; the LORD will allow his people an unrestrained familiarity with himself there.

Now they are in part made partakers of the divine nature; then they shall perfectly partake of it! that is to say, GOD will communicate to them his own image, make all his goodness not only pass before them, but pass into them, and stamp the image of all his perfections on them, so far as the creature is capable to receive the same; from whence shall result a perfect likeness to him, in all things in or about them, which completes the happiness of the creature. And this is what the

Psalmist seems to have had in view, Psalm xvii. 15. *I shall be satisfied, when I awake, with thy likeness*; the perfection of GOD's image, following upon the beatific vision. And so says John, 1 John iii. 2. *We shall be like him; for we shall see him as he is.* Hence there shall be a most close and intimate union betwixt GOD and the saints; GOD shall be in them, and they in GOD, in the way of a most glorious and perfect union; for then shall they dwell in love made perfect. *God is love, and he that dwelleth in love, dwelleth in God, and God in him*, 1 John iv. 16. How will the saints knit with GOD, and he with them; when he sees nothing in them, but his own image; when their love shall arrive at its perfection, no nature but the divine nature, being left in them; and all imperfection swallowed up in that glorious transformation into the likeness of GOD! their love to the LORD being purged from the dross of self-love, shall be most pure: so as they will love nothing but GOD, and in GOD. It shall be no more faint and languishing but burn like coals of juniper. It will be a light without darkness, a flaming fire without smoak. As the live-coal, when all the moisture is gone out of it, is all fire; so will the saints be all love, when they come to the full enjoyment of GOD in heaven, by intuitive and experimental knowledge of him, by sight and full participation of the divine goodness.

Lastly, From this glorious presence and enjoyment shall arise an unspeakable joy, which the saints shall be filled with. *In thy presence is fulness of joy*, Psalm xvi. 11. The saints sometimes enjoy GOD in the world, when their eyes being held, that they cannot perceive it, they have not the comfort of the enjoyment; but then, all mistakes being removed, they shall not only enjoy GOD, but rest in the enjoyment, with inexpressible joy and satisfaction. The desire of earthly things breeds torment, and the enjoyment of them often ends in loathing. But though the glorified saints shall ever desire more and more of GOD, their desires shall not be mixt with the least anxiety, since the fulness of the GOD-head stands always open to them; therefore they shall hunger no more, they shall not have the least uneasiness, in their eternal appetite after the hidden manna; neither shall continued enjoyment breed loathing; they shall never think they have too much; therefore it is added, *Neither shall the sun light on them, nor any heat*, Rev. vii. 16. The enjoyment of GOD and the Lamb will be ever fresh and new to them, through the ages of eternity; for they shall drink of living fountains of waters, where new waters are continually springing up in abundance, ver. 17. They shall eat of the tree of life, which for variety, affords twelve manner of fruits, and these always new and fresh, for it yields every month, Re-

xxii. 2. Their joy shall be pure and unmixed, without any dregs of sorrow; not slight and momentary, but solid and everlasting, without interruption. They will enter into joy. Mat. xxv. 21. *Enter thou into the joy of thy Lord.* The expression is somewhat unusual, and brings me in mind of that word of our suffering Redeemer, Mark xiv. 24. *My soul is exceeding sorrowful, unto death.* His soul was *beset with sorrows*, as the word, there used, will bear; the floods of sorrow went round about him, encompassing him on every hand; whithersoever he turned his eyes, sorrow was before him; it sprang in upon him, from heaven, earth, and hell, all at once; thus was he entered into sorrow, and therefore saith, Psal. lxix. 2. *I am come in deep waters, where the floods overflow me.* Now, wherefore all this, but that his own might enter into joy? Joy sometimes enters into us now, with much ado to get access, while we are compassed with sorrows; but then joy shall not only enter into us, but we shall enter into it, and swim for ever in an ocean of joy; where we will see nothing but joy, whithersoever we turn our eyes. The presence and enjoyment of GOD and the Lamb, will satisfy us with pleasures for evermore; and the glory of our souls and bodies, arising from thence, will afford us everlasting delight. The spirit of heaviness, how closely soever it cleaves to any of the saints now, shall drop off then; their weeping shall be turned into songs of joy, and bottles of tears shall issue in rivers of pleasure. Happy they who now sow in tears, which shall spring up in joy in heaven, and bow their heads there, with a weight of glory upon them.

Thus far of the Society in this kingdom of the saints.

X. In the *last* place, The kingdom shall endure for ever. As every thing in it is eternal, so the saints shall have an undoubted certainty and full assurance of the eternal duration of the same. This is a necessary ingredient in perfect happiness; for the least uncertainty, as to the continuance of any good with one, is not without some fear, anxiety and torment; and, therefore, is utterly inconsistent with perfect happiness. But the glorified shall never have fear, nor cause of fear, of any loss; they shall be ever with the LORD, 1 Thess. iv. 17. They shall all attain the full persuasion, that nothing shall be able to separate them from the love of GOD, nor from the full enjoyment of him, for ever. The inheritance, reserved in heaven, is incorruptible; it hath no principle of corruption, in itself, to make it liable to decay, but endures for evermore: It is undefiled; nothing from without, can mar its beauty, nor is there any thing in itself, to offend those who enjoy it: And therefore it fadeth not away, but ever remains in its native lustre, and primitive beauty, 1 Pet. i. 4. Hitherto of the nature of the kingdom of heaven.

SECONDLY, Proceed we now, to speak of the Admission of the saints into this their kingdom; where I shall briefly touch upon two things: (1.) The formal admission, in the call unto them from the Judge, to come to their kingdom. (2.) The Quality in which they are admitted and introduced to it.

I. Their Admission, the text shews to be by a voice from the throne: the King calling to them from the throne, before angels and men, to come to their kingdom. *Come* and *go* are but short words, but they will be such as will afford matter of tho't to all mankind, through the ages of eternity; since upon the one depends everlasting happiness, and upon the other, everlasting misery. Now our LORD bids the worst of sinners, who hear the gospel, *Come*: but the most part will not come unto him. Some few, whose hearts are touched by his Spirit, do embrace the call, and their souls within them say, *Behold! we come unto thee*; they give themselves to the LORD, forsake the world and their lusts for him; they bear his yoke, and cast it not off, no not in the heat of the day, when the weight of it, perhaps, makes them sweat the blood out of their bodies. Behold the fools! saith the carnal world; whither are they going? But stay a little, O foolish world! From the same mouth, whence they had the call they are now following, another call shall come which will make amends for all; *Come, ye blessed of my Father, inherit the kingdom*, &c.

The saints shall find an inexpressible sweetness in this call, to come: (1.) Hereby JESUS CHRIST shews his desire of their society in the upper house, that they may be ever with him there. Thus he will open his heart unto them, as sometimes he did to his Father concerning them, saying, *Father, I will that they—be with me, where I am*, &c. John xvii. 24. Now the travail of his soul stands before the throne, not only the souls, but the bodies he has redeemed; and they must come, for he must be completely satisfied.——(2.) Hereby they are solemnly invited to the marriage-supper of the Lamb. They were invited to the lower table, by the voice of the servants, and the secret workings of the Spirit within them; and they came, and did partake of the feast of divine communications in the lower house: but JESUS CHRIST, in person, shall invite them, before all the world, to the higher table. (3.) By this he admits them into the mansions of glory. The keys of heaven hang at the girdle of our royal Mediator: All power in heaven is given to him, Mat. xxviii. 18. and none get in thither, but whom he admits. When they were living on earth, with the rest of the world, he opened the everlasting doors of their hearts, entered into them himself, and shut them again, so as sin could never re-enter, to reign there as formerly: and now he opens heaven's doors to them, draws his doves into the ark, and shuts them in there; so as the law, death and hell, can never get them out again. The saints, in this life, were still labouring to enter into that rest; but Satan was always pulling them back, their corruption always drawing them down; in so much, that they have sometimes been left to hang by a hair of a promise, if I may be allowed the expression, not without fears of falling into the lake of fire: but now CHRIST gives the word for their admission: they are brought in, and put beyond all hazard. *Lastly,* Thus he speaks to them, as the person introducing them into the kingdom, into the presence-chamber of the great King, and unto the throne. JESUS CHRIST is the great Secretary of heaven, whose it is to bring the saints into the gracious presence of GOD; and to whom alone it belongs, to bring them into the glorious presence of GOD in heaven. Truly heaven would be a strange place to them, if JESUS was not there: but the Son will introduce his brethren into his Father's kingdom; they shall go in with him to the marriage, Mat. xxv. 10.

II. Let us consider in what Quality they are introduced by him.

First, He brings them in as the blessed of his Father; so runs the call from the throne: *Come, ye blessed of my Father,* &c. It is CHRIST's Father's house, they are to come into; therefore he puts them in mind, that they are blessed of his Father; dear to the Father, as well as to himself. This is it, that makes heaven home to them; namely, that it is CHRIST's Father's house, where we may be assured of welcome, being married to the Son, and being his Father's choice for that very end. He brings them in for his Father's sake, as well as for his own; they are the blessed of his Father, who, as he is the fountain of the Deity, is also the fountain of all blessings conferred on the children of men. They are these to whom GOD designed well from eternity. They were blessed in the eternal purpose of GOD, being elected to everlasting life; at the opening of the book of life, their names were found written therein. So that, bringing them to the kingdom, he doth but bring them to what the Father, from all eternity, designed for them: being saved by the Son, they are saved according to his (*i. e.* the Father's) purpose, 2 Tim. i. 9. They are these, to whom the Father has spoken well. He spake well to them in his word, which must now receive its full accomplishment. They had his promise of the kingdom, lived and died in the faith of it: and now they come to receive the thing promised. Unto them he has done well: A gift is often, in Scripture, called a blessing; and GOD's blessing is ever real, like Isaac's blessing, by which Jacob became his heir: they were all by grace justified, sanctified, and made to persevere unto the end; now they are raised up in glory, and, being tried, stand in the judgment: what remains then, but that GOD crown his own work of grace in them, in giving them their kingdom, in the full enjoyment of himself for ever? *Finally*, They are these, whom GOD has consecrated; the which, also, is a Scripture-notion of blessing, 1 Cor. x. 16. GOD set them apart for himself, to be kings and priests unto him; and the Mediator introduceth them, as such, to their kingdom and priesthood.

Secondly, CHRIST introduceth them as heirs of the kingdom to the actual possession of it: *Come, ye bless'd, inherit the kingdom, &c.* They are the children of GOD, by regeneration and adoption: *And if children, then heirs; heirs of God, and joint heirs with Christ*, Rom. viii. 17. Now is the general assembly of the first-born before the throne: their minority is overpast, and the time appointed of the Father, for their receiving of their inheritance is come. The Mediator purchased the inheritance for them, with his own blood; their rights and evidences were drawn long ago, and registered in the Bible: nay, they had infeftment of their inheritance, in the person of JESUS CHRIST, as their proxy, when he ascended into heaven, whither the Fore-runner is for us entered, Heb. vi. 20. Nothing remaineth, but that they enter into personal possession thereof; which, begun at death, is perfected at the last day; when the saints, in their bodies as well as their souls, go into their kingdom.

Lastly, They are introduced to it, as these it was prepared for from the foundation of the world. The kingdom was prepared for them in the eternal purpose of GOD, before they or any of them had a being; which shews it to be a gift of free grace to them. It was, from eternity, the divine purpose, that there should be such a kingdom for the elect; and that all impediments, which might mar their access to it, should be removed out of the way; and withal, by the same eternal decree, every one's place in it, was determined and set apart, to be reserved for him, that each of the children coming home at length into their Father's house, might find his own place awaiting him, and ready for him; as, at Saul's table, David's place was empty, when he was not there, to occupy it himself, 1 Sam. xx. 25.— And now that the appointed time is come, they are brought in to take their several places in glory, set apart and reserved for them, till they should come at them.

Use. I shall shut up my discourse on this subject, with a word of Application: (1.) To all who claim a right to this kingdom. (2.) To these who have indeed a right to it. (3.) To these who have not a right thereto.

First, Since it is evident, there is no promiscuous admission into the kingdom of heaven, and none do obtain it, but those whose claim is formally tried by the great Judge, and after tri-

Application. 355

al, sustained as good and valid; it is necessary that all of us impartially try and examine, whether, according to the laws of the kingdom, contained in the holy Scriptures, we can verify and make good our claim to this kingdom? The hopes of heaven, which most men have, are built on such sandy foundations, as can never abide the trial; having no ground in the word, but in their own deluded fancy; such hopes will leave those who entertain them, miserably disappointed at last.— Wherefore, it is not only our duty, but our interest, to put the matter to a fair trial in time. If we find, we have no right to heaven, indeed we are yet in the way; and what we have not, we may obtain; but if we find we have a right to it, we will then have the comfort of a happy prospect into eternity, which is the greatest comfort one is capable of in the world. If ye enquire, how ye may know whether ye have a right to heaven, or not? I answer, ye must know that by the state ye are now in. If ye are yet in your natural state, ye are children of wrath, and not children of this kingdom; for that state, to them who live and die in it, issues an eternal misery. If you be brought into the state of grace, you have a just claim to the state of glory; for grace will certainly issue in glory at length.

This kingdom is an inheritance, which none but the children of GOD can justly claim; now we become the children of GOD, by regeneration and union with CHRIST his Son: *And if children, then heirs, heirs of God, and joint heirs with Christ,* Rom. viii. 17. These then are the great points, upon which ones evidences for the state of glory do depend. And therefore I refer you to what is said on the state of grace, for clearing of you as to your right to glory.

If you be heirs of glory, the kingdom of GOD is within you, by virtue of your regeneration and union with CHRIST. (1.) The kingdom of heaven has the throne in thy heart, if thou hast a right to that kingdom: CHRIST is in thee, & GOD is in thee; and having chosen him for thy portion, thy soul has taken up its everlasting rest in him, and gets no kindly rest but in him; as the dove, until she came into the ark. To him the soul habitually inclines, by virtue of the new nature, the divine nature, which the heirs of glory are partakers of, Psal. lxxiii. 25. *Whom have I in heaven but thee. And there is none upon earth, that I desire besides thee.* (2.) The laws of heaven are in thy heart, if thou art an heir of heaven, Heb. viii. 10. *I will put my laws into their mind, and write them in their hearts.* Thy mind is enlightened in the knowledge of the laws of the kingdom, by the Spirit of the LORD, the instructor of all the heirs of glory; for whoever may want instruction, sure an heir to a crown shall not want it. *It is written in the prophets, And they shall all be*

Y

taught of God, John vi. 45. **Therefore,** though father and mother leave them early, or be in no concern about their Christian education, and they be soon put to work for their daily bread; yet they shall not lack teaching. Withal thy heart is changed, and thou bearest GOD's image which consists in righteousness and true-holiness, Eph. iv. 24. Thy soul is reconciled to the whole law of GOD, and at war with all known sin.—— In vain do they pretend to the holy kingdom, who are not holy in heart and life; for, *Without holiness no man shall see the Lord*, Heb. xii. 14. If heaven is a rest, it is for spiritual labourers, and not for loiterers. If it is an eternal triumph, they are not in the way to it, who avoid the spiritual warfare, and are in no care to subdue corruption, resist temptation, and to cut their way to it, thro' the opposition made by the devil, the world, and the flesh. (3.) The treasure in heaven is the chief in thy esteem and desire, for it is your treasure; and, *Where your treasure is, there will your heart be also*, Matth. vi. 21. If it is not the things that are seen, but the things that are not seen, which thy heart is in greatest care and concern to obtain; if thou art driving a trade with heaven, and thy chief business lies there; it is a sign thy treasure is there, for thy heart is there. But if thou art of these who wonder why so much ado, about heaven and eternal life, as if less might serve the turn; thou art like to have nothing to do with it at all. Carnal men value themselves most on their treasures upon earth; with them, the things that are not seen, are weighed down by the things that are seen; and no losses do so much affect them as earthly losses; but the heirs of the crown of glory, will value themselves most on their treasures in heaven, and will not put their private estate in the balance with their kingdom: nor will the loss of the former go so near their hearts, as the thoughts of the loss of the latter. Where these first-fruits of heaven are to be found, the eternal weight of glory will surely follow after; while the want of them must be admitted, according to the word, to be an incontestible evidence of an heir of wrath.

Secondly, Let the heirs of the kingdom behave themselves suitable to their character and dignity. Live as having the faith and hope of this glorious kingdom: let your conversation be in heaven, Phil. iii. 20. Let your souls delight in communion with GOD, while ye are on earth, since ye look for your happiness in communion with him in heaven. Let your speech & actions favour of heaven: and in your manner of life, look like the country to which ye are going; that it may be said of you, as of Gideon's brethren, Judges viii. 28. each one resembled the children of a king. Maintain a holy contempt of the world, & of the things of the world. Altho' others whose earthly things are their best things, do set their hearts upon them; yet it becomes you to set your feet on them since your best things are above. This world is but the country, thro' which lies your road to Immanuel's land; therefore pass through it as pilgrims and strangers, and dip not into the incumbrances of it, so as to retard you in your journey. It is unworthy of one born to a palace, to set his heart on a cottage, to dwell there; and of one running for a prize of gold, to go off his way, to gather the stones of the brook; but much more is it unworthy of an heir of the kingdom of heaven, to be hid among the stuff of this world, when he should be going on to receive his crown. The prize set before you, challengeth your utmost zeal, activity and diligence; and holy courage, resolution, and magnanimity, become those who are to inherit the crown. Ye cannot come at it, without fighting your way to it, through difficulties from without, and from within; but the kingdom before you is sufficient to balance them all, tho' ye should be called to resist even unto blood. Prefer CHRIST's cross before the world's crown: and wants in the way of duty before ease and wealth in the way of sin; *Choose rather to suffer affliction with the people of God, than to enjoy the pleasures of sin for a season,* Heb. xi. 25. In a common Inn, strangers (perhaps) fare better than the children; but here lies the difference, the children are to pay nothing for what they have got, but the strangers get their bill, and must pay compleatly for all they have had. Did we consider the wicked's after reckoning, for all the smiles of common providence they meet with in the world, we would not grudge them their good things here; nor take it amiss that GOD keeps our best things last. Heaven will make up all the saints' losses, and all tears shall be wiped away from their eyes there.

It is worth observing, that there is such a variety of scripture notions of heaven's happiness, as may suit every afflicted case of the saints. Are they oppressed? The day cometh, in which they shall have the dominion. Is their honour laid in the dust? A throne to sit upon, a crown on their head, and a sceptre in their hand, will raise it up again. Are they reduced to poverty? Heaven is a treasure. If they be forced to quit their own habitations, yet CHRIST's Father's house is ready for them. Are they driven to the wilderness? There is a city prepared for them. Are they banished from their native country? They shall inherit a better country. If they are deprived of public ordinances, the LORD GOD Almighty, and the Lamb are the temple there, whither they are going; a temple, the doors of which none can shut. If their life be

principalities and powers, is indeed great; but a glorious triumph is awaiting them. If the toil and labours of the Christian life be great, there is an everlasting rest for them in heaven. Are they judged unworthy of society in the world? They shall be admitted into the society of angels in heaven. Do they complain of frequent interruptions of their communion with GOD? There they shall go no more out, but shall see his face forever more. If they are in darkness here, eternal light is there. If they grapple with death, there they shall have everlasting life. And to sum up all in one word, *he that overcometh, shall inherit all things*, Rev. xxi. 7. He shall have peace and plenty, profit and pleasure, every thing desirable; full satisfaction to his most enlarged desires. Let the expectants of heaven, then, lift up their heads with joy, gird up their loins, and so run as they may obtain; trampling on every thing that may hinder them, in the way to the kingdom. Let them never account any duty too hard, nor any cross too heavy, nor any pains too much, so as they may obtain the crown of glory.

Lastly, Let those who have no right to the kingdom of heaven, be stirred up to seek it with all diligence. Now is the time, wherein the children of wrath may become heirs of glory; and when the way to everlasting happiness is opened, it is no time to sit still and loiter. Raise up your hearts towards the glory that is to be revealed; and do not always lie along on this perishing earth. What can all your worldly enjoyments avail you, while you have no solid ground to expect heaven, after this life is gone? These riches and honours, profits and pleasures, that must be buried with us, and cannot accompany us into another world, are but a wretched portion, and will leave men comfortless at long-run. Ah! why are men so fond, in their life-time to receive their good things? why are they not rather in care, to secure an interest in the kingdom of heaven, which would never be taken from them, but afford them a portion, to make them happy through the ages of eternity! If you desire honour, there you may have the highest honour, and which will last, when the world's honours are laid in the dust; if riches, heaven will yield you a treasure; and, there are pleasures for evermore. O! be not despisers of the pleasant land, neither judge yourselves unworthy of eternal life; but marry the heir, and heaven shall be your dowry; close with CHRIST, as he is offered to you in the gospel, and ye shall inherit all things. Walk in the way of holiness, and it will lead you to the kingdom. Fight against sin and Satan, and ye shall receive the crown. Forsake the world, and the doors of heaven will be open to receive you.

HEAD VI.

HELL.

MATTHEW xxv. 41.

Then shall he say also unto them on the left hand, Depart from me ye cursed, into everlasting fire, prepared for the devil and his angels.

WERE there no other place of eternal lodging but heaven, I should here have closed my discourse of man's eternal state; but seeing in the other world, there is a prison for the wicked, as well as a palace for the saints, we must also enquire into that state of everlasting misery; the which the worst of men may well bear with, without crying, *Art thou come to torment us before the time?* Since there is yet access to fly from the wrath to come; and all that can be said of it, comes short of what the damned will feel; for who knoweth the power of GOD's anger?

The last thing our LORD did, before he left the earth was, He lift up his hands, and blessed his disciples, Luke xxiv. 50, 51. But the last thing he will do, before he leave the throne, is to curse and condemn his enemies; as we learn from the text, which contains the dreadful sentence, wherein the everlasting misery of the wicked is wrapt up. In which three things may be taken notice of. *First*, The quality of the condemned, *ye cursed.* The Judge finds the curse of the law upon them as transgressors, and sends them away with it, from his presence into hell, there to be fully executed upon them. *Secondly*, The punishment which they are adjudged to, and to which they were always bound over, by virtue of the curse. And it is two-fold, the punishment of Loss, in separation from GOD and CHRIST, *Depart from me*; and the punishment of Sense, in most exquisite and extreme torment, *Depart from me into fire.* *Thirdly*, The aggravation of their torments. (1.) They are ready for them, they are not to expect a moment's respite. The fire is prepared, and ready to catch hold of those who are thrown into it. (2.) They will have the society of devils in their torments, being shut up with them in hell. They must depart into the same fire prepared for Beelzebub, the prince of devils, and his angels; namely, other reprobate angels who fell with him, and became devils. It is said to be prepared for them, because they sinned, and were condemned to hell, before man sinned. This speaks further terror to the damned, that they must go into the same torments and place of torment, with the devil and his angels. They hearkened to his temptations, and they must partake in his torments; his works they would do, and they must receive the wages, which is death. In this life they joined with devils, in enmity against GOD and CHRIST, and the way of holiness; and in the other they must lodge with them. Thus all the goats shall be shut up together; for that name is common to devils and wicked men, in scripture, Lev. xvii. 7. Where the word rendered devils, properly signifies hairy ones or goats, in the shape of which creatures, devils delighted much to appear to their worshippers. (3.) The last aggravation of their torment, is the eternal duration thereof, they must depart into everlasting fire. This is it that puts the cape-stone upon their misery, namely, that it shall never have an end.

DOCTRINE.

The Wicked shall be shut up under the curse of God, in everlasting Misery, with the Devils in Hell.

After having evinced that there shall be a resurrection of the body, and a general judgment, I think it not needful to insist to prove the truth of future punishments. The same conscience there is in men of a future judgment, bears witness also of the truth of future punishment. And that the punishment of the damned shall not be annihilation, or a reducing them to nothing, will be clear in the progress of our discourse. In treating of this awful subject, I shall enquire into these four things; (1.) The curse under which the damned shall be shut up. (2.) Their misery under that curse. (3.) Their society with devils, in this miserable state. (4.) The eternity of the whole.

I. As to the curse under which the damned shall be shut up in hell; it is the terrible sentence of the law, by which they are bound over to the wrath of GOD, as transgressors. This curse does not first seize them, when, standing before the tribunal, they receive their sentence; but they were born under it, they led their life under it, in this world; they died under it; rose with it, out of their graves; and the Judge finding it upon them, sends them away with it, into the pit; where it shall lie on them through the ages of eternity. By nature all men are under the curse; but it is removed from the elect, by virtue of their union with CHRIST. It abides on the rest of sinful mankind; and by it they are devoted to destruction, separated to evil, as one may describe the curse, from Deut. xxix. 21. *And the Lord shall separate him unto evil.* Thus shall the damned, for ever, be persons devoted to destruction; separate and set apart, from among the rest of mankind, unto evil, as vessels of wrath, set up for marks to the arrows of divine wrath; and made the common receptacle and shore of vengeance.

This curse hath its first fruits on earth, which are a pledge of the whole lump that is to follow. And hence it is, that as temporal and eternal benefits are bound up together, under the same expressions in the promise to the LORD's people, as Isa. xxxv. 10. *And the ransomed of the Lord shall return, and come to Zion,* &c. relating both to the return from Babylon, and to the saints going to their eternal rest in heaven; even so temporal and eternal miseries, on the enemies of GOD, are sometimes wrapt up under one and the same expression in the threatning, as Isa. xxx. 33. *For Tophet is ordained of old; yea, for the king it is prepared; he hath made it deep and large; the pile thereof is fire and much wood; the breath of the Lord, like a stream of brimstone, doth kindle it.* Which relates both to the temporal and eternal destruction of the Assyrians, who fell by the hand of the angel before Jerusalem. See also, Isa. lxvi. 24. What is that judicial blindness, to which many are given up, *In whom the God of this world hath blinded their eyes,* 2 Cor. iv. 4. but the first fruits of hell, and of the curse? Their sun is going down at noon-day; their darkness increasing, as if it would not stop, till it issue in utter darkness. Many a lash in the dark, doth conscience give the wicked, which the world doth not hear of; and what is that, but that the never-dying worm is already begun to gnaw them? And there is not one of these, but they may call it *Joseph,* for *the Lord shall add another*; or rather, *Gad,* for *a troop cometh.* These drops of wrath, are terrible forebodings of the full shower which is to follow. Sometimes they are given up to their vile affections, that they have no more command over them, Rom. i. 26. So their lusts grow up more and more towards perfection, if I may so speak. As in heaven grace comes to its perfection, so in hell sin arrives at its highest pitch; and as sin is thus advancing upon the man, he is the nearer and the liker to hell. There are three things that have a fearful aspect here. *First*, When every thing that might do good to mens souls, is blasted to them; so that their blessings are cursed, Mal. ii. 2. Sermons, prayers, admonitions, and reproofs, **which** are powerful towards others, are quite inefficacious to them. *Secondly*, When men go on sinning still, in the face of plain rebukes from the LORD, in ordinances and providences; GOD meets them with rods, in the way of their sin, as it were striking them back; yet they rush forward. What can be more like hell, where the LORD is always smiting, and the damned always sinning against him? *Lastly*, When every thing in one's lot is turned into fuel to one's lusts. Thus adversity and prosperity, poverty and wealth, the want of ordinances, and the enjoyment of them, do all but nourish the corruptions of many. Their vicious stomachs corrupt whatsoever they receive, and all does but increase noxious humors.

But the full harvest follows, in that misery which they shall forever lie under in hell; that wrath, which by virtue of the curse, shall come upon them to the uttermost; the which, is the curse fully executed. This black cloud opens upon them, and the terrible thunder-bolt strikes them, by that dreadful voice from the throne, *Depart from me, ye cursed*, &c. Which will give the whole wicked world a dismal view of what is in the bosom of the curse. (1.) It is a voice of extreme indignation and wrath, a furious rebuke from the Lion of the tribe of Judah. His looks will be most terrible to them; his eyes will cast flames of fire on them; and his words will pierce their hearts, like envenomed arrows. When he will thus speak them out of his presence for ever, and, by his word, chase them away from before the throne; they will see how keenly wrath burns in his heart against them for their sins. (2.) It is a voice of extreme disdain and contempt from the LORD. Time was, when they were pitied, besought to pity themselves, and to be the LORD's; but they despised him, they would none of him: but now shall they be barred out of his sight, under everlasting contempt. (3.) It is a voice of extreme hatred. Hereby the LORD shuts them out of his bowels of love and mercy: *Depart, ye cursed*, as if he should say, I cannot endure to look at you; there is not one purpose of good to you in mine heart; nor shall ye ever hear one word more of hope from me. *Lastly*, It is a voice of eternal rejection from the LORD. He commands them to be gone, and so casts them off for ever. Thus the doors of heaven are shut against them; the gulf is fixed between them and it, and they are driven to the pit. Now should they cry with all possible earnestness, *Lord, Lord, open to us*; they will hear nothing but, *Depart, depart, ye cursed.* Thus shall the damned be shut up under the curse.

USE *First*, Let all these who, being yet in their natural state, are under the curse, consider this, and flee to JESUS CHRIST betimes, that they may be delivered from it. How can ye sleep in that state, being wrapt up in the curse! JESUS CHRIST is now saying unto you, Come, ye cursed; I will take the curse from off you, and give you the blessing. The waters of the sanctuary are now running, to heal the cursed ground; take heed to improve them for that end to your own souls, and fear it as hell, to get no spiritual advantage thereby. Remember that *the miry places*, which are neither sea, nor dry land, a fit emblem of hypocrites; *and the marshes*, that neither breed fishes, nor bear trees; but the waters of the sanctuary leave them as they find them, in their barrenness; *shall not be healed*; seeing they spurn the only remedy; *they shall be given to salt*, left under eternal barrenness, set up for the monuments of the wrath of GOD, and concluded for ever under the curse, Ezek. xlvii. 11. *Secondly*, Let all cursers consider this, whose mouths are filled with cursing themselves and others. He that clothes himself with cursing, shall find the curse come into his bowels like water, and like oil into his bones, Psalm cix. 18. if repentance prevent it not. He shall get all his imprecations against him fully answered, in that day wherein he stands before the tribunal of GOD; and shall find the killing weight of the curse of GOD, which he makes light of now.

II. I proceed to speak of the Misery of the damned, under that curse: a misery which the tongues of men and angels cannot sufficiently express. GOD always acts like himself; no favours can be equal to his, and his wrath and terror, are without a parallel. As the saints in heaven are advanced to the highest pitch of happiness, so the damned in hell arrive at the height of misery. Two things here, I shall soberly enquire into; the punishment of Loss, and the punishment of Sense, in hell. But since these also are such things as eye has not seen, nor ear heard, we must, as Geographers do, leave a large void for the unknown land, which the day will discover.

First, The punishment of Loss, which the damned shall undergo, is separation from the LORD; as we learn from the text: *Depart from me, ye cursed.* This will be a stone upon their grave's mouth, as the talent of lead, Zech. v. 7, 8. that will hold them down for ever. They shall be eternally separated from GOD and CHRIST. CHRIST is the way to the Father: but the way, as to them, shall be everlastingly blocked up; the bridge shall be drawn, and the great gulf fixed; so shall they be shut up in a state of eternal separation from GOD the Father, Son, and holy Ghost. They will be locally separated from the Man CHRIST, and shall never come into the seat of the blessed, where he appears in his glory but be cast out into utter darkness, Matth. xxii. 13. They cannot indeed be locally separated from GOD: they cannot be in a place where he is not, since he is, and will be present everywhere: *If I make my bed in hell,* says the Psalmist, *behold thou art there,* Psalm cxxxix. 8. But they shall be miserable beyond expression, in a relative separation from GOD. Tho' he will be present in the very centre of their souls, if I may so express it, while they are wrapt up in fiery flames, in utter darkness, it shall not only be to feed them with the vinegar of his wrath, to entertain them with the emanations of his revenging justice; but they shall never taste more of his goodness and bounty, nor have the least glimpse of hope from him. They will see his heart to be absolutely alienated from them; and that it cannot be towards them; but that they are the party against whom the LORD will have an indignation for ever. They shall be deprived of the glorious presence and enjoyment of GOD: they shall have no part in the beatific vision, nor see any thing in GOD towards them, but one wave of wrath rolling at the back of another. This will bring upon them, overwhelming floods of sorrow for evermore. They shall never taste of the rivers of pleasures the saints in heaven enjoy: but shall have an everlasting winter, and a perpetual night because the Sun of righteousness has departed from them, and so they are left in utter darkness. So great as heaven's happiness is, so great will their loss be: for they can have none of it for ever.

This separation of the wicked from GOD, will be, (1.) An involuntary separation. Now they depart from him, they will not come to him, though they are called, intreated, and obtested to come; but then they shall be driven away from him when they would gladly abide with him. Although the question, *What is thy Beloved, more than another beloved?* is frequent now amongst the despisers of the gospel, there will be no such question among all the damned crew: for then they will see, that man's happiness is only to be found in the enjoyment of GOD; and that the loss of him, is a loss that can never be balanced. (2.) It will also be a total and utter separation. Albeit the wicked are in this life separated from GOD, yet there is a kind of intercourse betwixt them; he gives them many good gifts, and they give him, at least, some good words; so that the peace is not altogether hopeless. But then there shall be a total separation, the damned being cast into utter darkness, where there will not be the least gleam of light or favour from the LORD; the which will put an end unto all their fair words to him. *Lastly*, It shall be a final separation: they will part with him, never more to meet: being shut up under everlasting horror and despair. The match betwixt JESUS CHRIST and unbelievers, which has so often been carried forward, and put back again, shall then be broken for ever; and never shall one message of favour or good-will, go betwixt the parties any more.

This punishment of Loss, in a total and final separation from GOD, is a misery beyond what mortals can conceive, and which the dreadful experience of the damned can only sufficiently unfold. But that we may have some conception of the horror of it, let the following things be considered.

1st, GOD is the chief good, and therefore to be separated from him, must be the chief evil. Our native country, our relations, and our life, are good; and, therefore, to be deprived of them, we reckon a great evil; and the better any thing is, so much the greater evil is the loss of it; wherefore, GOD being the chief good, and no good comparable to him, there can be no loss so great, as the loss of GOD. The full enjoyment of him, is the highest pinnacle of happiness, the creature is capable of arriving at; to be fully and finally separated from him, must then be the lowest step of misery, which the rational creature can be reduced to. To be cast off by men, by good men, by the best of men, is heavy: what must it then be, to be rejected of GOD, of goodness itself!

2dly, GOD is the fountain of all goodness, from which all goodness flows unto the creatures, and by which it is continued in them, and to them. Whatever goodness or perfection, natural as well as moral, is in any creature, it is from GOD, and depends upon him, as the light is from, and depends on the sun; for every created being, as such, is a dependent one. Wherefore a total separation from GOD, wherein all comfortable communication, betwixt GOD and a rational creature, is absolutely blocked up, must of necessity bring along with it a total eclipse of all light of comfort and ease whatsoever. If there is but one window, or open place, in a house, and that be quite shut up; it is evident there can be nothing but darkness in that house. Our LORD tells us, Matth. xix. 17. *There is none good but one, that is God.* Nothing good or comfortable is, originally, from the creature: whatever good or comfortable thing, one finds in one's self, as health of body, or peace of mind; whatever sweetness, rest, pleasure, or delight, one finds in other creatures, as in meat, drink, arts and sciences; all these are but some faint rays of the divine perfections, communicated from GOD unto the creature, and depending on a constant influence from him, for their conservation; which failing, they would immediately be gone: for it is impossible that any created thing can be to us more or better, than what GOD makes it to be. All the rivulets of comfort we drink of, within or without ourselves, come from GOD, as their spring-head; the course of which, towards us, being stopt, of necessity they must all dry up. So that, when GOD goes, all that is good and comfortable goes with him; all ease and quiet of body or mind. Hof. ix. 12. *Wo also unto them, when I depart from them.* When the wicked are totally and finally separated from him, all that is conformable in them, or about them, returns to its fountain, as the light goes away with the sun, and darkness succeeds in the room thereof. Thus, in their separation from GOD, all peace, is removed far away from them; and pain in body, and anguish of soul, succeed to it; all joy goes, and unmixed sorrow settles in them: all quiet and rest separate from them, and they are filled with horror and rage; hope flees away, and despair seizeth them; common operations of the Spirit, which now restrain them, are withdrawn for ever, and sin comes to its utmost height. And thus we have a dismal view, of the horrible spectacle of sin and misery, which a creature proves, when totally separated from GOD, and left to itself; and one may see this separation to be the very hell of hell.

Being separated from GOD, they are deprived of all good. The good things which they set their heart upon, in this world, are beyond their reach there. The covetous man cannot enjoy his wealth there; nor the ambitious man his honours; nor the sensual man his pleasures; no not a drop of water to cool his tongue, Luke xvi. 24, 25. No meat nor drink there, to strengthen the faint; no sleep to refresh the weary; and no music nor pleasant company, to comfort and chear up the sorrowful. And as for these good things, they despised in the world, they shall never more hear of them, nor see them. No offers of CHRIST there, no pardons, no peace; no wells of salvation, in the pit of destruction. In one word, they shall be deprived of whatsoever might comfort them, being totally and finally separated from God, the fountain of all goodness.

2dly, Man naturally desires to be happy, being withal conscious to himself, that he is not self-sufficient; and therefore has ever a desire of something without himself, to make him happy; and the soul being, by its natural make and constitution, capable of enjoying God, and nothing else being commensurable to its desires; it can never have true and solid rest, till it rest in the enjoyment of God. This desire of happiness, the rational creature can never lay aside, no not in hell. Now, while the wicked are on earth, they seek their satisfaction in the creature; and when one fails they go to another; thus they put off their time in the world, deceiving their own souls, and luring them on with vain hopes. But, in the other world, all comfort in the creatures having failed together at once; and the shadows they are now pursuing, having all of them, evanished in a moment; they shall be totally and finally separated from God, and see they have thus lost him. So the doors of earth and heaven both, are shut against them at once. This will create them unspeakable anguish, while they shall live under an eternal gnawing hunger after happiness, which, they certainly know, shall never be in the least measure satisfied, all doors being closed on them. Who, then, can imagine, how this separation from God shall cut the damned to the heart! How they will roar and rage under it! and how it will sting them and gnaw them, through the ages of eternity!

4thly, The damned shall know, that some are perfectly happy in the enjoyment of that God, from whom they themselves are separate: And this will aggravate the sense of their loss, that they can never have any share with these happy ones. Being separated from God, they are separated from the society of the glorified saints and angels. They may see Abraham afar off, and Lazarus in his bosom, Luke xvi. 23. but can never come into their company; being, as unclean lepers, thrust out without the camp, and excommunicated from the presence of the Lord, and of all his holy ones. It is the opinion of some, that every person in heaven or hell, shall hear and see all that passeth in either state. Whatever is to be said of this, we have ground from the word to conclude, that the damned shall have a very exquisite knowledge of the happiness of the saints in heaven; for what else can be meant by the rich man in hell, his seeing Lazarus in Abraham's bosom? One thing is plain in this case, that their own torments will give them such notions of the happiness of the saints, as a sick man has of health, or a prisoner has of liberty. And as they cannot fail of reflecting on the happiness of those in heaven, more than they can attain to contentment with their own lot; so every tho't of that happiness, will aggravate their loss. It would be a mighty torment to a hungry man, to see others liberally feasting, while he is so chained up, as he cannot have one crumb to stay his gnawing appetite. To bring music and dancing before a man labouring under extreme pains, would but encrease his anguish; how then will the songs of the blessed, in their enjoyment of God, make the damned roar, under their separation from him!

5thly, They will remember, that time was, when they might have been made partakers of the blessed state of the saints, in their enjoyment of God: And this will aggravate their sense of the loss. All may remember, there was once a possibility of it; that sometime they were in the world, in some corners of which, the way of salvation was laid open to men's view; and may wish they had gone round the world, till they had found it out. Despisers of the gospel will remember with bitterness, that Jesus Christ, with all his benefits, was offered to them; that they were exhorted, intreated, and pressed to accept, but would not; and that they were warned of the misery they feel, and obtested to flee from the wrath to come, but they would not hearken. The gospel-offer slighted, will make a hot hell; and the loss of an offered heaven, will be a sinking weight on the spirits of unbelievers, in the pit. Some will remember, that there was a probability of their being eternally happy; that sometime they seemed to stand fair for it, and were not far from the kingdom of God; that they had once almost consented to the blessed bargain; the pen in their hand, as it were, to sign the marriage-contract betwixt Christ and their souls; but, unhappily, they dropped it, and turned back from the Lord to their lusts again. And others will remember, that they thought themselves sure of heaven, but, being blinded with pride and self-conceit, they were above ordinances, and beyond instruction, and would not examine their state, which was their ruin: But then they shall in vain wish, they had reputed themselves the worst of the congregation in which they lived; and curse the fond conceit they had of themselves, and that others had of them too. Thus it will sting the damned, that they might have escaped this loss.

Lastly, They will see the loss to be irrecoverable; that they must eternally lie under it, never, never to be repaired. Might the damned, after millions of ages in hell, regain what they have lost, it would be some ground of hope; but the prize is gone, and can never be recovered. And there are two things here, which will pierce them to the heart. (1.) That they never knew the worth of it, till it was irrecoverably lost. Should a man give away an earthen pot full of gold for a trifle, never knowing what was in it, till it were quite gone from him, and past recovery; how would this foolish action gall him, upon the discovery of the riches in it; such an one's case may be a faint resemblance of the case of despisers of the gospel, when in hell they lift up their eyes, and behold that, to their torment, which they will not see now, to their salvation. (2.) That they have lost it for loss and dung! sold their part of heaven, and not enriched themselves with the prize. They lost heaven for earthly profits and pleasures, and now both are gone together from them. The drunkard's cups are gone, the covetous man's gain, the voluptuous man's carnal delights, and the sluggard's ease; nothing is left them to comfort them now. The happiness they lost remains indeed, but they can have no part in it for ever.

USE. Sinners, be persuaded to come to GOD through JESUS CHRIST, uniting with him through a Mediator; that ye may be preserved from this fearful separation from him. O be afraid to live in a state of separation from GOD, lest that which ye now make your choice, become your eternal punishment hereafter! Do not reject communion with GOD, cast not off the communion of saints; for it will be the misery of the damned, to be driven out from that communion. Cease to build up the wall of separation betwixt GOD and you, by continuing in your sinful courses; repent rather in time, and so pull it down, lest the cape-stone be laid upon it, and it stand for ever betwixt you and happiness. Tremble at the thoughts of rejection and separation from GOD. By whomsoever men are rejected on the earth, they ordinarily find some pity to them; but if ye be thus separated from GOD, ye will find all doors shut against you. Ye will find no pity from any in heaven: neither saints nor angels will pity them whom GOD has utterly cast off; none will pity you in hell, where there is no love but lothing; all being loathed of GOD, loathing him, and loathing one-another. This is a day of losses and fears. I shew you a loss, ye would do well to fear in time: be afraid lest you lose GOD; if ye do, a long eternity will be spent in roaring out lamentations for this loss. O horrid stupidity! men are in a mighty care and concern to prevent worldly losses: but they are in hazard of losing heaven, the communion of the blessed, and all good things for soul and body in another world; yet as careless in that matter, as if they were incapable of thought. O! compare this day with

370 *The Punishment of*

the day our text aims it. This day is heaven opened to them, who hitherto have rejected CHRIST, yet there is room, if they will come; but that day the doors shall be shut. Now CHRIST is saying unto you, *Come*, then he will say, *Depart*; seeing ye would not come when ye were bidden. Now pity is shown; the LORD pities you, his servants pity you, and tell you, that the pit is before you, and cry to you, that ye do yourselves no harm; but then ye shall have no pity from GOD nor man.

Secondly, The damned shall be punished in hell with the punishment of Sense; they must depart from GOD into everlasting fire. I am not in a mind to dispute, what kind of fire it is which they shall depart into, and be tormented by for ever, whether a material fire, or not? Experience will more than satisfy the curiosity of those, who are disposed rather to dispute about it, than to seek how to escape it. Neither will I meddle with that question, Where is it? It is enough, that the worm which never dieth, and the fire that is never quenched, will be found somewhere by impenitent sinners. But (1.) I shall evince that, whatever kind of fire it is; it is more vehement and terrible than any fire, we, on earth, are acquainted with. (2.) I shall condescend on some properties of these fiery torments.

As to the 1st of these; burning is the most terrible punishment, and brings the most exquisite pain and torment with it. By what reward could a man be induced to hold but his hand, in the flame of a candle for an hour? All imaginary pleasure on earth, would never prevail with the voluptuous man, to venture to lodge but one half hour in a burning fiery furnace; nor would all the wealth in the world, prevail with the most covetous to do it. Yet, on much lower terms, do most men in effect, expose themselves to everlasting fire in hell, which is more vehement and terrible, than any fire we on earth are acquainted with; as will appear by the following considerations.

1. As in heaven, grace being brought to its perfection, profit and pleasure do also arrive at their height there; so sin being come to its height in hell, the evil of punishment doth also arrive at its perfection there. Wherefore, as the joys in heaven are far greater, than any joys which the saints obtain on earth, so the punishments of hell must be greater, than any earthly torments whatsoever; not only in respect of the continuance of them, but also in respect of vehemency and exquisiteness.

2. Why are the things of the other world represented to us in an earthly dress, in the world; but that the weakness of

which are so mightily prized on earth, but something more excellent, than these finest and most precious things in the world; when therefore we **hear** of hell-fire, it is necessary we understand by it something more vehement, piercing, and tormenting, than any fire ever seen by our eyes. And here it is worth considering, that the tormenss of hell are held forth, under several other notions than that of fire simply; and the reason of it is plain; namely, that hereby, what of horror is wanting in one notion of hell, is supplied by another. Why is heaven's happiness represented under the various notions of a treasure, a paradise, a feast, a rest, &c. but that there is not one of these things sufficient to express it? Even so, hell-torments are represented under the notion of fire; which the damned are cast into. A dreadful representation indeed! yet not sufficient to express the misery of the state of sinners in them. Wherefore we hear also of the second death, Rev. xx. 6. for the damned in hell shall be ever dying; of the wine-press of the wrath of GOD, ch. xiv. 19. wherein they will be trodden in anger, trampled in the LORD's fury, Isa. lxiii. 3. pressed, broken, & bruised, without end; the worm that dieth not, Mark ix. 44. which shall eternally gnaw them; a bottomless pit, where they will be ever sinking, Rev. xx. 3. It is not simply called a fire, but the lake of fire and brimstone, ver. 19. a lake of fire burning with brimstone, ch. xix. 20. than which, one can imagine nothing more dreadful. Yet, because fire gives light, and light, as Solomon observes, Ec. xi. 7. is sweet, there is no light there, but darkness, utter darkness, Mat. xxv. 30. For they must have an everlasting night, since nothing can be there, which is in any measure comfortable or refreshing.

3. Our fire cannot affect a spirit, but by way of sympathy with the body, to which it is united; but hell-fire will not only pierce into the bodies, but directly into the souls of the damned; for it is prepared for the devil & his angels, these wicked spirits, whom no fire on earth can hurt. Job complains heavily, under the chastisement of GOD's fatherly hand, saying, *The arrows of the Almighty are within me, the poison whereof drinketh up my spirit*, Job vi. 4. But how will the spirits of the damned be pierced with the arrows of revenging justice! how will they be drunk up with the poison of the curse of these arrows! how vehement must that fire be, that pierceth directly into the soul, and makes an everlasting burning in the spirit, the most lively and tender part of a man, wherein wounds or pain are most intolerable!

Lastly, The preparation of this **fire**, evinceth the inexpressible vehemency & dreadfulness of it. **The text** calls it prepared fire,

paring, the product of infinite wisdom on a particular design, to demonstrate the most strict and severe divine justice against sin; which may sufficiently evidence to us, the inconceivable exquisiteness thereof. GOD always acts in a peculiar way, becoming his own infinite greatness, whether for or against the creature; and, therefore, as the things he hath prepared for them that love him, are great and good, beyond expression or conception; so, one may conclude, that the things he hath prepared against those who hate him, are great and terrible, beyond what men can either say, or think of them. The pile of Tophet, is fire and much wood, (the coals of that fire are coals of juniper, a kind of wood, which set on fire, burns most fiercely, Psf. cxx. 4.) and the breath of the LORD, like a stream of brimstone, doth kindle it, Isa. xxx. 33. Fire is more or less violent, according to the matter of it, and the breath by which it is blown; what heart, then, can fully conceive the horror of coals of juniper, blown up with the breath of the LORD? Nay, GOD himself will be a consuming fire, Deut. iv. 24. to the damned; intimately present, as a devouring fire, in their souls and bodies. It is a fearful thing to fall into a fire, or to be shut up in a fiery furnace, on earth; but the terror of these evanisheth, when one considers, how fearful it is to fall into the hands of the living GOD, which is the lot of the damned; for, *Who shall dwell with the devouring fire? Who shall dwell with everlasting burnings?* Isa. xxxiii. 14.

As to the second point proposed, namely, the properties of the fiery torments in hell.

1. They will be universal torments, every part of the creature being tormented in that flame. When one is cast into a burning fiery furnace, the fire makes its way into the very bowels, and leaves no member untouched; what part, then, can have ease, when the damned swim in a lake of fire burning with brimstone? There will their bodies be tormented, and scorched for ever. And as they sinned, so shall they be tormented, in all the parts thereof; that they shall have no sound side to turn them to; for what soundness or ease can be to any part of that body, which being separated from GOD, and all refreshment from him, is still in the pangs of the second death, ever dying, but never dead? But as the soul was chief in sinning, it will be chief in suffering too, being filled brimful of the wrath of a sin-revenging GOD. The damned shall ever be under deepest impressions of GOD's vindictive justice against them; and this fire will melt their souls within them, like wax. Who knows the power of that wrath, which had such an effect on the Mediator,

trary to the will of GOD's precepts, so GOD, in his dealings with them, in the other world, shall have war with their will for ever. What they would have, they shall not in the least obtain; but what they would not, shall be bound upon them, without remedy. Hence no pleasant affection shall ever spring up in their hearts any more; their love of complacency, joy, and delight, in any object whatsoever, shall be pluckt up by the root; and they will be filled with hatred, fury and rage, against GOD, themselves, and their fellow-creatures, whether happy in heaven, or miserable in hell, as they themselves are. They will be sunk in sorrow, racked with anxiety, filled with horror, galled to the heart with fretting, and continually darted with despair; which will make them weep, gnash their teeth, and blaspheme for ever, Mat. xxii. 13. *Bind him hand and foot, and take him away, and cast him into utter darkness; there shall be weeping and gnashing of teeth.* Rev. xvi. 21. *And there fell upon men, a great hail, out of heaven, every stone about the weight of a talent; and men blasphemed God, because of the hail; for the plague thereof was exceeding great.* Conscience will be a worm to gnaw and prey upon them; remorse for their sins, shall seize them and torment them for ever; and they shall not be able to shake it off, as sometimes they did; for in hell, their worm dieth not, Mark ix. 45, 46. Their memory will serve but to aggravate their torment, and every new reflection will bring another pang of anguish, Luke xvi. 25. *But Abraham said,* viz. to the rich man in hell, *Son, remember that thou in thy life-time receivedst thy good things.*

2. The torments in hell are manifold. Put the case, that a man were, at one and the same time, under the violence of the gout, gravel, and whatsoever diseases and pains have ever met together in one body; the torment of such a one would be but light in comparison with the torments of the damned. For, as in hell, there is an absence of all that is good and desirable, so there is the confluence of all evils there; since all the effects of sin and of the curse, take their place in it, after the last judgment, Rev. 20. 14. *And death and hell were cast into the lake of fire.* There they will find a prison, they can never escape out of; a lake of fire, wherein they will be ever swimming and burning; a pit, where they will never find a bottom. The worm that dieth not, shall feed on them, as on bodies which are interred; the fire that is not quenched, shall devour them, as dead bodies which are burned. Their eyes shall be kept in blackness of darkness, without the least comfortable gleam of

ing weeping, wailing, and gnashing of teeth, Mat. xiii. 42. and xxii. 13. They are represented to us, under the notion of pangs in travail, which are very sharp and exquisite. So says the rich man in hell, Luke xvi. 24. *I am tormented*, viz. as one in the pangs of child-bearing, *in this flame*. Ah! dreadful pangs! horrible travail! in which both soul and body are in pangs together! helpless travail! hopeless and endless! The word used for *hell*, Mat. v. 22. and in divers other places of the New Testament, properly denotes *the valley of Hinnom*; the name being taken from the valley of the children of Hinnom, in which was Tophet, 2 Kings xxiii. 10. where idolaters offered their children to Moloch. This is said to have been a great brazen idol, with arms like a man's; the which being heated by fire within it, the child was set in the burning arms of the idol; and, that the parents might not hear the shrieks of the child burning to death, they beat drums in the time of the horrible sacrifice; whence the place had the name of Tophet. Thus the exquisiteness of the torments in hell, are pointed out to us. Some have endured grievous tortures on earth, with a surprizing obstinacy and undaunted courage; but mens courage will fail them there, when they find themselves fallen into the hands of the living GOD, and no out-gate to be expected for ever. It is true, there will be degrees of torment in hell. *It shall be more tolerable, for Tyre and Sidon, than for Chorazin and Bethsaida*, Mat. xi. 21, 22. But the least load of wrath there, will be insupportable; for how can the heart of the creature endure, or his hands be strong, when GOD himself is a consuming fire to him? When the tares are bound in bundles for the fire, there will be bundles of covetous persons, of drunkards, profane swearers, unclean persons, formal hypocrites, unbelievers, and despisers of the gospel, and the like; the several bundles being cast into hell-fire, some will burn more keenly than others, according as their sins have been more heinous than those of others; a fiercer flame will seize the bundle of the profane, than the bundle of the unsanctified moralists; the furnace will be hotter to those who sinned against light, than to these who lived in darkness, Luke xii. 37, 38. *That servant which knew his Lord's will, and prepared not himself, neither did according to his will, shall be beaten with many stripes. But he that knew not, and did commit things worthy of stripes, shall be beaten with few stripes*. But the sentence common to them all, *Bind them in bundles to burn them*, Mat. xiii. 30. speaks the greatest vehemency and exquisiteness of the lowest degree of torment in hell.

4. They will be uninterrupted; there is no intermission there; no ease, no not for a moment. *They shall be tormented day and night, for ever and ever*, Rev. xx. 10. Few are so toiled in this world, but sometimes they get rest; but the damned shall get none; they took their rest, in the time appointed of GOD for labour. No storms are readily seen, but there is some space between showers; but no intermission in the storm that falls on the wicked in hell. There deep will be calling unto deep, and the waves of wrath continually rolling over them. There the heavens will be always black to them, and they shall have a perpetual night, but no rest, Rev. xiv. 10. *They shall have no rest, day nor night*.

5. They will be unpitied. The punishments inflicted on the greatest malefactors on earth, do draw forth some compassion from them, who behold them in their torments; but the damned shall have none to pity them. GOD will not pity them, but laugh at their calamities, Prov. i. 26. The blessed company in heaven, shall rejoice in the execution of GOD's righteous judgment, and sing while the smoak riseth up for ever, Rev. xix. 3. *And again they said, Allelujah; and her smoke rose up, for ever and ever*. No compassion can be expected from the devil and his angels, who delight in the ruin of the children of men, and are, and will be, for ever void of pity. Neither will one pity another there, where every one is weeping and gnashing his teeth, under his own insupportable anguish and pain. There natural affections will be extinguished; the parents will not love their children, nor children their parents; the mother will not pity the daughter in these flames, nor will the daughter pity the mother; the son will shew no regard to his father there, nor the servant to his master, where every one will be roaring under his own torment.

Lastly, To complete their misery their torments shall be eternal, Rev. xiv. 11. *And the smoke of their torment, ascendeth up for ever and ever*. Ah! what a frightful case is this, to be tormented in the whole body and soul, and that not with one kind of torment, but many; all of these most exquisite, and all this without any intermission, and without pity from any! what heart can conceive those things without horror? Nevertheless, if this most miserable case were at length to have an end, that would be some comfort; but the torments of the damned will have no end; of the which more afterwards.

USE. Learn from this, (1.) The evil of sin. It is a stream that will carry down the sinner, till he be swallowed up in an ocean of wrath. The pleasures of sin are bought too dear, at the rate of everlasting burnings. What availed the rich man's purple clothing and sumptuous fare, when, in hell, he was wrapt up in purple flames, and could not have a drop of water to cool his tongue? Alas! that men should indulge themselves in sin, which will be such bitterness in the end; that they should drink so great dily of the poisonous cup, and hug that serpent in their bosom, that will sting them to the heart, and gnaw out their bowels at length! (2.) What a GOD he is, with whom we have to do; what a hatred he bears to sin, and how severely he punisheth it. Know the LORD to be most just, as well as most merciful, and think not that he is such an one as you are; away with that fatal mistake before it be too late, Ps. l. 21, 22. *Thou thoughtest that I was altogether such an one as thyself; but I will reprove thee, and set them in order before thine eyes. Now consider this, ye that forget God, lest I tear you in pieces, and there be none to deliver.* The fire prepared for the devil and his angels, as dark as it is, will serve to discover GOD to be a severe revenger of sin. *Lastly,* The absolute necessity of fleeing to the LORD JESUS CHRIST by faith; the same necessity of repentance, and holiness of heart and life. The avenger of blood is pursuing thee, O sinner! haste and escape to the city of refuge. Wash now in the fountain of the Mediator's blood, that you may not perish in the lake of fire. Open thy heart to him, lest the pit close its mouth on thee. Leave thy sins, else they will ruin thee; kill them, else they will be thy death for ever.

Let not the terror of hell-fire, put thee upon hardening thy heart more, as it may do, if thou entertain that wicked thought, viz. *There is no hope,* Jer. ii. 25. which, perhaps, is more rife among the hearers of the gospel, than many are aware of. But there is hope for the worst of sinners, who will come unto JESUS CHRIST. If there are no good qualifications in thee, (as certainly there can be none in a natural man, none in any man, but what are received from CHRIST in him) know, that he has not suspended thy welcome on any good qualifications; do thou take himself and his salvation, freely offered unto all, to whom the gospel comes. *Whosoever will, let him take of the water of life freely,* Rev. xxii. 16. *Him that cometh to me, I will in no ways cast out,* John vi. 37. It is true, thou art a sinful creature, and canst not repent; thou art unholy, and canst not make thyself holy; nay, thou hast essayed to repent, to forsake sin, and to be holy, but still missed of repentance, reformation, and holiness; and therefore, *Thou saidst, there is no hope. No, for I have loved strangers, and after them will I go.* Truly, no marvel, that the success has not answered thy expectation, since thou hast always begun thy work amiss. But do thou, first of all, honour GOD, by believing the testimony he has given of his Son, namely, that eternal life is in him; and honour the Son of GOD, by believing on him, that is, embracing and falling in with the free offer of CHRIST, and of his salvation, from sin and from wrath, made to thee in the gospel, trusting in him confidently for righteousness to thy justification, and also for sanctification; seeing of GOD he is made unto us both righteousness and sanctification, 1 Cor. i. 30. Then, if thou hadst as much credit to give to the word, as thou wouldst allow to the word of an honest man offering thee a gift, and saying, take it, and it is thine; thou mayst believe that GOD is thy GOD, CHRIST is thine, his salvation is thine, thy sins are pardoned, thou had strength in him for repentance and for holiness; for all these are made over to thee in the free offer of the gospel. Believing on the Son of GOD, thou art justified, the curse is removed. And while it lies upon thee, how is it possible, thou shouldst bring forth the fruits of holiness? But, the curse is removed, that death, which seized on thee with the first Adam, according to threatning, Gen. ii. 17. is taken away. In consequence of which, thou shalt find the bands of wickedness, now holding thee fast in impenitency, broken asunder, as the bands of death; so as thou wilt be able to repent indeed from the heart; thou shalt find the spirit of life, on whose departure, that death ensued, returned to thy soul, so as thenceforth thou shalt be enabled to live unto righteousness. No man's case is so bad, but it may be mended this way, in time, to be perfectly right in eternity; & none's so good, but another way being taken, it will be marred for time and eternity too.

III. The damned shall have the society of devils in their miserable state in hell; for they must depart into fire prepared for the devil and his angels. O horrible company! O frightful association; who would chuse to dwell in a palace haunted by devils? To be confined to the most pleasant spot of earth, with the devil and his infernal furies, would be a most terrible confinement. How would mens hearts fail them, and their hair stand up, finding themselves environed with the hellish crew, in that case! but ah! how much more terrible must it be, to be cast with the devils into one fire, locked up with them in one dungeon, shut up with them in one pit! to be closed up in a den of roaring lions, girded about with serpents, surrounded with venomous asps, and to have the bowels eaten out by vipers, all together and at once, is a comparison too low, to shew the misery of the damned, shut up in hell with the devil and his angels. They go about now as roaring lions, seeking whom they may devour; but then shall they be confined in their dens with their prey, they shall be filled to the brim with the wrath of GOD, and receive the full torment, Mat. viii. 29. which they tremble in expectation of, Jam. ii. 19. being cast into the fire prepared for them. How will these lions roar and tear! how will these serpents hiss! these dragons vomit out fire? what horrible anguish will seize the damned, finding themselves in the lake of fire, with the devil who deceived them; drawn hither with the silken cords of temptation, by these wicked spirits, and bound with them in everlasting chains under darkness! Rev. xx. 10. *And the devil that deceived them, was cast into the lake of fire and brimstone, where the beast, and the false prophet are, and shall be tormented day and night for ever.*

O! that men would consider this in time, renounce the devil and his lusts, and join themselves to the LORD in faith and holiness. Why should men chuse that company in this world, and delight in that society, they would not desire to associate with in the other world? Those who like not the company of the saints on earth, will get none of it in eternity; but as godless company is their delight now, they will afterwards get enough of it; when they have an eternity to pass, in the roaring and blaspheming society of devils and reprobates in hell. Let those who use to invocate the devil to take them, soberly consider, that the company so often invited will be terrible at last, when come.

IV. And *Lastly*, Let us consider the eternity of the whole, the everlasting continuance of the miserable state of the damned in hell.

First, If I could, I should shew what eternity is, I mean, the creature's eternity. But who can measure the waters of the ocean, or who can tell you the days, years, and ages of eternity, which are infinitely more than the drops of the ocean? None can comprehend eternity, but the eternal GOD. Eternity is an ocean, whereof we will never see the shore: it is a deep, where we can find no bottom; a labyrinth, from whence we cannot extricate ourselves, and where we shall ever lose the door. There are two things one may say of it, (1.) It has a beginning. GOD's eternity has no beginning, but the creature's eternity has. Sometimes there was no lake of fire; and those who have been there, for some thousands of years, were once, in time, as we now are. (2.) It shall never have an end. The first who entered into the eternity of woe, is as far from the end of it, as the last, who shall go thither, will be at his entry. They who have launched out farthest into that ocean, are as far from land, as they were the first moment they went into it; and thousands of ages after this, they will be as far from it as ever. Wherefore, eternity, which is before us, is a duration that hath a beginning, but no end. It is a beginning without a middle, a beginning without an end. After millions of years, still it is a beginning. GOD's wrath, in hell, will ever be the wrath to come. But there is no middle in eternity. When millions of ages are past in eternity, what is past bears no proportion to what is to come; no not so much as one drop of water, falling from the tip of one's finger, bears to all the waters of the ocean. There is no end of it, while GOD is, it shall be. It is an entry without an out-gate, a continual succession of ages, a glass always running, which shall never run out.

Observe the continual succession of hours, days, months and years, how one still follows upon another; and think of eternity, wherein there is a continual succession without end. When you go out in the night, and behold the stars of heaven, how they cannot be numbered for multitude, think of the ages of eternity; considering withal, there is a certain definite number of the stars, but no number of the ages of eternity. When you

wheel, have an emblem of eternity before them; for to which part soever of the ring or wheel one looks, one will still see another part beyond it; and on whatsoever moment of eternity you condescend, there is still another beyond it. When you are abroad in the fields, and behold the piles of grass upon the earth, which no man can reckon: think with yourselves, that, were as many thousands of years to come, as there are piles of grass on the ground, even those would have an end at length, but eternity will have none. When you look to a mountain, imagine in your hearts, how long would it be, ere that mountain should be removed, by a little bird coming once every thousand years, and carrying away but one grain of the dust at once: the mountain would at length be removed that way, and bro't to an end, but eternity will never end. Suppose this with respect to all the mountains of the earth; nay, with respect to the whole globe of the earth; the grains of dust, whereof the whole earth is made up, are not infinite, and therefore the last grain would at long run come to be carried away, in the way supposed; but when that slowest work would be brought to an end, eternity would be, in effect but beginning.

These are some rude draughts of eternity; and now add misery and woe to this eternity, what tongue can express it? What heart can conceive? In what balance can that misery and that woe be weighed?

Secondly, Let us take a view of what is eternal, in the state of the damned in hell. Whatsoever is included in the fearful sentence, determining their eternal state, is everlasting; therefore all the doleful ingredients of their miserable state, will be everlasting: they will never end. The text expresly declares the fire, into which they must depart, to be everlasting fire. And our LORD elsewhere tells us, that in hell, the fire shall never be quenched, Mark ix. 43. with an eye to the valley of Hinnom, in which besides the already mentioned fire, for burning of the children of Moloch, there was also another fire, burning continually, to consume the dead carcases, and filth of Jerusalem; so the Scripture representing hell-fire by the fire of that valley,

continuance of the fire, is an aggravation of the misery of the damned; but surely, if they be annihilated, or substantially destroyed, it is all a case to them, whether the fire be everlasting or not. Nay, but they depart into everlasting fire, to be everlastingly punished in it, Mat. xxv. 46. *They shall go away into everlasting punishment.* Thus the execution of the sentence, is a certain discovery of the meaning of it. The worm that dieth not, must have a subject to live in; they who shall have no rest, day nor night, Rev. xiv. 11. but shall be tormented day & night, for ever and ever, chap. xx. 10. will certainly have a being for ever and ever, and not be brought into a state of eternal rest in annihilation. Destroyed indeed they shall be, but their destruction will be an everlasting destruction, 2 Thes. i. 9. a destruction of their well being, but not of their being. What is destroyed, is not therefore annihilated: *Art thou come to destroy us?* said the devil unto Jesus Christ, Luke iv. 34. Howbeit, the devils are afraid of torment, not of annihilation, Mat. viii. 29. *Art thou come hither to torment us?* The state of the damned, is indeed a state of death; but such a death it is, as is opposite only to a happy life; as is clear from other notions of their state, which necessarily include an eternal existence, of which before. As they, who are dead in sin, are dead to God and holiness, yet live to sin; so dying in hell, they live, but separated from God, and his favour, in which life lies, Pf. xxx. 5. They shall ever be under the pangs of death: ever dying, but never dead, or absolutely void of life. How desirable would such a death be to them! but it will fly from them for ever. Could each one kill another, or could they, with their own hands, rent themselves into lifeless pieces, their misery would quickly be at an end; but there they must live, who chused death, and refused life; for their death lives, and the end ever begins.

2*dly*, The curse shall fly upon them eternally, as the everlasting chain, to hold them in the everlasting fire; a chain that shall never be loosed, being fixed for ever about them, by the dreadful sentence of the eternal judgment. This chain, which spurns the united force of devils held fast by it, is too strong to be broken by men, who being solemnly anathematized, and devoted to destruction, can never be recovered to any other use.

3*dly*, Their punishment shall be eternal, Mat. xxv. 46. *They shall go away into everlasting punishment.* They will be, for ever, separate from God and Christ, and from the society of the holy angels and saints; between whom and them, an impassible gulf will be fixed, Luke xvi. 26. *Between us and you,* says Abraham, in the parable, to the rich man in hell, *there is a great gulf fixed; so that they which would pass from hence to you, cannot; neither can they pass to us, that would come from thence.* They shall, for ever, have the horrible society of the devil and his angels. There will be no change of company for evermore, in that region of **darkness.** Their torment in the fire, will be everlasting; they must live for ever in it. Several authors, both ancient and modern, tell of earthen-flax, of Salamander's hair; that cloth made of it, being cast into the fire, is so far from being burnt or consumed, that it is only made clean thereby, as other things are by washing. But, however that is, it is certain, the damned shall be tormented for ever and ever in hell-fire, and not substantially destroyed, Rev. xx. 10. And indeed nothing is annihilated by fire, but only dissolved. Of what nature soever hell-fire is, no question but the same God who kept the bodies of the three children from burning in Nebuchadnezzer's fiery furnace, can also keep the bodies of the damned from any such dissolution by hell-fire, as may infer privation of life.

Lastly, Their knowledge and sense of their misery, shall be eternal; and they shall assuredly know, that it will be eternal. How desirable would it be to them, to have their senses for ever locked up, and lose the consciousness of their own misery; as one may rationally suppose it to fare at length with some, in the punishment of death inflicted on them on earth, and as it is with some mad people, in their miserable case! But that agrees not with the notion of torment for ever and ever, nor the worm that dieth not. Nay, they will ever have a lively feeling of their misery, and strongest impressions of the wrath of God against them. And that dreadful intimation, of the eternity of their punishment, made to them by the Judge, in their sentence, will fix such impressions of the eternity of their miserable state upon their minds, as they will never be able to lay aside, but will continue with them evermore, to complete their misery. This will fill them with everlasting despair, a most tormenting passion, which will continually rent their hearts, as it were, in a thousand pieces. To see floods of wrath ever coming, and never to cease; to be ever in torment, and withal, to know there shall never, never be a release, will be the capestone put on the misery of the damned. If *hope deferred, maketh the heart sick*, Prov. xiii. 12. how killing will be, hope rooted up, slain outright, and buried for ever out of the creature's sight! This will fill them with hatred & rage against God, their known, irreconcilable enemy; and under it, they will roar for ever, like wild bulls in a net, and fill the pit with blasphemies evermore.

Lastly, I might here shew the reasonableness of the eternity of the punishment of the damned; but having already spoke of it, in vindicating the justice of God, in his subjecting men, in their natural state, to eternal wrath, I only remind you of three things; (1.) The infinite dignity of the party offended by sin, requires an infinite punishment to be inflicted, for the vindication of his honour; since the demerit of sin riseth according to dignity and excellency of the person against whom it is committed. The party offended, is the great God, the chief good; the offender, a vile worm: in respect of perfection, infinitely distant from God, to whom he is indebted for all that ever he had, implying any **good**, or perfection whatsoever. This then requires an infinite punishment to be inflicted on the sinner; the which, since it cannot, in him, be infinite in value, must needs be infinite in duration, that is to say, eternal. Sin is a kind of infinite evil, as it wrongs an infinite God: and the guilt and defilement thereof is never taken away, but endures for ever, unless the Lord himself in mercy do remove it. God who is offended, is eternal; his being never comes to an end; the sinful soul is immortal, and the man shall live for ever; the sinner being without strength, Rom. v. 6. to expiate his guilt, can never put away the offence; therefore it ever remains, unless the Lord do put it away himself, as in the elect, by his Son's blood. Wherefore the party offended, the offender, and the offence, ever remaining, the punishment cannot but be eternal. (2.) The sinner would have continued the course of his provocations against God, for ever, without end, if God had not put a check to it by death. As long as they were capable to act against him, in this world, they did it; and therefore, justly, he will act against them, while he is; that is, for ever. God, who judgeth of the will, intents, and inclinations of the heart, may justly do against sinners, in punishing, as they would have done against him, in sinning.

Lastly, Tho' I put not the stress of the matter here, yet, it is just and reasonable, the damned suffer eternally, since they will sin eternally in hell, gnashing their teeth, Mat. viii. 12. under their pain, in rage, envy and grudge, compare Acts vii. 54. Pſ. cxii. 10. Luke xiii. 28. and blaspheming God there, Rev. xvi. 21. whither they are driven away in their wickedness, Pro. xiv. 42. That the wicked be punished for their wickedness, is just; and it is nothing inconsistent with justice, that the being of the creature be continued for ever; wherefore, it is just, that the damned, continuing wicked eternally, do suffer eternally for their wickedness. The misery, under which they sin, can neither free them from the debt of obedience, nor excuse their sinning, and make it blameless. The creature, as a creature, is bound unto obedience to his Creator; and no punishment, inflicted on him, can free him from it, more than the malefactor's prisons, irons, whipping, and the like, do set him at liberty, to commit anew the crimes for which he is imprisoned, or whipt. Neither can the torments of the damned, excuse or make blameless their horrible sinning under them, more than exquisite pains, inflicted upon men on earth, can excuse their murmuring, fretting, and blaspheming against God under them: for it is not the wrath of God, but their own wicked nature, that is the true cause of their sinning under it; and so the holy Jesus bore the wrath of God, without so much as one unbecoming thought of God, and far less any unbecoming word.

Use I. Here is a measuring Reed; O! that men would apply it. *First*, Apply it to your time in **this** world, and you will you will see your age is as nothing. ... siderable point is sixty, eighty, or a hundred years, in respect of eternity? Compared with eternity, there is a greater disproportion, than between a hair's breadth, and the circumference of the whole earth. Why do we sleep then in such a short day, while we are in hazard of losing rest, through the long night of eternity? *Secondly*, Apply it to your endeavours for salvation, and they will be found very scanty. When men are pressed to diligence in their salvation-work, they are ready to say, *To what purpose is this waste?* Alas! if it were to be judged by our diligence, what is it that we have in view; as to the most part of us, no man could thereby conjecture, that we have eternity in view. If we duly considered eternity, we could not but conclude, that, to leave no means appointed of God unessayed, till we get our salvation secured; to refuse rest or comfort in any thing, till we are sheltered under the wings of the Mediator; to pursue our great interest with the utmost vigour, to cut off lusts dear as right hands & right eyes, to set our faces resolutely against all difficulties, and fight our way through all the opposition made by the devil, the world, & the flesh, are, all of them together, little enough for eternity.

USE II. Here is a balance of the sanctuary, by which one may understand the lightness, of what is falsly tho't weighty; and the weight of some things, by many reckoned to be very light.

First, Some things seem very weighty, which weighed in this balance, will be found very light. (1.) Weigh the world, and all that is in it, the lust of the flesh, the lust of the eyes, and the pride of life, and the whole will be found light, in the balance of eternity. Weigh herein all worldly profits, gains and advantages; and you will quickly see, that a thousand worlds will not quit the cost of an eternity of woe. *For what is a man profited, if he shall gain the whole world, and lose his own soul?* Mat. xvi. 26. Weigh the pleasures of sin, which are but for a season, with the fire that is everlasting, and you must account yourselves fools and madmen, to run the hazard of the one for the other. (2.) Weigh your afflictions in this balance, and you will find the heaviest of them very light, in respect of the weight of eternal anguish. Impatience under affliction, especially when worldly troubles do so imbitter mens spirits, that they cannot relish the glad tidings of the gospel, speaks great regardlessness of eternity. As a small and inconsiderable loss will be very little at heart with him, who sees himself in hazard of losing his whole estate; so troubles in this world, will appear but light to him, who has a lively view of eternity. Such a one will stoop,

& take up his cross, whatever it be, thinking it enough to escape eternal wrath. (3.) Weigh the most difficult and uneasy duties of religion here, and you will no more reckon the yoke of CHRIST insupportable. Repentance and bitter mourning for sin on earth, very light in comparison of eternal weeping, wailing and gnashing of teeth in hell. To wrestle with GOD in prayer, weeping, and making supplication for the blessing in time, is far easier than to lie under the curse thro' all eternity. Mortification of the most beloved lust is a light thing, in comparison with the second death in hell. *Lastly*, Weigh your convictions in this balance. O! how heavy do these lie upon many, till they get them shaken off! They are not disposed to fall in with them, but strive to get clear of them, as of a mighty burden. But the worm of an ill conscience, will neither die nor sleep in hell, tho' one may now lull it asleep for a time. And certainly, it is easier to entertain the sharpest convictions in this life, so as they may lead one to CHRIST, than to have them fixed for ever in the conscience, while in hell one is totally and finally separated from him.

Secondly, But on the other hand, (1.) Weigh sin in this balance; and, tho' now it seems but a light thing to you, ye will find it a weight sufficient to turn up an eternal weight of wrath upon you. Even idle words, vain thoughts, and unprofitable actions, weighed in this balance, and considered as following the sinner into eternity, will each of them be heavier than the sand of the sea; time idly spent will make a weary eternity. Now is your seed-time; tho'ts, words and actions are the seed sown; eternity is the harvest; tho' the seed now lies under the clod, unregarded by most men, even the least grain shall spring up at length; and the fruit will be according to the seed. Gal. iv. 8. *For he that soweth to his flesh, shall of the flesh reap corruption,* i. e. destruction; *but he that soweth to the Spirit, shall of the Spirit reap life everlasting.* (2.) Weigh in this balance your time, and opportunities of grace and salvation, and you will find them very weighty. Precious time, and seasons of grace, sabbaths, communions, prayers, sermons, and the like, are by many now a-days made light of; but the day is coming, when one of these will be reckoned more valuable than a thousand worlds, by those who now have the least value for them. When they are gone for ever, and the loss cannot be retrieved; these will see the worth of them, who will not now see it.

USE III. and *last*. Be warned and stirred up to flee from the wrath to come. Mind eternity, and closely ply the work of your salvation. What are you doing, while you are not so doing? Is heaven a fable, or hell a mere scare-crow? Must we live eternally, and will we be at no more pains to escape everlasting misery? Will faint wishes take the kingdom of heaven by force? And will such drowsy endeavors, as most men satisfy themselves with, be accounted flying from the wrath to come? Ye who have all ready fled to CHRIST, up, and be doing; ye have begun the good work, go on, loiter not, but work out your salvation with fear and trembling, Ph. ii. 12. *Fear him, which is able to destroy both body and soul in hell*, Mat. x. 28. Remember, ye are not yet ascended into heaven; ye are but in your middle state: The everlasting arms have drawn you out of the gulf of wrath ye were plunged into, in your natural state; they are still underneath you, that ye can never fall down into it again; nevertheless, ye have not yet got up to the top of the rock; the deep below you is frightful; look at it, and hasten your ascent. Ye who are yet in your natural state, lift up your eyes, and take a view of the eternal state. Arise, ye profane persons, ye ignorant ones, ye formal hypocrites, strangers to the power of godliness, flee from the wrath to come. Let not the young adventure to delay a moment longer, nor the old put off this work any more. *To day if ye will hear his voice, harden not your hearts*, lest he swear in his wrath, that ye shall never enter into his rest. It is no time to linger in a state of sin, as in Sodom, when fire and brimstone are coming down on it from the LORD. Take warning in time; they who are in hell, are not troubled with such warnings, but are enraged against themselves, for that they slighted the warning, when they had it.

Consider, I pray you, (1.) How uneasy it is to lie one whole night on a soft bed, in perfect health, when one very fain would have sleep, but cannot get it; sleep being departed from him. How often will one in that case wish for rest! How full of tossings to and fro! But ah! how dreadful must it then be, to lie in sorrow, wrapt up in scorching flames thro' a long eternity, in that place, where they have no rest day nor night! (2.) How terrible would it be, to live under violent pains of the cholic or gravel, for 40 or 60 years together, without any intermission? Yet that is but a very small thing, in comparison of eternal separation from GOD, the worm that never dieth, and the fire that it never quenched. (3.) Eternity is an awful tho't; O long, long, endless eternity! But will not every moment, in eternity of woe, seem a month, and every hour a year, in that most wretched and desperate condition? Hence ever and ever, as it were a double eternity. The sick man in the night, tossing to and fro on his bed, says, it will never be day; complains that his pain ever continues, never, never abates. Are these petty time-eternities which men form to themselves, in their own imaginations, so very grievous? Alas! then how grievous, how utterly insupportable must real eternity of woe, and all manner of miseries be! *Lastly*, There will be space enough there, to reflect on all the ills of one's heart and life, which one cannot get time to think of now; and to see that all that was said of the impenitent sinner's hazard, was true, and that the half was not told. There will be space enough in eternity to think on delayed repentance, to rue one's follies when it is too late; and in a state past remedy, to speak forth their fruitless wishes; O that I had never been born! That the womb had been my grave, and I had never seen the sun! O that I had taken warning in time, and fled from his wrath, while the door of mercy was standing open to me! O that I had never heard the gospel, that I had lived in some corner of the world, where a Saviour and the great salvation were not once named! But all in vain. What is done cannot be undone; the opportunity is lost, and can never be retrieved; time is gone, and cannot be recalled. Wherefore improve time, while you have it, and do not wilfully ruin yourselves, by stopping your ear to the gospel call.

And now if ye would be saved from the wrath to come, and never go into this place of torment, take no rest in your natural state; believe the sinfulness and misery of it, and labour to get out of it quickly, fleeing unto Jesus Christ by faith. Sin in you is the seed of hell; and if the guilt and reigning power of it, be not removed in time, they will bring you to the second death in eternity. There is no way to get them removed, but by receiving of CHRIST, as he is offered in the gospel, for justification and sanctification; and he is now offered to you with all his salvation, Rev. xxii. 12. 17. *And behold, I come quickly, and my reward is with me, to give every man according as his work shall be. And the Spirit and the bride say, Come. And let him that heareth say, Come. And let him that is athirst,* **Come.** *And whosoever will, let him take the water of life freely.* JESUS CHRIST is the Mediator of peace, and the Fountain of holiness; he it is who delivereth us from the wrath to come.—— *There is therefore now no condemnation to them which are in Christ Jesus, who walk not after the flesh, but after the Spirit,* Rom. viii. 1. And the terrors of hell, as well as the joys of heaven, are set before you, to stir you up to a cordial receiving of him, with all his salvation; and to determine you into the way of faith and holiness, in which alone you can escape the everlasting fire. May the LORD himself, make them effectual to that end.

Thus far of man's Eternal State; the which, because it is eternal, admits of no succeeding one for ever.

www.ingramcontent.com/pod-product-compliance
Lightning Source LLC
Chambersburg PA
CBHW030345230426
43664CB00007BB/539